FRIENDSHIP

Philosophic Reflections on a Perennial Concern

(Second Edition)

D1565503

Edited by

Philip Blosser
Marshell Carl Bradley

University Press of America, Inc.
Lanham • New York • Oxford

Copyright © 1997 by
University Press of America,® Inc.
4720 Boston Way
Lanham, Maryland 20706

12 Hid's Copse Rd.
Cummor Hill; Oxford OX2 9JJ

All rights reserved
Printed in the United States of America
British Library Cataloguing in Publication Information Available

Library of Congress Cataloging-in-Publication Data

Friendship : philosophic reflections on a perennial concern / edited by
Philip Blosser and Marshell Carl Bradley.--2nd ed.
p. cm.
Rev. ed of: Of friendship. 1989.
Includes bibliographical references and index.
I. Blosser, Philip. II. Bradley, Marshell Carl. III. Of friendship
BJ1533.F8042 1997 177'.62--dc21 97-21695 CIP

ISBN: 978-0-7618-0818-3

⊖™ The paper used in this publication meets the minimum
requirements of American National Standard for information
Sciences—Permanence of Paper for Printed Library Materials,
ANSI Z39.48—1984

Dedicated to the esteemed

TANABATATSUME ORIHIME, R.D.

a human being of matchless magnanimity,
compassion, and infectious love of life,
in gratitude for uncommon friendship,
and with prayer for eternal sunshine

Easter, 1997

CONTENTS

LATE MODERN

CONTEMPORARY

Preface to the Second Edition

Just what is "friendship"? What makes a relationship a *friendship* as opposed to something else? An understanding" between two people? A feeling? A moral obligation? Sympathy? Love? Esteem? How does friendship differ from the affection that exists between lovers, brothers, sisters, or parents and children? Or, if these are different species of friendship, what is the *genus?* Is friendship a matter of self-interest or of altruism; or something of each? Is friendship a *duty?* How does a friendship that exists for its own sake differ from one that exists for the sake of pleasure or utility? How can one tell a true friend from a false one, or friendship from flattery? Does authentic friendship exclude other people? Can friendship be jeopardized by too much intimacy?

Friendship is one of the most fascinating subjects that anyone can study. It is one of those subjects that is so close to us, so much a part of our everyday lives, that we hardly ever take notice of it. Like Heidegger's "being" or Augustine's "time," it is something so close at hand that we rarely give it a thought. Like "time," we are quite sure we know what it is until, suddenly, we are asked; and then, as Augustine noted when asked about "time," we are no longer sure. Or, as Heidegger noted of "being," we suddenly realize we have been overlooking it for so long that we are in danger of letting it slip into oblivion and forgetting what it is altogether.

Friendship was exalted in times past. Most everyone has heard of the celebrated friendships of Socrates and Plato, David and Jonathan, Jesus and John, the "beloved disciple." Others familiar with classical literature may recall Pylades and Orestes, Roland and Oliver, Amis and Amile, and perhaps Augustine and the death of his friend memorialized in his *Confessions.* The subject of friendship had a noble and eminent place in ancient times. Treatises, dialogues, essays—entire books—were devoted to the subject by philosophers and other classical writers. Plato devoted an entire dialogue, *Lysis,* to the subject. Aristotle offered an extensive analysis of it in Books VIII and IX of his *Nicomachean Ethics.* Cicero wrote a treatise, *On Friendship,* and numerous essays and discussions can be found among the works of Xenophon, Epicurus, Epictetus, Plutarch, St. Thomas Aquinas, and many others.

If friendship was exalted in ancient times and, to a degree, even in medieval times, it has become curiously marginal in modern times, especially in the contemporary world. In the hustle and bustle of our lives, it is almost as if we have ceased to have time for friendship, if not forgotten altogether what it is to be a friend. Certainly there has been a decline in philosophical reflection on the subject. Why this is so, is hard to say. Some, like Eric Fromm, have suggested the alienating nature of our industrial-capitalist society as the culprit. Others, like C. S. Lewis, have suggested various other reasons—that friendship is the least natural and biological of loves, which in our day gives it a pale and thin appearance, like "a sort of vegetarian substitute for the more organic loves"; that friendship cannot produce evolutionist "certificates of an animal origin and of survival value"; or that friendship is essentially selective and exclusive, running counter to egalitarian, democratic and collectivist values.

Whatever the cause, the eclipse of friendship as a subject of reflection, until recently, is unfortunate. For, whatever the shifting winds of ideology and cultural values may bring, friendship remains a basic and universal human concern—probably as basic as sex, money, or power. It is a concern that modern philosophy could meaningfully address but has largely overlooked. And this especially is ironic; for the philosophical tradition furnishes some of the richest resources available for anyone wishing to understand the issue. With the resurgence of interest in questions of personal character and "ethics of virtue" signaled by the milestone publication of Alasdair MacIntyre's *After Virtue* (1981), the subject of friendship has begun to find a readier audience once again, not only among professional philosophers and others in the academic community, but among the thinking public at large. As the widespread popularity of such titles as *Habits of the Heart* and *The Culture of Narcissism* over the past decade suggests, there are many beyond the walls of academe who are capable of appreciating how community or interpersonal ties enrich, rather than diminish, the individual. And the publication in rapid succession of new philosophical anthologies on friendship, such as the editions by Michael Pakaluk (*Other Selves: Philosophers on Friendship*, 1991), Neera K. Badhwar (*Friendship: A Philosophical Reader*, 1993), and

Leroy S. Rouner (*The Changing Face of Friendship*, 1994), illustrates the growing interest of the professional community since the first edition of the present work appeared in 1989. Even so, a proper philosophical accounting for a book on a subject such as this is still in order, beyond its practical justification of being the most comprehensive historical survey to date.

Why "friendship"?

A book on this subject may appear to be an oddity. One might ask: What could be more philosophically secondary than the matter of friendship?

Yet, the philosopher, sophisticated or not, might find herein a work which either inspired him or her to the discipline in the first instance; or which simply speaks to an element in our nature which more "rigorous" work simply does not or cannot. That said, this book is especially designed for those who are coming to philosophy for the first time. It might even be deemed proper that a work on "friendship" greet the would-be friend of wisdom first and foremost.

It might be suggested that the topic of friendship is self-evident; that everyone knows what a friend is and is not. Yet, perhaps "friendship" is not altogether different from the mysterious nature of "time" itself in this sense; perhaps "friendship" is far more complicated than one would think; and is anything but self-evident.

This analogy between time and friendship itself bears another complexity. For, in virtually every given human life, friendship has a certain priority in time. Before we are spouses, lovers, parents, or citizens proper, we are in some way friends; and, of course, *while* we assume all of those roles and relations, we are, in some manner, friends of someone, or something. That friendship has a certain priority in time is obvious. This book would address the manners in which it has priority in purpose as well.

It might be argued that the topic of friendship is a topic too narrow and too rhapsodical to be worthy of a work unto itself. Yet, as noted above, since the appearance of the first edition of this book under the title *Of Friendship* (Longwood, 1989), there have been various publications resembling it or emphatic of the theme.

While "friendship" would seem to be a rather idle topic or a category of "Ethics," earnest investigation of the topic soon reveals that it is as dynamic as are great friendships themselves. Students of "Business Ethics," "Politics" in general, or "Social Psychology" will find here works that delve into the "flip-side" of the more obviously forensic emphasis in those disciplines. Indeed, students and practitioners of "Business Administration" and "Political Science" should consider a serious look at this work. For what is an effective business environment if not a system of "friendships of utility"? And what is a well-ordered state if not a society of "friends" as much as a society of laws?

So, to whomever might take up this work, for whatever end, it is hoped that these writings will serve as springboards to greater advances in both life and letters; and to those quite accustomed to philosophic thought, may these readings on friendship be friendly desserts laid out overabundantly upon an already rich table.

This second edition of this work has been revised to take into account the suggestions made by those concerned with its classroom use. In this connection, the suggestions especially of Professor Richard J. Klonoski of the University of Scranton have proved invaluable. Without detailing the specific rationale for each revision at this point, perhaps it would be of interest to readers, nevertheless, to know what changes were made. (1) In the first section (Ancient and Medieval), a selection from Xenophon's *Memorabilia* has been omitted, and the following pieces were added: a brief selection from Hesiod's *Theogony,* a chapter containing two readings from Seneca's *Epistulae Morales,* and a chapter devoted to St. Aelred of Rievaulx's *De Spiritali Amicitia.* (2) In the second section (Early Modern), a selection from Descartes' *Correspondence* was omitted. (3) In the third section (Late Modern), no chapters were omitted, though the chapters on Schopenhauer and Kierkegaard were significantly shortened. (4) In the last section (Contemporary), two selections were omitted—Paul Weiss' discussion of "The Primary Ethical Principle" from his book, *Man's Freedom;* and a selection from Janice Raymond's fine study, *A Passion for Friends.* Added selections include the incisive feminist piece by Mary Hunt and the charming selection by Gilbert Milander, which includes a discussion of some of the issues raised by her. The current selection by Hanna Arendt replaces her discussions, in the previous edition, of "The Two-in-One" and of "Augustine, the First Philosopher of the Will"— both from her splendid book, *The Life of the Mind.* A number of selections have been shortened or amended in some way, including those of Aquinas, Montaigne, Spinoza, Hume, Kant, Santayana, Kierkegaard, and Schopenhauer. It is hoped that these changes will make this new edition of this work even more serviceable for contemporary classroom use. Finally, in this edition, the notes have been moved to the end of each chapter, and the bibliographical material has been placed at the back of the book.

For their generous assistance in various ways and at various stages of the production of the second edition of this book, we are indebted to many friends. We owe a debt of gratitude to Dr. Larry Yoder, for his assistance with a Lineberger Foundation Grant, and to the good offices of Dr. Robert Spuller, Academic Dean of Lenoir-Rhyne College, for generous financial support towards the publication of the work; to Fran Thomas and Sonnie Cooke for computer support in the task of formatting the final product; to my erstwhile colleague Ritalinda D'Andrea for friendship, inspiration and encouragement, not least in her passionate suggestion that we include an appropriate and representative selection from a feminist perspective; to Carol LaHurd, for help in locating a number of selections, including the one we included by Mary Hunt; to Professor Richard Klonoski of the University of Scranton, for his detailed recommendations of the selections by Hesiod, Seneca, Aelred, Arendt, Hunt, and Meilaender; and to Edie Ashman and Burl McCuiston of the Lenoir-Rhyne College Library for help in obtaining needed resources. For their help in producing the first edition of the work, we owe a continued debt of gratitude to Mr. Wyatt Benner, of Longwood Publishing, for his patient help as copy editor of the first edition; to Sonnie Cooke, for her invaluable assistance in typing much of the original manuscript; to Dawna Cooke, and Christopher and Jonathan Blosser, for their help in typing several of the selections; to Lori Blosser, for her painstaking assistance in proofreading all of the original selections; to some very special individuals (such as Mrs. Ursula A. Gray and Mrs. Gerda M. Seligson) whose help was indispensable in obtaining permissions for some of the invaluable selections in this book; to Robert Winter, Sr. Marie Annunciata, Eija-Riitta Korhola, Tapio Puolimatka, for steadfast friendship, and especially to the esteemed Tanabatatsume Orihime, R.D., to whom this book is dedicated in enduring gratitude and friendship.

The Editors:
Philip Blosser
Marshell Carl Bradley
Easter, March 1997

Acknowledgements

Gilgamesh: Reprinted by permission of The Bodley Head, Random House UK Ltd., from *Gilgamesh and Other Babylonian Tales*, translated and edited by Jennifer Westwood, New York: Cowan-McCann Press, 1970.

Excerpts from Augustine: Reproduced from *AUGUSTINE: Confessions and Enchiridion*, EDITED BY Albert Cook Outler (*Library of Christian Classics*). Used by permission of Westminster John Knox Press.

Excerpt from Aelred of Rievaulx: "The Origin of Friendship," translated by Mary Eugenia Laker, pages 51-66 in Aelred of Rievaulx's *Spiritual Friendship*, Cistercian Fathers Series Number 5. © Cistercian Publications, Kalamazoo, Michigan, 1974. Reproduced by permission of the publisher.

Excerpts from St. Thomas Aquinas: *Summa Theologica*, translated by the Fathers of the English Dominican Province, Vol. II. Copyright © 1947 Benziger Brothers, Inc. Excerpts reproduced by kind permission of the Benziger Publishing Company.

Excerpts from Nicolas Malebranche: Material from *The Search After Truth and Elucidations of the Search After Truth*, translated by Thomas M. Lennon and Paul J. Olscamp, is reprinted by permission. Copyright 1980 by the Ohio State University Press. All rights reserved.

Excerpts from David Hume: Material from *An Enquiry Concerning the Principles of Morals*, Vol. 4 of *Philosophical Works by David Hume*, edited by T. H. Green and T. H. Grose. Copyright © Scientia Verlag, Aalen, Germany, 1964. Reproduced by permission of the publisher.

Excerpts from Immanuel Kant: Excerpts as specified (pages 140-146) from *The Doctrine of Virtue*, by Immanuel Kant. English translation copyright © 1964 by Mary J. Gregor. Foreword Copyright © 1964 by H. J. Paton. Reprinted by permission of Harper & Row, Publishers, Inc.

Excerpts from G.W.F. Hegel: from *Early Theological Writings*, translated by T.M. Knox, published by The University of Chicago Press, 1948. Copyright © 1948 Richard Kroner. Reproduced by the kind permission of Gerda M. Seligson for the estate of Richard Kroner.

Excerpts from Arthur Schopenhauer: Material from *The World as Will and Representation,* 2 vols., translated by E.F.J. Payne. Copyright © 1958 The Falcon's Wing Press; copyright © 1969 Dover Publications, Inc. Selected portions reprinted by permission of Dover Publications, Inc., New York.

Excerpts from Søren Kierkegaard: Kierkegaard, Søren; *Either/Or.* Copyright © 1987 by Postscript Inc. Reprinted by permission of Princeton University Press.

Excerpt from C.S. Lewis: "Friendship" from *The Four Loves* by C. S. Lewis, copyright © 1960 by Helen Joy Lewis, reprinted by permission of Harcourt Brace Jovanovich, Inc.

Excerpt from Jean-Paul Sartre: Originally published in *Les Temps Modernes,* October, 1961. Reprinted in Jean-Paul Sartre, *Situations,* translated by Benita Eisler (New York: George Braziller, 1958). Copyright © 1964 by Éditions Gallimard. Reprinted by permission of Georges Borchardt, Inc.

Excerpt from J. Glenn Gray: *The Warriors: Reflections on Men in Battle* (New York: Harcourt, Brace & Co., 1959). Copyright © 1959 J. Glenn Gray, © 1987 Ursula A. Gray. Excerpts reprinted from "Love: War's Ally and Foe," pp. 64-95, by the kind permission of Mrs. Ursula A. Gray for the estate of J. Glenn Gray.

Excerpt from Hannah Arendt: "On Humanity in Dark Times: Thoughts about Lessing," from MEN IN DARK TIMES, translated by Richard and Clara Winston, copyright © 1968 by Hannah Arendt and renewed 1996 by Kotte Kohler, reprinted by permission of Harcourt Brace & Company.

Excerpt from Mary E. Hunt: From *The Changing Faces of Friendship,* edited by Leroy S. Rouner. © 1994 by the University of Notre Dame Press. Used by permission.

Excerpt from Gilbert Meilaender: From *The Changing Faces of Friendship,* edited by Leroy S. Rouner. © 1994 by the University of Notre Dame Press. Used by permission.

Chapter 1

The Epic of Gilgamesh

In justification for beginning a book of philosophic selections on friendship with a "myth" one may perhaps heed the words of the "philosopher" himself:

> *For it is owing to their wonder that men both now begin and at first began to philosophize; they wondered originally at the obvious difficulties, then advanced little by little and stated difficulties about the greater matters, e.g. about the phenomena of the moon and those of the sun and the stars, and about the genesis of the whole. And a man who is puzzled and wonders thinks himself ignorant, whence even a lover of myth is in a sense a lover of wisdom, for the myth is composed of wonders; therefore, since they philosophized in order to escape from ignorance, evidently they were pursuing science in order to know, and not for any utilitarian end . . .*
> *For all men begin, as we said, by wondering that things are as they are. . . .*
> *—Aristotle,* **Metaphysica***, Book I,*
> *Chap. 2, 982b 11-22, 983a 15.*

Indeed, in anticipation of the selections from Aristotle included in Chapter 4, in which Aristotle treats friendship as something of a **necessity** *in human existence, we have here, in the foreground of this and every other philosophical undertaking worthy of the name, fundamental questions concerning both wonder and necessity.*

In the first instance, then, perhaps one may legitimately wonder, by and with the myth, about the seeming necessity of friendship itself, for the very contemplation of the possibility of true friendship carries with it something of a feeling of the **infinite** *in our midst, while the responsibilities that are born with any kind of friendship whatsoever carry with them something which bears a sense of an astonishing* **finitude.**

These opposing forces of the **infinite** *and the* **finite** *are bound to clash within every soul, and they certainly clash dramatically in the characters depicted in* **The Epic of Gilgamesh.**

The following selection is a Sumerian epic poem dating from the second millennium B.C. As the product of a predominantly oral tradition, it cannot be pinned down precisely in date and cannot be ascribed to one "author" in particular. However, the work proceeds with a wondrous ingenuity and may well be the most sublime "mythical" treatment of friendship to be found in all of literature. The powerfully simple tale of the friendship of the near god-king Gilgamesh and his opposite, the near beast-man Enkidu is a "myth" whose truth is truly unforgettable.

Gilgamesh

Listen to the tale of Gilgamesh, of Gilgamesh the golden, King of Kings, who carved his name where great men's names were carved; and where no names were, there he built an altar to the gods.

He was the King in Uruk, where he raised great walls and ramparts, and the temple of Eanna for the father of the gods, Anu, Lord of all the Firmament, and for Ishtar, Queen of War and Love. There was no city on the face of earth more splendid than Uruk; there was no king more brave and strong than Gilgamesh, its lord. But he was two parts god and one part man, his human form unable to contain the restless vigour of divinity. So he became a tyrant and he took the young men of the city from their homes to labour on the temples and the walls, performing tasks that were beyond their strength. Sons lost fathers, fathers lost their sons—but worse than this in all the people's eyes was that he forced young maidens and new brides to be his own wives, leaving those they loved and those who loved them stricken with despair. The old men grumbled in their houses every day:

'Such is the shepherd of his flock, such is our king! No ravening wolf that slaughters the young lambs is crueller than he is, for he leaves no son to his old father and no bride to her new-wedded husband. Is there none who can restrain this tyrant, and relieve the sorrow that is weighing on our hearts, through the fault of Gilgamesh the King?'

The Making of Enkidu

The gods heard lamentations rising up out of the city, and they went before the throne of Anu, god of Uruk.

'Lord,' they said, 'in Uruk sons lose fathers, fathers sons, husbands lose wives upon their marriage-day, all through the fault of Gilgamesh the King.'

The goddess of creation, Aruru, was standing by, and they all turned on her: '*You* made him, Aruru, now you must make a match for him, his equal, strength for strength. Let them strive together, wild heart with wild heart, and in their striving let the city rest.'

The goddess formed an image in her mind. She washed her hands and, pinching off some clay, she shaped it to the pattern she had made and cast it on the plains, where it became a man like none those lands had ever seen. His name was Enkidu. He had Ninurta's strength, but his hair hung down his back as thick as grain, and long as any woman's. He was huge, and had a shaggy hide like Samuqan the cattle god. He roamed the plains and drank at water-holes with wild gazelle, neither he nor they knowing that he was of human-kind.

But a trapper met him one day, face to face, down at a water-hole; a second day, and then a third day they met. The trapper's face was frozen with cold fear. He took his game and went home to his house. His fear locked up his heart; he could not speak, but seeing him look strange, his father said: 'What has befallen you, my son?'

'Father,' said the trapper, 'a wild man roams the plains and drinks at water-holes with the gazelle. He eats grass like the beasts and sucks their milk. He sets them free from all my traps, fills in the pits. I am afraid to hunt. What shall I do?'

His father said: 'Go now to Gilgamesh, the King of Uruk, and tell *him* your tale. Then he will send a temple-woman here, for if she sits at evening by the wells the wild man, seeing her, will draw to her, attracted by her beauty; he will know that he is one of her kind. Then the beasts will run from him, as from all other men, and he will leave the plains.'

The trapper went, and told the King his tale.

'Lord,' said the trapper, 'a wild man roams the plains and drinks at water-holes with the gazelle. He eats grass like the beasts and sucks their milk. He sets them free from all my traps, fills in the pits. I am afraid to hunt. What shall I do?'

'Take back a temple-woman to the plains, for if she sits at evening at the wells the wild man, seeing her, will draw to her, attracted by her beauty; he will know that he is one of her kind. Then the beasts will run from him, as from all other men, and he will leave the plains.'

The trapper took a temple-woman back. They journeyed to the wells and there sat down to wait for Enkidu. He did not come the first day, nor the next, but on the third he came with the gazelle down from the plains, at evening, at the setting of the sun. When he saw the temple-woman, she seemed fairer than the beasts; when she spoke, her voice seemed sweeter than the birds'. The wild man stayed for six days by the wells and from the woman learned the speech of men, but when he would have gone back to his herd, the wild beasts ran from him, as they would run from any man. He grieved and was perplexed, for now he could not run as fast as they. He went back to the wells, and there sat down at the woman's feet, to learn what he must do.

In Uruk, Gilgamesh awoke from sleep and, rising, went to seek his mother out in her temple. When he came there, he bowed down and said: 'My mother, I have dreamed a dream. A star fell out of heaven at my feet. I tried to lift it but I was too weak. I tried to move it but could not prevail. All the land had gathered round the star, the men thronged round it and some kissed its feet. I put my forehead to it, raised it up. I lifted it and carried it to you, and you put it on a par with me, your son.'

Ninsun, the wise one, answered Gilgamesh: 'The star of heaven which fell down at your feet, which I myself put on a par with you, is the wild man of the plains and like a star is his great strength. He is the friend who, wild heart for wild heart, will equal you and be your second self, to guard your back in battle and in peace sit by your side; to laugh when you laugh and to share your grief. He will not forsake you.'

That same night, Gilgamesh dreamed again and, waking, went to Ninsun in her temple.

'Mother, I have dreamed another dream. In Uruk lay an axe, and the people thronged about it in the street. I laid it at your feet and you yourself put it on a par with me, your son.'

Ninsun, the wise one, answered Gilgamesh: 'The axe you saw is the wild man of the plains. His strength is like an axe. He is the friend who, wild heart for wild heart, will equal you and be your second self, to guard your back in battle and in peace sit by our side; to laugh when you laugh and to share your grief. He will not forsake you.'

'May I be granted such a friend,' said Gilgamesh.

Meanwhile, the woman talked to Enkidu.

'*You* are no beast to crop the grass,' she said, 'or drink at water-holes with the gazelle. You are no wild man now. Come, Enkidu, come with me into Uruk, where the king is Gilgamesh the Tyrant, whose vast strength is such that nowhere can he find his match. Now, therefore, he prevails over his people like some great wild ox, not caring for their pain.'

Enkidu grew eager at her words. He longed to find a friend—could this be he? Could this be one to share his secret thoughts?

He told the woman: 'Take me to Uruk, where Gilgamesh walks restless in his strength. I will challenge him and cry: "I am the one born on the plains, the strongest of all men, come here to change the proud ways of the tyrant Gilgamesh!"'

'You have no cause to boast,' the woman said, 'for though you may be the strongest of all *men,* yet he is two parts god, and stronger still. Never does he rest by night or day. But I will show you him, if you will come to Uruk, where each day is holiday and people walk the streets in gay attire, as bright as butterflies; where all the air is filled with scents of spices and perfumes; where wines abound to make your heart rejoice; where all would be as joyous as the sun, if Gilgamesh the King would mend his ways.'

The woman halved her robe and clothed the man. She led him, like a mother, by the hand down to the sheep-folds, where the shepherds were. They gathered round to see him, brought him bread; he stared at it, because he did not know how he was to eat it. They brought wine, but he was used to drink milk from the beasts and when he tried to lap like any dog, the shepherds laughed and made a mock of him. When they had taught him both to eat and drink, he rubbed his hairy body down with oil and then put on a garment. Now, indeed, he seemed to them the comeliest of men. He was the shepherds' watchman; since he had come they slept at night, while he caught the wolves and lions that fell upon their flocks.

But one day, by the sheep-folds where he sat, he lifted up his eyes and saw a man come running from the city, and he said: 'Woman, go bring him to me. Ask him why he comes here.'

She called out: 'Why do you come here?'

'For help,' the man replied. 'There is to be a wedding at the meeting-house, and Gilgamesh will surely come and carry off the bride to be his wife. Will you not stop him, Enkidu?'

The wild man shook, his face went white with anger at the stranger's words. He set out with the woman and they hastened to Uruk. They entered into the city and, when they reached the market-place, the people gathered round. Some said: 'He looks like Gilgamesh!'

'No, he is much shorter, though heavier of bone, I think.'

'They *say* he roamed the plains and ate the grass like any beast!'

The people made him welcome: 'A mighty man has come to us. He has arisen like a god to be a match for Gilgamesh!'

And when the King came through the town to the meeting-house of Uruk, his way was barred by Enkidu, who stood there in the street and would not move aside for him. He blocked the doorway with his foot to prevent the King from going in. The two began to fight. They grappled with each other, both snorting like two mighty bulls. They broke the doorpost, and the wall was shaken by their blows. They wrestled in the doorway, in the street, and in the market-place, till Gilgamesh, because he was part-god, threw Enkidu. He threw him to the ground and, standing there, he looked at him. Then his anger was abated and he turned to go away. After he had turned, the fallen Enkidu called out to him: 'Your mother, Ninsun, bore a son exalted over all! Enlil himself decreed for you your kingship over Uruk. There is none like you, for your strength is more than that of man.'

'It is a god's,' said Gilgamesh. 'I could not so have thrown you had it been otherwise, and yet I found it hard to do. Truly, you are my equal! Will you be my companion, the friend to know my secret thoughts?'

'I will,' said Enkidu, and they sealed a pact of friendship which would endure between them in happiness and sorrow, while both their lives should last.

The Slaying of Humbaba

Gilgamesh sat in Uruk and was sad, pondering the life of men, and death. He fell asleep at last and dreamed a dream of his own dying, because he was one third a mortal man and shared their bitter fate. He woke to sorrow, and he told his dream to Enkidu, his dear friend.

'Do not grieve,' said Enkidu. 'You will not live for ever, yet still yours is the kingship, yours the power to rule. Deal justly by your people, win their love, and leave behind you an everlasting name.'

'My name will not endure without brave deeds,' said Gilgamesh, 'and therefore let us go into the Cedar Forest to win fame.'

Enkidu sighed bitterly.

'Why set your heart on this?'

'In that forest dwells Humbaba, the great giant, set there by Enlil to safeguard the trees, but he has grown too proud. So let us go and fell him, cut him down, uproot the evil that is in that land.'

'When I was as a beast and roamed the plains, I saw that land. The Cedar Forest runs a full ten thousand leagues from side to side, and if some creature stirs within its depths, Humbaba hears though sixty leagues away. What man would venture into his dark realm, would choose to meet the keeper of the trees, whose breath is hot as fire, whose mighty roar is like the fearful thunder of the storm? No man on earth can equal *him* in strength, for Enlil made him perilous to men. Weakness takes hold of those who enter in his dark dominions. We shall not return.'

'What man can live for ever, Enkidu? Our days are numbered and our time runs fast, and all our deeds are but a breath of wind. Already, in the city, you fear death—what has become of all your manly strength? I will walk before you. You may call: "Gilgamesh, go on! Be not afraid!" from where you stand in safety. If I fall, my name will live for ever. They will say: "Gilgamesh has fallen in fight with the terrible Humbaba," and sons as yet unborn will speak my name with pride in days to come. Your fearfulness afflicts my heart with grief, but I shall still go on, still put my hand to this great task and cut the cedar down. I shall give orders to my armourers; they will forge for us weapons fit for gods, so come with me.'

Gilgamesh set his armourers to work. Great swords they cast, and made them sheaths of gold; forged monstrous axes for a giant's bane. When all was ready, each of them would arm with massive weapons of ten talents' weight.

Gilgamesh called the elders of Uruk and said: 'O elders, listen to your King. I wish to see him of whom all men talk, him with whose dread name the lands are filled. In the Cedar Forest I will vanquish him and cause the lands to hear of Gilgamesh.'

The elders of Uruk said to their King: 'You are young, O Gilgamesh. Your heart is rash. You do not know what you propose to do. Humbaba is no man like other men! Who is there that can stand against his might? His roar is like the storm, his mouth holds fire, and he breathes out death to all mankind. Why must you do this thing? For you must fail.'

Gilgamesh looked at Enkidu, and laughed.

'What shall I tell them? That I am afraid? Would you have us sit here all our days, each growing old in fear and idleness?'

The elders said: 'If you must go, then may your patron god protect you; may he bring you safely home; to the quay of Uruk cause you to return.'

Gilgamesh bowed himself down to the ground before the sun-god, Shamash, and he prayed: 'I go, O Shamash, and I raise my hands to you in prayer. Let it be well with me. Bring me back to Uruk. Keep me safe.'

Gilgamesh called his friend to go with him and in the temple have the omens read. He came out weeping, tears ran down his face, for the omens spelled disaster.

'Must I walk alone, down a road which I have never gone before without your guidance, Shamash?' cried the King.

His workmen brought the weapons, the massive swords and axes, and placed a bow of Anshan in his hand. The elders gave their blessing once again, and for the journey counselled Gilgamesh.

'Do not trust in your strength! Let Enkidu go on before you. He has seen the way, has walked the road that leads up to the Gate. He who goes before will save his friend. May Shamash grant you victory. May he cause your eyes to see the fulfillment of the vows that you have made. May he open up closed paths, and send propitious dreams, and cause you to slay Humbaba like a child. In the river of the forest, wash your feet. Every evening dig a well and let there be pure water always in your water-skin for an offering to Shamash.'

Enkidu said: 'Come, friend. Let us set out on our way. Let your heart be not afraid, but follow me.'

Gilgamesh said: 'First, we must take farewell of Ninsun, my wise mother. Let us go into the temple Egalmah, her home.'

The friends went hand in hand to Egalmah, the palace of the goddess.

'Hear me, Mother,' said King Gilgamesh, 'for I must tread a strange road from today, and from today face dangers unforeseen, until the day when I return again. I must slay the keeper of the trees to win myself an everlasting name, so pray for me to Shamash that I may uproot the evil that is in his land.'

Ninsun the Queen put on her finest robes, and on her head the royal diadem. She mounted to the roof of Egalmah, where stood the Sun Lord's altar, nearest Heaven, and throwing incense on the sacred fire, she sent her prayers up with the winding smoke.

'Why did you give my son a restless heart? Now that you have touched him and he walks a strange road, facing dangers unforeseen, guard him until the day that he returns. When you have turned your eye away from earth, entrust him to the Watchmen of the Night till you come back with Aya, Bride of Dawn, and your bright glances watch the world again.'

Ninsun put out the incense and went down to where her son still stood with Enkidu.

'Enkidu,' she said, 'from this day on, you are my child. I have adopted you. Here is my amulet; it is a pledge that I have taken you to be my son. Into your keeping I give Gilgamesh, your brother; keep him safe, and bring him back to me when all is done.'

The friends bade her farewell. They set out now, and as they left the gates, the elders cried: 'In our assembly we have paid heed to your words; pay heed to ours in turn, O Gilgamesh! Let Enkidu protect the friend he loves.'

'Fear not,' said Enkidu. 'All will be well.'

For twenty leagues they walked before they ate; and thirty more before they stopped for sleep. A journey of six weeks was made by them in just three days, and after they had crossed the seventh mountain in their path, they saw ahead the Gate into the Forest. It was shut, and guarded by a watchman, set there by Humbaba, the great giant; less in size, but as terrible of aspect as it seemed the giant could be, and Gilgamesh fell back.

'Remember the vows you made!' cried Enkidu. 'Stand forth and slay this watchman!'

At his words, the King took heart and said: 'We must be quick. He is used to put on seven coats of mail when he goes into battle. One is on. If we delay, he will be fully armed, and how then shall we take his life from him?'

Like a furious wild ox, the watchman roared, and cried out: 'Go! You may not enter in! This is the Cedar Forest, and the realm of Humbaba the giant. Mortal men may not pass by these gates.'

'Yet we shall pass,' said Gilgamesh the King.

The two advanced and struck the watchman down. As yet he had put on but one mail coat, and so his life was taken, though he was the servant of the giant, great of strength and towering of stature. Enkidu stepped forward to the Gate, when once its keeper lay dead on the ground. Such was its beauty and its craftsmanship that he could not bear to strike it with his axe, but pushed it open with his outstretched hand.   He sprang back with a cry, for on the Gate lay deep enchantments.

Enkidu cried out: 'O let us not go down into the Forest; see my hand! When I touched the Gate, my hand lost all its strength and now it hangs down lifeless at my side. Some deep enchantment lies about this Gate. Let us not pass inside!'

'Should we turn back, now we have come so far?' asked Gilgamesh. 'Would you remain behind? No, stay with me. The weakness will soon pass. Together we will go into the depths of this great Forest and perform the task for which we came. Forget your thoughts of death.'

They passed inside the Gate and caught their breath. Their words were stilled to silence. They were still, and gazed upon the Forest, the green mountain. They beheld the height of the cedars and the broad path through the trees where the giant was used to walk in the cool and pleasant shade.   Greener were the shadows of the Mountain of the Cedar than of any other place, and Gilgamesh the King dug a well at sunset there, to offer up to Shamash waters from the earth. He poured out meal and prayed: 'Mountain of the Cedar, send me a dream to show me if my fate be good or bad.'

The two lay down to sleep.   When midnight came, Gilgamesh awoke and roused his friend: 'Enkidu, I dreamed that we two stood within deep gorges, when a mountain fell and by its side we seemed as small as flies. I dreamed again; again the mountain fell. It struck me down; the mountain caught my foot. Then light blazed out and in it was a form more beautiful than any in the land. He took the mountain off me, pulled me out, and giving me water, set me on my feet.'

Enkidu said: 'This dream was fortunate.   The mountain was Humbaba. It must mean that we shall likewise bring about his fall, and by the help of Shamash, Lord of Light.'

They travelled on next day, and once again Gilgamesh, at evening, dug a well in honour of the Sun God, and again he scattered meal upon the ground. This time he prayed: 'Mountain, bring a dream for Enkidu, to show him if his fate be good or bad.'

The Mountain sent a dream to Enkidu. He thought that in his dream a cold rain fell, but he kept silent, for he was afraid. Then Gilgamesh awoke. He said: 'My friend, did you not call me? Did you not touch me, or has some god now passed this way? I have dreamed a third dream.   In it lightning filled the air.   Heaven thundered, earth resounded, daylight failed and darkness fell. The brightness vanished and the fire went out. Then death rained down and turned the world to ashes and to dust.'

'My friend, be not afraid,' said Enkidu. 'For this dream too, may mean that we shall slay Humbaba, and his fall will be as dreadful as the storms that you have seen.'

Though he spoke cheerful words, his heart was cold. The two resolved to go on with their task. Gilgamesh took an axe up in his hand and he cut down a cedar. Far away, the giant Humbaba heard the noise. He grew enraged: 'Who has come among my trees? Who is cutting down my cedar?'

Then from Heaven the Sun God Shamash called: 'Be not afraid! Go forward without fear—you have my help.'

The two advanced. With great strides from his house the giant Humbaba came and horror fell upon the two friends' hearts, for he was huger than the tales had made him and more terrible. He fastened on the King the eye of death. The strength of Gilgamesh began to fail and, with his one sound hand, Enkidu his friend could not hope to defend him. Gilgamesh the King called out to heavenly Shamash: 'Help me, Lord! I have honoured you! I have pursued the road decreed by fate which brought me to this place, here to cut down Humbaba, who is evil in your sight, to root out all the evil in your land.'

The Sun God heard, and called from their far caves the Great Wind, and the Whirlwind, the Tempest and the Storm, the North, the South, the Freezing Wind, the Burning Wind—all eight rose up against Humbaba and beat against his evil eyes. He was unable to go forward, unable to turn back. He was helpless, and he pleaded: 'Let me go, O Gilgamesh. You shall be my master if you spare me, I your slave. I will cut down the cedars which I have tended on the Mountain, and build a palace for you. Have mercy, Gilgamesh!'

The King was moved by his strong pleas. He said: 'Is it not right for us to set the prisoner free, for us to send the captive back to his mother's house, and to return the caught bird to his nest?'

'It is not right to set *this* prisoner free, to send *this* captive back to his mother's house, and to return *this* caught bird to his nest, if you would see *your* mother once again. Where is your judgment? What use is your strength if wisdom does not guide it? If we do not slay him, then he will turn on us. Do not listen to his pleading. He is evil and must die.'

'It will be as in the dream,' said Gilgamesh, 'the brightness of our fame will be eclipsed and all our deeds as ash, if we kill him.'

'It is not so. Our fame will be as great. The giant must die or us, and you must choose.'

Gilgamesh struck first; next Enkidu; and at the third blow Humbaba lay still.

But he was the keeper of the cedar trees, whose power made forests tremble; now his death caused the whole world to shudder, mountains move, and hills and valleys be put from their place. Yet Gilgamesh still cut the cedars down and Enkidu hacked out the twining roots as far as the Euphrates. Then they turned their faces from the Forest and went home.

The Bull of Heaven

Time passed on in peace and quietness till one day Ishtar, cruel Queen of Love, looked from Eanna to where King Gilgamesh sat on his royal throne in robes of state. She looked and loved.

'O Gilgamesh,' she said, 'if you would be my husband, I would harness to the storm a chariot of lapis lazuli and gold; on golden wheels would you ride earth and air, and all the kings and princes of the world would bow themselves before you, and give praise.'

'How could I take the Queen of Heaven for wife? Would you wear earthly garments, eat our bread? And, Lady, all men know that you break faith. For Tammuz, your young husband, women wail at the ending of the year: who let him die? You loved the roller once—and broke his wing; now he stands crying *"kappi"* in the groves. What happened to the shepherd of the herd who daily heaped up sacrifice to you? You cursed him and you turned him into a wolf. His herd boys chase him off and his own dogs tear at his flanks. Then there was Ishullanu—what of him? You offered him your love, but he refused, so in your injured pride you struck him down, and turned your father's gardener to a mole. If I became your husband, you would soon grow tired of me and treat me like to them.'

A great wrath fell on Ishtar. She ascended into Heaven. She stood raging before Anu, her father, and she said: 'Gilgamesh has cursed me, and taunted me with all my deeds. He has *refused* to be my husband!'

'And if he has?' Lord Anu said. 'Have you not deserved his taunts?'

'I will have vengeance! Father—make me the Bull of Heaven, that Gilgamesh may be destroyed! If you will not do this, I will break down the Door of the Underworld and cause the dead to rise again, and they will be more numerous than the living upon earth.'

'If I do this,' said Anu, 'there will be drought for seven years. Have you fodder for the cattle and grain to feed mankind?'

'There is enough,' said Ishtar.

'Be it so, then,' Anu said.

The Bull of Heaven descended and an army marched against it. Its first snort killed six hundred men; its second snort killed more; at its third snort it saw Enkidu and charged, but he was ready. He seized it by the horns and cried out: 'Gilgamesh, be quick! Run your sword between its nape and horns.'

The Bull foamed at the mouth and tore the ground up in its rage, but Enkidu held fast and swiftly Gilgamesh thrust in his sword. The Bull fell dead. The brothers cut the heart out of the beast and offered it to Shamash, the bright sun, then took their rest.

But from the walls of Uruk went up the cry of Ishtar: 'Accursed be he who killed the Bull! Let Gilgamesh beware, for twice now he has scorned me!'

Enkidu turned toward her, tore off the right thigh of the bull and cast it in her face: 'Thus would I do with you if only I were able to catch hold of you,' he shouted.

Ishtar sent up a wail. She called her temple-women and they set up lamentations over the right thigh of the Bull. Beside the monstrous corpse stood the King with all his craftsmen. They cut off the huge horns and hung them on the palace wall. Then the brothers washed their hands in the waters of Euphrates and rode in triumph through the streets where crowds had gathered thick, hoping to see the heroes.

The King cried out to them: 'Who is the greatest?'

'The greatest of men is Gilgamesh, and next is Enkidu!'

But Enkidu was troubled in his dreams that night and, when day came, he went and told all he had dreamt to Gilgamesh the King.

'My friend, hear what a dream I had last night, when I saw Heaven. All the gods were there in council and I heard Lord Anu say: "The brothers have offended twice. First they killed Humbaba, and then the Bull of Heaven, so one of them must die."

'Enlil said: "Not Gilgamesh; he is the King. Take Enkidu."

'Shamash answered: "He is innocent. Why, therefore, should he die? It was at *my* command these two cut down the giant Humbaba, for although he was *your* servant, the cedar-land is *mine*."

'Enlil raged at heavenly Shamash: "You go down there to earth each day and grow more man than god! They share the guilt, but Gilgamesh is King, set over Uruk by my own decree. And he is two parts god. Therefore you shall not take him. Take the one who is no more than man."'

When Enkidu had told this dream, a fever came and daily spread outward from the cankered hand that had touched the Forest Gate. Gilgamesh sat over him and grieved: 'Why do the gods take you instead of me? Though I sit and wait outside the doors of death, yet you and I will never meet again.'

Enkidu burned with fever and he cursed the Forest Gate: 'I saw you from afar, and I marvelled at your beauty, for you were made in Nippur by skilled craftsmen and your size was so exceeding great that there could not be another like you anywhere. And so I would not hurt you. O Gate, had I but known that by your beauty you would cause my death, I would not thus have spared you, would not have touched your timbers with my bare hand, but instead I would have raised my axe and hewed you down.'

Then he cursed the temple-woman, for it was she who first had brought him into Uruk and to Gilgamesh: 'May she be cast out! Let her be driven from the temple, let her haunt the shadow of the wall, let the streets become her dwelling-place. Let each hand strike her cheek!'

When Shamash heard these words, he called from Heaven: 'Why do you curse the woman? It was she who clothed your body with her garments, taught you speech, how to eat bread, and drink wine from a cup. It was she who gave you Gilgamesh the King, to be your friend and your own brother. And from him you received the high seat in his palace, the seat at his left side, so that the princes of the earth should kiss your feet. Over you the King will cause Uruk to wail; over you, when you are buried, he will mourn. He will let his hair grow long, put on a lion-skin, and wander in the desert for your sake.'

Enkidu's anger left him when he heard the words of Shamash. He lifted off the curse and gave a blessing in its place. He lay there growing weaker, with the fever burning in him and his dreams became more terrible with every night that passed.

One night, he woke and called out to his friend: 'Gilgamesh, last night the heavens groaned and the earth rang echoing with the sound. I stood alone before some dreadful thing whose face was dark as any bird of storm; who seized me in strong talons, held me fast, and choked my life out with his eagle-claw. And then he turned my arms to feathered wings and led me down that path which none walks twice, to the house of Ereshkigal, Queen of Death, to the house which the man who enters never leaves. The people there are clothed with wings like birds. They sit in darkness for eternity. Their food is dust and clay their sustenance. And there I saw the princes of the earth, their splendour brought to ashes and to dust. The Queen of Darkness sat upon her throne and, before her, squatting at her feet, was Belit-sheri, she who is the Scribe and keeps the register of all the dead. She was reading from a tablet which she held, but raised her head and saw me. She got up and stretching out her hand, took me away. And at that, I awoke. I am afraid.'

Gilgamesh said: 'Dear friend, your dream has shown that darkness is the end of mortal life.'

Enkidu's pain increased from day to day, and on the twelfth he called to Gilgamesh: 'Because of Ishtar's wrath I lie here now upon a bed of shame, not like a man who falls in battle and is blessed. But as for me, I die dishonoured.' And he spoke no more.

As soon as the first light of morning came, Gilgamesh cried: 'Elders of Uruk! It is for Enkidu my friend that I now weep. It is for Enkidu that I shed bitter tears. He was my axe, the bow in my right hand, the shield that was before me, and my joy. An evil foe has robbed me of my friend, my younger brother, who once ran with the wild ass and the panther of the plain. We two ascended mountains, we killed the Bull of Heaven, and we slew Humbaba, the keeper of the trees. O, Enkidu, where are you? Are you lost out in the darkness? What sleep has taken hold of you? Can you not hear my voice?'

Gilgamesh touched the heart of Enkidu. It did not beat.

The King then veiled his brother like a bride. Back and forth he paced before his friend and like a lion lifted up his voice, or a lioness robbed of her young cubs. He tore his hair, cast off his royal robes and wept: 'I gave to you the seat at my left side, so that the princes of the earth should kiss your feet. Now I will cause the people of Uruk to weep and wail for you, and over you, when you are buried, I will mourn. I will let my hair grow long, put on a lion-skin, and wander in the desert for your sake.'

For seven days and seven nights he wept, before he gave his brother to the earth. And then he left Uruk, and went away to wander in the wilderness in grief.

The Search for Everlasting Life

Gilgamesh wept bitterly for Enkidu his friend, and roamed the desert waste.

'Where is there any rest for me,' he cried, 'now Enkidu is dead, for black despair gnaws at my heart. As he is, I shall be. I am afraid, and therefore I will go to seek out Utnapishtim, the one man whom the gods saved from the flood that drowned the world. For him, whom men call Faraway, they set in Dilmun, in the Garden of the Gods, and gave him the gift of everlasting life. He will tell me how to win it for myself.'

He set out on his journey, wandering far till he reached the mountain Mashu which stands guard over the rising and the setting of the sun. Its peaks stretched up to Heaven, but its roots pierced down into the gloomy Underworld. The Scorpion-people kept watch at its gate; ringed with flame, their gaze was death to men. But Gilgamesh, his face dark with dismay, covered his eyes but for a moment's space against their fiery aureoles, then advanced. He gathered up his courage and bowed low.

'This is a god who comes on unafraid,' said the Scorpion-man, but his wife answered him: 'He is but two parts god and one part man.'

The Scorpion-man called out to Gilgamesh. He asked: 'Why have you come here, come so far, out here to Mashu on the rim of earth?'

Gilgamesh said: 'I had a friend who died. Because of him, I travelled to this place. My life is empty now that he is dead and as he is, so one day shall I be. I shall lie down and never rise again. So I seek Utnapishtim, for they say that he alone has everlasting life; he will tell me how to win it for myself.'

'No living man before you has dared to go into the mountain Mashu, for inside there stretch twelve leagues of darkness without light, from the rising to the setting of the sun.'

'Yet I must go,' said Gilgamesh. 'In sorrow or in pain, in sighing or in weeping, I must go.'

'The gate is open for you. Enter in. And may you safely, at the ending of your journey, return this way again.'

Gilgamesh entered in. He took the road that the Sun God walks at midnight while men sleep. The first league, there was darkness and no light before him or behind; the second league, thick was the darkness and there was no light before him or behind; and at the eighth league, Gilgamesh cried out, for there was darkness still, and still no light before him or behind. But at the ninth, he felt the North Wind blow upon his face; at the eleventh he saw light; and after twelve came out into the sun.

He came into the garden of the sun, where Shamash walks at evening, where each leaf is made of lapis lazuli, where vines bear dark carnelians. It was there that Shamash saw him and his heart was troubled.

'No living man has passed this way,' he said, 'nor will again, and you will never find what you are looking for, while this world lasts, because the gods decreed that darkness be the end of mortal life.'

Gilgamesh answered: 'Should I rest my head in the midst of earth and sleep for all the years when I have come so far? Should I stay here? I must go on. But let me see the sun, though I am as a dead man in this place, far from the land of living. Let me look, till I can look no longer, at its fire, for there is only darkness after death.'

Down by the shore of the sea, there was a house where sat Siduri, Woman of the Vine, using the golden jug and golden vat the gods had given her, to make their wine. When she looked up, she saw a man approach and, even from a distance, she could see that, though he had the stature of a god, despair was in his heart, and on his face was the look of one who traveled without hope. She took counsel with herself.

'Surely,' she said, 'this man must be a murderer who comes here. Why else should he be wandering in this place?'

She barred her gate. Gilgamesh heard the heavy bolt shoot home. He said: 'Siduri, what was it you saw that made you bar your gate? Do you not know that I am Gilgamesh, who killed Humbaba, cut the cedar down, and seized and slew the Bull that came from Heaven?'

Siduri said: 'If *you* are Gilgamesh, who killed Humbaba, cut the cedar down, and seized and slew the Bull that came from Heaven, why are your cheeks so thin, why are they burnt with cold and heat, why do you wander in the desert and the plain? Why is despair within your heart and on your face the look of one who travels without hope?'

He said to her: 'Why should these things not be? My friend, my younger brother, who once ran wild with the wild ass and the panther of the plain, who ascended mountains with me, killed the Bull and slew Humbaba, keeper of the trees; my friend whom I loved dearly, and who went beside me through all hardships—he is dead. The fate of man has overtaken him. For seven days and seven nights I wept, and would not give him up for burial, thinking: "My friend will rise at my lament." But the Annunaki, Judges of the Dead, seized him. He is gone, and now my life is empty, so I roam the grassy plains and deserts, far and wide. How can I be silent, when my friend, my younger brother whom

I loved, has turned to clay? And I, shall I not like him soon lie down and never rise again? I am afraid.'

'Gilgamesh, where are you running? You will never find what you are looking for while this world lasts, because the gods decreed that darkness be the end of mortal life. And you, great King, must learn to live your life from day to day, and look no further than the evening's rest. Short pleasures can be sweet. Take food and wine, be merry and rejoice. Go now again the way you came, return to your dear wife and to the child that holds you by the hand, for love was granted men as well as death.'

'I loved my brother Enkidu. He died. How can I rest, when I must die as he? Tell me the road to Utnapishtim. O, tell me how to find him! I will cross the sea and if I cannot cross, roam in the desert waste, for I have heard that he alone has everlasting life. He will tell me how to win it for myself.'

Siduri said: 'No man has ever crossed. None who has come here since the days of old has crossed the sea, save Shamash in his course. Hard is the passage; bitter, dark and deep are the Waters of Death that bar the way to land, that flow between the sea and Dilmun's shore. But Gilgamesh, go down into the woods, and look for Urshanabi. He is there, close by the Images of Stone which keep him safe as Utnapishtim's Boatman. It may be that he will take you over, but if not, turn back, go home. There is no other way.'

Gilgamesh grew fretful at her words and went down to the edges of the sea. With his axe he struck, in senseless rage, the Images of Stone that stood nearby and shattered them. He then walked further on and came upon the Boatman in the woods, as he was carving a new prow. He rose and said: 'My name is Urshanabi. Who are you?'

'Do you not know that I am Gilgamesh, who killed Humbaba, cut the cedar down, and seized and slew the Bull that came from Heaven?'

The Boatman said: 'If *you* are Gilgamesh, who killed Humbaba, cut the cedar down, and seized and slew the Bull that came from Heaven, why are your cheeks so thin, why are they burnt with cold and heat, why do you wander in the desert and the plain? Why is despair within your heart and on your face the look of one who travels without hope?'

He said to him: 'Why should these things not be? My friend, my younger brother, who once ran with the wild ass and the panther of the plain, who ascended mountains with me, killed the Bull and slew Humbaba, keeper of the trees; my friend, whom I loved dearly, and who went beside me through all hardships—he is dead. The fate of man has overtaken him. For seven days and seven nights I wept and would not give him up for burial, thinking: "My friend will rise again at my lament." But the Annunaki seized him. He has gone, and now my life is empty, so I roam the grassy plains and deserts, far and wide. How can I be silent, when my friend, my younger brother whom I loved, has turned to clay? And I, shall I not like him soon lie down and never rise again? I am afraid. So take me to Utnapishtim! Ferry me across, for he alone has everlasting life and will tell me how to win it for myself.'

Urshanabi said: 'We cannot go. You broke the Images of Stone that kept me safe. The passage is now dangerous—but yet go down into the woods, and with your axe cut out a hundred and twenty poles; each one must be full sixty cubits long. We may yet cross.'

Gilgamesh went at once into the woods and cut the poles, in number and in size just as the Boatman said. They launched the boat and glided on the sea, and in three days had made a journey of six weeks. When they had crossed the sea, they ran at last into the Waters of Death that barred the way to land, and flowed between the sea and Dilmun's shore. Then Urshanabi said: 'Take up a pole and thrust it deep. Now cast the thing away, for it is wet to almost its full length. You must not touch the Waters with your hands or you will die. Now take a second up, and now a third, a fourth, a fifth, a sixth, a seventh, an eighth.'

Gilgamesh pushed the boat on with the poles until the last was used, but still they were far out upon the Waters, far from land. So then the King stood up and spread his arms, and with his garment for a sail they reached the shore.

The Flower of Youth

Utnapishtim, called the Faraway, was sitting at his ease upon the slopes of Dilmun, in the Garden of the Gods, and when he saw the boat come in to land, he took counsel with himself, and in his heart said: 'Who has destroyed the Images of Stone that used to guard the ship? Who is this man who comes here with my boatman on the sea? He is none of mine!'

As they approached, he called: 'Who are you, and what is it you seek, that you have crossed such waters on your way?'

'Do you not know that I am Gilgamesh, who killed Humbaba, cut the cedar down, and seized and slew the Bull that came from Heaven?'

Utnapishtim said: 'If *you* are he, who killed Humbaba, cut the cedar down, and seized and slew the Bull that came from Heaven, why are your cheeks so thin, why are they burnt with cold and heat, why do you wander in the desert and the plain? Why is despair within your heart and on your face the look of one who travels without hope?'

He answered him: 'Why should these things not be? My friend, my younger brother who once ran with the wild ass and the panther of the plain, who ascended mountains with me, killed the Bull and slew Humbaba, keeper of the trees; my friend whom I loved dearly, and who went beside me through all hardships—he is dead. The fate of man has overtaken him. For seven days and seven nights I wept, and would not give him up for burial, thinking: "My friend will rise at my lament." But the Annunaki, Judges of the Dead, seized him. He is gone, and now my life is empty, so I roam the grassy plains and deserts, far and wide. How can I be silent when my friend, my younger brother whom I loved, has turned to clay? And I, shall I not like him soon lie down and never rise again? I am afraid.'

'Gilgamesh, where are you running? You will never find what you are looking for while this world lasts, because the gods decreed that darkness be the end of mortal life. For do we build a house to last for ever, make a law to last for ever—from the days of old there is no permanence. The river brings a flood but then it falls; the sun comes out then hides behind a cloud; the gods allotted life but also death. How like they are—the sleeping and the dead; both picture death, a lesser and a great. Sleep is the sign of your mortality.'

'I have crossed mountains, I have crossed the seas and never had my fill of restful sleep. I was wearied out with walking and my clothing hung in rags before I reached Siduri of the Vine. I have killed the lion and tiger, the bear, the panther and the stag, the ibex and hyena, and the creatures of the plain, to eat their flesh and wear their skins, since I set out to find you. For you alone can tell me how to win immortal life, life everlasting. *You* look like a man, you are no different from myself, and yet you live. In my heart I thought that you would seem a god, a mighty man of battle—here you lie idly on your side out in the sun! Tell me how you got the precious gift of everlasting life and entered into the company of the gods.'

Utnapishtim said: 'I will reveal a hidden thing, a secret of the gods, and tell how Ea saved me from the Flood.'

He told him how the gods had drowned the world, but for his piety had taken him to live for ever in fair Dilmun.

'As for you,' he said, 'what can we do to help you win this life for which you seek? First we must see if you can pass the test and overcome the little death of sleep. Six days and seven nights you must not sleep.'

But Gilgamesh had walked the desert waste and he was weary; sleep came falling down, sleep came like a rainstorm blew on him; he slept.

Utnapishtim said: 'Look at the man who thought that he could win eternal life! Sleep like a rainstorm blows on him; he sleeps, and sleeping proves he is no more than man. Did I not say the sleeping and the dead both picture death? Wife, see him where he lies! If Gilgamesh cannot even conquer sleep, a little dying, how much less shall he withstand its image, true death, when it comes.'

Utnapishtim's wife said: 'Touch the man that he may awake, that he may now return upon the road by which he came, to his own land.'

'Deceitful is mankind! This man will try to deceive us by denying that he slept. We must give him proof. Therefore bake loaves of bread and each day stand a fresh one by his head to mark the passing time as he sleeps on.'

So she baked loaves of bread and every day stood one beside the King, till the day came when the first was hard as stone, the third still moist, the sixth one freshly baked, the seventh unmade. Then Utnapishtim touched the sleeping man and he awoke.

'I hardly slept,' he said.

'Count up the loaves and see how many days.'

'Where shall I go now, and what shall I do? Wherever I set my foot, death comes behind! For if I cannot even conquer sleep, a little dying, how much less shall I be able to withstand its image, death?'

Utnapishtim told his Boatman that he must take the King down to the washing-place to bathe him and to cleanse his matted hair.

'And I will give him garments such that they will show no sign of wear until he comes into Uruk again. You must go with him; since you brought him here, across the boundaries of life and death, and broke the rule established by the gods, you cannot stay, you can no longer be my Boatman. Urshanabi, you must leave.'

Urshanabi did as he was told and when the King was washed and clothed anew, they launched the boat to make the journey back. But Utnapishtim's wife said: 'Gilgamesh was weary when he came and weary goes. What will you give him now for all his pains, to take back to his land?'

So Utnapishtim called to them; the King took up a pole and brought the boat back in towards the bank.

'Gilgamesh, you were weary when you came and weary go. What would you have of me for all your pains, to take back to your land? I will reveal to you a hidden thing, a secret of the gods, so listen well. Beneath the waters in a certain place there grows a little plant with spines as sharp as any thorn or rose. If you can pluck it, then your hands will hold the Flower of Youth, to make you young again.'

Utnapishtim told him where to look and, with the Boatman, Gilgamesh set out. When they reached the place that they were looking for, Gilgamesh tied stones upon his feet and leapt into the waters. Down and down, into the deepest channels of the sea he sank, and there he saw the plant. He grasped its stem; although it pricked his hands, he plucked it from its roots, cut off the stones, and let the waters bear him to the light.

He said to Urshanabi: 'See this plant. It is the Flower of Youth, and by its power old men grow young again. I will return to Uruk and there give this magic plant to all the old to eat and at the last, when I have reached old age, I too shall eat and have back all my strength.'

So Gilgamesh and Urshanabi sailed over the sea towards Uruk again, and after fifty leagues they stopped to rest because the night had come. They pulled to shore. There was a pool of cool, clean water near, and Gilgamesh the King went down to bathe, leaving the Flower of Youth upon the bank. But deep down in the pool, a serpent lay that smelled the Flower. It rose up, seized it, ate. It sloughed its skin, becoming young again.

Then Gilgamesh sat down and wept aloud: 'Was it for this that I have laboured? Has the life-blood of my heart been spent all for a serpent? This my prize? Though everlasting life could not be mine, yet in my hand I held the Flower of Youth. Now I have lost it there is nothing left.

'Come with me, Urshanabi, to Uruk; let us leave the boat and make our way by land. I will show you my great city. There at least, my toil has not been fruitless. Its high walls and the ramparts I have raised— these things will be all there is left of me when I am dead.'

So Gilgamesh the golden, King of Kings, resigned himself to death, the fate of men. He came back weary from his wandering and wrote on brick this tale of ancient days. Though he was mortal man, he set his name where great men's names were set, and where no names were, there he built an altar to the gods.

Chapter 2

Hesiod, *Theogony*

*Hesiod (fl. c. 700 BC) was one of the earliest Greek poets, often called the "father of Greek didactic poetry." Two of his complete epics have survived—***Theogony** *(relating myths of the gods) and* **Works and Days** *(describing peasant life).*

Not much is known about Hesiod. He was a native of Boeotia, a district of central Greece to which his father had migrated from Cyme in Asia Minor. It is said that he may have been a rhapsodist—a professional reciter of poetry—learning the technique and vocabulary of the epic by memorizing and reciting heroic songs. Hesiod himself attributes his poetic gifts to the Muses who, he says, appeared to him while he was tending sheep, giving him a poet's staff and endowing him with a poet's voice, and bidding him to "sing of the race of the blessed gods immortal."

In apparent fulfillment of this request, the earlier of his extant works, the **Theogony**, *recounts the history of the gods beginning with Chaos, Gaea (Earth), and Eros. Gaea gives birth to Uranus (Heaven), mountains, Pontus (the Sea), and later, after uniting herself with Uranus, other deities. One of these is Titan Cronus, who rebels against Uranus, emasculating him, then ruling until overpowered by Zeus. The story of crime and revolt is the fundamental subject of the* **Theogony**; *and Hesiod's authorship of the work is now beyond doubt.*

The present selection, from the **Theogony**, *portrays Friendship as emerging from the abyss of darkness and death surrounding the original birth narratives of the gods. First there was Chaos, and with Chaos' first yawn, the great Mother Earth* (Gaea) *and* Eros *were born. But Chaos yawned again, and* Erebos, *the Dark, and his sister Night*

23

*came forth; and Night gave birth to the dreadful likes of Doom, Fate,
Death, Blame, Woe, and Nemesis, Deceit, Strife, and Friendship. Thus,
Hesiod's world-order emerges from the chasm of darkness, strife, and
death; and amidst this dark and dreadful abyss, the only light
discernible among the offspring of Night is Friendship.*

Theogony

And Night bare hateful Doom and black Fate and Death, and she
bare Sleep and the tribe of Dreams. And again the goddess murky
Night, though she lay with none, bare Blame and painful Woe, and the
Hesperides who guard the rich, golden apples and the trees bearing fruit
beyond glorious Ocean. Also she bare the Destinies and ruthless
avenging Fates, Clotho and Lachesis and Atropos,[1] who gave men at
their birth both evil and good to have, and they pursue the
transgressions of men and of gods: and these goddesses never cease
from their dread anger until they punish the sinner with a sore penalty.
Also deadly Night bare Nemesis (Indignation) to afflict mortal men,
and after her, Deceit and Friendship and hateful Age and hard-hearted
Strife.

But abhorred Strife bare painful Toil and Forgetfulness and Famine
and tearful Sorrows, Fightings also, Battles, Murders, Manslaughters,
Quarrels, Lying Words, Disputes, Lawlessness and Ruin, all of one
nature, and Oath who most troubles men upon earth when anyone
willfully swears a false oath.

Notes

[1] Clotho (the Spinner) is she who spins the thread of man's life; Lachesis (the
Disposer of Lots) assigns to each man his destiny; Atropos (She who cannot be
turned) is the "Fury with the abhorred shears."

Chapter 3

Plato, *Lysis,* or *Friendship*

Plato, (427-347 B.C.) is usually regarded as the most famous 'disciple' of Socrates. Plato abandoned a more obvious political career rather early in life, choosing to devote his life to philosophy instead. Yet, he did not leave the affairs of 'the city' behind. He founded the Academy in Athens, perhaps the most significant school of 'higher learning,' which survived some nine hundred years before it was closed by Justinian in 529.

To some, Plato, not Aristotle, deserves the title "the philosopher," and to this day he remains the most widely read and quoted thinker on record. His **Republic** *is regarded the most influential book in Western civilization, next to the Bible, and it is but one of many dialogues equally profound if not as ambitious in scope.*

One 'minor' dialogue is **Lysis,** *a dialogue devoted entirely to the topic of friendship. To some, this dialogue is frustrating, because in the end the question of what a friend truly is remains undefined, while the definitions that are entertained along the way are extraordinarily subtle.*

One of the reasons why this little dialogue on such an 'obvious' topic is so difficult lies with the dramatic setting of the dialogue itself. That which one would learn from this dialogue must be learned by a careful reading 'between the lines,' as it were, as Socrates 'wrestles with speech' with youths who are rather busily learning to wrestle merely with their bodies. Thus, does Socrates play 'the mid-wife' for them, giving them ultimately no 'final' solution to their inquiry. Rather, he displays for his young interlocutors the questioning way by which one is engaged in a philosophic question. It is no accident that

*Plato has the dialogue occur as Socrates is distracted, in a 'friendly'
way, from his bee-line from the Academy to the Lyceum, in such a way
that he enters a wrestling hall. In the end, no one can quite 'pin down'
the definition of a true friend, though Socrates has shown the young
men in the course of the dialogue examples of both the sophistry they
will someday have to wrestle with in the Lyceum and the wise
questioning procedure to be followed in philosophy proper, a manner
of questioning to be learned from the Academy.*

*Thus, in the end, Socrates appears to have **said** nothing particularly
positive in the question concerning the friend; yet the drama of the
dialogue suggests that he has shown something very definite as to what
a friend must wrestle with indeed, if one would ultimately be a friend of
wisdom.*

Lysis (or *Friendship*)

Persons of the Dialogue

SOCRATES, *who is the narrator*
MENEXENUS
HIPPOTHALES
LYSIS
CTESIPPUS

Scene: A newly-erected palaestra[1] outside the walls of Athens.

I was going from the Academy straight to the Lyceum by the outer
road, which is close under the wall. When I came to the postern gate of
the city, which is by the fountain of Panops, I fell in with Hippothales,
the son of Hieronymus, and Ctesippus, from the deme[2] of Paeania, and
a company of young men who were standing with them. Hippothales,
seeing me approach, asked whence I came and whither I was going.

I am going, I replied, from the Academy straight to the Lyceum.

Then come straight to us, he said, and turn in here; you may as well.

Who are you, I said; and where am I to come?

Here, he said, showing me an enclosed space and an open door over
against the wall. This is the place where we all meet: and a goodly
company we are.

And what is this place, I asked; and what sort of entertainment have you?

It is a newly-erected palaestra, he replied; and the entertainment is generally conversation, to which you are welcome.

Thank you, I said; and who is your teacher?

Your old friend and admirer, Miccus, he said.

Indeed, I replied; he is a very eminent professor.

Are you disposed, he said, to go with me and see them?

Yes, I said; but I should like to know first, what is expected of me, and who is the favourite among you?

Some persons have one favourite, Socrates, and some another, he said.

And who is yours? I asked. Tell me that, Hippothales.

At this question he blushed; and I said to him, O Hippothales, son of Hieronymus! you need not say that you are, or that you are not, in love; the confession is too late; for I see that you are not only in love, but are already far gone in your love. Unintelligent and unpractical as I am, the Gods have given me the power of quickly detecting a lover and his beloved.

Whereupon he blushed more and more.

Ctesippus said: I like to see you blushing, Hippothales, and hesitating to tell Socrates the name; why, if he is with you but a very short time, you will have plagued him to death by talking about nothing else. Indeed, Socrates, he has deafened us and stopped our ears with talking of Lysis; and if he is a little intoxicated, there is every likelihood that we shall be woken up, thinking we hear the name of Lysis. His talk, bad as it is, might be worse; but when he drenches us with his poems and his prose, it is unbearable; and worse still is his manner of singing them to his love; he has a voice which is truly appalling, and we are forced to endure it: and now being asked straight out by you, he is blushing.

I suppose, I said, this Lysis must be quite young; for the name does not recall anyone to me.

Why, he said, his father being a very well-known man, he is known as his father's son, and is not as yet commonly called by his own name; but, although you do not know his name, I am sure that you must know his face, for that is quite enough to distinguish him.

But tell me whose son he is, I said.

He is the eldest son of Democrates, of the deme of Aexonè.

Ah, Hippothales, I said; what a noble and wholly ingenuous love you have found! I wish that you would favour me with the exhibition which you have been giving to the rest of the company, and then I shall be able to judge whether you know what a lover ought to say about his love, either to the youth himself, or to others.

Nay, Socrates, said Hippothales; you surely do not attach any importance to what Ctesippus is saying.

Do you mean, I said, that you disown the love of the person whom he says that you love?

No; but I deny that I make verses or write prose compositions to him.

He is not in his right mind, said Ctesippus; he is talking nonsense, and is stark mad.

O Hippothales, I said, I do not want to hear any verses or songs you have composed in honour of your favourite; but I want to know the purport of them, that I may be able to judge of your mode of approaching your beloved.

Ctesippus will be able to tell you, he said; for if, as he avers, the sound of my words is always dinning in his ears, he must have a very accurate knowledge and recollection of them.

Yes, indeed, said Ctesippus; I know only too well, and very ridiculous the tale is: for although he is a lover, and most devotedly in love, he has nothing particular to talk about to his beloved which a child might not say. Now is not that ridiculous? He can only speak of what the whole city celebrates, the wealth of Democrates, and of Lysis, the boy's grandfather, and of all the other ancestors of the youth, and their stud of horses, and their victories at the Pythian games, and at the Isthmus, and at Nemea in chariot and horse races—these are the tales which he composes and repeats, and even more prehistoric stories still. Only the day before yesterday he made a poem in which he described the entertainment of Heracles, telling how in virtue of his relationship to the family he was hospitably received by an ancestor of Lysis; for this ancestor was himself begotten by Zeus of the daughter of the founder of the deme. And these are the sort of old wives' tales which he sings and recites to us, and compels us to listen to him.

When I heard this, I said: O ridiculous Hippothales! How can you be making and singing hymns in honour of yourself before you have won?

But my songs and verses, he said, are not in honour of myself, Socrates.

You think not?

What do you mean?

Most assuredly, I said, those songs are all in your own honour; for if you win your beautiful love, your discourses and songs will be a glory to you, and may be truly regarded as hymns of praise composed in honour of yourself who have conquered and won such a love; but if he slips away from you, the more you have praised him, the more ridiculous you will look at having lost this fairest and best of blessings; and therefore the wise lover does not praise his beloved until he has won him, because he is afraid of what may come. There is also another danger; the fair, when anyone praises or magnifies them, are filled with the spirit of pride and vain-glory. Do you not agree with me?

Yes, he said.

And the more vain-glorious they are, the more difficult is the capture of them?

Naturally.

What should you say of a hunter who frightened the animals away, and made the capture of his prey more difficult?

He would be a bad hunter, undoubtedly.

Yes; and to infuriate a lover instead of soothing him with words and songs, would show a great want of art: do you not agree?

Yes.

And now reflect, Hippothales, and see whether you are not guilty of all these errors in writing your poetry. For I can hardly suppose that you will affirm a man to be a good poet who injures himself by his poetry.

Assuredly not, he said; such a poet would be a fool. And this is the reason why I take you into my counsels, Socrates, and I shall be glad of any further advice which you may have to offer. Will you tell me by what words or actions a man might become endeared to his love?

That is not easy to determine, I said; but if you will enable me to talk with your love, I may perhaps be able to show you how to converse with him, instead of singing and reciting in the fashion of which you are accused.

There will be no difficulty there, he replied. If you will only go with Ctesippus into the palaestra, and sit down and talk, I believe that he will come of his own accord; for he is very fond of listening, Socrates. And as this is the festival of the Hermaea, the young men and boys are all together. He will be sure to come; but if he does not come of himself, let Ctesippus call him; for he knows him well, and his cousin Menexenus is Lysis' great friend.

That will be the way, I said. Thereupon I led Ctesippus into the palaestra, and the rest followed.

Upon entering we found that the boys had just been sacrificing; and the ceremony was nearly at an end. They were all in their best array, and games at dice were going on among them. Most of them were in the outer court amusing themselves; but some were in the corner of the apodyterium[3] playing at odd and even with a number of dice, which they took out of little wicker baskets. There was also a circle of lookers-on; among them was Lysis. He was standing with the other boys and youths, having a wreath upon his head, lovely to look at, and not less worthy of praise for his look of gentle breeding than for his beauty. We left them, and went over to the opposite side of the room, where, finding a quiet place, we sat down; and then we began to talk. This attracted Lysis, who was constantly turning round to look at us— he was evidently wanting to come to us. For a time he hesitated and had not the courage to come alone; but afterwards, his friend Menexenus, in the course of his game, entered the palaestra from the court, and when he saw Ctesippus and myself proceeded to take a seat by us; and then Lysis, seeing him, followed, and sat down by his side; and the other boys joined. And Hippothales too, when he saw the crowd standing by us, got behind them, where he thought that he would be out of sight of Lysis, lest he should anger him; and there he stood and listened.

I turned to Menexenus, and said: Son of Demophon, which of you two youths is the elder?

That is a matter of dispute between us, he said.

And which is the nobler? Is that also a matter of dispute?

Yes, certainly. ·

And do you also dispute which is the fairer?

The two boys laughed.

I shall not ask which is the richer of the two, I said; for you are friends, are you not?

Certainly, they replied.

And friends have all things in common, so that one of you can be no richer than the other, if you say truly that you are friends.

They assented. I was about to ask which was the juster and which the wiser of the two; but at this moment Menexenus was called away by someone who came and said that the gymnastics-master wanted him. I suppose that he had to offer sacrifice. So he went away, and I asked Lysis some more questions. I dare say, Lysis, I said, that your father and mother love you very much.

Certainly, he said.

And they would wish you to be as happy as possible.

Yes.

But do you think that anyone is happy who is in the condition of a slave, and who could not do what he liked?

I should think not indeed, he said.

And if your father and mother love you, and desire that you should be happy, it is quite clear that they are eager to promote your happiness.

Certainly, he replied.

And do they then permit you to do what you like, and never rebuke you or hinder you from doing what you desire?

Yes, indeed, Socrates; there are a great many things which they hinder me from doing.

What do you mean? I said. Do they want you to be happy, and yet hinder you from doing what you like? For example, if you want to mount one of your father's chariots, and take the reins at a race, would they refuse to allow you to do so and prevent you?

Certainly, he said, they would not allow me to do so.

Whom then will they allow?

There is a charioteer, whom my father pays for driving.

And do they trust a hireling more than you to do what he likes with the horses? And do they pay him for this as well?

They do.

But I dare say that you may take the whip and guide the mule-cart if you like;—they would permit that?

Permit me! indeed they would not.

Then, I said, may no one else use the whip to the mules?

Yes, the muleteer.[4]

And is he a slave or a free man?

A slave.

And do they esteem a slave of more value than you who are their son? And do they entrust their property to him rather than to you? and allow him to do what he likes, when they prohibit you? Answer me now: Are you your own master, or do they not even allow that?

Nay, he said, of course they do not allow it.

Then you have a master?

Yes, my tutor; there he is.

And is he a slave?

To be sure; he is our slave, he replied.

Surely, I said, this is a strange thing, that a free man should be governed by a slave. And what does he do with you?

He takes me to my teachers.

You do not mean to say that your teachers also rule over you?

Of course they do.

Then I must say that your father is pleased to inflict many lords and masters on you. But at any rate when you go home to your mother, she lets you have your own way, and does not interfere with your happiness; her wool, or the piece of cloth which she is weaving, is at your disposal: I am sure that she does not hinder you from touching her wooden spathe, or her comb, or any other of her spinning implements.

Nay, Socrates, he replied, laughing; not only does she hinder me, but I should be beaten if I were to touch one of them.

Well, I said, this is amazing. And did you ever behave ill to your father or your mother?

No, indeed, he replied.

But why then are they so terribly anxious to prevent you from being happy, and doing as you like?—keeping you all day long in subjection to another, and, in a word, allowing you to do nothing which you desire; so that you get no good, as would appear, out of their great possessions, which are under the control of anybody rather than of you, and have no use of your own fair person, which is tended and taken care of by another; while you, Lysis, are master of nobody, and can do nothing you wish?

Why, he said, Socrates, the reason is that I am not of age.

I doubt whether that is the real reason, I said; for I should imagine that your father Democrates, and your mother, do permit you to do some things already, and do not wait until you are of age: for example, if they want anything read or written, you, I presume, would be the first person in the house set to that task.

Very true.

And you would be allowed to write or read the letters in any order which you please, or to take up the lyre and tighten or loosen any of the strings and play it with your fingers or strike it with the plectrum, exactly as you please, and neither father nor mother would interfere with you.

That is true, he said.

Then what can the reason be, Lysis, I said, why they allow you to do the one and not the other?

I suppose, he said, because I understand the one, and not the other.

Yes, my dear youth, I said, then the reason is not any deficiency of years, but a deficiency of knowledge; and the very day when your father thinks that you are wiser than he is, he will instantly commit himself and his possessions to you.

I expect so.

Aye, I said; and your neighbor, too, will he not observe the same rule about you as your father? As soon as he is satisfied that you know more about the management of family business than he does, will he continue to administer his affairs himself, or will he commit them to you?

I think that he will commit them to me.

Will not the Athenian people, too, entrust their affairs to you when they see that you have wisdom enough to manage them?

Yes.

And oh! let me put another case, I said. There is the great king, and he has an eldest son, who is the Prince of Asia;—suppose that you and I go to him and establish to his satisfaction that we are better cooks than his son, will he not entrust to us the prerogative of making soup, and putting in anything that we like while the pot is boiling, rather than to his son?

To us, clearly.

And we shall be allowed to throw in salt by handfuls, whereas the son will not be allowed to put in even a pinch?

Of course.

Or suppose again that the son has bad eyes, would he allow him, or not, to touch his own eyes if he thinks that he has no knowledge of medicine?

He would not allow him.

Whereas, if he supposed us to have a knowledge of medicine, he would allow us to do what we like with him—even to open the eyes wide and sprinkle ashes upon them, because he supposed that we knew the right treatment?

That is true.

And everything in which we appear to him to be wiser than himself or his son he would commit to us?

Of course, Socrates, he replied.

This then is how it stands, my dear Lysis; in things which we know everyone will trust us—Hellenes and barbarians, men and women; we may do as we please about them, and no one if he can help it will interfere with us; we shall be free, and masters of others; and these things will be really ours, for we shall be benefited by them. But in things of which we have no understanding, no one will trust us to do as seems good to us—they will hinder us as far as they can; and not only strangers, but father and mother, and even a nearer relation if there be one, and in these matters we shall be subject to others; and these things will not be ours, for we shall not be benefited by them. Do you agree?

He assented.

And shall we be friends to others, and will any others love us, in matters where we are useless to them?

Certainly not.

Then neither does your father love you, nor does anybody love anybody else, in so far as he is useless to him?

It seems not.

And therefore, my boy, if you become wise, all men will be your friends and kindred, for you will be useful and good; but if you are not wise, neither father, nor mother, nor kindred, nor anyone else, will be your friends. And in matters of which one has as yet no knowledge, can he have any conceit of knowledge?

That is impossible, he replied.

And you, Lysis, if you require a teacher, have not yet attained to wisdom.

True.

And therefore you are not conceited, having no knowledge of which to be conceited.

Indeed, Socrates, I think not.

When I heard him say this, I turned to Hippothales, and was very nearly making a blunder, for I was going to say to him: That is the way, Hippothales, in which you should talk to your beloved, humbling and lowering him, and not as you do, puffing him up and spoiling him. But I saw that he was in great distress and confusion at what had been said, and I remembered that, although he was in the neighborhood, he did not want to be seen by Lysis; so upon second thoughts I refrained.

In the meantime Menexenus came back and sat down in his place by Lysis; and Lysis, in a childish and affectionate manner, whispered privately in my ear, so that Menexenus should not hear: Do, Socrates, tell Menexenus what you have been telling me.

Suppose that you tell him yourself, Lysis, I replied; for I am sure that you were attending.

Certainly, he replied.

Try, then, to remember the words, and be as exact as you can in repeating them to him, and if you have forgotten anything, ask me again the next time that you see me.

I will be sure to do so, Socrates; but do tell him something new, and let me listen till it is time to go home.

I certainly cannot refuse, I said, since you ask me; but then, as you know, Menexenus is very pugnacious, and therefore you must come to the rescue if he attempts to upset me.

Yes, indeed, he said; he is very pugnacious, and that is the reason why I want you to argue with him.

That I may make a fool of myself?

No, indeed, he said; but I want you to put him down.

That is no easy matter, I replied; for he is a terrible fellow—a pupil of Ctesippus. And there is Ctesippus himself: do you not see him?

Never mind, Socrates, please start arguing with him.

Well, I suppose that I must, I replied.

Hereupon Ctesippus complained that we were talking in secret, and keeping the feast to ourselves.

I shall be happy, I said, to let you have a share. Here is Lysis, who does not understand something that I was saying, and wants me to ask Menexenus, who, as he thinks, is likely to know.

And why do you not ask him? he said.

Very well, I said, I will; and do you, Menexenus, answer. But first I must tell you that I am one who from my childhood upward have set my heart upon a certain possession. All people have their fancies; some desire horses, and others dogs; and some are fond of gold, and others of honour. Now, I have no violent desire of any of these things; but I have a passion for friends; and I would rather have a good friend than the best cock or quail in the world: I would even go further, and say the best horse or dog. Yea, by the dog of Egypt, I should greatly prefer a real friend to all the gold of Darius, or even to Darius himself: I am such a lover of friends as that. And when I see you and Lysis, at your early age, so easily possessed of this treasure and so soon, he of you, and you of him, I am amazed and reckon you happy, seeing that I myself am so far from having made a similar acquisition that I do not even know in what way a friend is acquired. But this is just what I want to ask you about, for you have experience. Tell me then, when one loves another, is the lover or the beloved the friend; or may either be the friend?

Either may, I should think, be the friend of either.

Do you mean, I said, that when only one of them loves the other, they are mutual friends?

Yes, he said; that is my meaning.

But what if the lover is not loved in return? which is a very possible case.

Yes.

Or is, perhaps, even hated? for this does sometimes seem to happen to lovers in relation to their beloved. Nothing can exceed their love;

and yet they imagine either that they are not loved in return, or even that they are hated. Is not that true?

Yes, he said, quite true.

In that case, the one loves, and the other is loved?

Yes.

Then which is the friend of which? Is the lover the friend of the beloved, whether he be loved in return, or hated; or is the beloved the friend; or is there no friendship at all on either side, unless they both love one another?

This is what I think is the case.

Then this notion is not in accordance with our previous one. We were saying that both were friends, if one only loved; but now, unless they both love, neither is a friend.

That appears to be so.

Then nothing which does not love in return is beloved by a lover?

I think not.

Then they are not lovers of horses, whom the horses do not love in return; nor lovers of quails, nor of dogs, nor of wine, nor of gymnastic exercises, who have no return of love; no, nor of wisdom, unless wisdom loves them in return. Or shall we say that they do love them, although they are not beloved by their friends; and that the poet was wrong who sings—'Happy the man to whom his children are dear,[5] and steeds having single hoofs, and dogs of chase, and the stranger of another land'?

I do not think that he is wrong.

You think that he was right?

Yes.

Then, Menexenus, the conclusion is, that what is beloved, whether loving or hating, may be dear to the lover of it: for example, very young children, too young to love, or even hating their father or mother when they are punished by them, are never dearer to them than at the time when they are hating them.

I think that what you say is true.

And, if so, not the lover, but the beloved, is the friend or dear one?

Yes.

And the hated one, and not the hater, is the enemy?

It seems so.

Then many men are loved by their enemies and hated by their friends, and are the friends of their enemies and the enemies of their friends, seeing that it is the beloved and not the lover who is the friend.

Yet, how absurd, my dear friend, or indeed impossible is this paradox of a man being an enemy to his friend or a friend to his enemy.

What you say, Socrates, does seem to be true.

But if this cannot be, the lover will be the friend of that which is loved?

So it appears.

And the hater will be the enemy of that which is hated?

Certainly.

Well then, we must reach the same conclusion and acknowledge in this as in the preceding instance, that a man may often be the friend of one who is not his friend or who may be his enemy, when he loves that which does not love him or which even hates him. And he may be the enemy of one who is not his enemy, and is even his friend: for example, when he hates that which does not hate him, or which even loves him.

That appears to be true.

But if the lover is not a friend, nor the beloved a friend, nor those who both love and are loved, what are we to say? Whom are we to call friends to one another? Are there any others?

Indeed, Socrates, I cannot think of any.

But, O Menexenus! I said, may we not have been altogether wrong in our line of search?

I am sure we have been wrong, Socrates, said Lysis. And he blushed as he spoke, the words seeming to come from his lips involuntarily, because his whole mind was taken up with the argument; there was no mistaking his attentive look while he was listening.

I was pleased at the interest which was shown by Lysis, and I wanted to give Menexenus a rest, so I turned to him and said, I think, Lysis, that what you say is true, and that, if we were right in our line of search, we should never be wandering as we are; let us proceed no further in this direction (for the road seems to be getting difficult), but take the other path into which we turned, and follow the poets' road; for they are to us in a manner our fathers and guides in wisdom, and in their account of the essence of friendship they make a very lofty claim; God himself, they say, creates friends and draws them to one another; and this they express, if I am not mistaken, in the following words, 'God is ever drawing like towards like,' and so making them acquainted. I dare say that you have heard the verse.

Yes, he said; I have.

And have you not also met with the writings of wise men who say just the same, that like must love like? They are the people who argue and write about nature and the universe.

Very true, he replied.

And are they right in saying this?

They may be.

Perhaps, I said, about half, or possibly altogether, right, if their meaning were correctly apprehended by us. For the more a bad man has to do with a bad man, and the more nearly he is brought into contact with him, the more he will be likely to be at enmity with him, for he injures him; and injurer and injured cannot be friends. Is not that true?

Yes, he said.

Then one half of the saying is untrue, if the wicked are like one another?

That is true.

But the real meaning of the saying, as I imagine, is that the good are like one another, and friends to one another; and that the bad, as is often said of them, are never at unity with one another or with themselves; for they are passionate and restless, and anything which is at variance and enmity with itself can scarcely be like, and therefore friendly to, any other thing. Do you not agree?

Yes, I do.

Then, my friend, those who say that the like is friendly to the like mean to intimate, if I rightly apprehend them, that the good man only is the friend of the good, and of him only; but that the evil man never attains to any real friendship, either with a good man or an evil one. Do you agree?

He nodded assent.

Then now we know how to answer the question 'Who are friends?' for the argument declares 'That the good are friends'.

Yes, he said, I think so.

Yes, I replied; and yet I am not quite satisfied with this answer. For heaven's sake, let us face what I suspect. Assuming that like, inasmuch as he is like, is the friend of like, and useful to him—or rather let me try another way of putting the matter: Can like do any good or harm to like which he could not do to himself, or suffer anything from his like which he would not suffer from himself? And if neither can be of any use to the other, how can they feel affection for one another? Can they now?

They cannot.

And can that be dear to you, for which you feel no affection?

Certainly not.

Then the like is not the friend of the like in so far as he is like; but perhaps the good may be the friend of the good in so far as he is good?

Perhaps.

But then again, will not the good, in so far as he is good, be sufficient for himself? Certainly he will. And he who is sufficient wants nothing—that is implied in the word sufficient.

Of course not.

And he who wants nothing will feel affection for nothing?

He will not.

Neither can he love that for which he has no affection?

He cannot.

And he who loves not is not a lover or friend?

Clearly not.

What place then is there for any friendship at all between good men, if, when absent, they do not feel the loss of one another (for even when alone they are sufficient for themselves), and when present have no use of one another? How can such persons ever value one another?

They cannot.

And friends they cannot be, unless they value one another?

Very true.

But see now, Lysis, where we are mistaken in all this—are we not on the wrong tack?

How so? he replied.

I have heard some one say, as I just now recollect, that the like is the greatest enemy of the like, the good of the good—yes, and he quoted the authority of Hesiod, who says, 'Potter quarrels with potter, bard with bard, beggar with beggar', and of all other things he affirmed, in like manner, 'That of necessity the most like are most full of envy, strife, and hatred of one another, and the most unlike, of friendship. For the poor man is compelled to be the friend of the rich, and the weak requires the aid of the strong, and the sick man of the physician; and everyone who is ignorant feels affection for, and loves, him who knows.' And indeed he went on to say, even more impressively, that the idea of friendship existing between similars is not the truth, but the very reverse of the truth, and that the most opposed are the most friendly; for that everything desires not like but that which is most unlike: for example, the dry desires the moist, the cold the hot, the bitter the sweet, the sharp the blunt, the void the full, the full the void, and so of all other things; for the opposite is the food of the opposite, whereas like gets no profit from like. And I thought that he who said this was a clever man, and that he spoke well. What do the rest of you say?

I should say, at first hearing, that he is right, said Menexenus.

Then we are to say that the greatest friendship is of opposites?

Exactly.

Well, Menexenus, will not that be a monstrous answer? and will not those omniscient lovers of disputation be down upon us in triumph, and ask whether friendship is not the very opposite of enmity; and what answer shall we make to them—must we not admit that they speak the truth?

We must.

Is then the enemy (they will proceed) the friend of the friend, or the friend the friend of the enemy?

Neither, he replied.

Again, is a just man the friend of the unjust, or the temperate of the intemperate, or the good of the bad?

I do not see how that is possible.

And yet, I said, if friendship goes by contraries, these contraries must be friends.

They must.

Then neither like and like nor unlike and unlike are friends.

I suppose not.

Let us ask a further question: may not all these notions of friendship be erroneous? But may not that which is neither good nor evil still in some cases be the friend of the good?

How do you mean? he said.

Why really, I said, the truth is that I do not know; but my head is dizzy with the puzzles of the argument, and therefore I hazard the conjecture, that 'the beautiful is the friend', as the old proverb says. Beauty is certainly a soft, smooth, slippery thing, and therefore of a nature which easily slips through our hands and escapes us. Well, I affirm that the good is beautiful. You will agree to that?

Yes.

I say then, as a kind of inspiration, that what is neither good nor evil is the friend of the beautiful and the good, and I will tell you how I get this inspiration: I assume that there are three categories—the good, the bad, and that which is neither good nor bad. You would agree—would you not?

I agree.

And neither is the good the friend of the good, nor the evil of the evil, nor the good of the evil;—these alternatives are excluded by the previous argument; and therefore, if there be such a thing as friendship or love at all, we must infer that what is neither good nor evil must be the friend, either of the good, or of that which is neither good nor evil, for nothing can be the friend of the bad.

True.

But neither can like be the friend of like, as we were just now saying.

True.

And if so, that which is neither good nor evil can have no friend which is neither good nor evil.

It seems not.

It follows that only that which is neither good nor evil is the friend of the good, and of the good alone.

That may be assumed to be certain.

And does not this seem to lead us in the right way? Just remark, that the body which is in health requires neither medical nor any other aid, but has what it needs; and the healthy man has no love of the physician, because he is in health.

He has none.

But the sick loves him, because he is sick?

Certainly.

And sickness is an evil, and the art of medicine a good and useful thing?

Yes.

But the human body, regarded as a body, is neither good nor evil?

True.

And the body is compelled by reason of disease to court and make friends with the art of medicine?

Yes.

Then that which is neither good nor evil becomes the friend of good, by reason of the presence of evil?

So we may infer.

And clearly this must have happened before it had become evil through the evil in it. When once it had become evil, it could no longer desire and love the good; for, as we were saying, evil cannot be the friend of the good.

Impossible.

Further, I must observe that some substances are assimilated to others when these others are present with them; and there are some which are not assimilated; take, for example, the case of a colour which is put on another substance; the colour is then present with it.

Very good.

At such a time, is the thing itself which is painted really of the same colour as the paint which is on it?

What do you mean? he said.

This is what I mean: Suppose that I were to cover your auburn locks with white lead, would they be really white, or would they only appear to be white?

They would only appear to be white, he replied.

And yet whiteness would be present in them?

True.

But that would not make them at all the more white; not withstanding the presence of white in them, they would not be white any more than black?

No.

But when old age infuses whiteness into them, then they become assimilated, and are white by the presence of white.

Certainly.

Now I want to know whether in all cases a substance is assimilated by the presence of another substance; or must the presence be after a peculiar sort?

The latter, he said.

Then that which is neither good nor evil may be in the presence of evil, but not as yet evil, or it may already have become evil?

And when anything is in the presence of evil, not being as yet evil, the presence of evil in this sense arouses the desire of good in that thing; but the presence which actually makes a thing evil, takes away the desire and friendship of the good; for that which was once neither good nor evil has now become evil, and the good was supposed to have no friendship with the evil?

None.

And therefore we say that those who are already wise, whether gods or men, are no longer lovers of wisdom; nor can they be lovers of wisdom who are ignorant to the extent of being evil, for no evil or ignorant person is a lover of wisdom. There remain those who suffer from the evil of ignorance, but are not yet hardened in their ignorance or void of understanding, and are still aware that they do not know what they do not know: and therefore those who are as yet neither good nor bad are the lovers of wisdom. But the bad do not love wisdom any more than the good; for, as we have already seen, neither is unlike the friend of unlike, nor like of like. You remember that?

Yes, they both said.

And so, Lysis and Menexenus, we have discovered the nature of friendship—there can be no doubt of it: Friendship is the love which the neither good nor evil, when it is in the presence of evil, has for that which is good, either in soul, in body, or in any other way.

They both agreed and entirely assented, and for a moment I rejoiced and was satisfied like a huntsman just holding fast his prey. But then a most unaccountable suspicion came across me, and I felt that the conclusion was untrue. I was pained, and said, Alas! Lysis and Menexenus, I am afraid that we have been grasping at a shadow only.

Why do you say so? said Menexenus.

I am afraid, I said, that our arguments about friendship have, like some men, proved impostors.

How do you mean? he asked.

Well, I said; look at the matter in this way: a friend is the friend of someone; is he not?

Certainly he is.

And has he a motive and object in being a friend, or has he no motive and object?

He has a motive and object.

And is the object which makes him a friend, dear to him, or neither dear nor hateful to him?

I do not quite follow you, he said.

I do not wonder at that, I said. But perhaps, if I put the matter in another way, you will be able to follow me, and my own meaning will be clearer to myself. The sick man, as I was just now saying, is the friend of the physician—is he not?

Yes.

And he is the friend of the physician because of disease, and for the sake of health?

Yes.

And disease is an evil?

Certainly.

And what of health? I said. Is that good or evil, or neither?

Good, he replied.

And we were saying, I believe, that the body being neither good nor evil, because of disease, that is to say because of evil, is the friend of medicine, and medicine is a good: and medicine has entered into this friendship for the sake of health, and health is a good.

True.

And is health a friend, or not a friend?

A friend.

And disease is an enemy?

Yes.

Then that which is neither good nor evil is the friend of the good because of the evil and hateful, and for the sake of the good and the friend?

So it seems.

Then it is for the sake of the friend, and because of the enemy, that the friend is a friend of the friend?

That is to be inferred.

Very well, said I, then at this point, my boys, let us take heed, and be on our guard against deceptions. I will pass over the difficulty that the friend is the friend of the friend, and therefore the like of the like, which has been declared by us to be an impossibility; but in order that this new statement may not delude us, let us attentively examine another point: Medicine, as we were saying, is a friend, or dear to us, for the sake of health?

Yes.

And health is also dear?

Certainly.

And if dear, then dear for the sake of something?

Yes.

And surely this object must also be dear, as is implied in our previous admissions?

Yes.

And that something dear involves something else dear?

Yes.

But then, must we not either continue in this way till our strength fails, or arrive at some first principle of friendship or dearness which is not capable of being referred to any other, for the sake of which, as we maintain, all other things are dear.

We must.

My fear is that all those other things, which, as we say, are dear for the sake of another, are illusions and deceptions only, but where that first principle is, there is the true ideal of friendship. Let me put the matter thus: Suppose the case of a great treasure (this may be a son, who is more precious to his father than all his other treasures); would not the father, who values his son above all things, value other things also for the sake of his son? I mean, for instance, if he knew that his son had drunk hemlock, and the father thought that wine would save him, he would value the wine?

Of course.

And also the vessel which contains the wine?

Certainly.

But does he therefore value the three measures of wine, or the earthen vessel which contains them, equally with his son? Is not this rather the true state of the case? All his anxiety has regard not to the means which are provided for the sake of an object, but to the object for the sake of which they are provided. And although we may often say that gold and silver are highly valued by us, that is not the truth; for there is a further object, whatever it may be, which we value most of all, and for the sake of which gold and all our other possessions are acquired by us. Am I not right?

Yes, certainly.

And may not the same be said of the friend? That which is only dear to us for the sake of something else is improperly said to be dear, but the truly dear is that in which all these so-called dear friendships terminate.

That, he said, appears to be true.

Then that which is truly dear is not dear for the sake of something else which is dear.

True.

Then we have done with the notion that that which is dear, is so on account of something else which is dear. Now, may we take it that the good is dear?

I think so.

Well then, is the good loved because of the evil? Let me put the case in this way: Suppose that of the three categories, good, evil, and that which is neither good nor evil, there remained only the good and the neutral, and that evil were banished far away, and in no way affected soul or body, nor ever at all that class of things which, as we say, are neither good nor evil in themselves;—would the good be of any use, or other than useless to us? For if there were nothing to hurt us any longer, we should have no need of anything that would do us good. Then it would be clearly seen that we did but love and desire the good because of the evil, and as the remedy of the evil, which was the disease; but if there is no disease, there is no need of a remedy. Is it true that of its nature the good is loved because of the evil by us who are placed between the two, and that there is no use in the good for its own sake?

It does look like this.

Then that final principle of friendship in which all other friendships terminated, those, I mean, which are relatively dear and for the sake of something else, is of another and a different nature from them. For they are called dear because of another dear or friend. But with the true friend or dear, the case is quite the reverse; for that is proved to be dear because of the hated, and if the hated were away it would be no longer dear.

Very true, he replied; at any rate not if our present view holds good.

But, oh! will you tell me, I said, whether if evil were to perish, we should hunger any more, or thirst any more, or have any similar desire? Or may we suppose that hunger will remain while men and animals remain, but not so as to be hurtful? And the same of thirst and the other desires,—that they will remain, but will not be evil because evil has perished? Or rather shall I say, that to ask what either will be then or will not be is ridiculous, for who knows? This we do know, that in our present condition hunger may injure us, and may also benefit us:—Is not that true?

Yes.

And in like manner thirst or any similar desire may sometimes be an advantage and sometimes a disadvantage to us, and sometimes neither one nor the other?

To be sure.

But is there any reason why, because evil perishes, that which is not evil should perish with it?

None.

Then, even if evil perishes, the desires which are neither good nor evil will remain?

So it seems.

And must not a man love that which he desires and longs for?

He must.

Then, even if evil perishes, there may still remain some things which are dear?

Yes.

But not if evil is the cause of friendship: for in that case nothing will be the friend of any other thing after the destruction of evil; for the effect cannot remain when the cause is destroyed.

True.

And have we not admitted already that the friend loves something, and that for a reason? And at the time of making the admission we were of the opinion that the neither good nor evil loves the good because of the evil?

Very true.

But now our view is changed, and we conceive that there must be some other cause of friendship?

I suppose so.

May not the truth be rather, as we were saying just now, that desire is the cause of friendship; for that which desires is dear to that which is desired at the time of desiring it? And may not the other theory have been only a long story about nothing?

Likely enough.

But surely, I said, he who desires, desires that of which he is in want?

Yes.

And that of which he is in want is dear to him?

True.

And he is in want of that of which he is deprived?

Certainly.

Then love and desire and friendship would appear to be of the natural or congenial. Such, Lysis and Menexenus, is the inference.

They assented.

Then if you are friends, you must have natures which are congenial to one another?

Certainly, they both said.

And I say, my boys, that no one who loves or desires another would ever have loved or desired or longed for him if he had not been in some way congenial to him, either in his soul, or in his character, or in his manners, or in his form.

Yes, yes, said Menexenus. But Lysis was silent.

Then, I said, the conclusion is, that ;what is of a congenial nature must be loved.

It follows, he said.

Then the lover, who is true and no counterfeit, must of necessity be loved by his love.

Lysis and Menexenus gave a reluctant assent to this; and Hippothales changed into all manner of colours with delight.

Here, intending to review the argument, I said: Can we point out any difference between the congenial and the like? For if that is possible, then I think, Lysis and Menexenus, there may be some sense in our argument about friendship. But if the congenial is only the like, how will you get rid of the other argument, of the uselessness of like to like in as far as they are like? (for to allow that what is useless is dear, would be absurd). Suppose, then, that we agree to distinguish between the congenial and the like—in the intoxication of argument, that may perhaps be allowed.

Very true.

And shall we further say that the good is congenial, and the evil uncongenial to everyone? Or again that the evil is congenial to the evil, and the good to the good; and that which is neither good nor evil to that which is neither good nor evil?

They agreed to the latter alternative.

Then, my boys, we have again fallen into the old discarded error; for the unjust will be the friend of the unjust, and the bad of the bad, just as much as the good of the good.

That appears to be the result.

But again, if we say that the congenial is the same as the good, in that case the good and he only will be the friend of the good.

True.

But that too was a position of ours which, as you will remember, has been already refuted by ourselves.

We remember.

Then what is to be done? Or rather is there anything to be done? I can only, like the wise men who argue in courts, sum up the arguments:—If neither the beloved, nor the lover, nor the like, nor the unlike, nor the good, nor the congenial, nor any other of whom we spoke—for there were such a number of them that I cannot remember all—if none of these are friends, I know not what remains to be said.

Here I was going to invite the opinion of some older person, when suddenly we were interrupted by the bodyguards of Lysis and Menexenus, who came upon us, like tutelary genii,[6] bringing with them the boys' brothers, and bade them go home, as it was getting late. At first, we and the bystanders tried to drive them off; but afterwards, as they would not mind, and only went on shouting in their foreigners' Greek, and got angry, and kept calling the boys—they appeared to us to have been drinking rather too much at the Hermaea, which made them difficult to manage—we fairly gave way and broke up the company.

I said, however, a few words to the boys at parting: O Menexenus and Lysis, how ridiculous that you two boys, and I, an old man, who venture to range myself with you, should imagine ourselves to be friends—this is what the bystanders will go away and say—and as yet we have not been able to discover what is a friend!

Notes

[1] In ancient Greece, a public place for training and practice in wrestling and other athletics.

[2] One of the townships in ancient Attica.

[3] A dressing-room or robing-room for those preparing for the bath.

[4] A mule-driver.

[5] The Greek word *philos* is used both in the active sense of "friend" and in the passive sense of "dear."

[6] Guardian spirits.

Chapter 4

Aristotle, *Nicomachean Ethics*

Aristotle, born in 384 B.C., in Stagira in Macedonia, is sometimes called "the philosopher." Few minds in the whole of history have been both so systematic and encyclopedic as that of Aristotle. Virtually every basic modern science can trace its influences back to a treatise with Aristotle's name at the heading.

The son of a physician, Aristotle, at the age of eighteen, trekked to Athens where he enrolled in Plato's Academy. He remained there for twenty years, leaving shortly after Plato's death. He traveled to Asia Minor where he married the niece of a local king and eventually returned to Macedonia where he would become tutor to the young Alexander the Great.

The **Nicomachean Ethics** *is one of two major treatises on ethical theory from Aristotle. The other, the* **Eudemian Ethics**, *concludes with a grand section of friendship, though much of that part of the work is a repetition of the treatment of friendship contained in books 8 and 9 of the* **Nicomachean Ethics**, *the selection to be found below.*

Many of Aristotle's works have been lost to us, and while Cicero and others have provided testimony to the fact that Aristotle was as much of a great literary stylist as was Plato, such more "poetically" expressed works have never turned up. The following selection, as in the case in most of Aristotle's works, be the topic metaphysics, physics, psychology or biology, seems to be a compilation of lecture notes edited by students, though in this particular instance the editor has been thought to be Aristotle's son, Nicomachus.

Having discussed the difference between intellectual and moral virtues, and pleasure and pain, Aristotle addresses the topic of friendship at considerable length. In keeping with his usual world-view, Aristotle finds a natural hierarchical arrangement in the various forms of friendship, from which one may see at work both "the philosopher's" worldly sobriety and rather sublime theological bent.

Nicomachean Ethics

Book VIII

Chapter 1. It will be natural to discuss friendship next, for friend-ship is a kind of virtue or implies virtue. It is also indispensable to life. For without friends no one would choose to live, even though he possessed every other good. It even seems that people who are rich and hold official and powerful positions have the greatest need of friends; for what is the good of this sort of prosperity without some opportunity for generosity, which is never so freely or so admirably displayed as toward friends? Or how can prosperity be preserved in safety and security without friends? The greater a person's importance, the more liable it is to disaster. And in poverty and other misfortunes our friends are our only refuge. Again, when we are young, friends are a help to us, in saving us from error, and when we grow old, in taking care of us and doing the things for us we are too feeble to do for ourselves. When we are all in the prime of life, they prompt us to noble actions, as the line runs, "Two going together,"[1] for two people are better than one both in thought and in action.

Friendship or love seems the natural instinct of a parent toward a child, and of a child toward a parent, not only among men but among birds and animals generally. . . .

Again, it seems that friendship is the bond which holds states together, and that lawmakers set more store by it than by justice; for harmony is something like friendship, and it is harmony that they especially try to promote, and discord that they try to expel, as the enemy of the state. When people are friends there is no need of justice between them; but when they are just, they yet need friendship too. Indeed justice, in its supreme form, assumes the character of friendship.

Nor is friendship indispensable only; it is also noble. We praise those who love their friends, and to have many friends is thought to be a fine thing. Some people hold that to be a friend is the same thing as to be a good man.

The subject of friendship gives room for a good many differences of opinion. Some define it as a sort of likeness, and say people are friends because they are like each other. Hence the sayings, "Like seeks like," "Birds of a feather," and so on. Others, on the contrary, say "Two of a trade never agree." So philosophical thinkers indulge in more profound physical speculations on the subject . . . Heraclitus declares that "contending things draw together," that "harmony most beautiful is formed of discords," and that "all things are by strife engendered." Others, among whom is Empedocles, take the opposite view and insist that "like desires like," . . .

Chapter 2. It is possible, I think to shed light on the subject of friendship, by determining what is lovable or an object of love. For plainly not everything is loved, but only that which is lovable, which is what is good or pleasant or useful. A thing too is useful if it is a means of gaining something good or pleasant. If so, it follows that it is the good and the pleasant that are lovable because they are ends.

We may ask, then, do we love what is good in itself, or what is good for us? For there is sometimes a difference between them. The same question may be asked in regard to what is pleasant. It is said that everyone loves what is good for himself, and that, while the good is lovable in an absolute sense, it is what is good for each individual that is lovable in his eyes. It may even be said that a man loves not what is good for him but what seems good. But this will make no difference; for in that case, what is lovable will be what seems lovable.

Now there are three motives for love. We do not, it must be noted, apply the term "love" to our feeling for lifeless things. The reason is (1) that they are incapable of returning our affection, and (2) that we do not wish their good; for it would, of course, be ridiculous to wish good to the wine. If we wish it at all, it is only in the sense of wishing the wine to keep well, so that we may enjoy it ourselves. But everyone knows that we ought to wish our friend's good for his sake. If we wish people good in this sense, we call it good will, unless our good wishes are returned; reciprocal good will we call friendship.

We must add too that the good will must not be unknown. A person often wishes well to people whom he has not seen, but whom he supposes to be good or useful; and it is possible that one of these persons may entertain the same feelings toward him. Such people, then, it is clear, wish well to one another; but they cannot properly be called friends, so long as their feeling is unknown to each other. If they are to be friends, they must feel good will to each other and wish each other's good for one of the motives aforesaid, and each of them must know that the other wishes him well.

Chapter 3. Now as the reasons for friendship differ in kind, so accordingly do the corresponding kinds of affection and friendship. The kinds of friendship therefore are three, being equal in number to the things which are lovable or the objects of friendship, for every such object may arouse a reciprocal affection between two persons.

People who love each other wish each other's good up to the point on which their love is fixed. Accordingly, those who love each other for reasons of utility do not love each other for themselves, but only as far as they get some benefit from one another. So with those who love for pleasure's sake. They are fond of witty people, not for their character, but because they are pleasant to them. People then who love for utility's sake are moved to affection by what is good for themselves, and people who love for pleasure, by what is pleasant to themselves. They love a person not for what he is in himself, but only for being useful or pleasant to them. Such friendships then are friendships incidentally only; for the person loved is not loved for being what he is, but merely for being a source of some good or pleasure. Such friendships accordingly are easily dissolved, if the parties do not continue always the same; for they cease loving once they cease to be pleasant or useful to each other.

Now utility is not a permanent quality; it varies at different times. Hence when the reason for the friendship disappears, the friendship itself is dissolved, since it depended on that reason. Friendship of this kind seems to arise especially among old people, for in old age we look for profit rather than pleasure, and also among those in the prime of life or youth who have an eye to their own interest. Friends of this kind do not generally live together; for sometimes they are not even congenial. Nor do they want such companionship, except when they are of use to one another, since the pleasure they give each other goes no further than the hopes they entertain of getting benefit from it. Among these friendships we may count the friendship which exists between host and guest.

The friendship of the young is based apparently on pleasure; for they live by emotion and are inclined to pursue most the pleasure of the moment. But as their age increases, their pleasures alter with it. They are therefore quick at making friendships and quick at abandoning them; for their friendships shift with the object that pleases them, and their pleasure is liable to sudden change. Young people are amorous too, amorousness being generally a matter of emotion and pleasure. Hence they fall in love and soon afterwards fall out of love, passing from one condition to another many times in a single day. But amorous people wish to spend their days and lives together, since thus they attain the object of their friendship.

Perfect friendship is the friendship of people who are good and alike in virtue; for they are alike in wishing each other's good, inasmuch as they are good and good in themselves. Those who wish the good of their friends for their friend's sake are in the truest sense friends, since their friendship is the consequence of their own character, and not an accident. Their friendship therefore lasts as long as their goodness, and goodness is a permanent quality. So each of them is good in an absolute sense, and good in relation to his friend. For good men are not only good in an absolute sense, but helpful to each other. They are pleasant too; for the good are pleasant in an absolute sense, and pleasant to one another. For everybody finds pleasure in actions proper to him and in others like him, and all good people act alike or nearly alike.

Such a friendship is naturally permanent, for it unites in itself all the right conditions of friendship. For the aim of all friendship is good or pleasure, either absolute or relative to the person who feels the affection; and it is founded on a certain similarity. In the friendship of good men all the conditions just described are realized in the friends themselves; other friendships bear only a resemblance to the perfect friendship. That which is good in an absolute sense is pleasant also in an absolute sense. They are too the most lovable objects of affection, and for this reason love and friendship in this highest and best sense are found most among such men.

Friendships of this kind are likely to be rare; for such people are few. Such friendships require time and familiarity too; for, as the adage puts it, men cannot know one another until they have eaten salt together; nor can they admit one another to friendship, or be friends at all, until each has been proved lovable and trustworthy by the other. People who are quick to treat one another as friends wish to be friends but are not so really, unless they are lovable and know each other to be so; for the wish to be friends may arise in a minute, but not friendship.

Chapter 4. This kind of friendship then is perfect as regards durability and in all other respects; and each friend receives from the other in every way the same or nearly the same treatment as he gives, which is as it ought to be. Friendship based on pleasure has a certain resemblance to it, for the good too are pleasant to one another. So also with friendship based on utility, for the good are useful, too, to one another. Here likewise friendships are most permanent when the two persons get the same thing, such as pleasure, from one another; and not only the same thing, but from the same source, as happens between two wits, though not between a lover and his beloved. For these do not find pleasure in the same things; the pleasure of one is in beholding the object of his love, and of the other in being courted by his lover.[2] Then when beauty passes away, the friendship sometimes passes away too; for the lover then finds no pleasure in the sight of his beloved, and the beloved is no more courted by his lover. On the other hand, lovers often remain friends, if their characters are similar, and familiarity has taught them to love each other's character. But those who give and receive not pleasure but profit are both less true and less constant friends. Friendships based on utility are dissolved as soon as the advantage comes to an end, for in them there is no love of a person, but only a love of profit.

For pleasure or profit then it is possible that even bad men may be friends to one another, and good people to bad, and one who is neither good nor bad to any sort of person; but clearly none but the good can be friends for the friends' own sake, since bad people do not delight in one another unless to gain something thereby.

It is only, too, the friendship of good men that cannot be destroyed by slander. For it is not easy to believe what anyone says about a person whom we have tested ourselves for many years, and found to be good. In the friendship of the good too there is confidence, and the assurance that neither of the two friends will do injury to the other, and whatever else is required by true friendship. But in other friendships there is no protection against slander and injury. . . .

Chapter 6. . . . It is impossible to be friends with a great number of people in the perfect sense of friendship as it is to be in love with a great number of people at once. For perfect friendship is in some sense an excess, and such excess of feeling is natural toward one individual, but it is not easy for a great number of people to give intense pleasure to the same person at the same time, or, I may say, to seem even good to him at all. Friendship too involves experience and familiarity, which are very difficult. But it is possible to find a great number of acquaintances who are simply useful or pleasant or agreeable; for people of this kind are numerous and their services do not take much time.

Among such acquaintanceships one that is based on pleasure more nearly resembles a friendship, when each party renders the same services to the other, and is delighted with the other or with the same things, as they are in friendships of the young; for a generous spirit is especially characteristic of these friendships.

Friendships that rest on utility are for commercial characters. Fortunate people, however, do not want what is useful but what is pleasant. They want people to live with; and though for a short time they may put up with disagreeableness, nobody would stand it continuously. Nobody would stand the good itself continuously, if it were disagreeable to him. Hence they require their friends to be pleasant. They ought perhaps to require them also to be good, and not only so, but good for themselves; because then they would have all the qualities which friends ought to have.

People in positions of authority can make a distinction between their friends. Some are useful to them, and others pleasant, though the same people are not usually both useful and pleasant. They do not look for friends who are good as well as pleasant, or who will help them to attain noble ends; they want to be pleased and look partly for amusing people and partly for those who are clever at doing what they are told. These qualities are hardly ever combined in the same person.

We have said that a good man is at once pleasant and useful. But such a man does not become the friend of one superior to him in rank, unless he is himself superior to that person in goodness. Otherwise there is no equality, such as does occur when his superiority in virtue is proportionate to his inferiority in some other respect. Friendships of this kind, however, are exceedingly rare.

Chapter 7. . . . There is another kind of friendship that is based on inequality, such as the friendship of a father for his son, or of any elder person for a younger, or of a husband for his wife, or of a ruler for a subject. These friendships are of different sorts; for the friendship of parents for children is not the same as that of rulers for subjects, nor is even the friendship of a father for his son the same as that of a son for his father, nor that of a husband for his wife the same as a wife's for her husband. For in each of these there is a different virtue and a different function, and the motives of each are different; hence the friendships also are different. It follows that the services rendered by each party to the other in these friendships are not the same, nor is it right to expect they should be; but when children render to parents what is due to the authors of their being, and parents to children what is due to them, then their friendships are permanent and good.

In all friendships that involve the principle of inequality, the love also should be proportional; the better or the more useful party, or whoever may be the superior, should receive more love than he gives. For when the love is proportional to the merit, a sort of equality is established; and this equality seems to be a condition of friendship.

Equality in justice is apparently not the same as equality in friendship. In justice, equality proportioned to merit is the prime consideration, and quantitative equality the second, but in friendship quantitative equality is first and proportion to merit second. This is clearly seen when there is a wide distinction between two persons as regards virtue, vice, wealth, or anything else. For persons so widely different cease to be friends; they do not even expect to be. And nowhere is this so conspicuous as in the case of the gods; for they are vastly superior to us in all good things. It is clear too in the case of kings; for people who are much their inferiors do not expect to be their friends. Nor again do worthless people expect to be friends with the best or wisest of mankind. No doubt in such cases it is impossible to define exactly the point up to which friendship may be continued; it may suffer much from unevenness and yet keep on. But where the gulf is as wide as between a god and a man, it ceases to be. . . .

Chapter 8. Friendship seems to consist rather in loving than in being loved. This may be shown by the delight mothers have in loving; for mothers sometimes give their children to be brought up by others, and so long as they know about them and love them, do not look for love in return (if they cannot have both), but are content, it seems, to see their children doing well, and to give them their love, even if the children in their ignorance do them none of the services that are a mother's due. Then if friendship consists in loving rather than in being loved, and people who love their friends are praised, it is evidently the particular virtue of friends to love. Hence only where there is love in adequate measure are friends permanent and their friendship lasting.

In this way, even people who are unequal can be friends, for they will be equalized. And equality and likeness make friendship, especially the likeness of the good; for the good, being constant themselves, remain unchanged in relation to one another, and neither ask others to do wrong nor do it themselves. They may even be said to prevent it; for good people do no wrong nor allow their friends to do it. But in wicked friends there is no stability; for they do not remain the same themselves for long. And if they become friends, it is only for a short time, and for the satisfaction they take in each other's wickedness....

Chapter 11. ... Under perverted forms of government justice does not go far, and neither does friendship. Nowhere is its field so limited as under the worst of governments, for in a tyranny friendship does not exist, or hardly exists. Where there is nothing in common between ruler and subject, there cannot be friendship between them, as there cannot be justice either. The relation is like that between craftsman and tool, or soul and body, or master and slave. These latter get some benefit from the people who use them, but there can be no friendship or justice in our relation to lifeless things, or to a horse or an ox or a slave as slave. For there is nothing in common between a master and his tool, and a slave is a living tool and a tool a lifeless slave. One cannot therefore be friends with a slave as slave, though one can with a slave as man. For there seems a possibility of justice between a man and any other who is capable of taking part in a system of law and mutual agreements. Therefore one can be friends with him, so far as he is man. However, in tyrannies friendships and justice exist only to a slight extent and have only a narrow range. Their range is widest in democracies, because when people are equals they have most in common.

Chapter 12. All forms of friendship, as has been said, imply association. We may, however, properly distinguish the friendships of kinsmen and of comrades from other friendships. As for the friendships of fellow citizens, fellow tribesmen, fellow sailors and such, they are more like simple friendships of association, since they seem based on a sort of compact. We may class them with the friendship of host and guest.

The friendship of kinsmen appears to be of various kinds, but to depend all in all on the friendship of parent for child; for parents love their children as parts of themselves, and children their parents as the author of their being. Parents know their offspring better than the children know that they are their begetters; and the author of another's being feels more closely united to his child than the child to his parent; for the product of any person belongs to its producer, as a tooth or a hair or anything to its owner, but the producer does not belong to his product, or does not in the same degree. There is a difference between them too of time, for parents love their children as soon as they are born, but children do not love their parents until they have lived some time and gained intelligence or sense. From these considerations it is clear too why mothers love their children more than fathers do.

Parents then love their children as themselves, for their offspring are like second selves—second in the sense of being separate. And children love their parents as being born of them; and brothers love one another as being born of the same parents. For the identity of children with their parents constitutes an identity between the children themselves. Hence we use phrases like "the same blood," "the same stock," and so on, in speaking of brothers and sisters. They are therefore in a sense the same, though separate beings. It is a great help to friendship to have been brought up together, and to be of the same age; for "two of an age agree," as the saying is, and boys brought up together become comrades; hence the friendship of brothers resembles the friendship of comrades. Cousins and all other kinsmen have a bond of union, as springing from the same source. They are more or less closely united according as their first common ancestor is near or remote.

The love of children for parents and of men for the gods is a love for what is good and higher than themselves; for parents are the authors of the greatest benefit to their children, since to them children owe their existence and nurture and education from the day of their birth. There is both more pleasure and more utility in such a friendship than in the friendship of strangers, for their lives have more in common.

The characteristics of friendship between brothers are the same as between comrades. They are intensified when brothers are good but exist always in consequence of their likeness; for brothers are more nearly related to each other and love one another naturally from birth. There is the greatest similarity of character among children of the same parents, who are brought up together and receive a similar education; and they have stood the strong and sure test of time. The elements of friendship between other kinsmen are in proportion to the nearness of their kinship.

Between husband and wife friendship seems to be a law of nature, since man is even more naturally inclined to contract a marriage than to set up a state. The household comes before and is more necessary than the state, and the procreation of children is the universal function of animals. In the case of other animals this is the limit of their married union; but men unite not only for the production of children but for other purposes of life. As soon as a man and a woman unite, a distribution of functions takes place. Some are proper to the husband and others to the wife; hence they supply one another's needs, each contributing his special gifts to the common stock. Accordingly, both utility and pleasure are found in this friendship. But its basis will be virtue too, if the husband and wife are good; for each has his or her own virtue, and both delight in that as right. Children, too, are seemingly a bond of union between them; hence marriages that are childless are more easily dissolved. For children are a blessing common to both parents, and this community of interests binds them together. . . .

Book IX

Chapter 3. Another question that presents a problem is whether we ought or ought not to break off friendships with people whose character is no longer what it once was. If the motive of the friendship was utility or pleasure, then when the utility or the pleasure comes to an end, there is nothing unreasonable in breaking off the friendship. For it was the utility or the pleasure that we loved, and when they have ceased to exist, it is only reasonable that our love should come to an end too.

But a man would have ground for complaint, if a friend who had loved him for his usefulness or pleasantness had pretended to love him for his character. For, as we said at the outset, differences arise between friends most often when the actual grounds of the friendship are not what they suppose it to be. Now if a person, A, has deceived himself into imagining it was his character which won him B's affection, although there was nothing in B's conduct to warrant such an idea, he has only himself to blame. But if he was deluded by pretense on B's part, he has a right to complain of him as an impostor and to denounce him more bitterly than he would a man who counterfeits money, inasmuch as this felony affects something more precious than money.

But suppose we take a person into our friendship, believing him to be a good man, and he turns out and is recognized as a rascal, is it still our duty to love him? Love, it would seem, is now an impossibility, because not everything, but only the good is lovable. Evil neither can nor ought to be loved; for it is not our duty to love the wicked, or to make ourselves like bad men. We have said already that like loves like. Is it right then in such circumstances to break off the friendship at once? Or, perhaps, if not in all cases, at least where the vice is incurable? If there is any possibility of reforming the friend who has gone wrong, we should indeed come to the help of his character even more than of his property, since character is a better thing than property and enters more closely into friendship. Still a person who breaks off a friendship under these circumstances is not thought to be acting at all unreasonably. He was not a friend of the person as that person is now; therefore, if his friend has altered and it is impossible to reclaim him, he lets him go.

Again, suppose A stays as he was but B becomes better and vastly superior to A in virtue. Ought B then to treat A still as a friend? It is, I think, impossible. The case becomes clearest when the distance is wide between the two friends, as happens with childhood friendships, when one of two friends remains a child in mind and the other is a fully developed man. How can they be friends, when they sympathize with each other neither in their ideas nor in their pleasures and pains? There will be no personal understanding between them, and without understanding it is impossible, as we saw, to be friends, for it is impossible for two people to live together. But this point has been already discussed.

Is it right then, when two friends cease to be sympathetic, for one to treat the other exactly as if he had never been his friend? Surely we must not entirely forget the old intimacy, but even as we think we should oblige friends rather than strangers, so for old friends we should show some consideration for the sake of the past friendship, provided that the break in the friendship was not caused by some extraordinary wickedness. . . .

Chapter 8. The question is also asked whether a man should love himself or someone else most. We criticize people who are exceedingly fond of themselves, and call them "self-lovers" by way of reproach; for a bad man has an eye to his own interest in all that he does, and the more so the worse he is. So we accuse him of doing nothing except for his own advantage. A good man, on the other hand, is moved by a feeling of honor, and the better he is, the more strongly he is so moved. He acts in his friend's interest, disregarding his own. . .

It is therefore reasonable to ask, which of these two views we should follow, since there is something plausible in both. Perhaps then we ought to analyze them and determine how far and in what sense they are each right. The truth will, I think, become clear if we make plain the meaning of the word "self-love" in them both. When people use it as a term of reproach, they give the name "self-lovers" to men who grasp for themselves a larger share of money, honors, and bodily pleasures than belongs to them. These things are what men in general desire. These they believe to be the best goods, on these they set their hearts, and for these they compete. So the men who work to get an unfair share of these things are gratifying their appetites and emotions generally, or, in other words, the irrational parts of their souls. Most men are like this and therefore most self-love is bad. Hence the term "self-love" has come to be used in a bad sense. It is right then to disapprove of men who love themselves in this sense. People ordinarily apply the term "self-love" to those who snatch for themselves an unfair share of these things.

But a man who sets his heart always on doing above all what is just or temperate or virtuous in any respect, and who always and in every way chooses for himself the noble part, is never accused of self-love or blamed for it. Yet such a man, more than the other, would seem a lover of himself. At all events, he takes for himself what is noblest and best, and gratifies the highest part of his nature and yields it unqualified obedience. And as the highest element in a state or any other corporation seems to be in the truest sense the state or corporation itself, so with a man. He is then in the truest sense a lover of himself, who loves and gratifies the higher part of his being. . . .

Now when any persons are especially intent on doing noble acts, we all approve and applaud them. If all people were eager to do what is noble and exerted themselves to the utmost in the noblest deeds, then the state would have the greatest of all goods, since virtue is the greatest good. We conclude then that a good man should be a lover of self, for by his noble deeds he will benefit himself and serve others, but that a wicked man should not be a lover of self, for he will injure himself and other people too by following his evil passions. . . .

It is true of the good man that he will act often in the interest of his friends and of his country, and, if need be, will even die for them. He will give up money, honor, and all the goods for which the world contends, reserving only nobility for himself, because he would rather enjoy an intense pleasure for a short time than a moderate pleasure for long, have one year of noble life than many years of ordinary existence, and perform one great and lofty act than many trifling ones. It is true of one who dies for another that he chooses a great nobility for his own. Such a man will spend his riches gladly to enrich his friends; for while his friend gets money, he wins nobility, and so obtains the greater good for himself. The same with honor and offices of state. All these he will surrender to his friend, for the surrender is noble and laudable for himself.

It is right to call such a man good, for he chooses nobility above everything. He may give up even the opportunity for a good act to a friend. It may be nobler for him to inspire his friend to act than to act himself. In whatever field men deserve praise, a good man assigns to himself the greater share of noble conduct. In this sense then a man should be a lover of self, but not in the sense in which ordinary people love themselves. . . .

Chapter 10. Should we then have as many friends as possible? Or is it with friendship generally as with hospitality, of which it has been neatly said, "Give me not many guests, nor give me none."[3] That is, should a man neither be friendless nor again have an excessive number of friends?

In the case of friends whose friendship we make from motives of utility, the saying is perfectly applicable, for to return the services of many people is a laborious task and life is not long enough. A larger number of such friends, then, than one needs for one's own life would be superfluous and an obstacle to noble living. We therefore do not want them. As for friends made because they seem pleasant or sweet to us, a few are enough, as a little sweetening is enough in our diet.

But taking only good friends, we may ask, "Should we have as many as possible, or is there a limit fixed to the size of a circle of friends, as there is to the size of a city state?"[4] For although ten people would not be enough to compose such a state, still if the population rose to a hundred thousand, it would cease to be a city state. The number of citizens, however, cannot probably be precisely fixed, but may be anything within certain definite limits. So, too, to the number of friends there will be a limit, namely, the largest number with whom one can live. For the sharing of life together, we saw, was a special characteristic of friendship. Obviously a person cannot live with many people and distribute himself among them.

Again, a person's friends must be friends of one another, if they are all to pass their days together; and this condition can hardly be carried out by many people at a time. It is hard too for one person to sympathize fittingly with many people in their joys and sorrows; for probably at the very time he is called on to rejoice with one he will be summoned to sorrow with another.

Perhaps then it is well not to try to have the largest number of friends possible, but only as many as suffice for a life together, since apparently no one can be a devoted friend to many people at once. So too no one can love several people at once; for love is in idea a sort of exaggerated friendship and no person can feel this friendship for more than one individual. So too one cannot be a devoted friend of more than a few people. This seems actually to be the case. We do not find people having many friends as intimate with themselves as comrades. The classical friendships[5] of story too have all been friendships between two persons. People who have a host of friends and take everybody to their arms seem to be nobody's friends, unless indeed in the sense in which all fellow citizens are friends. If they have such a host of friends we call them easily suited.

Although then one may simply as a fellow citizen be a friend of many people, and yet not be too easygoing but truly good, one cannot have with many people a friendship based on virtue and on the merits of our friends themselves. We must be content if we find a few such friends.

Notes

[1] Homer, *Iliad,* X, where Diomed expresses his desire for a companion in invading the camp of the Trojans.

[2] In the time of Plato and Aristotle, the only love that was considered dignified and taken seriously was that between two men, not between man and woman. On this subject see Plato's *Symposium,* as well as chapters 12, 25 and 30 of this book.

[3] From Hesiod, *Works and Days.*

[4] In Aristotle's view, large cities of the kind we have today would have seemed unwieldy and barbaric. A Greek "city state" or *polis,* by contrast, was small—small enough, in Aristotle's view, to be organized and governed in a civilized manner.

[5] For example, the famous friendships of Achilles and Patroclus, Damon and Pythias, or of Pylades and Orestes.

Chapter 5

Seneca, *Epistulae Morales*

Lucius Annaeus, called Seneca the Younger (c. 4 BC-AD 65), was a Roman philosopher, statesman, orator, and tragedian. He was Rome's leading intellectual figure in the mid-first-century AD, when he and his friends virtually ruled the Roman world from 54-62 during the first part of the emperor Nero's reign.

Born in Corduba, Spain, the second son of a wealthy and famous teacher of rhetoric, Seneca is celebrated as the first of the "Spanish" philosophers. Some time after moving to Rome, he was banished by emperor Claudius in 41 to Corsica on a charge of adultery with princess Julia Livilla, the Emperor's niece. In this environment, he studied natural science, philosophy, and wrote three treatises entitled **Consolationes.** *He was recalled to Rome because of the influence of the Emperor's wife, Agrippina, in 49. He became praetor in 50, married Pompeia Paulina, a wealthy woman, built a powerful group of friends, including the new prefect of the general, Sextus Africanius Burrus, and became tutor to the future emperor Nero. The Murder of Claudius pushed Seneca and Burrus into positions of power under Nero. On the one hand, they introduced fiscal and judicial reforms and fostered more humane attitudes toward slaves. On the other hand, in 59 they condoned—or contrived—the murder of Agrippina, Nero's mother. Upon the death of Burrus in 62, Seneca retired and wrote some of his best philosophical works. In 65 his enemies denounced him as a party to a conspiracy. He was ordered to commit suicide, and met his death with fortitude and composure.*

His best-written and most compelling writings are his **Epistulae Morales,** *from which the present selection is taken. This work consists*

*of 124 brilliant essays covering a range of moral problems, in the form
of letters addressed to Lucilius. The spread of Stoicism in the Roman
Empire kept his philosophy alive. He was found to have Christian
influences in his thinking, and it the belief that he may have known St.
Paul. His works were studied by St. Augustine, St. Jerome, and
consoled Boethius in prison. His moral treatises were edited by
Erasmus, and the first complete English translation of them appeared
as early as 1614.*

On Philosophy and Friendship: Epistle IX

You desire to know whether Epicurus is right when, in one of his
letters,[1] he rebukes those who hold that the wise man is self-sufficient
and for that reason does not stand in need of friendships. This is the
objection raised by Epicurus against Stilbo and those who believe[2] that
the Supreme Good is a soul which is insensible to feeling.

We are bound to meet with a double meaning if we try to express
the Greek term "lack of feeling" summarily, in a single word, rendering
it by the Latin word *impatientia*. For it may be understood in the
meaning the opposite to that which we wish it to have. What we mean
to express is, a soul which rejects any sensation of evil; but people will
interpret the idea as that of a soul which can endure no evil. Consider,
therefore, whether it is not better to say "a soul that cannot be harmed"
or "a soul entirely beyond the realm of suffering." There is this
difference between ourselves and the other school[3] our ideal wise man
feels his troubles, but overcomes them; their wise man does not even
feel them. But we and they alike hold this idea,—that the wise man is
self-sufficient. Nevertheless, he desires friends, neighbours, and
associates, no matter how much he is sufficient unto himself. And
mark how self-sufficient he is; for on occasion he can be content with a
part of himself. If he lose a hand through disease or war, or if some
accident puts out one or both of his eyes, he will be satisfied with what
is left, taking as much pleasure in his impaired and maimed body as he
took when it was sound. But while he does not pine for these parts if
they are missing, he prefers not to lose them. In this sense the wise
man is self-sufficient, that he can do without friends, not that he desires
to do without them. When I say "can," I mean this: he endures the loss
of a friend with equanimity.

But he need never lack friends, for it lies in his own control how soon he shall make good a loss. Just as Phidias, if he lose a statue, can straightaway carve another, even so our master in the art of making friendships can fill the place of a friend he has lost. If you ask how one can make oneself a friend quickly, I will tell you, provided we are agreed that I may pay my debt[4] at once and square the account, so far as this letter is concerned. Hecato[5] says: "I can show you a philtre, compounded without drugs, herbs, or any witch's incantation: 'If you would be loved, love.'" Now there is a great pleasure, not only in maintaining old and established friendships, but also in beginning and acquiring new ones. There is the same difference between winning a new friend and having already won him, as there is between the farmer who sows and the farmer who reaps. The philosopher Attalus used to say: "It is more pleasant to make than to keep a friend, as it is more pleasant to the artist to paint than to have finished painting." When one is busy and absorbed in one's work, the very absorption affords great delight; but when one has withdrawn one's hand from the completed masterpiece, the pleasure is not so keen. Henceforth it is the fruits of his art that he enjoys; it was the art itself that he enjoyed while he was painting. In the case of our children, their young manhood yields the more abundant fruits, but their infancy was sweeter.

Let us now return to the question. The wise man, I say, self-sufficient through he be, nevertheless desires friends if only for the purpose of practicing friendship, in order that his noble qualities may not lie dormant. Not, however, for the purpose mentioned by Epicurus[6] in the letter quoted above: "That there may be someone to sit by him when he is ill, to help him when he is in prison or in want;" but that he may have someone by whose sick-bed he himself may sit, someone a prisoner in hostile hands whom he himself may set free. He who regards himself only, and enters upon friendships for this reason, reckons wrongly. The end will be like the beginning: he has made friends with one who might assist him out of bondage; at the first rattle of the chain such a friend will desert him. These are the so-called "fair-weather" friendships; one who is chosen for the sake of utility will be satisfactory only so long as he is useful. Hence prosperous men are blockaded by troops of friends; but those who have failed stand amid vast loneliness, their friends fleeing from the very crisis which is to test their worth. Hence, also, we notice those many shameful cases of persons who, through fear, desert or betray. The beginning and the end cannot but harmonize. He who begins to be your friend because it pays will also cease because it pays. A man will be attracted by some reward offered in exchange for his friendship, if he be attracted by aught in friendship other than friendship itself.

For what purpose, then, do I make a man my friend? In order to have someone for whom I may die, whom I may follow into exile, against whose death I may stake my own life, and pay the pledge, too. The friendship which you portray is a bargain and not a friendship; it regards convenience only, and looks to the results. Beyond question the feeling of a lover has in it something akin to friendship; one might call it friendship run mad. But, though this is true, does anyone love for the sake of gain, or promotion, or renown? Pure[7] love, careless of all other things, kindles the soul with desire for the beautiful object, not without the hope of a return of the affection. What then? Can a cause which is more honourable produce a passion that is base? You may retort: "We are not now discussing the question whether friendship is to be cultivated for its own sake." On the contrary, nothing more urgently requires demonstration; for if friendship is to be sought for its own sake, he may seek it who is self-sufficient. "How, then," you ask, "does he seek it?" Precisely as he seeks an object of great beauty, not attracted to it by desire for gain, nor yet frightened by the instability of Fortune. One who seeks friendship for favourable occasions, strips it of all its nobility.

The wise man is self-sufficient." This phrase, my dear Lucilius, is incorrectly explained by many; for they withdraw the wise man from the world, and force him to dwell within his own skin. But we must mark with care what this sentence signifies and how far it applies; the wise man is sufficient unto himself for a happy existence, but not for mere existence. For he needs many helps towards mere existence; but for a happy existence he needs only a sound and upright soul, one that despises Fortune.

I should like also to state to you one of the distinctions of Chrysippus,[8] who declares that the wise man is in want of nothing, and yet needs many things.[9] "On the other hand," he says, "nothing is needed by the fool, for he does not understand how to use anything, but he is in want of everything." The wise man needs hands, eyes, and many things that are necessary for his daily use; but he is in want of nothing. For want implies a necessity, and nothing is necessary to the wise man. Therefore, although he is self-sufficient, yet he has need of friends. He craves as many friends as possible, not, however, that he may live happily; for he will live happily even without friends. The Supreme Good calls for no practical aids from outside; it is developed at home, and arises entirely within itself. If the good seeks any portion of itself from without, it begins to be subject to the play of Fortune.

People may say: "But what sort of existence will the wise man have, if he be left friendless when thrown into prison, or when stranded in some foreign nation, or when delayed on a long voyage, or when cast upon a lonely shore? "His life will be like that of Jupiter, who, amid the dissolution of the world, when the gods are confounded together and Nature rests for a space from her work, can retire into himself, and give himself over to his own thoughts.[10] In some such way as this the sage will act; he will retreat into himself, and live with himself. As long as he is allowed to order his affairs according to his judgment, he is self-sufficient—and marries a wife; he is self-sufficient—and brings up children; he is self-sufficient—and yet could not live if he had to live without the society of man. Natural promptings, and not his own selfish needs, draw him into friendships. For just as other things have for us an inherent attractiveness, so has friendship. As we hate solitude and crave society, as nature draws men to each other, so in this matter also there is an attraction which makes us desirous of friendship. Nevertheless though he sage may love his friends dearly, often comparing them with himself, and putting them ahead of himself, yet all the good will be limited to his own being, and he will speak the words which were spoken by the very Stilbo[11] whom Epicurus criticizes in his letter. For Stilbo, after his country was captured and his children and his wife lost, as he emerged from the general desolation alone and yet happy, spoke as follows to Demetrius, called Sacker of Cities because of the destruction he brought upon them, in answer to the question whether he had lost anything: "I have all my goods with me!" There is a brave and stout-hearted man for you! The enemy conquered, but Stilbo conquered his conqueror. "I have lost nothing!" Aye, he forced Demetrius to wonder whether he himself had conquered after all. "My goods are all with me!" In other words, he deemed nothing that might be taken from him to be a good.

We marvel at certain animals because they can pass through fire and suffer no bodily harm; but how much more marvelous is a man who has marched forth unhurt and unscathed through fire and sword and devastation! Do you understand now how much easier it is to conquer a whole tribe than to conquer one man? This saying of Stilbo makes common ground with Stoicism; the Stoic also can carry his goods unimpaired through cities that have been burned to ashes; for he is self-sufficient. Such are the bounds which he sets to his own happiness.

But you must not think that our school alone can utter noble words; Epicurus himself, the reviler of Stilbo, spoke similar language[12]; put it down to my credit, though I have already wiped out my debt for the present day.[13] He says: "Whoever does not regard what he has as most ample wealth, is unhappy, though he be master of the whole world." Or, if the following seems to you a more suitable phrase,—for we must try to render the meaning and not the mere words: "A man may rule the world and still be unhappy, if he does not feel that he is supremely happy." In order, however, that you may know that these sentiments are universal,[14] suggested, of course, by Nature, you will find in one of the comic poets this verse: "Unblest is he who thinks himself unblest."[15] For what does your condition matter, if it is bad in your own eyes? You may say: "What then? If yonder man, rich by base means, and yonder man, lord of many but slave of more, shall call themselves happy, will their own opinion make them happy?" It matters not what one says, but how one feels at all times. There is no reason, however, why you should fear that this great privilege will fall into unworthy hands; only the wise man is please with his own. Folly is ever troubled with weariness of itself. Farewell.

On Grief for Lost Friends: Epistle LXII

I am grieved to hear that your friend Flaccus is dead, but I would not have you sorrow more than is fitting. That you should not mourn at all I shall hardly dare to insist; and yet I know that it is the better way. But what man will ever be so blessed with that ideal steadfastness of soul, unless he has already risen far above the reach of Fortune? Even such a man will be stung by and event like this, but it will be only a sting. We, however, may be forgiven for bursting into tears, if only our tears have not flowed to excess, and if we have checked them by our own efforts. Let not the eyes be dry when we have lost a friend, nor let them overflow. We may weep, but we must not wail.

Do you think that the law which I lay down for you is harsh, when the greatest of Greek poets has extended the privilege of weeping to one day only, in the lines where he tells us that even Niobe took thought of food?[16] Do you wish to know the reason for lamentations and excessive weeping? It is because we seek the proofs of our bereavement in our tears, and do not give way to sorrow, but merely parade it. No man goes into mourning for his own sake. Shame on our ill-timed folly! There is an element of self-seeking even in our sorrow.

"What," you say, "am I to forget my friend?" It is surely a short-lived memory that you vouchsafe to him, if it is to endure only as long as your grief; presently that brow of yours will be smoothed out in laughter by some circumstance, however casual. It is to a time no more distant than this that I put off the soothing of every regret, the quieting of even the bitterest grief. As soon as you cease to observe yourself, the picture of sorrow which you have contemplated will fade away; at present you are keeping watch over your own suffering. But even while you keep watch it slips away from you, and the sharper it is, the more speedily it comes to an end.

Let us see to it that the recollection of those whom we have lost becomes a pleasant memory to us. No man reverts with pleasure to any subject which he will not be able to reflect upon without pain. So too it cannot but be that the names of those whom we have loved and lost come back to us with a sort of sting; but there is a pleasure even in this sting. For, as my friend Attalus[17] used to say: "The remembrance of lost friends is pleasant in the same way that certain fruits have an agreeably acid taste, or as in extremely old wines it is their very bitterness that pleases us. Indeed, after a certain lapse of time, every thought that gave pain is quenched, and the pleasure comes to us unalloyed." If we take the word of Attalus for it, "to think of friends who are alive and well is like enjoying a meal of cakes and honey; the recollection of friends who have passed away gives a pleasure that is not without a touch of bitterness. Yet who will deny that even these things, which are bitter and contain an element of sourness, do serve to arouse the stomach?" For my part, I do not agree with him. To me, the thought of my dead friends is sweet and appealing. For I have had them as if I should one day lose them; I have lost them as if I have them still.

Therefore, Lucilius, act as befits your own serenity of mind, and cease to put a wrong interpretation on the gifts of Fortune. Fortune has taken away, for Fortune has given. Let us greedily enjoy our friends, because we do not know how long this privilege will be ours. Let us think how often we shall leave them when we go upon distant journeys, and how often we shall fail to see them when we tarry together in the same place; we shall thus understand that we have lost too much of their time while they were alive. But will you tolerate men who are most careless of their friends, and then mourn them most abjectly, and do not love anyone unless they have lost him? The reason why they lament too unrestrainedly at such times is that they are afraid lest men doubt whether they really have loved; all too late they seek for proofs of their emotions. If we have other friends, we surely deserve ill at their hands and think ill of them, if they are of so little account that they fail to console us for the loss of one. If, on the other hand, we have no other friends, we have injured ourselves more than Fortune has injured us; since Fortune has robbed us of one friend, but we have robbed ourselves of every friend whom we have failed to make. Again, he who has been unable to love more than one, has had none too much love even for that one.[18] If a man who has lost his one and only tunic through robbery chooses to bewail his plight rather than look about him for some way to escape the cold, or for something with which to cover his shoulders, would you not think him an utter fool?

You have buried one whom you loved; look about?? for someone to love. It is better to replace your friend than to weep for him. What I am about to add is, I know, a very hackneyed remark, but I shall not omit it simply because it is a common phrase: A man ends his grief by the mere passing of time, even if he has not ended it of his own accord. But the most shameful cure for sorrow, in the case of a sensible man, is to grow weary of sorrowing. I should prefer you to abandon grief, rather than have grief abandon you; and you should stop grieving as soon as possible, since, even if you wish to do so, it is impossible to keep it up for a long time. Our forefathers[19] have enacted that, in the case of women, a year should be the limit for mourning; not that they need to mourn for so long, but that they should mourn no longer. In the case of men, no rules are laid down, because to mourn at all is not regarded as honourable. For all that, what woman can you show me, of all the pathetic females that could scarcely be dragged away from the funeral-pile or torn from the corpse, whose tears have lasted a whole month? Nothing becomes offensive so quickly as grief; when fresh, it finds someone to console it and attracts one another to itself; but after becoming chronic, it is ridiculed, and rightly. For it is either assumed or foolish.

He who writes these words to you is no other than I, who wept so excessively for my dear friend Annaeus Serenus[20] that, in spite of my wishes, I must be included among the examples of men who have been overcome by grief. To-day, however, I condemn this act of mine, and I understand that the reason why I lamented so greatly was chiefly that I had never imagined it possible for his death to precede mine. The only thought which occurred to my mind was that he was the younger, and much younger, too,—as if the Fates kept to the order of our ages!

Therefore let us continually think as much about our own morality as about that of all those we love. In former days I ought to have said: "My friend Serenus is younger than I; but what does that matter? He would naturally die after me, but he may precede me." It was just because I did not do this that I was unprepared when Fortune dealt me the sudden blow. Now is the time for you to reflect, not only that all things are mortal, but also that their mortality is subject to no fixed law. Whatever can happen at any time can happen to-day. Let us therefore reflect, my beloved Lucilius, that we shall soon come to the goal which this friend, to our own sorrow, has reached. And perhaps, if only the tale told by wise men is true[21] and there is a bourne to welcome us, then he whom we think we have lost has only been sent on ahead. Farewell.

Notes

[1] Frag. 174 Usener.

[2] *i.e.,* the Cynics.

[3] *i.e.,* the Cynics.

[4] *i.e.,* the *diurna mercedula;* see *Ep.* vi. 7.

[5] Frag. 27 Fowler.

[6] Frag. 175 Usener.

[7] "Pure love," *i.e.,* love in its essence, unalloyed with other emotions.

[8] *Cf.* his *Frag. moral.* 674 von Arnim.

[9] The distinction is based upon the meaning of *egere,* "to be in want of" something indispensable, and *opus esse,* "to have need of" something which one can do without.

[10] This refers to the Stoic conflagration; after certain cycles their world was destroyed by fire. *Cf.* E.V. Arnold, *Roman Stoicism,* pp. 192f.; *cf.* also Chrysippus, *Frag. phys.* 1065 von Arnim.

[11] *Gnomologici Vaticani* 515a Sternberg.

[12] Frag. 474 Usener.

[13] *Cf.* above, § 6.

[14] *i.e.,* not confined to the Stoics, etc.

[15] Author unknown; perhaps, as Buecheler thinks, adapted from the Greek.

[16] Homer, Iliad, xix. 229 and xxiv. 602.

[17] The teacher of Seneca, often mentioned by him.

[18] The reason is, as Lipsius observed, that friendship is essentially a social virtue, and not confined to one object. The pretended friendship for one and only one is a form of self-love, and is not unselfish love.

[19] According to tradition, from the time of Numa Pompilius.

[20] An intimate friend of Seneca, probably a relative, who died in the year 63 for eating poisoned mushrooms (Pliny, *N.H.* xxii. 96). Seneca dedicated to Serenus several of his philosophical essays.

[21] *Cf.* the closing chapter of the *Agricola* of Tacitus: *si, ut sapientibus placet, non cum corpore extinguuntur magnae animae,* etc.

Chapter 6

Epictetus, *The Discourses*

Epictetus (c. 50-110 A.D.) was the most influential of all philosophers who are generally regarded as "Stoics." The history of Stoicism can be traced back to the Greek philosopher Zeno, who lived in the third century B.C. As the Romans conquered Greece, Rome, in time, had Stoicism as one of its more unusual imports and eventually such figures as Seneca and Marcus Aurelius took up this form of philosophy which, risking oversimplification, could be called a 'philosophy of austere resignation.'

While Stoicism, like any other form of thought, has its complexities, if one were to simplify it by definition, it may have the character of being a rather rigid form of thought praising austerity and self-denial, in part through the apparent belief that this was not only the best way of life but one to which the best men were almost fated.

Indeed, even in the 20th century, one can hear of the influence of Stoicism almost daily, when one who has been confronted by a situation which is beyond his control simply throws up his hands and the observer, not being familiar with philosophic thought in the least, says that the baffled or defeated fellow has 'decided to be philosophical about it.' The observer would better say 'Stoical' in such a case (though even this word would probably be too complex for the situation), as philosophy is never reducible to Stoicism as such, except, of course, for the practicing Stoic.

The actual life of Epictetus is somewhat sketchy as is expected in the case of a man who chooses almost defiantly to withdraw from the affairs of 'the world' for the most part. Yet it is known that as a child Epictetus was sold into slavery, though because of his unusual intellectual abilities, he was granted an education. Though eventually lettered, Epictetus devoted himself almost exclusively to the living and teaching of his very austere ethic. He apparently never wrote, but his 'disciples' compiled many of his teachings and sayings into **The Enchiridion** *(the manual) and* **The Discourses,** *works which were hardly systematic but which did try to sum up the general teachings of the Stoical way of life.*

Epictetus' devout belief in God and his recommendations against the pleasures of 'the world,' one of which was friendship apparently, made him comparable to many early Christians. Indeed, many historians and theologians suggest that, in fact, many of the early Christian writers were themselves either consciously or unconsciously deeply influenced by the precepts of Stoicism.

Discourses (*Of Friendship*)

To whatever objects a person devotes his attention, these objects he probably loves. Do men ever devote their attention, then, to [what they think] evils? By no means. Or even to things indifferent? No, nor this. It remains, then, that good must be the sole object of their attention; and if of their attention, of their love too. Whoever, therefore, understands good, is capable likewise of love; and he who cannot distinguish good from evil, and things indifferent from both, how is it possible that he can love? The wise person alone, then, is capable of loving.

"How so? I am not this wise person, yet I love my child."

I protest it surprises me that you should, in the first place, confess yourself unwise. For in what are you deficient? Have not you the use of your senses? Do you not distinguish the semblances of things? Do you not provide such food and clothing and habitation as are suitable to you? Why then do you confess that you want wisdom? In truth, because you are often struck and disconcerted by semblances, and their speciousness gets the better of you; and hence you sometimes suppose the very same things to be good, then evil, and lastly, neither; and, in a word, you grieve, you fear, you envy, you are disconcerted, you change. Is it from this that you confess yourself unwise? And are you not changeable too in love? Riches, pleasure, in short, the very same things, you sometimes consider good, and at other times evil. And do you not consider the same persons too alternately as good and bad, at one time treating them with kindness, at another with enmity; at one time commending, and at another censuring them?

"Yes. This too is the case with me."

Well, then; can he who is deceived in another be his friend, think you?

"No, surely."

Or does he who loves him with a changeable affection bear him genuine good will?

"Nor he, neither."

Or he who now vilifies, then admires him?

"Nor he."

Do you not often see little dogs caressing and playing with each other, so that you would say nothing could be more friendly? But to learn what this friendship is, throw a bit of meat between them, and you will see. Do you too throw a bit of land between you and your son, and you will see that he will quickly wish you under ground, and you him; and then you, no doubt, on the other hand will exclaim, What a son have I brought up! He would bury me alive! Throw in a pretty girl, and the old fellow and the young one will both fall in love with her; or let fame or danger intervene, the words of the father of Admetus will be yours: "*You love to see the light. Doth not your father? You fain would still behold it. Would not he?* "[1]

Do you suppose that he did not love his own child when it was little; that he was not in agonies when it had a fever, and often wished to undergo that fever in its stead? But, after all, when the trial comes home, you see what expression he uses. Were not Eteocles and Polynices born of the same mother and of the same father? Were they not brought up, and did they not live and eat and sleep, together? Did they not kiss and fondle each other? So that anyone who saw them would have laughed at all the paradoxes which philosophers utter about love. And yet when a kingdom, like a bit of meat, was thrown between them, see what they say—

> *Polynices.* Where wilt thou stand before the towers?
> *Eteocles.* Why askest thou this of me?
> *Pol.* I will oppose myself to thee, to slay thee.
> *Et.* I too am seized by this desire.[2]

Such are the prayers they offer. Be not therefore deceived. No living being is held by anything so strongly as by its own needs. Whatever therefore appears a hindrance to these, be it brother or father or child or mistress or friend, is hated, abhorred, execrated; for by nature it loves nothing like its own needs. This motive is father and brother and family and country and God. Whenever, therefore, the gods seem to hinder this, we vilify even them, and throw down their statues, and burn their temples; as Alexander ordered the temple of Aesculapius to be burned, because he had lost the man he loved.

When, therefore, anyone identifies his interest with those of sanctity, virtue, country, parents, and friends, all these are secured; but whenever he places his interest in anything else than friends, country, family, and justice, then these all give way, borne down by the weight of self-interest. For wherever *I* and *mine* are placed, thither must every living being gravitate. If in body, that will sway us; if in our own will, that; if in externals, these. If, therefore, I rest my personality in the will, then only shall I be a friend, a son, or a father, such as I ought. For in that case it will be for my interest to preserve the faithful, the modest, the patient, the abstinent, the beneficent character; to keep the relations of life inviolate. But if I place my personality in one thing, and virtue in another, the doctrine of Epicurus will stand its ground, that virtue is nothing, or mere opinion.

From this ignorance it was that the Athenians and Lacedemonians quarreled with each other, and the Thebans with both; the Persian king with Greece, and the Macedonians with both; and now the Romans with the Getes. And in still remoter times the Trojan war arose from the same cause. Alexander [Paris] was the guest of Menelaus; and whoever had seen the mutual proofs of good will that passed between them would never have believed that they were not friends. But a tempting bait, a pretty woman, was thrown in between them; and over her arose a war. At present, therefore, when you see that dear brothers have, in appearance, but one soul, do not immediately pronounce upon their love; not though they should swear it, and affirm it was impossible to live apart. For the governing faculty of a bad man is faithless, unsettled, undiscriminating, successively vanquished by different semblances. Do not inquire, as others do, whether they were born of the same parents, and brought up together, and under the same teacher; but this thing only, in what they place their interest—in externals or in their own wills. If in externals, you can no more pronounce them friends, than you can call them faithful, or constant, or brave, or free; nay, nor even truly men, if you are wise. For it is no principle of humanity that makes them bite and vilify each other, and take possession of public assemblies, as wild beasts do of solitudes and mountains; and convert courts of justice into dens of robbers; that prompts them to be intemperate, adulterers, seducers; or leads them into other offenses that men commit against each other—all from that one single error, by which they risk themselves and their own concerns on things uncontrollable by will.

But if you hear that these men in reality suppose good to be placed only in the will, and in a right use of things as they appear, no longer take the trouble of inquiring if they are father and son, or old companions and acquaintances; but boldly pronounce that they are friends, and also that they are faithful and just. For where else can friendship be found, but where joined with fidelity and modesty, a devotion to virtue alone?

"Well; but such a one paid me the utmost regard for so long a time, and did he not love me?"

How can you tell, foolish man, if that regard be any other than he pays to his shoes, or his horse, when he cleans them? And how do you know but that when you cease to be a necessary utensil, he may throw you away, like a broken platter?

"Well; but it is my wife, and we have lived together many years."

And how long did Eriphyle live with Amphiaraus, becoming the mother of many children? But a necklace came between them. What does a necklace signify? One's conviction concerning such things. This turned her into a savage animal; this cut asunder all love, and allowed her to remain neither the wife nor the mother.[3]

Whoever, therefore, among you studies either to be or to gain a friend, let him dig out all false convictions by the root, hate them, drive them utterly out of his soul. Thus, in the first place, he will be secure from inward reproaches and contests, from vacillation and self-torment. Then, with respect to others, to every like-minded person he will be without disguise; to such as are unlike he will be patient, mild, gentle, and ready to forgive them, as failing in points of the greatest importance; but severe to none, being fully convinced of Plato's doctrine, that the soul is never willingly deprived of truth. Without all this, you may, in many respects, live as friends do; and drink and lodge and travel together, and even be born of the same parents; and so may serpents too; but neither they nor you can ever be really friends, while your accustomed principles remain brutal and execrable.

Notes

[1] Euripides, *Alcestis,* v. 691. Pheres, the father of Admetus, is defending himself for not consenting to die in place of his son.

[2] Euripides, *Phoenissae,* v. 630, 631.

[3] Amphiaraus married Eriphyle, the sister of Adrastus, king of Argos, and was betrayed by her for a golden chain.

Chapter 7

Cicero, *Treatise on Friendship*

Marcus Tullius Cicero (106 B.C.-43 B.C.) is often called the greatest of all Roman orators and the supreme master of Latin prose style. Indeed, Cicero's contributions to philosophy are for the most part limited to his rigorous synthesis of philosophy and rhetoric. He himself would acknowledge that he could add little that would be "original" philosophically, as he deferred at almost every turn to the Greek masters. But Cicero did take it upon himself, as far as both a citizen and statesman could, to educate "the people" in philosophy and letters as far as possible. He believed that a profound liberal education, with philosophy at its basis, was essential for the very health and survival of the Roman Empire.

In 76 B.C., Cicero was elected to the office of quaestor in Sicily, and in 70 B.C., he successfully prosecuted the corrupt praetor Verres, who had subjected the Sicilians to extortion and oppression. Thus was Cicero's political career launched.

In 64 B.C., a year in which he was elected consul by a large majority, Cicero uncovered the plot by Catiline and others which was designed to seize the chief offices of the state. From such positions, Catiline and the others intended to sell wholesale certain goods of the state in order to cover their personal debts from their lives lived in considerable excess. Cicero saved the day, but his political fortune would turn sour with time and resentment from others.

In 58 B.C., under the rule of "the first triumvirate," Pompey, Caesar, and Crassus, Cicero was banished and a "temple of Liberty" which was being constructed on the site of his house was destroyed.

Wavering in and out of the political arena thereafter, Cicero was eventually beheaded upon the establishment of the triumvirate of Antony, Octavius, and Lepidus, who concluded that, among other things, Cicero must have approved of the cause of the conspirators against both Caesar and Antony.

The selection below is the work **De Amicitia** *or* **Of Friendship,** *mainly a recollection of a conversation on the topic among Cicero's elders, Fannius, Laelius, and Scaevola.*

Treatise on Friendship

The augur Quintus Mucius Scaevola used to recount a number of stories about his father-in-law Gaius Laelius, accurately remembered and charmingly told; and whenever he talked about him always gave him the title of "the wise" without any hesitation. . . . Among many other occasions I particularly remember one. He was sitting on a semicircular garden-bench, as was his custom, when I and a very few intimate friends were there, and he chanced to turn the conversation upon a subject which about that time was in many people's mouths. You must remember, Atticus, for you were very intimate with Publius Sulpicius, what expressions of astonishment, or even indignation, were called forth by his mortal quarrel, as tribune, with the consul Quintus Pompeius, with whom he had formerly lived on terms of the closest intimacy and affection. Well, on this occasion, happening to mention this particular circumstance, Scaevola detailed to us a discourse of Laelius on friendship delivered to himself and Laelius's other son-in-law Gaius Fannius, son of Marcus Fannius, a few days after the death of Africanus. The points of that discussion I committed to memory, and have arranged them in this book at my own discretion. For I have brought the speakers, as it were, personally on to my stage to prevent the constant "said I" and "said he" of a narrative, and to give the discourse the air of being orally delivered in our hearing. . . .

Gaius Fannius and Quintus Mucius come to call on their father-in-law after the death of Africanus. They start the subject; Laelius answers them. And the whole essay on friendship is his. In reading it you will recognize a picture of yourself.

2. *Fannius.* You are quite right, Laelius! there never was a better or more illustrious character than Africanus. But you should consider that at the present moment all eyes are on you. Everybody calls you

"the wise" *par excellence*, and thinks you so. . . . Your wisdom people believe to consist in this, that you look upon yourself as self-sufficing and regard the changes and chances of mortal life as powerless to affect your virtue. Accordingly they are always asking me, and doubtless also our Scaevola here, how you bear the death of Africanus. . . .

Scaevola. Yes, indeed, Laelius, I am often asked the question mentioned by Fannius. But I answer in accordance with what I have observed: I say that you bear in a reasonable manner the grief which you have sustained in the death of one who was at once a man of the most illustrious character and a very dear friend. That of course you could not but be affected—anything else would have been wholly unnatural in a man of your gentle nature—but that the cause of your non-attendance at our college meeting was illness, not melancholy.

Laelius. Thanks, Scaevola! You are quite right; you spoke the exact truth. . . .

4. . . . Yet such is the pleasure I take in recalling our friendship, that I look upon my life as having been a happy one because I have spent it with Scipio. With him I was associated in public and private business; with him I lived in Rome and served abroad; and between us there was the most complete harmony in our tastes, our pursuits, and our sentiments, which is the true secret of friendship . . . . What makes me care the more about this is the fact that in all history there are scarcely three or four pairs of friends on record; and it is classed with them that I cherish a hope of the friendship of Scipio and Laelius being known to posterity.

Fannius. Of course that must be so, Laelius. But since you have mentioned the word friendship, and we are at leisure, you would be doing me a great kindness, and I expect Scaevola also, if you would do as it is your habit to do when asked questions on other subjects, and tell us your sentiments about friendship, its nature, and the rules to be observed in regard to it.

Scaevola. I shall of course be delighted. Fannius has anticipated the very request I was about to make. So you will be doing us both a great favour.

5. *Laelius.* I should certainly have no objection if I felt confidence in myself. For the theme is a noble one, and we are (as Fannius has said) at leisure. . . . All I can do is to urge on you to regard friendship as the greatest thing in the world; for there is nothing which so fits in with our nature, or is so exactly what we want in prosperity or adversity.

But I must at the very beginning lay down this principle—*friendship can only exist between good men. . . .*

We mean then by the "good" *those whose actions and lives leave no question as to their honour, purity, equity, and liberality; who are free from greed, lust, and violence; who have the courage of their convictions. . . .*

Now this truth seems clear to me, that nature has so formed us that a certain tie unites us all, but that this tie becomes stronger from proximity. So it is that fellow-citizens are preferred in our affections to foreigners, relations to strangers; for in their case Nature herself has caused a kind of friendship to exist, though it is one which lacks some of the elements of permanence. Friendship excels relationship in this, that whereas you may eliminate affection from relationship, you cannot do so from friendship. Without it relationship still exists in name, friendship does not. You may best understand this friendship by considering that, whereas the merely natural ties uniting the human race are indefinite, this one is so concentrated, and confined to so narrow a sphere, that affection is ever shared by two persons only or at most by a few.

6. Now friendship may be thus defined: *a complete accord on all subjects human and divine, joined with mutual good-will and affection.* And with the exception of wisdom, I am inclined to think nothing better than this has been given to man by the immortal gods. There are people who give the palm to riches or to good health, or to power and office, many even to sensual pleasures. This last is the ideal of brute beasts; and of the others we may say that they are frail and uncertain, and depend less on our own prudence than on the caprice of fortune. Then there are those who find the "chief good" in virtue. Well, that is a noble doctrine. But the very virtue they talk of is the parent and preserver of friendship, and without it friendship cannot possibly exist.

Let us, I repeat, use the word virtue in the ordinary acceptation and meaning of the term, and do not let us define it in high-flown language. Let us account as good the persons usually considered so, such as Paulus, Cato, Gallus, Scipio, and Philus. Such men as these are good enough for everyday life; and we need not trouble ourselves about those ideal characters which are nowhere to be met with.

Well, between men like these the advantages of friendship are almost more than I can say. To begin with, how can life be worth living, to use the words of Ennius, which lacks that repose which is to be found in the mutual good-will of a friend? What can be more delightful than to have some one to whom you can say everything with the same absolute confidence as to yourself? Is not prosperity robbed of half its value if you have no one to share your joy? On the other hand, misfortunes would be hard to bear if there were not some one to feel them even more acutely than yourself. In a word, other objects of ambition serve for particular ends—riches for use, power for securing homage, office for reputation, pleasure for enjoyment, health for freedom from pain and the full use of the functions of the body. But friendship embraces innumerable advantages. Turn which way you please, you will find it at hand. It is everywhere; and yet never out of place, never unwelcome. Fire and water themselves, to use a common expression, are not of more universal use than friendship. I am not now speaking of the common or modified form of it, though even that is a source of pleasure and profit, but of that true and complete friendship which existed between the select few who are known to fame. Such friendship enhances prosperity, and relieves adversity of its burden by halving and sharing it.

7. And great and numerous as are the blessings of friendship, this certainly is the sovereign one, that it gives us bright hopes for the future and forbids weakness and despair. In the face of a true friend a man sees as it were a second self. So that where his friend is he is; if his friend be rich, he is not poor; though he be weak, his friend's strength is his; and in his friend's life he enjoys a second life after his own is finished. This last is perhaps the most difficult to conceive. But such is the effect of the respect, the loving remembrance, and the regret of friends which follow us to the grave. While they take the sting out of death, they add a glory to the life of the survivors. Nay, if you eliminate from nature the tie of affection, there will be an end of house and city, nor will so much as the cultivation of the soil be left. If you don't see the virtue of friendship and harmony, you may learn it by observing the effects of quarrels and feuds. Was any family ever so well established, any State so firmly settled, as to be beyond the reach of utter destruction from animosities and factions? This may teach you the immense advantage of friendship. . . .

8. Well, then, it has very often occurred to me when thinking about friendship, that the chief point to be considered was this: is it weakness and want of means that make friendship desired? I mean, is its object an interchange of good offices, so that each may give that in which he is strong, and receive that in which he is weak? Or is it not rather true that, although this is an advantage naturally belonging to friendship, yet its original cause is quite other, prior in time, more noble in character, and springing more directly from our nature itself? The Latin word for

friendship—*amicitia*—is derived from that for love—*amor;* and love is certainly the prime mover in contracting mutual affection. For as to material advantages, it often happens that those are obtained even by men who are courted by a mere show of friendship and treated with respect from interested motives. But friendship by its nature admits of no feigning, no pretense: as far as it goes it is both genuine and spontaneous. Therefore I gather that friendship springs from a natural impulse rather than a wish for help: from an inclination of the heart, combined with a certain instinctive feeling of love, rather than from a deliberate calculation of the material advantage it was likely to confer. The strength of this feeling you may notice in certain animals. They show such love to their offspring for a certain period, and are so beloved by them, that they clearly have a share in this natural, instinctive affection. But of course it is more evident in the case of man: first, in the natural affection between children and their parents, an affection which only shocking wickedness can sunder; and next, when the passion of love has attained to a like strength—on our finding, that is, some one person with whose character and nature we are in full sympathy, because we think that we perceive in him what I may call the beacon-light of virtue. For nothing inspires love, nothing conciliates affection, like virtue. . . .

10. Well, then, my good friends, listen to some conversations about friendship which very frequently passed between Scipio and myself. I must begin by telling you, however, that he used to say that the most difficult thing in the world was for a friendship to remain unimpaired to the end of life. So many things might intervene: conflicting interests; differences of opinion in politics; frequent changes in character, owing sometimes to misfortunes, sometimes to advancing years. He used to illustrate these facts from the analogy of boyhood, since the warmest affections between boys are often laid aside with the boyish toga; and even if they did manage to keep them up to adolescence, they were sometimes broken by a rivalry in courtship, or for some other advantage to which their mutual claims were not compatible. Even if the friendship was prolonged beyond that time, yet it frequently received a rude shock should the two happen to be competitors for office. For while the most fatal blow to friendship in the majority of cases was the lust of gold, in the case of the best men it was a rivalry for office and reputation, by which it had often happened that the most violent enmity had arisen between the closest friends.

Again, wide breaches and, for the most part, justifiable ones were caused by an immoral request being made of friends, to pander to a man's unholy desires or to assist him in inflicting a wrong. A refusal, though perfectly right, is attacked by those to whom they refuse compliance as a violation of the laws of friendship. Now the people who have no scruples as to the requests they make to their friends, thereby allow that they are ready to have no scruples as to what they will do *for* their friends; and it is the recriminations of such people which commonly not only quench friendships, but give rise to lasting enmities. "In fact," he used to say, "these fatalities overhang friendship in such numbers that it requires not only wisdom but good luck also to escape them all."

12. We may then lay down this rule of friendship—*neither ask nor consent to do what is wrong.* For the plea "for friendship's sake" is a discreditable one, and not to be admitted for a moment. This rule holds good for all wrong-doing, but more especially in such as involves disloyalty to the republic. . . . Bad men must have the fear of punishment before their eyes: a punishment not less severe for those who follow than for those who lead others to crime . . . .

We conclude, then, not only that no such confederation of evilly disposed men must be allowed to shelter itself under the plea of friendship, but that, on the contrary, it must be visited with the severest punishment, lest the idea should prevail that fidelity to a friend justifies even making war upon one's country. . . .

13. Let this, then, be laid down as the first law of friendship, that *we should ask from friends, and do for friends, only what is good.* But do not let us wait to be asked either: let there be ever an eager readiness, and an absence of hesitation. Let us have the courage to give advice with candor. In friendship, let the influence of friends who give good advice be paramount; and let this influence be used to enforce advice not only in plain-spoken terms, but sometimes, if the case demands it, with sharpness; and when so used, let it be obeyed.

I give you these rules because I believe that some wonderful opinions are entertained by certain persons who have, I am told, a reputation for wisdom in Greece. There is nothing in the world, by the way, beyond the reach of their sophistry. Well, some of them teach that we should avoid very close friendships, for fear that one man should have to endure the anxieties of several. Each man, say they, has enough and to spare on his own hands; it is too bad to be involved in the cares of other people. The wisest course is to hold the reins of friendship as loose as possible; you can then tighten or slacken them at your will. For the first condition of a happy life is freedom from care, which no one's mind can enjoy if it has to travail, so to speak, for others besides itself. Another sect, I am told, gives vent to opinions still less generous. I briefly touched on this subject just now. They affirm that friendships should be sought solely for the sake of the assistance they give, and not at all from motives of feeling and affection; and that therefore just in proportion as a man's power and means of support are lowest, he is most eager to gain friendships: thence it comes that weak women seek the support of friendship more than men, the poor more than the rich, the unfortunate rather than those esteemed prosperous. What noble philosophy! You might just as well take the sun out of the sky as friendship from life; for the immortal gods have given us nothing better or more delightful.

But let us examine the two doctrines. What is the value of this "freedom from care"? It is very tempting at first sight, but in practice it has in many cases to be put on one side. For there is no business and no course of action demanded from us by our honour which you can consistently decline, or lay aside when begun, from a mere wish to escape from anxiety. Nay, if we wish to avoid anxiety we must avoid virtue itself, which necessarily involves some anxious thoughts in showing its loathing and abhorrence for the qualities which are opposite to itself—as kindness for ill-nature, self-control for licentiousness, courage for cowardice. Thus you may notice that it is the just who are most pained at injustice, the brave at cowardly actions, the temperate at depravity. It is then characteristic of a rightly ordered mind to be pleased at what is good and grieved at the reverse. Seeing then that the wise are not exempt from the heart-ache (which must be the case unless we suppose all human nature rooted out of their hearts), why should we banish friendship from our lives, for fear of being involved by it in some amount of distress? If you take away emotion, what difference remains I don't say between a man and a beast, but between a man and a stone or a log of wood, or anything else of that kind?

Neither should we give any weight to the doctrine that virtue is something rigid and unyielding as iron. In point of fact it is in regard to friendship, as in so many other things, so supple and sensitive that it expands, so to speak, at a friend's good fortune, contracts at his misfortunes. We conclude then that mental pain which we must often encounter on a friend's account is not of sufficient consequence to banish friendship from our life, any more than it is true that the cardinal virtues are to be dispensed with because they involve certain anxieties and distresses.

14. . . . Again, the believers in the "interest" theory appear to me to destroy the most attractive link in the chain of friendship. For it is not

so much what one gets by a friend that gives one pleasure, as the warmth of his feeling; and we only care for a friend's service if it has been prompted by affection. And so far from its being true that lack of means is a motive for seeking friendship, it is usually those who being most richly endowed with wealth and means, and above all with virtue (which, after all, is a man's best support), are least in need of another, that are most open-handed and beneficent. Indeed I am inclined to think that friends ought at times to be in want of something. For instance, what scope would my affections have had if Scipio had never wanted my advice or cooperation at home or abroad? It is not friendship, then, that follows material advantage, but material advantage friendship.

15. We must not therefore listen to these superfine gentlemen when they talk of friendship, which they know neither in theory nor in practice. For who, in heaven's name, would choose a life of the greatest wealth and abundance on condition of neither loving or being beloved by any creature? That is the sort of life tyrants endure. They, of course, can count on no fidelity, no affection, no security for the goodwill of any one. For them all is suspicion and anxiety; for them there is no possibility of friendship. Who can love one whom he fears, or by whom he knows that he is feared? Yet such men have a show of friendship offered them, but it is only a fair-weather show. If it ever happen that they fall, as it generally does, they will at once understand how friendless they are. So they say Tarquin observed in his exile that he never knew which of his friends were real and which sham, until he had ceased to be able to repay either. Though what surprises me is that a man of his proud and overbearing character should have a friend at all. And as it was his character that prevented his having genuine friends, so it often happens in the case of men of unusually great means—their very wealth forbids faithful friendships. For not only is Fortune blind herself; but she generally makes those blind also who enjoy her favours. They are carried, so to speak, beyond themselves with self-conceit and self-will; nor can anything be more perfectly intolerable than a successful fool. You may often see it. Men who before had pleasant manners enough undergo a complete change on attaining power of office. They despise their old friends; devote themselves to new. . . .

16. To turn to another branch of our subject. We must now endeavour to ascertain what limits are to be observed in friendship— what is the boundary-line, so to speak, beyond which our affection is not to go. On this point I notice three opinions, with none of which I

agree. One is *that we should love our friend just as much as we love ourselves, and no more;* another, *that our affection to them should exactly correspond and equal theirs to us;* a third, *that a man should be valued at exactly the same rate as he values himself.* To not one of these opinions do I assent. The first, which holds that our regard for ourselves is to be the measure of our regard for our friend, is not true; for how many things there are which we would never have done for our own sakes, but do for the sake of a friend! We submit to make requests from unworthy people, to descend even to supplication; to be sharper in invective, more violent in attack. Such actions are not creditable in our own interests, but highly so in those of our friends. There are many advantages too which men of upright character voluntarily forego, or of which they are content to be deprived, that their friends may enjoy them rather than themselves.

The second doctrine is that which limits friendship to an exact equality in mutual good offices and good feelings. But such a view reduces friendship to a question of figures in a spirit far too narrow and illiberal, as though the object were to have an exact balance in a debtor and creditor account. True friendship appears to me to be something richer and more generous than that comes to; and not to be so narrowly on its guard against giving more than it receives. In such a matter we must not be always afraid of something being wasted or running over in our measure, or of more than is justly due being devoted to our friendship.

But the last limit proposed is the worst, namely, that a friend's estimate of himself is to be the measure of our estimate of him. It often happens that a man has too humble an idea of himself, or takes too despairing a view of his chance of bettering his fortune. In such a case a friend ought not to take the view of him which he takes of himself. Rather he should do all he can to raise his drooping spirits, and lead him to more cheerful hopes and thoughts. . . .

17. The real limit to be observed in friendship is this: the characters of the two friends must be stainless. There must be complete harmony of interests, purpose, and aims, without exception. Then if the case arises of a friend's wish (not strictly right in itself) calling for support in a matter involving his life or reputation, we must make some concession from the straight path—on condition, that is to say, that extreme disgrace is not the consequence. Something must be conceded to friendship. And yet we must not be entirely careless of our reputation, nor regard the good opinion of our fellow-citizens as a weapon which we can afford to despise in conducting the business of

our life, however lowering it may be to tout for it by flattery and smooth words. We must by no means abjure virtue, which secures us affection. . . .

18. Now, what is the quality to look out for as a warrant for the stability and permanence of friendship? It is loyalty. Nothing that lacks this can be stable. We should also in making our selection look out for simplicity, a social disposition, and a sympathetic nature, moved by what moves us. These all contribute to maintain loyalty. You can never trust a character which is intricate and tortuous. Nor, indeed, is it possible for one to be trustworthy and firm who is unsympathetic by nature and unmoved by what affects ourselves. We may add, that he must neither take pleasure in bringing accusations against us himself, nor believe them when they are brought. All these contribute to form that constancy which I have been endeavouring to describe. And the result is, what I started by saying, that friendship is only possible between good men.

Now there are two characteristic features in his treatment of his friends that a good (which may be regarded as equivalent to a wise) man will always display. First, he will be entirely without any make-believe or pretense of feeling; for the open display even of dislike is more becoming to an ingenuous character than a studied concealment of sentiment. Secondly, he will not only reject all accusations brought against his friend by another, but he will not be suspicious himself either, nor be always thinking that his friend has acted improperly. Besides this, there should be a certain pleasantness in word and manner which adds no little flavour to friendship. A gloomy temper and unvarying gravity may be very impressive; but friendship should be a little less unbending, more indulgent and gracious, and more inclined to all kinds of good-fellowship and good-nature. . . .

20. . . . As a general rule, we must wait to make up our mind about friendships till men's characters and years have arrived at their full strength and development. People must not, for instance, regard as fast friends all whom in their youthful enthusiasm for hunting or football they liked for having the same tastes. By that rule, if it were a mere question of time, no one would have such claims on our affections as nurses and slave-tutors. Not that they are to be neglected, but they stand on a different ground. It is only these mature friendships that can be permanent. For difference of character leads to difference of aims, and the result of such diversity is to estrange friends. The sole reason, for instance, which prevents good men from making friends with bad,

or bad with good, is that the divergence of their characters and aims is the greatest possible.

Another good rule in friendship is this: do not let an excessive affection hinder the highest interests of your friends. This very often happens. I will go again to the region of fable for an instance. Neoptolemus could never have taken Troy if he had been willing to listen to Lycomedes, who had brought him up, and with many tears tried to prevent his going there. Again, it often happens that important business makes it necessary to part from friends: the man who tries to balk it, because he thinks that he cannot endure the separation, is of a weak and effeminate nature, and on that very account makes but a poor friend. There are, of course, limits to what you ought to expect from a friend and to what you should allow him to demand of you. And these you must take into calculation in every case.

21. Again, there is such a disaster, so to speak, as having to break off friendship. And sometimes it is one we cannot avoid. For at this point the stream of our discourse is leaving the intimacies of the wise and touching on the friendship of ordinary people. It will happen at times that an outbreak of vicious conduct affects either a man's friends themselves or strangers, yet the discredit falls on the friends. In such cases friendships should be allowed to die out gradually by an intermission of intercourse. They should, as I have been told that Cato used to say, rather be unstitched than torn in twain; unless, indeed, the injurious conduct be of so violent and outrageous a nature as to make an instant breach and separation the only possible course consistent with honour and rectitude. . . .

Our first object, then, should be to prevent a breach; our second, to secure that, if it does occur, our friendship should seem to have died a natural rather than a violent death. Next, we should take care that friendship is not converted into active hostility, from which flow personal quarrels, abusive language, and angry recriminations. These last, however, provided that they do not pass all reasonable limits of forbearance, we ought to put up with, and, in compliment to an old friendship, allow the party that inflicts the injury, not the one that submits to it, to be in the wrong. Generally speaking, there is but one way of securing and providing oneself against faults and inconveniences of this sort—not to be too hasty in bestowing our affection, and not to bestow it at all on unworthy objects.

Now, by "worthy of friendship" I mean those who have in themselves the qualities which attract affection. This sort of man is rare; and indeed all excellent things *are* rare; and nothing in the world is so hard to find as a thing entirely and completely perfect of its kind. But most people not only recognize nothing as good in our life unless it is profitable, but look upon friends as so much stock, caring most for those by whom they hope to make most profit. Accordingly they never possess that most beautiful and most spontaneous friendship which must be sought solely for itself without any ulterior object. They fail also to learn from their own feelings the nature and the strength of friendship. For every one loves himself, not for any reward which such love may bring, but because he is dear to himself independently of anything else. But unless this feeling is transferred to another, what a real friend is will never be revealed; for he is, as it were, a second self. But if we find these two instincts showing themselves in animals,— whether of the air or the sea or the land, whether wild or tame,—first, a love of self, which in fact is born in everything that lives alike; and, secondly, an eagerness to find and attach themselves to other creatures of their own kind; and if this natural action is accompanied by desire and by something resembling human love, how much more must this be the case in man by the law of his nature? For man not only loves himself, but seeks another whose spirit he may so blend with his own as almost to make one being of two.

22. But most people unreasonably, not to speak of modesty, want such a friend as they are unable to be themselves, and expect from their friends what they do not themselves give. The fair course is first to be good yourself, and then to look out for another of like character. It is between such that the stability in friendship of which we have been talking can be secured; when, that is to say, men who are united by affection learn, first of all, to rule those passions which enslave others, and in the next place to take delight in fair and equitable conduct, to bear each other's burdens, never to ask each other for anything inconsistent with virtue and rectitude, and not only to serve and love but also to respect each other. I say "respect"; for if respect is gone, friendship has lost its brightest jewel. And this shows the mistake of those who imagine that friendship gives a privilege to licentiousness and sin. Nature has given us friendship as the handmaid of virtue, not as a partner in guilt: to the end that virtue, being powerless when isolated to reach the highest objects, might succeed in doing so in union and partnership with another. Those who enjoy in the present, or have enjoyed in the past, or are destined to enjoy in the future such a partnership as this, must be considered to have secured the most excellent and auspicious combination for reaching nature's highest good. This is the partnership, I say, which combines moral rectitude,

fame, peace of mind, serenity: all that men think desirable because with them life is happy, but without them cannot be so. This being our best and highest object, we must, if we desire to attain it, devote ourselves to virtue; for without virtue we can obtain neither friendship nor anything else desirable. In fact, if virtue be neglected, those who imagine themselves to possess friends will find out their error as soon as some grave disaster forces them to make trial of them. Wherefore, I must again and again repeat, you must satisfy your judgment before engaging your affections: not love first and judge afterwards. We suffer from carelessness in many of our un-dertakings: in none more than in selecting and cultivating our friends. . . .

27. . . . This is all I had to say on friendship. One piece of advice on parting. Make up your minds to this. Virtue (without which friendship is impossible) is first; but next to it, and to it alone, the greatest of all things is Friendship.

Chapter 8

Plutarch, *How to Tell a Flatterer from a Friend*
(*from Moralia*)

Plutarch of Chaeronea (c. 46-120), a Greek biographer and essayist, is known primarily for his authorship of **The Lives of the Noble Grecians and Romans.** *Born in Chaeronea, Boeotia, not far from Delphi, he studied at the Academy in Athens, traveled in Egypt and Italy, was appointed to various diplomatic missions, and was among the most educated men of his day. For a time he settled in Rome where he taught philosophy and achieved professional and social success, attaining also the rank of honorary consular. But at the height of his success, Plutarch abandoned life in the fast lane, returning to his provincial home town of Chaeronea, where he became a market inspector, established a small philosophical school for the young men of the neighborhood, and became a priest of the temple of Delphi. The reasons underlying this career change rest at the heart of Plutarch's personal philosophy.*

By the time Plutarch reached maturity, virtually all the works of poetry and philosophy and art of Greece and Rome that the world calls classical had been completed. What Plutarch wanted to do was to preserve, practice and promulgate the classical Hellenistic way of life in such a way that its fate would not be tied to the fortunes of a particular political order. His attachment to the Delphic cult, his participation in the public life of his home town, and his interest in the philosophical education of youth can only be understood within the context of the values of his Greek tradition and heritage. His **Lives** *were themselves written to inspire loyalty to Hellenism; and they display evident pride in the culture and greatness of the men of*

Greece, even though they are always fair and honest in their treatment of the Romans.

Plutarch's extant writings include 46 biographies, collected in the **Lives** *for which he is most well known, and 65 dialogues, treatises and philosophical essays on miscellaneous ethical, literary and historical subjects, collected in the* **Moralia.** *An early English translation of the* **Lives** *by Sir Thomas North had a profound influence on English literature; it supplied, among other things, the material for Shakespeare's* **Coriolanus, Julius Caesar, Antony and Cleopatra, and Timon of Athens.**

Plutarch's philosophical position is a form of Platonism expanded to include elements from the Pythagoreans, Peripatetics, Stoics, and even Epicureans and Cynics. On the other hand, some of his dialogues contain denunciations of certain views of Epicureans and Stoics. Throughout his writings, in any case, Plutarch exhibits an exceptional warmth, sympathy and charm, which, unlike many of the more austere classics, renders his work unusually accessible. His continual attention to the details of human character and its moral implications, his personal style and use of anecdotal material, his broad-ranging allusions to the classics—all these continue to make for delightful reading.

Our selection, "How to Tell a Flatterer from a Friend," is taken from the **Moralia.** *Plutarch's warm family feeling is particularly evident in the Moralia. In an essay on "Brotherly Love," Plutarch makes the unusually personal point of mentioning his own brother Timon, perhaps with the intention of emulating Plato, who honored his brothers Glaucon and Adimantus by mentioning them in his best dialogues. In "Flattery and Friendship" Plutarch sets forth various criteria for distinguishing between the genuine friend and the mere flatterer. The latter part of the treatise is devoted to "outspokenness" (or frankness), which true friends exhibit and which false friends distort to their own uses, often presenting a plausible imitation of authentic friendship. The full title of the work is, appropriately, "How One May Distinguish between Flatterer and Friend."*

How to Tell a Flatterer from a Friend

1. Plato[1] says, my dear Antiochus Philopappus, that everyone grants forgiveness to the man who avows that he dearly loves himself, but he also says that along with many other faults which are engendered thereby the most serious is that which makes it impossible for such a man to be an honest and unbiased judge of himself. "For Love is blind as regards the beloved,"[2] unless one, through study, has acquired the habit of respecting and pursuing what is honourable rather than what is inbred and familiar. This fact affords to the flatterer a very wide field within the realm of friendship,[3] since in our love of self he has an excellent base of operations against us. It is because of this self-love that everybody is himself his own foremost and greatest flatterer, and hence finds no difficulty in admitting the outsider to witness with him and to confirm his own conceits and desires. For the man who is spoken of with opprobrium as a lover of flatterers is in high degree a lover of self, and, because of his kindly feeling toward himself, he desires and conceives himself to be endowed with all manner of good qualities; but although the desire for these is not unnatural, yet the conceit that one possesses them is dangerous and must be carefully avoided. Now if Truth is a thing divine, and, as Plato[4] puts it, the origin "of all good for gods and all good for men," then the flatterer is in all likelihood an enemy to the gods and particularly to the Pythian god. For the flatterer always takes a position over against the maxim "Know thyself," by creating in every man deception towards himself and ignorance both of himself and of the good and evil that concerns himself; the good he renders defective and incomplete, and the evil wholly impossible to amend.

2. If the flatterer, then, like most other evils, attacked solely or mostly the ignoble and mean, he would not be so formidable or so hard to guard against. But the fact is, that as bore-worms make their entrance chiefly into the delicate and sweet-scented kinds of wood, so it is ambitious, honest, and promising characters that receive and nourish the flatterer as he hangs upon them. Moreover, just as Simonides says, "The rearing of horses consorts not with Zacynthus, but with wheat-bearing acres, " so we observe that flattery does not attend upon poor, obscure, or unimportant persons, but makes itself a stumbling-block and a pestilence in great houses and great affairs, and oftentimes overturns kingdoms and principalities. Wherefore it is no small task, nor a matter requiring but slight foresight, to subject it to examination, so that, being thoroughly exposed, it may be prevented from injuring or

discrediting friendship. Vermin depart from dying persons and forsake their bodies, as the blood, from which the vermin derive their sustenance, loses its vitality; and so flatterers are never so much as to be seen coming near where succulence and warmth are lacking, but where renown and power attend, there do they throng and thrive; but if a change come, they slink away quickly and are gone. But we must not wait until that experience shall befall, which is a thing profitless, or rather injurious and not devoid of danger. For it is cruel to discover friends that are no friends at a crucial time which calls for friends, since there is then no exchanging one that is untrustworthy and spurious for the true and trustworthy. But one's friend, like a coin, should have been examined and approved before the time of need, not proved by the need to be no friend. For we must not wait for injury to open our eyes, but to avoid injury we must gain acquaintance with the flatterer and learn how to detect him; otherwise we shall be in the same case with those who try to learn about deadly drugs by tasting them first, and so ruin and destroy themselves in order to reach their decision. We do not, of course, commend such persons, nor again those who rate the friend as something noble and beneficial, and so imagine that all who are socially agreeable at once stand openly convicted of being flatterers. For a friend is not unpleasant or absolute, nor is it bitterness and sternness that give dignity to friendship, but this very nobility and dignity in it is sweet and desirable. "Close by its side have the Graces and Longing established their dwelling,"[5] and not merely for one who is in misfortune, "'Tis sweet to gaze into a kind man's eyes," as Euripides[6] has it, but when friendship attends us, it brings pleasure and delight to our prosperity no less than it takes away the griefs and the feeling of helplessness from adversity. As Evenus[7] has remarked that fire is the best of sauce, so God, by commingling friendship with our life, has made everything cheerful, sweet and agreeable, when friendship is there to share in our enjoyment. Indeed, how the flatterer could use pleasures to insinuate himself, if he saw that friendship was nowhere ready to welcome what is pleasant, no man can explain. But just as false and counterfeit imitations of gold imitate only its brilliancy and lustre, so apparently the flatterer, imitating the pleasant and attractive characteristics of the friend, always presents himself in a cheerful and blithe mood, with never a whit of crossing or opposition. But that is no reason why persons who express commendation should instantly be suspected of being simply flatterers. For commendation at the right time is no less becoming to friendship than is censure, or we may express it better by saying that complaining and fault-finding generally is unfriendly and unsociable, whereas the kindly feeling that ungrudgingly and readily bestows commendation for noble acts inclines us, at some later time, cheerfully and without distress to bear admonishment and frankness of speech, since we believe, and are content, that the man who is glad to commend blames only when he must.

3. One might say, then, that it is difficult to distinguish flatterer and friend, if neither pleasure nor praise shows the difference; indeed, in services and courtesies we may often observe that friendship is outstripped by flattery. How can it be helped, will be our answer, if we are in quest of the real flatterer, who takes hold of the business with adroitness and skill, and if we do not, like most people, regard as flatterers merely those self-ministering[8] trencher-slaves, so called, whose tongue will be wagging, as one man has put it, as soon as the water is brought for the hands,[9] for whom one dish and one glass of wine is enough to show their ill breeding with its display of vulgarity and offensiveness? Surely there was no need to press the case against Melanthius, the parasite of Alexander of Pherae, who, in answer to those who asked how Alexander was slain, said, "By a stab through his ribs that hit me in my belly"; nor those who throng round a rich man's table whom "Not fire, nor steel, nor bronze can keep from coming each day to dine,"[10] nor the flatteresses in Cyprus, Athenaeus who when they had crossed over into Syria, acquired the nickname of "ladderesses," because by prostrating themselves they afforded by their bodies a means for the women of the royal household to mount their carriages.

4. Against whom, then, must we be on our guard? Against the man who does not seem to flatter and will not admit that he does so, the man who is never to be found hanging round the kitchen, never caught noting the shadow on the sun-dial to see if it is getting towards dinner-time, never gets drunk and drops down in a heap on the floor; he is usually sober, he is always busy, and must have a hand in everything; he has a mind to be in all secrets, and in general plays the part of friend with the gravity of a tragedian and not like a comedian or a buffoon. For as Plato[11] says, "it is the height of dishonesty to seem to be honest when one is not," and so the flattery which we must regard as difficult to deal with is that which is hidden, not that which is openly avowed, that which is serious, not that which is meant as a joke. For such flattery infects even true friendship with distrust, unless we give heed, for in many respects it coincides with friendship. Now it is true that Gobryas, having forced his way into a dark room along with the fleeing Magian, and finding himself engaged in a desperate struggle, called

upon Darius, who had stopped beside them and was in doubt what to do, to strike even though he should pierce them both; but we, if we can by no means approve the sentiment, "Down with a foe though a friend go too," have great cause to fear in seeking to detach the flatterer, who through many similarities is closely interlocked with the friend, lest in some way we either cast out the useful along with the bad, or else, in trying to spare what is close to our hearts, we fall upon what is injurious. So, I think, when wild seeds which have a shape and size approximating to wheat have got mixed with it, the process of cleaning is difficult (for either they do not pass out through a finer sieve, or else they do pass out through a coarser, and the wheat along with them); in like manner, flattery which blends itself with every emotion, every movement, need, and habit, is hard to separate from friendship.

5. For the very reason, however, that friendship is the most pleasant thing in the world, and because nothing else gives greater delight, the flatterer allures by means of pleasures and concerns himself with pleasures. And just because graciousness and usefulness go with friendship (which is the reason why they say that a friend is more indispensable than fire and water), the flatterer thrusts himself into services for us, striving always to appear earnest, unremitting, and diligent. And inasmuch as that which most especially cements a friendship begun is a likeness of pursuits and characters, and since to take delight in the same things and avoid the same things is what generally brings people together in the first place, and gets them acquainted through the bond of sympathy, the flatterer takes note of this fact, and adjusts and shapes himself, as though he were so much inert matter, endeavoring to adapt and mould himself to fit those whom he attacks through imitation; and he is so supple in changes and so plausible in his copyings that we may exclaim: "Achilles' self thou art and not his son."

But the most unprincipled trick of all that he has is this: perceiving that frankness of speech, by common report and belief, is the language of friendship especially (as an animal has its peculiar cry), and, on the other hand, that lack of frankness is unfriendly and ignoble, he does not allow even this to escape imitation, but, just as clever cooks employ bitter extracts and astringent flavourings to remove the cloying effect of sweet things, so flatterers apply a frankness which is not genuine or beneficial, but which, as it were, winks while it frowns, and does nothing but tickle. For these reasons, then, the man is hard to detect, as is the case with some animals to which Nature has given the faculty of changing their hue, so that they exactly conform to the colours and objects beneath them. And since the flatterer uses resemblances to deceive and to wrap about him, it is our task to use the differences in order to unwrap him and lay him bare, in the act, as Plato[12] puts it, of "adorning himself with alien colours and forms for want of any of his own" . . .

7. What, then, is the method of exposing him, and by what differences is it possible to detect that he is not really like-minded, or even in a fair way to become like-minded, but is merely imitating such a character? In the first place, it is necessary to observe the uniformity and permanence of his tastes, whether he always takes delight in the same things, and commends always the same things, and whether he directs and ordains his own life according to one pattern, as becomes a free-born man and a lover of congenial friendship and intimacy; for such is the conduct of a friend. But the flatterer, since he has no abiding-place of character to dwell in, and since he leads a life not of his own choosing but another's, moulding and adapting himself to suit another, is not simple, not one, but variable and many in one, and, like water that is poured into one receptacle after another, he is constantly on the move from place to place, and changes his shape to fit his receiver.

The capture of the ape, as it seems, is effected while he is trying to imitate man by moving and dancing as the man does; but the flatterer himself leads on and entices others, not imitating all persons alike, but with one he joins in dancing and singing, and with another in wrestling and getting covered with dust; if he gets hold of a huntsman fond of the chase, he follows on, all but shouting out the words of Phaedra: "Ye gods, but I yearn to encourage the hounds, as I haste on the track of the dapple deer."[13] He does not trouble himself in regard to the quarry, but he goes about to net and ensnare the huntsman himself. But if he is on the track of a scholarly and studious young man, now again he is absorbed in books, his beard grows down to his feet, the scholar's gown is the thing now and a stoic indifference, and endless talk about Plato's numbers and right-angled triangles. At another time, if some easy-tempered man fall in his way, who is a hard drinker and rich, "Then stands forth the wily Odysseus stripped of his tatters;[14] off goes the scholar's gown, the beard is mowed down like an unprofitable crop; it's wine-coolers and glasses now, bursts of laughter while walking in the streets, and frivolous jokes against the devotees of philosophy. Just so at Syracuse, it is said, after Plato had arrived, and an insane ardour for philosophy laid hold on Dionysius, the king's palace was filled with dust by reason of the multitude of men that were drawing their geometrical diagrams in it; but when Plato fell out of favour, and Dionysius, shaking himself free from philosophy, returned post-haste to wine and women and foolish talk and licentiousness, then grossness and forgetfulness and fatuity seized upon the whole people as though they had undergone a transformation in Circe's house. A further testimony is to be found in the action of the great flatterers and the demagogues, of whom the greatest was Alcibiades. At Athens he indulged in frivolous jesting, kept a racing-stable, and led a life full of urbanity and agreeable enjoyment; in Lacedaemon he kept his hair cropped close, he wore the coarsest clothing, he bathed in cold water; in Thrace he was a fighter and a hard drinker; but when he came to Tissaphernes, he took to soft living, and luxury, and pretentiousness. So by making himself like to all these people and conforming his way to theirs he tried to conciliate them and win their favour. Not of this type, however, was Epameinondas or Agesilaus, who, although they had to do with a very large number of men and cities and modes of life, yet maintained everywhere their own proper character in dress, conduct, language, and life. So, too, Plato in Syracuse was the same sort of man as in the Academy, and to Dionysius he was the same as to Dion.

8. The changes of the flatterer, which are like those of a cuttle-fish, may be most easily detected if a man pretends that he is very changeable himself and disapproves the mode of life which he previously approved, and suddenly shows a liking for actions, conduct, or language which used to offend him. For he will see that the flatterer is nowhere constant, has no character of his own, that it is not because of his own feelings that he loves and hates, and rejoices and grieves, but that, like a mirror, he only catches the images of alien feelings, lives and movements. For he is the kind of man who, if you chance to blame one of your friends before him, will exclaim, "You've been slow in discovering the man's character; for my part I took a dislike to him long ago." But if, on the next occasion, you change about again and commend the man, then you may be sure the flatterer will avow that he shares your pleasure and thanks you for the man's sake, and that he believes in him. If you say that you must adopt some other sort of life, as, for example, by changing from public life to ease and quietness, then he says, "Yes, we ought long ago to have secured release from turmoils and jealousies." But again if you appear to be bent on public activity and speaking, then he chimes in, "Your thoughts are worthy of you; ease is a pleasant thing, but it is inglorious and mean." Without more ado we must say to such a man: "Stranger, you seem to me now a different man than aforetime."[15] I have no use for a friend that shifts

about just as I do and nods assent just as I do (for my shadow better performs that function), but I want one that tells the truth as I do, and decides for himself as I do.

This is one method, then, of detecting the flatterer; (9)[16] but here follows a second point of difference which ought to be observed, in his habits of imitation. The true friend is neither an imitator of everything nor ready to commend everything, but only the best things; "His nature 'tis to share not hate but love," as Sophocles[17] has it, and most assuredly to share also in right conduct and in love for the good, not in error and evil-doing, unless, as a result of association and close acquaintance, an emanation and infection, like that which comes from a diseased eye, contaminate him against his will with a touch of baseness or error. In a similar way it is said that close acquaintances used to copy Plato's stoop, Aristotle's lisp, and King Alexander's twisted neck as well as the harshness of his voice in conversation. In fact, some people unconsciously acquire most of their peculiarities from the traits or the lives of others. But the flatterer's case is exactly the same as that of the chameleon. For the chameleon can make himself like to every colour except white, and the flatterer, being utterly incapable of making himself like to another in any quality that is really worth while, leaves no shameful thing unimitated; but even as bad painters, who by reason of incompetence are unable to attain to the beautiful, depend upon wrinkles, moles, and scars to bring out their resemblances, so the flatterer makes himself an imitator of licentiousness, superstition, passionate anger, harshness toward servants, and distrust toward household and kinsmen. For by nature he is of himself prone to the worse, and he seems very far removed from disapproving what is shameful, since he imitates it. In fact it is those who follow a higher ideal and show distress and annoyance at the errors of their friends, who fall under suspicion. This is the thing that brought Dion into disfavour with Dionysius, Samius with Philip, Cleomenes with Ptolemy, and finally brought about their undoing. But the flatterer, desiring to be and to seem pleasant and loyal at the same time, affects to take greater delight in the worse things, as one who for the great love he bears will take no offence even at what is base, but feels with his friend and shares his nature in all things. For this reason flatterers will not be denied a share even in the chances of life which happen without our will; but they flatter the sickly by pretending to be afflicted with the same malady, and not to be able to see or hear distinctly if they have to do with those who are dim-sighted or hard of hearing, just as the flatterers of Dionysius, whose sight was failing, used to bump against one another and upset the dishes at dinner. And some seize upon afflictions rather as a means to insinuate themselves still more, and carry their fellow-feeling so far as to include inmost secrets. If they know, for example, that one or another is unfortunate in his marriage, or suspicious towards his sons or his household, they do not spare themselves, but lament over their own children or wife or kinsmen or household, divulging certain secret faults of theirs. For such similarity makes fellow-feeling stronger, so that the others, conceiving themselves to have received pledges, are more inclined to let out some of their own secrets to the flatterers, and having so done they take up with them, and are afraid to abandon the confidential relation. I personally know of one man who put away his wife after his friend had sent his own away; but he was caught visiting her in secret and sending messages to her after his friend's wife had got wind of what was going on. Quite unacquainted with a flatterer, then, was he who thought that these iambic verses applied to a flatterer rather than to a crab: "His body is all belly; eyes that look all ways; a beast that travels on its teeth." For such a description is that of a parasite, one of "The saucepan friends and friends postprandial," as Eupolis puts it.

10. However, let us reserve this matter for its proper place in our discussion. But let us not omit to note this clever turn which the flatterer has in his imitations, that if he does imitate any of the good qualities of the person whom he flatters, he gives him always the upper hand. The reason is this: between true friends there is neither emulation nor envy, but whether their share of success is equal or less, they bear it with moderation and without vexation. But the flatterer, mindful always that he is to play the second part, abates from his equality in the imitation, admitting that he is beaten and distanced in everything save what is bad. In bad things, however, he does not relinquish the first place, but, if the other man is malcontent, he calls himself choleric; if the man is superstitious he says of himself that he is possessed; that the man is in love, but that he himself is mad with passion. "You laughed inopportunely," he says, "but I nearly died of laughing." But in good things it is just the reverse. The flatterer says that he himself is a good runner, but the other man simply flies; that he himself is a fairly good horseman, "but what is that compared with this Centaur?" "I am a natural born poet, and I write verse that is not at all bad, yet 'To Zeus belongs the thunder, not to me'" (anonymous). Thus at the same time he thinks to show that the other's tastes are excellent by imitating them, and that his prowess is unrivalled by letting himself be outdone.

Thus, then, in the flatterer's attempts to conform himself to another, differences like these are found which distinguish him from a friend. . .

12. They say that the gad-fly finds lodgement with cattle close by the ear, as does the tick with dogs; so also the flatterer takes hold of ambitious men's ears with his words of praise, and once settled there, he is hard to dislodge.   Wherefore in this matter especially it is necessary to keep the judgment awake and on the alert, to see whether the praise is for the action or for the man. It is for the action if they praise us in absence rather than in our presence; also if they, too, cherish the same desires and aspirations themselves and praise not us alone but all persons for like conduct; also if they are not found doing and saying now this and now the opposite; but, chief of all, if we ourselves know that we feel no regret for those actions for which we are praised, no feeling of shame and no wish that we had said or done the opposite.   For if our own conscience protests and refuses to accept the praise, then it is not affected or touched, and is proof against assault by the flatterer.   Yet, in some way that passes my knowledge, most people have no patience with efforts to console them in their misfortunes, but are more influenced by those who commiserate and condole with them; and whenever these same people are guilty of mistakes and blunders, the man who by chiding and blaming implants the sting of repentance is taken to be an enemy and an accuser, whereas they welcome the man who praises and extols what they have done, and regard him as kindly and friendly.   Now those who unthinkingly praise and join in applauding an act or a saying, or anything offered by another, whether he be in earnest or in jest, are harmful only for the moment and for the matter at hand; but those who with their praises pierce to the man's character, and indeed even touch his habit of mind with their flattery, are doing the very thing that servants do who steal not from the heap[18] but from the seed-corn. For, since the disposition and character are the seed from which actions spring, such persons are thus perverting the very first principle and fountain-head of living, inasmuch as they are investing vice with the names that belong to virtue. Amid factions and wars, Thucydides says "they changed the commonly accepted meaning of words when applied to deeds as they thought proper.   Reckless daring came to be regarded as devoted courage, watchful waiting as specious cowardice, moderation as a craven's pretext, a keen understanding for everything as want of energy to undertake anything." And so in attempts at flattery we should be observant and on our guard against prodigality being called "liberality," cowardice "self-

reservation," impulsiveness "quickness," stinginess "frugality," the amorous man "companionable and amiable," the irascible and overbearing "spirited," the insignificant and meek "kindly." So Plato[19] somewhere says that the lover, being a flatterer of his beloved, calls one with a snub nose "fetching," one with a hooked nose "kingly," dark persons "manly," and fair persons "children of the gods"; while "honey-hued" is purely the creation of a lover who calls sallowness by this endearing term, and cheerfully puts up with it. And yet an ugly man who is made to believe that he is handsome, or a short man that he is tall, is not for long a party to the deception, and the injury that he suffers is slight and not irremediable. But as for the praise which accustoms a man to treat vices as virtues, so that he feels not disgusted with them but delighted, which also takes away all shame for his errors—this is the sort that brought afflictions upon the people of Sicily, by calling the savage cruelty of Dionysius and of Phalaris "hatred of wickedness"; this it is that ruined Egypt, by giving to Ptolemy's effeminacy, his religious mania, his hallelujahs, his clashing of cymbals, the name of "piety" and "devotion to the gods"; this it is that all but subverted and destroyed the character of the Romans in those days, by trying to extenuate Antony's[20] luxuriousness, his excesses and ostentatious displays, as "blithe and kind-hearted actions due to his generous treatment at the hands of Power and Fortune." What else was it that fastened the mouthpiece and flute upon Ptolemy? What else set a tragic stage for Nero, and invested him with mask and buskins? Was it not the praise of his flatterers? And is not almost any king called an Apollo if he can hum a tune, and a Dionysus if he gets drunk, and a Heracles if he can wrestle? And is he not delighted, and thus led on into all kinds of disgrace by the flattery?

13. For this reason we must be especially on our guard against the flatterer in the matter of his praises. But of this he is not unconscious himself, and he is adroit at guarding against the breath of suspicion. If, for example, he gets hold of some coxcomb, or a rustic wearing a thick coat of skin, he indulges his raillery without limit, just as Strouthias, in the play, walks all over Bias, and takes a fling at his stupidity by such praise as this: "More you have drunk than royal Alexander,"[21] and "Ha! ha! A good one on the Cyprian."[22] But as for the more clever people, he observes that they are particularly on the look-out for him in this quarter, that they stand well upon their guard in this place and region; so he does not deploy his praise in a frontal attack, but fetches a wide circuit, and "Approaches noiseless as to catch a beast," touching and handling him. Now he will report other people's praise of him, quoting

another's words as public speakers do, how he had the pleasure of meeting in the market-place with some strangers or elderly men, who recounted many handsome things of him and expressed their admiration; then again, he will fabricate and concoct some trivial and false accusation against him, which he feigns to have heard from others, and comes up in hot haste to inquire when it was he said this or when it was he did that. And if the man denies the thing, as he naturally will, then on the instant the flatterer seizes him and launches him into a flood of praise: "I wondered if you did speak ill of any of your good friends, since it is not your nature to speak ill even of your enemies, or if you did make any attempt on other's property when you give away so much of your own."

14. Others, like painters who set off bright and brilliant colours by laying on dark and sombre tints close beside them, covertly praise and foster the vices to which their victims are addicted by condemning and abusing, or disparaging and ridiculing, the opposite qualities. Among the profligate they condemn frugality as "rusticity"; and among avaricious evil-doers, whose wealth is gained from shameful and unscrupulous deeds, they condemn contented independence and honesty as "the want of courage and vigour for active life"; but when they associate with the easy-going and quiet people who avoid the crowded centres of the cities, they are not ashamed to call public life "a troublesome meddling with others' affairs," and ambition "unprofitable vainglory." Often enough a way to flatter a public speaker is to disparage a philosopher, and with lascivious women great repute is gained by those who brand faithful and loving wives as "cold" and "countrified." But here is the height of depravity, in that the flatterers do not spare their own selves. For as wrestlers put their own bodies into a lowly posture in order to throw their opponents, so flatterers, by blaming themselves, pass surreptitiously into admiration for their neighbours: "I am a miserable coward on the water, I have no stomach for hardships, I go mad with anger when anyone speaks ill of me; but for this man here," he says, "nothing has any terrors, nothing any hardship, but he is a singular person; he bears everything with good humour, everything without distress." But if there be somebody who imagines himself possessed of great sense, and desires to be downright and uncompromising, who because he poses as an upright man, forsooth, always uses as a defence and shield this line: "Son of Tydeus, praise me not too much, nor chide me,"[23] the accomplished flatterer does not approach him by this road, but there is another device to apply to a man of this sort. Accordingly the flatterer comes to consult with

him about his own affairs, as with one obviously his superior in wisdom, and says that while he has other friends more intimate yet he finds it necessary to trouble him. "For where can we resort who are in need of counsel, and whom can we trust?" Then having heard whatever the other may say, he asserts that he has received, not counsel, but the word of authority; and with that he takes his departure. And if he observes that the man lays some claim to skill in letters, he gives him some of his own writings, and asks him to read and correct them. Mithridates, the king, posed as an amateur physician, and some of his companions offered themselves to be operated upon and cauterized by him, thus flattering by deeds and not by words; for he felt that their confidence in him was a testimony to his skill. "In many a guise do the gods appear,"[24] and this class of dissimulated praise, which calls for a more cunning sort of precaution, is to be brought to light by deliberately formulating absurd advice and suggestions, and by making senseless corrections. For if he fails to contradict anything, if he assents to everything and accepts it, and at each suggestion exclaims "good" and "excellent," he makes it perfectly plain that he "The password asks, to gain some other end," his real desire being to praise his victim and to puff him up all the more.

15. Moreover, just as some have defined painting as silent poetry,[25] so there is a kind of praise that is silent flattery. For just as men engaged in hunting are less noticed by their quarry if they pretend not to be so engaged, but to be going along the road or tending flocks or tilling the soil, so flatterers gain the best hold with their praise when they pretend not to be praising, but to be doing something else. Take, for example, a man who yields his seat or his place at table to a new-comer, or if he is engaged in speaking to the popular assembly or the senate and discovers that someone of the wealthy wants to speak, suddenly lapses into silence in the midst of his argument, and surrenders the platform with his right to speak; such a man by his silence, far more than one who indulges in loud acclaim, makes it plain that he regards the rich person as his better and his superior in intelligence. This is the reason why such persons are to be seen taking possession of the front seats at entertainments and theatres, not because they think they have any right to them, but so that they may flatter the rich by giving up their seats. So, too, in an assemblage or a formal meeting they may be observed to begin a subject of discussion, and later to give ground as though before their betters, and to shift over with the utmost readiness to the other side, if the man opposing them be a person of power or wealth or repute. Herein lies the supreme test by

which we must detect such cases of cringing submission and giving way, in that deference is paid, not to experience or virtue or age, but to wealth and repute. . . .

20. One mode of protection, as it would seem, is to realize and remember always that our soul has its two sides: on the one side are truthfulness, love for what is honourable, and power to reason, and on the other side irrationality, love of falsehood, and the emotional element; the friend is always found on the better side as counsel and advocate, trying, after the manner of a physician, to foster the growth of what is sound and to preserve it; but the flatterer takes his place on the side of the emotional and irrational, and this he excites and tickles and wheedles, and tries to divorce from the reasoning powers by contriving for it divers low forms of pleasurable enjoyment. There are some sorts of food, for example, that are without affinity for either the blood or the breath, which add no vigour to nerves or marrow, but only excite the lower passions, arouse the appetite, and make unsound flesh that is morbid within. So the flatterer's talk adds nothing to the thinking and reasoning powers, but only promotes familiarity with some amorous pleasure, intensifies a foolish fit of temper, provokes envy, engenders an offensive and inane bulk of conceit, commiserates in distress, or, by a succession of slanders and forebodings, causes malice, illiberality and distrust to grow bitter, timorous, and suspicious; and these are all matters that will not escape the observant. For the flatterer is always covertly on the watch for some emotion, and pampering it, and his presence is like that of a tumour in that he ever comes immediately following some morbid or inflamed condition of the soul. "Are you angry? Punish then." "Do you crave a thing? Then buy it." "Are you afraid? Let's run away." "Have you a suspicion? Then give it credence." . . .

23. . . . You must have noticed the ape. He cannot guard the house like the dog, nor carry a load like the horse, nor plough the land like oxen; and so he has to bear abuse and scurrility, and endure practical jokes, thus submitting to be made an instrument of laughter. So also with the flatterer: unable to help another with words or money or to back him in a quarrel, and unequal to anything laborious or serious, yet he makes no excuses when it comes to underhand actions, he is a faithful helper in a love-affair, he knows exactly the price to be paid for a prostitute, he is not careless in checking up the charge for a wine supper, nor slow in making arrangements for dinners, he tries to be in the good graces of mistresses; but if bidden to be impudent toward a wife's relatives or to help in hustling a wife out of doors he is relentless

and unabashed. As a result the man is not hard to detect in this way, either; for if he is told to do any disreputable and dishonourable thing that you will, he is ready to be prodigal of himself in trying to gratify the man who tells him to do it.

24. The great difference between flatterer and friend may be most clearly perceived by his disposition towards one's other friends. For a friend finds it most pleasant to love and be loved along with many others, and he is always constant in his endeavours that his friend shall have many friends[26] and be much honoured; believing that "friends own everything in common" he thinks that no possession ought to be held so much in common as friends. But the flatterer is false, spurious, and debased, inasmuch as he fully understands that he is committing a crime against friendship, which in his hands becomes a counterfeit coin as it were. While he is by nature jealous, yet he employs his jealousy against his own kind, striving constantly to outdo them in scurrility and idle gossip, but he stands in awesome dread of his betters, not indeed because he is "Trudging afoot beside a Lydian chariot,"[27] but because, as Simonides puts it, he "Hath not even lead to show 'gainst gold refined and un-alloyed." Whenever, then, the flatterer, who is but a light and deceptive plated-ware, is examined and closely compared with genuine and solid-wrought friendship, he does not stand the test, but he is exposed, and so he does the same thing as the man who had painted a wretched picture of some cocks. For the painter bade his servant scare all real cocks as far away as possible from the canvas; and so the flatterer scares all real friends away, and does not allow them to come near; or if he cannot accomplish this, he openly cringes to them, pays them attentions, and makes a great show of respect for them as for superiors, but secretly he is suggesting and spreading some sort of calumny; and when secret talk has caused an irritating sore, even though he be not entirely successful at the outset, yet he remembers and observes the precept of Medius. This Medius was, if I may call him so, leader and skilled master of the choir of flatterers that danced attendance on Alexander, and were banded together against all good men. Now he urged them not to be afraid to assail and sting with their calumnies, pointing out that, even if the man who is stung succeeds in healing the wound, the scar of the calumny will still remain. In fact it was by such scars, or rather such gangrenes and cancers, that Alexander was consumed so that he destroyed Callisthenes, Parmenio, and Philotas, and put himself without reserve into the hands of men like Hagno, Bagoas, Agesias, and Demetrius, to be brought low, by submitting to be worshipped, bedecked and fantastically tricked out by

them, after the manner of a barbaric idol. So great is the power wielded by giving gratification, and it is greatest, apparently, with those who seem to be the greatest personages. For self-conceit regarding the noblest qualities, coupled with the wish to have them, gives both confidence and boldness to the flatterer. It is true that lofty places are difficult of approach and access for those who propose to capture them, but loftiness or conceit, in a mind which lacks sense because of the favours of Fortune or Nature, lies at the mercy of the insignificant and mean.

25. Wherefore I now urge, as I did at the beginning of this treatise, that we eradicate from ourselves self-love and conceit. For these, by flattering us beforehand, render us less resistant to flatterers from without, since we are quite ready to receive them. But if, in obedience to the god, we learn that the precept, "Know thyself," is invaluable to each of us, and if at the same time we carefully review our own nature and upbringing and education, how in countless ways they fall short of true excellence, and have inseparably connected with them many a sad and heedless fault of word, deed, and feeling, we shall not very readily let the flatterers walk over us. Now Alexander[28] said that two things moved him to discredit those who proclaimed him a god, his sleeping and his passion for women, evidently feeling that in these matters he revealed the more ignoble and susceptible side of himself; and so in our own case, if we are careful to observe many and many a fault of our own, shameful and grievous, both of omission and commission, we shall constantly be detecting our own need, not of a friend to commend and extol us, but of a friend to take us to task, to be frank with us, and indeed to blame us when our conduct is bad. For there are but few among many who have the courage to show frankness rather than favour to their friends. And again, among those few you cannot easily find men who know how to do this, but rather you shall find those who think that if they abuse and find fault they use frankness. Yet frankness, like any other medicine, if it be not applied at the proper time, does but cause useless suffering and disturbance, and it accomplishes, one may say, painfully what flattery accomplishes pleasantly. For people are injured, not only by untimely praise, but by untimely blame as well; and it is this especially that delivers them over, broadside on, to the flatterers, an easy prey, since like water they glide away from the steeps that repel toward the valleys that softly invite. Frankness, therefore, should be combined with good manners, and there should be reason in it to take away its excess and intensity, which may be compared to that of light, so that any who are exposed to it shall not,

for being disturbed and distressed by those who find fault with everything and accuse every one, take refuge in the shadow of the flatterer, and turn away towards what does not cause pain.

Notes

[1] *Laws*, 731 D, E.

[2] *Ibid.*; cited also in *Moralia*, 90 A, 92 E, and 1000 A.

[3] True friendship is, of course, proof against flattery, but friendship weakened by self-love is a sort of border-land between true friendship and flattery in which the flatterer can work.

[4] *Laws*, 730 c.

[5] Adapted from Hesiod, *Theogony*, 64.

[6] *Ion*, 732; again cited in *Moralia*, 69 A.

[7] Again cited in *Moralia*, 126 D, 697 D, and 1010 D.

[8] Men too poor to afford a servant, and hence obliged to carry their own bottle of oil to the bath. *Cf.* Demosthenes, *Against Conon*, § 16 (p. 1262).

[9] The ceremonial washing of the hands immediately before eating.

[10] From the *Flatterers* of Eupolis according to Plutarch, *Moralia*, 778 E.

[11] *Republic*, 361 A.

[12] *Phaedrus*, 239 D.

[13] Euripides, *Hippolytus*, 218.

[14] Homer, *Od.* xxii. 1.

[15] Homer, *Odyssey*, xvi. 181.

[16] Chapter 9 begins at this point in the text. [*Eds.*]

[17] Adapted from Sophocles, *Antigone*, 523.

[18] The grain, after being winnowed, was heaped on the threshing-floor.

[19] *Republic*, 474 E; cf. *Supra*, 45 A.

[20] See Plutarch, *Life of Antony*, chap. Ix. (920).

[21] From the *Flatterer* of Menander; Kock, *Com. Att. Frag.* Iii., *Menander*, No. 293.

[22] *Ibid.* No. 29.

[23] Homer, *Il.* X. 249.

[24] From the stock lines used at the close of the *Alcestis*, the *Andromache*, the *Bacchae*, and the *Helena*, of Euripides.

[25] A dictum attributed to Simonides by Plutarch, *Moralia*, 346 F.

[26] Plutarch has devoted a separate essay (*De amicorum multitudine*) to this subject (*Moralia*, 79 B-93 B).

[27] From Pindar according to Plutarch, *Life of Nicias*, chap. I. (523 B).

[28] *Cf.* Plutarch, *Life of Alexander*, chap. Xxii. (677 B) and *Moralia*, 717 B.

Chapter 9

St. Augustine, *Confessions*

St. Augustine (354-430) is unquestionably the most influential of all Christian theologians. Even Luther, the Protestant **par excellence,** *would ever sign his letters "Martin Luther, Augustinian."*

Born in North Africa, near Carthage, Aurelius Augustine had a tempestuous youth. With a pagan father and a Christian mother, a mother who was ever mindful to try and focus the young Aureluius' attention on the faith, Augustine almost seemed destined to live a colorful life full of contrasts. In his early years, Augustine was taken with the Manichean religion, a variation of Zoroastrianism, and was later heavily influenced by the mysticism of the Neo-Platonists.

After years of a tumultuous life and education in both Carthage and Rome, Augustine became a professor of rhetoric in Milan. There, he underwent his eventual conversion under the influence of the teaching of Saint Ambrose. In 395, Augustine became bishop of Hippo and remained in North Africa until his death.

The following selection is drawn from one of Augustine's major works, his **Confessions.** *In this work, written in the form of a prayer of confession addressed to God, the question of the friend comes up again and again in a variety of ways, ways by which Augustine is able to relate not only general observations about the will and the concept of radical evil in human nature, but also by which he is able to relate how a story of friends who underwent conversion caused him himself to undergo conversion with his friends also. Readers familiar with Augustine's* **Confessions** *will know why this passionate work is an all-time favorite and an established classic of the Western tradition.*

Confessions

Book Two

He concentrates here on his sixteenth year, a year of idleness, lust, and adolescent mischief. The memory of stealing some pears prompts a deep probing of the motives and aims of sinful acts. "I became to myself a wasteland."

Chapter I

1. I wish now to review in memory my past wickedness and the carnal corruptions of my soul—not because I still love them, but that I may love thee, O my God. For love of thy love I do this, recalling in the bitterness of self-examination my wicked ways, that thou mayest grow sweet to me, thou sweetness without deception! Thou sweetness happy and assured! Thus thou mayest gather me up out of those fragments in which I was torn to pieces, while I turned away from thee, O Unity, and lost myself among "the many."[1] For as I became a youth, I longed to be satisfied with worldly things, and I dared to grow wild in a succession of various and shadowy loves. My form wasted away, and I became corrupt in thy eyes, yet I was still pleasing to my own eyes—and eager to please the eyes of men.

Chapter II

2. But what was it that delighted me save to love and to be loved? Still I did not keep the moderate way of the love of mind to mind—the bright path of friendship. Instead, the mists of passion steamed up out of the puddly concupiscence of the flesh, and the hot imagination of puberty, and they so obscured and overcast my heart that I was unable to distinguish pure affection from unholy desire. Both boiled confusedly within me, and dragged my unstable youth down over the cliffs of unchaste desires and plunged me into a gulf of infamy. Thy anger had come upon me, and I knew it not. I had been deafened by the clanking of the chains of my mortality, the punishment for my soul's pride, and I wandered farther from thee, and thou didst permit me to do so. I was tossed to and fro, and wasted, and poured out, and I boiled over in my fornications—and yet thou didst hold thy peace, O my tardy Joy! Thou didst still hold thy peace, and I wandered still

farther from thee into more and yet more barren fields of sorrow, in proud dejection and restless lassitude. . . .

Chapter III

5. Now, in that year my studies were interrupted. I had come back from Madaura, a neighboring city[2] where I had gone to study grammar and rhetoric; and the money for a further term at Carthage was being got together for me. This project was more a matter of my father's ambition than of his means, for he was only a poor citizen of Tagaste.

To whom am I narrating all this? Not to thee, O my God, but to my own kind in thy presence—to that small part of the human race who may chance to come upon these writings. And to what end? That I and all who read them may understand what depths there are from which we are to cry unto thee.[3] For what is more surely heard in thy ear than a confessing heart and a faithful life?

Who did not extol and praise my father, because he went quite beyond his means to supply his son with the necessary expenses for a far journey in the interest of his education? For many far richer citizens did not do so much for their children. Still, this same father troubled himself not at all as to how I was progressing toward thee nor how chaste I was, just so long as I was skillful in speaking—no matter how barren I was to thy tillage, O God, who art the one true and good Lord of my heart, which is thy field.[4]

6. During that sixteenth year of my age, I lived with my parents, having a holiday from school for a time—this idleness imposed upon me by my parents' straitened finances. The thornbushes of lust grew rank about my head, and there was no hand to root them out. Indeed, when my father saw me one day at the baths and perceived that I was becoming a man, and was showing the signs of adolescence, he joyfully told my mother about it as if already looking forward to grandchildren, rejoicing in that sort of inebriation in which the world so often forgets thee, its Creator, and falls in love with thy creature instead of thee—the inebriation of that invisible wine of a perverted will which turns and bows down to infamy. But in my mother's breast thou hadst already begun to build thy temple and the foundation of thy holy habitation—whereas my father was only a catechumen, and that but recently. She was, therefore, startled with a holy fear and trembling: for though I had not yet been baptized, she feared those crooked ways in which they walk who turn their backs to thee and not their faces.

7. Woe is me! Do I dare affirm that thou didst hold thy peace, O my God, while I wandered farther away from thee? Didst thou really then hold thy peace? Then whose words were they but thine which by my mother, thy faithful handmaid, thou didst pour into my ears? None of them, however, sank into my heart to make me do anything. She deplored and, as I remember, warned me privately with great solicitude, "not to commit fornication; but above all things never to defile another man's wife." These appeared to me but womanish counsels, which I would have blushed to obey. Yet they were from thee, and I knew it not. I thought that thou wast silent and that it was only she who spoke. Yet it was through her that thou didst not keep silence toward me; and in rejecting her counsel I was rejecting thee—I, her son, "the son of thy handmaid, thy servant."⁵ But I did not realize this, and rushed on headlong with such blindness that, among my friends, I was ashamed to be less shameless than they, when I heard them boasting of their disgraceful exploits—yes, and glorying all the more the worse their baseness was. What is worse, I took pleasure in such exploits, not for the pleasure's sake only but mostly for praise. What is worthy of vituperation except vice itself? Yet I made myself out worse than I was, in order that I might not go lacking for praise. And when in anything I had not sinned as the worst ones in the group, I would still say that I had done what I had not done, in order not to appear contemptible because I was more innocent than they; and not to drop in their esteem because I was more chaste.

8. Behold with what companions I walked the streets of Babylon!⁶ I rolled in its mire and lolled about on it, as if on a bed of spices and precious ointments. And, drawing me more closely to the very center of that city, my invisible enemy trod me down and seduced me, for I was easy to seduce. My mother had already fled out of the midst of Babylon and was progressing, albeit slowly, toward its outskirts. For in counseling me to chastity, she did not bear in mind what her husband had told her about me. And although she knew that my passions were destructive even then and dangerous for the future, she did not think they should be restrained by the bonds of conjugal affection—if, indeed, they could not be cut away to the quick. She took no heed of this, for she was afraid lest a wife should prove a hindrance and a burden to my hopes. These were not her hopes of the world to come, which my mother had in thee, but the hope of learning, which both my parents were too anxious that I should acquire—my father, because he had little or no thought of thee, and only vain thoughts for me; my mother, because she thought that the usual course of study would not

only be no hindrance but actually a furtherance toward my eventual return to thee. This much I conjecture, recalling as well as I can the temperaments of my parents. Meantime, the reins of discipline were slackened on me, so that without the restraint of due severity, I might play at whatsoever I fancied, even to the point of dissoluteness. And in all this there was that mist which shut out from my sight the brightness of thy truth, O my God; and my iniquity bulged out, as it were, with fatness![7] ...

Chapter VIII

16. What profit did I, a wretched one, receive from those things which, when I remember them now, cause me shame—above all, from that theft, which I loved only for the theft's sake? And, as the theft itself was nothing, I was all the more wretched in that I loved it so. Yet by myself alone I would not have done it—I still recall how I felt about this then—I could not have done it alone. I loved it then because of the companionship of my accomplices with whom I did it. I did not, therefore, love the theft alone—yet, indeed, it was only the theft that I loved, for the companionship was nothing. What is this paradox? Who is it that can explain it to me but God, who illumines my heart and searches out the dark corners thereof? What is it that has prompted my mind to inquire about it, to discuss and to reflect upon all this? For had I at that time loved the pears that I stole and wished to enjoy them, I might have done so alone, if I could have been satisfied with the mere act of theft by which my pleasure was served. Nor did I need to have that itching of my own passions inflamed by the encouragement of my accomplices. But since the pleasure I got was not from the pears, it was in the crime itself, enhanced by the companionship of my fellow sinners.

Chapter IX

17. By what passion, then, was I animated? It was undoubtedly depraved and a great misfortune for me to feel it. But still, what was it? "Who can understand his errors?"[8]

We laughed because our hearts were tickled at the thought of deceiving the owners, who had no idea of what we were doing and would have strenuously objected. Yet, again, why did I find such delight in doing this which I would not have done alone? Is it that no one readily laughs alone? No one does so readily; but still sometimes, when men are by themselves and no one else is about, a fit of laughter will overcome them when something very droll presents itself to their sense or mind. Yet alone I would not have done it—alone I could not have done it at all.

Behold, my God, the lively review of my soul's career is laid bare before thee. I would not have committed that theft alone. My pleasure in it was not what I stole, but rather the act of stealing. Nor would I have enjoyed doing it alone—indeed I would not have done it! O friendship all unfriendly! You strange seducer of the soul, who hungers for mischief from impulses of mirth and wantonness, who craves another's loss without any desire for one's own profit or revenge—so that, when they say, "Let's go, let's do it," we are ashamed not to be shameless.

Book Three—The sto*ry of his student days in Carthage* . . .

Chapter I

1. I came to Carthage, where a caldron of unholy loves was seething and bubbling all around me. I was not in love as yet, but I was in love with love; and, from a hidden hunger, I hated myself for not feeling more intensely a sense of hunger. I was looking for something to love, for I was in love with loving, and I hated security and a smooth way, free from snares. Within me I had a dearth of that inner food which is thyself, my God—although that dearth caused me no hunger. And I remained without any appetite for incorruptible food—not because I was already filled with it, but because the emptier I became the more I loathed it. Because of this my soul was unhealthy; and, full of sores, it exuded itself forth, itching to be scratched by scraping on the things of the senses.[9] Yet, had these things no soul, they would certainly not inspire our love.

To love and to be loved was sweet to me, and all the more when I gained the enjoyment of the body of the person I loved. Thus I polluted the spring of friendship with the filth of concupiscence and I dimmed its luster with the slime of lust. Yet, foul and unclean as I was, I still craved, in excessive vanity, to be thought elegant and urbane. And I did fall precipitately into the love I was longing for. My God, my mercy, with how much bitterness didst thou, out of thy infinite goodness, flavor that sweetness for me! For I was not only beloved but also I secretly reached the climax of enjoyment; and yet I was joyfully bound with troublesome ties, so that I could be scourged with the burning iron rods of jealousy, suspicion, fear, anger, and strife. . . .

Chapter III

5. And still thy faithful mercy hovered over me from afar. In what unseemly iniquities did I wear myself out, following a sacrilegious curiosity, which, having deserted thee, then began to drag me down into the treacherous abyss, into the beguiling obedience of devils, to whom I made offerings of my wicked deeds. And still in all this thou didst not fail to scourge me. I dared, even while thy solemn rites were being celebrated inside the walls of thy church, to desire and to plan a project which merited death as its fruit. For this thou didst chastise me with grievous punishments, but nothing in comparison with my fault, O thou my greatest mercy, my God, my refuge from those terrible dangers in which I wandered with stiff neck, receding farther from thee, loving my own ways and not thine—loving a vagrant liberty!

6. Those studies I was then pursuing, generally accounted as respectable, were aimed at distinction in the courts of law—to excel in which, the more crafty I was, the more I should be praised. Such is the blindness of men that they even glory in their blindness. And by this time I had become a master in the School of Rhetoric, and I rejoiced proudly in this honor and became inflated with arrogance. Still I was relatively sedate, O Lord, as thou knowest, and had no share in the wreckings of "The Wreckers"[10] (for this stupid and diabolical name was regarded as the very badge of gallantry) among whom I lived with a sort of ashamed embarrassment that I was not even as they were. But I lived with them, and at times I was delighted with their friendship, even when I abhorred their acts (that is, their "wrecking") in which they insolently attacked the modesty of strangers, tormenting them by uncalled-for jeers, gratifying their mischievous mirth. Nothing could more nearly resemble the actions of devils than these fellows. By what name, therefore, could they be more aptly called than "wreckers"?— being themselves wrecked first, and altogether turned upside down. They were secretly mocked at and seduced by the deceiving spirits, in the very acts by which they amused themselves in jeering and horseplay at the expense of others . . . .

Book Four

This is the story of his years among the Manicheans. It includes the account of the poignant loss of a friend which leads to a searching analysis of grief and transience.

Chapter IV

7. In those years, when I first began to teach rhetoric in my native town, I had gained a very dear friend, about my own age, who was associated with me in the same studies. Like myself, he was just rising up into the flower of youth. He had grown up with me from childhood and we had been both school-fellows and playmates. But he was not then my friend, nor indeed ever became my friend, in the true sense of the term; for there is no true friendship save between those thou dost bind together and who cleave to thee by that love which is "shed abroad in our hearts through the Holy Spirit who is given to us."[11] Still, it was a sweet friendship, being ripened by the zeal of common studies. Moreover, I had turned him away from the true faith—which he had not soundly and thoroughly mastered as a youth—and turned him toward those superstitious and harmful fables which my mother mourned in me. With me this man went wandering off in error and my soul could not exist without him. But behold thou wast close behind thy fugitives—at once a God of vengeance and a Fountain of mercies, who dost turn us to thyself by ways that make us marvel. Thus, thou didst take that man out of this life when he had scarcely completed one whole year of friendship with me, sweeter to me than all the sweetness of my life thus far.

8. Who can show forth all thy praise[12] for that which he has experienced in himself alone? What was it that thou didst do at that time, O my God; how unsearchable are the depths of thy judgements! For when, sore sick of a fever, he long lay unconscious in a death sweat and everyone despaired of his recovery, he was baptized without his knowledge. And I myself cared little, at the time, presuming that his soul would retain what it had taken from me rather than what was done to his unconscious body. It turned out, however, far differently, for he was revived and restored. Immediately, as soon as I could talk to him—and I did this as soon as he was able, for I never left him and we hung on each other overmuch—I tried to jest with him, supposing that he also would jest in return about that baptism which he had received when his mind and senses were inactive, but which he had since learned

that he had received. But he recoiled from me, as if I were his enemy, and, with a remarkable and unexpected freedom, he admonished me that, if I desired to continue as his friend, I must cease to say such things. Confounded and confused, I concealed my feelings till he should get well and his health recover enough to allow me to deal with him as I wished. But he was snatched away from my madness, that with thee he might be preserved for my consolation. A few days after, during my absence, the fever returned and he died.

9. My heart was utterly darkened by this sorrow and everywhere I looked I saw death. My native place was a torture room to me and my father's house a strange unhappiness. And all the things I had done with him—now that he was gone—became a frightful torment. My eyes sought him everywhere, but they did not see him; and I hated all places because he was not in them, because they could not say to me, "Look, he is coming," as they did when he was alive and absent. I became a hard riddle to myself, and I asked my soul why she was so downcast and why this disquieted me so sorely.[13]   But she did not know how to answer me. And if I said, "Hope thou in God,"[14] she very properly disobeyed me, because that dearest friend she had lost was as an actual man, both truer and better than the imagined deity she was ordered to put her hope in. Nothing but tears were sweet to me and they took my friend's place in my heart's desire.

Chapter V

10. But now, O Lord, these things are past and time has healed my wound. Let me learn from thee, who art Truth, and put the ear of my heart to thy mouth, that thou mayest tell me why weeping should be so sweet to the unhappy. Hast thou—though omnipresent—dismissed our miseries from thy concern? Thou abidest in thyself while we are disquieted with trial after trial. Yet unless we wept in thy ears, there would be no hope for us remaining. How does it happen that such sweet fruit is plucked from the bitterness of life, from groans, tears, sighs, and lamentations? Is it the hope that thou wilt hear us that sweetens it? This is true in the case of prayer, for in a prayer there is a desire to approach thee. But is it also the case in grief for a lost love, and in the kind of sorrow that had then overwhelmed me? For I had neither a hope of his coming back to life, nor in all my tears did I seek this. I simply grieved and wept, for I was miserable and had lost my joy. Or is weeping a bitter thing that gives us pleasure because of our

aversion to the things we once enjoyed and this only as long as we loathe them?

Chapter VI

11. But why do I speak of these things? Now is not the time to ask such questions, but rather to confess to thee. I was wretched; and every soul is wretched that is fettered in the friendship of mortal things—it is torn to pieces when it loses them, and then realizes the misery which it had even before it lost them. Thus it was at that time with me. I wept most bitterly, and found a rest in bitterness. I was wretched, and yet that wretched life I still held dearer than my friend. For though I would willingly have changed it, I was still more unwilling to lose it than to have lost him. Indeed, I doubt whether I was willing to lose it, even for him—as they tell (unless it be fiction) of the friendship of Orestes and Pylades;[15] they would have gladly died for one another, or both together, because not to love together was worse than death to them. But a strange kind of feeling had come over me, quite different from this, for now it was wearisome to live and a fearful thing to die. I suppose that the more I loved him the more I hated and feared, as the most cruel enemy, that death which had robbed me of him. I even imagined that it would suddenly annihilate all men, since it had had such a power over him. This is the way I remember it was with me.

Look into my heart, O God! Behold and look deep within me, for I remember it well, O my Hope who cleansest me from the uncleanness of such affections, directing my eyes toward thee and plucking my feet out of the snare. And I marveled that other mortals went on living since he whom I had loved as if he would never die was now dead. And I marveled all the more that I, who had been a second self to him, could go on living when he was dead. Someone spoke rightly of his friend as being "his soul's other half"[16]—for I felt that my soul and his soul were but one soul in two bodies. Consequently, my life was now a horror to me because I did not want to live as a half self. But it may have been that I was afraid to die, lest he should then die wholly whom I had so greatly loved.

Chapter VII

12. O madness that knows not how to love men as they should be loved! O foolish man that I was then, enduring with so much rebellion the lot of every man! Thus I fretted, sighed, wept, tormented myself,

and took neither rest nor counsel, for I was dragging around my torn and bloody soul. It was impatient of my dragging it around, and yet I could not find a place to lay it down. Not in pleasant groves, nor in sport or song, nor in fragrant bowers, nor in magnificent banquetings, nor in the pleasures of the bed or the couch; not even in books or poetry did it find rest. All things looked gloomy, even the very light itself. Whatsoever was not what he was, was now repulsive and hateful, except my groans and tears, for in those alone I found a little rest. But when my soul left off weeping, a heavy burden of misery weighed me down. It should have been raised up to thee, O Lord, for thee to lighten and to lift. This I knew, but I was neither willing nor able to do; especially since, in my thoughts of thee, thou wast not thyself but only an empty fantasm. Thus my error was my god. If I tried to cast off my burden on this fantasm, that it might find rest there, it sank through the vacuum and came rushing down again upon me. Thus I remained to myself an unhappy lodging where I could neither stay nor leave. For where could my heart fly from my heart? Where could I fly from my own self? Where would I not follow myself? And yet I did flee from my native place so that my eyes would look for him less in a place where they were not accustomed to see him. Thus I left the town of Tagaste and returned to Carthage.

Chapter VIII

13. Time never lapses, nor does it glide at leisure through our sense perceptions. It does strange things in the mind. Lo, time came and went from day to day, and by coming and going it brought to my mind other ideas and remembrances, and little by little they patched me up again with earlier kinds of pleasure and my sorrow yielded a bit to them. But yet there followed after this sorrow, not other sorrows just like it, but the causes of other sorrows. For why had that first sorrow so easily penetrated to the quick except that I had poured out my soul onto the dust, by loving a man as if he would never die who nevertheless had to die? What revived and refreshed me, more than anything else, was the consolation of other friends, with whom I went on loving the things I loved instead of thee. This was a monstrous fable and a tedious lie which was corrupting my soul with its "itching ears,"[17] by its adulterous rubbing. And that fable would not die to me as often as one of my friends died. And there were other things in our companionship that took strong hold of my mind: to discourse and jest with him; to indulge in courteous exchanges; to read pleasant books together; to trifle

together; to be earnest together; to differ at times without ill-humor, as a man might do with himself, and even through these infrequent dissensions to find zest in our more frequent agreements; sometimes teaching, sometimes being taught; longing for someone absent with impatience and welcoming the homecomer with joy. These and similar tokens of friendship, which spring spontaneously from the hearts of those who love and are loved in return—in countenance, tongue, eyes, and a thousand ingratiating gestures—were all so much fuel to melt our souls together, and out of the many made us one.

Chapter IX

14. This is what we love in our friends, and we love it so much that a man's conscience accuses itself if he does not love one who loves him, or respond in love to love, seeking nothing from the other but the evidences of his love. This is the source of our moaning when one dies—the gloom of sorrow, the steeping of the heart in tears, all sweetness turned to bitterness—and the feeling of death in the living, because of the loss of the life of the dying.

Blessed is he who loves thee, and who loves his friend in thee, and his enemy also, for thy sake; for he alone loses none dear to him, if all are dear in Him who cannot be lost. And who is this but our God: the God that created heaven and earth, and filled them because he created them by filling them up? None loses thee but he who leaves thee; and he who leaves thee, where does he go, or where can he flee but from thee well-pleased to thee offended? For where does he not find thy law fulfilled in his own punishment? "Thy law is the truth"[18] and thou art Truth. . . .

Book Eight—*Conversion to Christ* . . .

Chapter III

7. What, then, happens in the soul when it takes more delight at finding or having restored to it the things it loves than if it had always possessed them? Indeed, many other things bear witness that this is so—all things are full of witnesses, crying out, "So it is." The commander triumphs in victory; yet he could not have conquered if he had not fought; and the greater the peril of the battle, the more the joy of the triumph. The storm tosses the voyagers, threatens shipwreck, and everyone turns pale in the presence of death. Then the sky and sea

grow calm, and they rejoice as much as they had feared. A loved one is sick and his pulse indicates danger; all who desire his safety are themselves sick at heart; he recovers, though not able as yet to walk with his former strength; and there is more joy now than there was before when he walked sound and strong. Indeed, the very pleasures of human life—not only those which rush upon us unexpectedly and involuntarily, but also those which are voluntary and planned—men obtain by difficulties. There is no pleasure in eating and drinking unless the pains of hunger and thirst have preceded. Drunkards even eat certain salt meats in order to create a painful thirst—and when the drink allays this, it causes pleasure. It is also the custom that the affianced bride should not be immediately given in marriage so that the husband may not esteem her any less, whom as his betrothed he longed for.

8. This can be seen in the case of base and dishonorable pleasure. But it is also apparent in pleasures that are permitted and lawful: in the sincerity of honest friendship; and in him who was dead and lived again, who had been lost and was found. The greater joy is everywhere preceded by the greater pain. What does this mean, O Lord my God, when thou art an everlasting joy to thyself, and some creatures about thee are ever rejoicing in thee? What does it mean that this portion of creation thus ebbs and flows, alternately in want and satiety? Is this their mode of being and is this all thou hast allotted to them: that, from the highest heaven to the lowest earth, from the beginning of the world to the end, from the angels to the worm, from the first movement to the last, thou wast assigning to all their proper places and their proper seasons—to all the kinds of good things and to all thy just works? Alas, how high thou art in the highest and how deep in the deepest! Thou never departest from us, and yet only with difficulty do we return to thee. . . .

Notes

[1] Yet another Plotinian phrase; cf. *Enneads,* I, 6, 9:1-2

[2] Twenty miles from Tagaste, famed as the birthplace of Apuleius, the only notable classical author produced by the province of Africa.

[3] Another echo of the *De profundis* (Ps. 130:1)—and the most explicit statement we have from Augustine of his motive and aim in writing these "confessions."

[4] Cf. I Cor. 3:9.

[5] Ps. 116:16.

[6] Cf. Jer. 51:6; 50:8.

---

[7] Cf. Ps. 73:7.

[8] Ps. 19:12.

[9] Cf. Job 2:7, 8.

[10] *Evertores*, "overturners," from *evertere*, to overthrow or ruin. This was the nickname of a gang of young hoodlums in Carthage, made up laregely, it seems, of students in the schools.

[11] Cf. Ps. 106:2.

[12] Cf. Ps. 106:2

[13] Cf. Ps. 42:5; 43:5.

[14] Ibid.

[15] Cf. Ovid, *Tristia*, IV, 4:74.

[16] Cf. Horace, Ode I, 3:8, where he speaks of Virgil, *et serves animae dimidium meae.* Augustine's memory changes the text here to *dimidium animae suae*.

[17] II Tim. 4:3.

[18] Ps. 119:142.

Chapter 10

Aelred of Rievaulx, *Spiritual Friendship* (*De Spiritali Amicitia*)

St. Aelred of Rievaulx (c. 1110-1167) born in Hexham, Northumberland, England, was a writer, historian, and outstanding Cistercian abbot of Rievaulx Abbey, Yorkshire, who influenced monasticism in medieval England, Scotland, and France.

Of noble birth, Aelred was reared in the court of King David I of Scotland, whose life story he later wrote, and from whom he was royal steward. He entered the Cistercian abbey of Rievaulx in c. 1134 and became abbot of Rievaulx in 1143. He served as adviser to kings and ecclesiastics. In 1162 he persuaded King Henry II of England to ally with Louis VII of France in support of Pope Alexander III against Holy Roman Emperor Frederick I Barbarossa.

Despite poor health and an ascetic life, he traveled widely to visit Cistercian houses in England, Scotland, and France. His Christocentric theology is considered among the finest of England during the European Middle Ages. His tremendous influence on the Cistercian order earned him the title of "Bernard of the north" (after Bernard of Clairvaux). By 1166, illness halted his missions. His feast day is February 3.

Those of his writings that survive deal with devotion and history. His historical works includes a genealogy of English kings and a life of St. Edward the Confessor. His **De Spirtali Amicitia**, *from which the present selection is taken, is considered his greatest work. It presents a distinctively Christian conception of the friendship described by Cicero's* **De Amicitia**, *which had impressed Aelred from his youth,* *designating Christ as the source and ultimate impetus of spiritual friendship.*

Spiritual Friendship

Book I: The Origin of Friendship

Aelred. Here we are, you and I, and I hope a third, Christ, is in our midst. There is no one now to disturb us; there is no one to break in upon our friendly chat, no man's prattle or noise of any kind will creep into this pleasant solitude. Come now, beloved, open your heart, and pour into these friendly ears whatsoever you will, and let us accept gracefully the boon of this place, time, and leisure.

2. Just a little while ago as I was sitting with the brethren, while all around were talking noisily, one questioning, another arguing—one advancing some point on Sacred Scripture, another information on vices, and yet another on virtue—you alone were silent. At times you would raise your head and make ready to say something, but just as quickly, as though your voice had been trapped in your throat, you would drop your head again and continue your silence. Then you would leave us for a while, and later return looking rather disheartened. I concluded from all this that you wanted to talk to me, but that you dreaded the crowd, and hoped to be alone with me.

3. *Ivo.*[1] That's it exactly, and I deeply appreciate your solicitude for your son. His state of mind and his desire have been disclosed to you by none other than the Spirit of Love. And would that your Lordship would grant me this favor, that, as often as you visit your sons here, I may be permitted, at least once, to have you all to myself and to disclose to you the deep feelings of my heart without disturbance.

4. *Aelred.* Indeed, I shall do that, and gladly. For I am greatly pleased to see that you are not bent on empty and idle pursuits, but that you are always speaking of things useful and necessary for your progress. Speak freely, therefore, and entrust to your friend all your cares and thoughts, that you may both learn and teach, give and receive, pour out and drink in.

5. *Ivo.* I am certainly ready to learn, not to teach; not to give, but to receive; to drink in, not to pour out; as indeed my youth demands of me, inexperience compels, and my religious profession exhorts. But that I may not foolishly squander on these considerations the time that I need for other matters, I wish that you would teach me something about

spiritual friendship, namely, its nature and value, its source and end, whether it can be cultivated among all, and, if not among all, then by whom; how it can be preserved unbroken, and without any disturbance of misunderstanding be brought to a holy end.

6. *Aelred.* I wonder why you think it proper to seek this information from me, since it is evident that there has been enough, and more, discussion on matters of this kind by ancient and excellent teachers; particularly since you spent your youth in studies of this sort, and have read Cicero's treatise, *On Friendship,* in which in a delightful style he treats at length all those matters which appear to pertain to friendship, and there he sets forth certain laws and precepts, so to speak, for friendship.

7. *Ivo.* That treatise is not altogether unknown to me. In fact, at one time I took great delight in it. But since I began to taste some of the sweetness from the honey comb of Holy Scripture, and since the sweet name of Christ claimed my affection for itself, whatever I henceforth read or hear, though it be treated ever so subtly and eloquently, will have no relish or enlightenment for me, if it lacks the salt of the heavenly books and the flavoring of that most sweet name. 8. Therefore, those things which have already been said, even though they are in harmony with reason, and other things which the utility of this discussion demands that we treat, I should like proved to me with the authority of the Scriptures. I should like also to be instructed more fully as to how the friendship which ought to exist among us begins in Christ, is preserved according to the Spirit of Christ, and how its end and fruition are referred to Christ. For it is evident that Tullius was unacquainted with the virtue of true friendship, since he was completely unaware of its beginning and end, Christ.

9. *Aelred.* I confess I have been won over, but, not knowing myself or the extent of my own ability, I am not going to teach you anything about these matters but rather to discuss them with you. For you yourself have opened the way for both of us, and have enkindled that brilliant light on the very threshold of our inquiry, which will not allow us to wander along unknown paths, but will lead us along the sure path to the certain goal of our proposed quest. 10. For what more sublime can be said of friendship, what more true, what more profitable, than that it ought to, and is proved to, begin in Christ, continue in Christ, and be perfected in Christ? Come now, tell me, what do you think ought to be our first consideration in this matter of friendship?

Ivo. In the first place, I think we should discuss the nature of friendship so as not to appear to be painting in emptiness, as we would, indeed, if we were unaware of the precise identity of that about which an ordered discussion on our part should proceed.

11. *Aelred.* But surely you are satisfied, as a starting point, with what Tullius says, are you not? "Friendship is mutual harmony in affairs human and divine coupled with benevolence and charity."

12. *Ivo.* If that definition satisfies you, I agree that is satisfies me.

13. *Aelred.* In that case, those who have the same opinion, the same will, in matters human and divine, along with mutual benevolence and charity, have, we shall admit, reached the perfection of friendship.

14. *Ivo.* Why not? But still, I do not see what the pagan Cicero meant by the word "charity" and "benevolence."

15. *Aelred.* Perhaps for him the word "charity" expresses an affection of the heart, and the word "benevolence," carrying it out in deed. For mutual harmony itself in matters human and divine ought to be dear to the hearts of both, that is, attractive and precious; and the carrying out of these works in actual practice ought to be both benevolent and pleasant.

16. *Ivo.* I grant that this definition pleases me adequately, except that I should think it applied equally to pagan and Jews, and even to bad Christians. However, I confess that I am convinced that true friendship cannot exist among those who live without Christ.

17. *Aelred.* What follows will make it sufficiently clear to us whether the definition contains too much or too little, so that it may either be rejected, or if, so to say sufficient and not over inclusive, be admitted. You can, however, get some idea of the nature of friendship from the definition, even though it should seem somewhat imperfect.

18. *Ivo.* Please, will I annoy you if I say that this definition does not satisfy me unless you unravel for me the meaning of the word itself?

19. *Aelred.* I shall be glad to comply with your wishes if only you will pardon my lack of knowledge and not force me to teach what I do not know. Now I think the word *amicus* (friend) comes from the word *amor* [love], and *amicitia* (friendship) from *amicus.* For love is a certain "affection" of the rational soul whereby it seeks and eagerly strives after some object to possess it and enjoy it. Having attained its object through love, it enjoys it with a certain interior sweetness, embraces it, and preserves it. We have explained the affections and movements of love as clearly and carefully was we could in our *Mirror*[2] with which you are already familiar.

20. Furthermore, a friend is called a guardian of love or, as some would have it, a guardian of the spirit itself. Since it is fitting that my friend be a guardian of our mutual love or the guardian of my own spirit so as to preserve all its secrets in faithful silence, let him, as far as he can, cure and endure such defects as he may observe in it; let him rejoice with his friend in his joys, and weep with him in his sorrows, and feel as his own all that his friend experiences.

21. Friendship, therefore, is that virtue by which spirits are bound by ties of love and sweetness, and out of many are made one. Even the philosophers of this world have ranked friendship not with things causal or transitory but with the virtues which are eternal. Solomon in the *Book of Proverbs* appears to agree with them when he says: "He that is a friend loves at all times" [Prov. 17:17] manifestly declaring that friendship is eternal if it is true friendship; but, if it should ever cease to be, then it was not true friendship, even though it seemed to be so.

22. *Ivo.* Why is it, then, that we read about bitter enmities arising between the most devoted friends?

23. *Aelred.* God-willing, we shall discuss that matter more amply in its own place. Meantime remember this: he was never a friend who could offend him whom he at one time received into his friendship; on the other hand, that other has not tasted the delights of true friendship who even when offended has ceased to love him whom he once cherished. For "he that is a friend loves at all times." 24. Although he be accused unjustly, though he be injured, though he be cast in the flames, though he be crucified, "he that is a friend loves at all times." Our Jerome speaks similarly: "A friendship which can cease to be was never true friendship."

25. *Ivo.* Since such perfection is expected of true friendship, it is not surprising that those were so rare whom the ancients commended as true friends. As Tullius says: "in so many past ages, tradition extols scarcely three or four pairs of friends." But if in our day, that is, in this age of Christianity, friends are so few, it seems to me that I am exerting myself uselessly in striving after this virtue which I, terrified by its admirable sublimity, now almost despair of ever acquiring.

26. *Aelred.* "Effort in great things," as someone has said, "is itself great." Hence it is the mark of a virtuous mind to reflect continually upon sublime and noble thoughts, that it may either attain the desired object or understand more clearly and gain knowledge of what ought to be desired. Thus, too, he must be supposed to have advanced not a little who has learned, by a knowledge of virtue, how far he is from virtue itself. 27. Indeed, the Christian ought not to despair of acquiring

any virtue since daily the divine voice from the Gospel reechoes: "Ask, and you shall receive...." [Mt. 7:7; Jn 16:24]. It is no wonder, then, that pursuers of true virtue were rare among the pagans since they did not know the Lord, the Dispenser of virtue, of whom it is written: "The Lord of hosts, he is the King of glory" [Ps. 23:10]. 28. Indeed, through faith in him they were prepared to die for one another—I do not say three or four, but I offer you thousands of pairs of friends—although the ancients declared or imagined the devotion of Pylades and Orestes a great marvel.[3] Were they not, according to the definition of Tullius, strong in the virtue of true friendship, of whom it is written: "And the multitude of believers had but one heart and one soul; neither did anyone say that aught was his own, but all things were common unto them"? [Acts 4:32]. 29. How could they fail to have complete agreement on all things divine and human with charity and benevolence, seeing that they had but one heart and one soul? How many martyrs gave their lives for their brethren! How many spared neither cost, nor even physical torments! I am sure you have often read—and that not dry-eyed—about the girl of Antioch rescued from a house of ill-repute by a fine bit of strategy on the part of a certain soldier. Sometime later he whom she had discovered as a guardian of her chastity in that house of ill-repute became her companion in martyrdom. 30. I might go on citing many examples of this kind, did not the danger of verboseness forbid, and their very abundance enjoin us to be silent. For Christ Jesus announced their coming. He spoke, and they were multiplied above number. "Greater love than this," he says, "no man has, that a man lay down his life for his friends." [Jn. 15:13].

31. *Ivo.* Are we then to believe that there is no difference between charity and friendship?

32. *Aelred.* On the contrary, there is a vast difference; for divine authority approves that more are to be received into the bosom of charity than into the embrace of friendship. For we are compelled by the law of charity to receive in the embrace of love not only our friends but also our enemies. But only those do we call friends to whom we can fearlessly entrust our heart and all its secrets; those, too, who, in turn, are bound to us by the same law of faith and security.

33. *Ivo.* How many persons leading a worldly existence and acting as partners in some form of vice, are united by a similar pact and find the bond of even that sort of friendship to be more pleasant and sweet than all the delights of this world!

34. I hope that you will not find it burdensome to isolate, as it were, from the company of so many types of friendship that one which we think should be called "spiritual" to distinguish it from the others with which it is to some extent bound up and confused and which accost and clamor for the attention of those who seek and long for it. For by contrasting them you would make spiritual friendship better known to us and consequently more desirable, and thus more actively rouse and fire us to its acquisition.

35. *Aelred.* Falsely do they claim the illustrious name of friends among whom there exists a harmony of vices; since he who does not love is not a friend, but he does not love his fellow-man who loves iniquity. "For he that loves iniquity" does not love, but "hates his own soul" [Ps. 10:6]. Truly, he who does not love his own soul will not be able to love the soul of another. 36. Thus it follows that they glory only in the name of friendship and are deceived by a distorted image and are not supported by truth. Yet, since such great joy is experienced in friendship which either lust defiles, avarice dishonors, or luxury pollutes, we may infer how much sweetness that friendship possesses which, in proportion as it is nobler, is the more secure; purer, it is the more pleasing; freer, it is the more happy. 37. Let us allow that, because of some similarity in feelings, those friendships which are not true, be, nevertheless, called friendships, provided, however, they are judiciously distinguished from that friendship which is spiritual and therefore true. 38. Hence let one kind of friendship be called carnal, another worldly, and another spiritual. The carnal springs from mutual harmony in vice; the worldly is enkindled by the hope of gain; and the spiritual is cemented by similarity of life, morals, and pursuits among the just.

39. The real beginning of carnal friendship proceeds from an affection which like a harlot directs its step after every passer-by, following its own lustful ears and eyes in every direction. By means of the avenues of these senses it brings into the mind itself images of beautiful bodies or voluptuous objects. To enjoy these as he pleases the carnal man thinks is blessedness, but to enjoy them without an associate he considers less delightful. 40. Then by gesture, nod, words, compliance, spirit is captivated by spirit, and one is inflamed by the other, and they are kindled to form a sinful bond, so that, after they have entered upon such a deplorable pact, the one will do or suffer any crime or sacrilege whatsoever for the sake of the other. They consider nothing sweeter than this type of friendship, they judge nothing more equable, believing community of like and dislike to be imposed upon

them by the laws of friendship. 41. And so, this sort of friendship is undertaken without deliberation, is tested by no act of judgment, is in no wise governed by reason; but through the violence of affection is carried away through divers paths, observing no limit, caring naught for uprightness, foreseeing neither gains nor losses, but advancing toward everything heedlessly, indiscriminately, lightly and immoderately. For that reason, goaded on, as if by furies, it is consumed by its own self, or is dissolved with the same levity with which it was originally fashioned.

42. But worldly friendship, which is born of a desire for temporal advantage or possessions, is always full of deceit and intrigue; it contains nothing certain, nothing constant, nothing secure; for, to be sure, it ever changes with fortune and follows the purse. 43. Hence it is written: "He is a fair-weather friend, and he will not abide in the day of your trouble" [Sir. 6:8]. Take away his hope of profit, and immediately he will cease to be a friend. This type of friendship the following lines very aptly deride: "A friend, not of the man, but of his purse is he, held fast by fortune fair, by evil made to flee."

44. And yet, the beginning of this vicious friendship leads many individuals to a certain degree of true friendship: those, namely, who at first enter into a compact of friendship in the hope of common profit while they cherish in themselves faith in baneful riches, and who, in so far as human affairs are concerned, reach an acme of pleasing mutual agreement. But a friendship ought in no wise be called true which is begun and preserved for the sake of some temporal advantage.

45. For spiritual friendship, which we call true, should be desired, not for consideration of any worldly advantage or for any extrinsic cause, but from the dignity of its own nature and the feelings of the human heart, so that its fruition and reward is nothing other than itself.[4] 46. Whence the Lord in the Gospel says: "I have appointed you that you should go, and should bring forth fruit" [Jn. 15:16f.], that is, that you should love one another. For true friendship advances by perfecting itself, and the fruit is derived from feeling the sweetness of that perfection. And so spiritual friendship among the just is born of a similarity in life, morals, and pursuits, that is, it is a mutual conformity in matters human and divine united with benevolence and charity.

47. Indeed, this definition seems to me to be adequate for representing friendship. If, however, "charity" is, according to our way of thinking, named in the sense that friendship excludes every vice, then "benevolence" expresses the feeling to love which is pleasantly roused interiorly. 48. Where such friendship exists, there, indeed, is a community of likes and dislikes, the more pleasant in proportion as it is

more sincere, the more agreeable as it is more sacred; those who love in this way can will nothing that is unbecoming, and reject nothing that is expedient. 49. Surely, such friendship prudence directs, justice rules, fortitude guards, and temperance moderates. But of these matters we shall speak in their place. Now, then, tell me whether you think enough has been said about the matter you first brought up, namely, the nature of friendship.

50. *Ivo.* Your explanation is certainly sufficient, and nothing else suggests itself to me for further inquiry. But before we go on to other things, I should like to know how friendship first originated among men. Was it by nature, by chance or by necessity of some kind? Or did it come into practice by some statute or law imposed upon the human race, and did practice then commend it to man?

51. *Aelred.* At first, as I see it, nature itself impressed upon the human soul a desire for friendship, then experience increased that desire, and finally the sanction of the law confirmed it. For God, supremely powerful and supremely good, is sufficient good unto himself, since his good, his joy, his glory, his happiness, is himself. 52. Nor is there anything outside himself which he needs, neither man, nor angel, nor heaven, nor earth, nor anything which these contain. To him every creature proclaims: "You are my God, for you have no need of my goods" [Ps. 15:2]. Not only is he sufficient unto himself, but he is himself the sufficiency of all things: giving simple being to some, sensation to other, and wisdom over and above these to still others, himself the Cause of all being, the Life of all sensation, the Wisdom of all intelligence. 53. And thus Sovereign Nature has established all natures, has arranged all things in their places, and has discreetly distributed all things in their own times. He has willed, moreover, for so his eternal reason has directed, that peace encompass all his creatures and society unite them; and thus all creatures obtain from him, who is supremely and purely one, some trace of that unity. For that reason he has left no type of beings alone, but out of many has drawn them together by means of a certain society.

54. Suppose we begin with inanimate creation—what soil or what river produces one single stone of one kind? Or what forest bears but a single tree of a single kind? And so even in inanimate nature a certain love of companionship, so to speak, is apparent, since none of these exists alone but everything is created and thrives in a certain society with its own kind.

And surely in animate life who can easily describe how clear the picture of friendship is, and the image of society and love? 55. And

4

though in all other respects animals are rated irrational, yet they imitate man in this regard to such an extent that we almost believe they act with reason. How they run after one another, play with one another, so express and betray their love by sound and movement, so eagerly and happily do they enjoy their mutual company, that they seem to prize nothing else so much as they do whatever pertains to friendship.

56. For the angels too divine Wisdom provided, in that he created not one but many. Among them pleasant companionship and delightful love created the same will, the same desire. Assuredly, since one seemed to be superior, the other inferior, there would have been occasion for envy, had not the charity of friendship prevented it. Their multitude thus excluded solitude, and the bond of charity among many increased their mutual happiness.

57. Finally, when God created man, in order to commend more highly the good of society, he said: "It is not good for man to be alone: let us make him a helper like unto himself" [Gen. 2:18]. It was from no similar, nor even from the same, material that divine Might formed this help mate, but as a clearer inspiration to charity and friendship he produced the woman from the very substance of the man [Gen. 2:21f.]. How beautiful it is that the second human being was taken from the side of the first, so that nature might teach that human beings are equal and, as it were, collateral, and that there is in human affairs neither a superior nor an inferior, a characteristic of true friendship. 58. Hence, nature from the very beginning implanted the desire for friendship and charity in the heart of man, a desire which an inner sense of affection soon increased with a taste of sweetness. But after the fall of the first man, when with the cooling of charity concupiscence made secret inroads and caused private good to take precedence over the common weal, it corrupted the splendor of friendship and charity through avarice and envy, introducing contentions, emulations, hates and suspicions because the morals of men had been corrupted. 59. From that time the good distinguished between charity and friendship, observing that love ought to be extended even to the hostile and perverse, while no union of will and ideas can exist between the good and wicked. And so friendship which, like charity, was first preserved among all by all, remained according to the natural law among the few good. They saw the sacred laws of faith and society violated by many and bound themselves together by a closer bond of love and friendship. In the midst of the evils which they saw and felt, they rested in the joy of mutual charity. 60. But in those in whom wickedness obliterated every feeling for virtue, reason, which could not be extinguished in them, left

the inclination toward friendship and society, so that without companionship riches could hold no charm for the greedy, nor glory for the ambitious, nor pleasure for the sensuous man. There are compacts—even sworn bonds—of union among the wicked which ought to be abhorred. These, clothed with the beautiful name of friendship, ought to have been distinguished from true friendship by law and precept, so that when true friendship was sought, one might not incautiously be ensnared among those other friendships because of some slight resemblance. 61. Thus friendship, which nature has brought into being and practice has strengthened, has by the power of law been regulated. It is evident, then, that friendship is natural, like virtue, wisdom, and the like, which should be sought after and preserved from their own sake as natural goods. Everyone that possesses them makes good use of them, and no one entirely abuses them.

61. *Ivo.* May I ask, do not many people abuse wisdom? Those, I mean, who desire to please men through it, or take pride in themselves by reason of the wisdom placed in them or certainly those who consider it a thing that can be sold, just as they imagine there is a source of revenue in piety.

63. *Aelred.* Our Augustine should satisfy you on that point. Here are his words: "He who pleases himself, pleases a foolish man, because, to be sure, he is foolish who pleases himself." But the man who is foolish is not wise; and he who is not wise is not wise because he does not possess wisdom. How then does he abuse wisdom who does not even possess it? And so proud chastity is no virtue, because pride itself, which is a vice, makes conformable to itself that which was considered a virtue. Therefore, it is not a virtue, but a vice.

64. *Ivo.* But I tell you, with your forbearance, that it does not seem consistent to me to join wisdom to friendship, since there is no comparison between the two.

65. *Aelred.* In spite of the fact that they are not coequal, very often lesser things are linked with greater, good with better, weaker with stronger. This is particularly true in the case of virtues. Although they vary by reason of a difference in degree, still they are close to one another by reason of similarity. Thus widowhood is near to virginity, conjugal chastity to widowhood. Although there is a great difference between these individual virtues, there is, nevertheless, a conformity in this, that they are virtues. 66. Now, then, conjugal chastity does not fail to be a virtue for the reason that widowhood is superior in continency. And whereas holy virginity is preferred to both, it does not thereby take

away the excellence of the others. And yet, if you consider carefully what has been said about friendship, you will find it so close to, even replete with, wisdom, that I might almost say friendship is nothing else but wisdom.

67. Ivo. I am amazed, I admit, but I do not think that I can easily be convinced of your view.

68. Aelred. Have you forgotten that Scripture says: "He that is a friend loves at all times"? Our Jerome also, as you recall, says: "Friendship which can end was never true friendship." That friendship cannot even endure without charity has been more than adequately established. Since then in friendship eternity blossoms, truth shines forth, and charity grows sweet, consider whether you ought to separate the name of wisdom from these three.

69. Ivo. What does this all add up to? Shall I say of friendship what John, the friend of Jesus, says of charity: "God is friendship"? [cf. 1 Jn. 4:16]

70. Aelred. That would be unusual, to be sure, nor does it have the sanction of the Scriptures. But still what is true of charity, I surely do not hesitate to grant to friendship, since "he that abides in friendship, abides in God, and God in him" [*Ibid.*]. That we shall see more clearly when we begin to discuss its fruition and utility. Now if we have said enough on the nature of friendship in view of the simplicity of our poor wit, let us reserve for another time the other points you proposed for solution.

71. Ivo. I admit that my eagerness finds such a delay quite annoying, but it is necessary since not only is it time for the evening meal, from which no one may be absent, but, in addition, there are the burdensome demands of the other religious who have a right to your care.

Notes

[1] Probably a monk of Wardon in Bedforshire, presumably at the request of whom Aelred wrote his *Jesus at the Age of Twelve.* See *The Works of Aelred of Rievaulx,* vol. I (Cistercian Fathers Series 1); and cf. E. Laker's critical edition of *Spiritual Friendship,* from which the present chapter is excerpted, for excellent and detailed notes. [*Eds.*]

[2] The *Mirror of Charity,* written by Aelred while he was still novice master of Rievaulx, at the command of his abbot, Bernard of Clairvaux. The third book of this work treats of friendship. [*Eds.*]

[3] Pylades helped Orestes, son of Agamemnon, to avenge the murder of his father; and when Orestes was condemned to death, Pylades proved the depth of his friendship by seeking to die in his place. [*Eds.*]

[4] Bernard of Clairvaux is said to have stated: "Love requires no other cause but itself, nor does it command a reward. Its reward is its enjoyment." [*Eds.*]

Chapter 11

St. Thomas Aquinas, *Summa Theologica*

St. Thomas Aquinas (c. 1225-1274) is the second most important figure in medieval Christianity behind Augustine. While the Christian faith was common to both St. Thomas and St. Augustine, the primary influences in their intellectual development were somewhat different, as were their times. Eight centuries separated Thomas from Augustine and it may generally be said that Augustine's Christian theology was expressed through the language of Neo-Platonism, while Thomas' world-view finds expression in terms of that of the work of Aristotle, whom he called, simply, "the Philosopher."

St. Thomas was born in Italy into a family of some nobility and was educated for a civil career in the prestigious Abbey of Monte Cassino, from which he later went to the University of Naples. At eighteen, much to the disgruntlement of his parents, Thomas joined the Dominican order. By a ruse, Thomas' parents lured him home, where they tried to talk him out of his theological leanings. They failed, but having the upper hand, they imprisoned Thomas for two long years in the family castle. When it became clear Thomas would not give up his philosophic and theological devotion, his mother helped him escape from prison.

Eventually Thomas made his way to Cologne to study with the most famous teacher of the day, Albertus Magnus, and afterward proceeded to the University of Paris, where he completed the vast majority of his work.

The fusing of the work of Aristotle with the Christian faith can be seen almost everywhere in the work of St. Thomas, even in the following selections from his major work, the **Summa Theologica.**

Here, the main thrust of Thomas' account of friend-ship has to do with the manner by which one, through **charity,** *may be a friend both to God and also, as far as is possible, to humanity as well.*

Summa Theologica

Question 23: Of Charity, Considered in Itself

First Article: Whether Charity Is Friendship?

We proceed thus to the First Article:—

Objection 1. It would seem that charity is not friendship. For nothing is so appropriate to friendship as to dwell with one's friend, according to the Philosopher (*Ethic.* viii. 5). Now charity is of man towards God and the angels, *whose dwelling* (Douay,—*conversation*) *is not with men* (Dan. ii. 11). Therefore charity is not friendship.

Obj. 2. Further, there is no friendship without return of love (*Ethic,* viii. 2). But charity extends even to one's enemies, according to Matth. v. 44: *Love your enemies.* Therefore charity is not friendship.

Obj. 3. Further, according to the Philosopher (*Ethic.* viii. 3) there are three kinds of friendship, directed respectively towards the delightful, the useful, or the virtuous. Now charity is not friendship for the useful or delightful; for Jerome says in his letter to Paulinus which is to be found at the beginning of the Bible: *True friendship cemented by Christ, is where men are drawn together, not by household interests, not by mere bodily presence, not by crafty and cajoling flattery, but by the fear of God, and the study of the Divine Scriptures.* No more is it friendship for the virtuous, since by charity we love even sinners, whereas friendship based on the virtuous is only for virtuous men (*Ethic.* viii). Therefore charity is not friendship.

On the contrary, It is written (Jo. xv. 15): *I will not now call you servants . . . but My friends.* Now this was said to them by reason of nothing else than charity. Therefore charity is friendship.

I answer that, According to the Philosopher (*Ethic.* viii. 2, 3), not every love has the character of friendship, but that love which is together with benevolence, when, to wit, we love someone so as to wish good to him. If, however, we do not wish good to what we love, but wish its good for ourselves, (thus we are said to love wine, or a horse, or the like) it is love not of friendship, but of a kind of concupiscence.

For it would be absurd to speak of having friendship for wine or for a horse.

Yet neither does well-wishing suffice for friendship, for a certain mutual love is requisite, since friendship is between friend and friend; and this well-wishing is founded on some kind of communication.

Accordingly, since there is a communication between man and God, inasmuch as He communicates His happiness to us, some kind of friendship must needs be based on this same communication, of which it is written (1 Cor. i. 9): *God is faithful: by Whom you are called unto the fellowship of His Son.* The love which is based on this communication, is charity: wherefore it is evident that charity is the friendship of man for God.

Reply Obj. 1. Man's life is twofold. There is his outward life in respect of his sensitive and corporeal nature; and with regard to this life there is no communication or fellowship between us and God or the angels. The other is man's spiritual life in respect of his mind, and with regard to this life there is fellowship between us and both God and the angels, imperfectly indeed in this present state of life, wherefore it is written (Phil. iii. 20): *Our conversation is in heaven.* But this *conversation* will be perfected in heaven, when *His servants shall serve Him, and they shall see His face* (Apoc. xxii. 3, 4). Therefore charity is imperfect here, but will be perfected in heaven.

Reply Obj. 2. Friendship extends to a person in two ways: first in respect of himself, and in this way friendship never extends but to one's friends: secondly, it extends to someone in respect of another, as, when a man has friendship for a certain person, for his sake he loves all belonging to him, be they children, servants, or connected with him in any way. Indeed, so much do we love our friends, that for their sake we love all who belong to them, even if they hurt or hate us; so that, in this way, the friendship of charity extends even to our enemies, whom we love out of charity in relation to God, to Whom the friendship of charity is chiefly directed.

Reply Obj. 3. The friendship that is based on the virtuous is directed to none but a virtuous man as the principal person, but for his sake we love those who belong to him, even though they be not virtuous: in this way charity, which above all is friendship based on the virtuous, extends to sinners, whom, out of charity, we love for God's sake.

Question 25: Of the Object of Charity

Sixth Article: Whether We Ought to Love One Neighbor More Than Another?

We proceed thus to the Sixth Article:—

Objection 1. It would seem that we ought not to love one neighbor more than another. For Augustine says (*De Doctr. Christ.* i. 28): *One ought to love all men equally. Since, however, one cannot do good to all, we ought to consider those chiefly who by reason of place, time or any other circumstance, by a kind of chance, are more closely united to us.* Therefore one neighbor ought not to be loved more than another.

Obj. 2. Further, where there is one and the same reason for loving several, there should be no inequality of love. Now there is one and the same reason for loving all one's neighbors, which reason is God, as Augustine states (*De Doctr. Christ.* i. 27). Therefore we ought to love all our neighbors equally.

Obj. 3. Further, to love a man is to wish him good things, as the Philosopher states (*Rhet.* ii. 4). Now to all our neighbors we wish an equal good, viz. everlasting life. Therefore we ought to love all our neighbors equally.

On the contrary, One's obligation to love a person is proportionate to the gravity of the sin one commits in acting against that love. Now it is a more grievous sin to act against the love of certain neighbors, than against the love of others. Hence the commandment (Lev. xx. 9), —*He that curseth his father or mother, dying let him die*, which does not apply to those who cursed others than the above. Therefore we ought to love some neighbors more than others.

I answer that, There have been two opinions on this question: for some have said that we ought, out of charity, to love all our neighbors equally, as regards our affection, but not as regards the outward effect. They held that the order of love is to be understood as applying to outward favors, which we ought to confer on those who are connected with us in preference to those who are unconnected, and not to the inward affection, which ought to be given equally to all including our enemies.

But this is unreasonable. For the affection of charity, which is the inclination of grace, is not less orderly than the natural appetite, which is the inclination of nature, for both inclinations flow from Divine wisdom. Now we observe in the physical order that the natural inclination in each thing is proportionate to the act or movement that is becoming to the nature of that thing: thus in earth the inclination of gravity is greater than in water, because it is becoming to earth to be beneath water. Consequently the inclination also of grace which is the effect of charity, must needs be proportionate to those actions which have to be performed outwardly, so that, to wit, the affection of our charity be more intense towards those to whom we ought to behave with greater kindness.

We must, therefore, say that, even as regards the affection we ought to love one neighbor more than another. The reason is that, since the principle of love is God, and the person who loves, it must needs be that the affection of love increases in proportion to the nearness to one or the other of those principles. For as we stated above (A. 1), wherever we find a principle, order depends on relation to that principle.

Reply Obj. 1. Love can be unequal in two ways: first on the part of the good we wish our friend. In this respect we love all men equally out of charity: because we wish them all one same generic good, namely everlasting happiness. Secondly love is said to be greater through its action being more intense: and in this way we ought not to love all equally.

Or we may reply that we have unequal love for certain persons in two ways: first, through our loving some and not loving others. As regards beneficence we are bound to observe this inequality, because we cannot do good to all: but as regards benevolence, love ought not to be thus unequal. The other inequality arises from our loving some more than others: and Augustine does not mean to exclude the latter inequality, but the former, as is evident from what he says of beneficence.

Reply Obj. 2. Our neighbors are not all equally related to God; some are nearer to Him, by reason of their greater goodness, and those we ought, out of charity, to love more than those who are not so near to Him.

Reply Obj. 3. This argument considers the quantity of love on the part of the good which we wish our friends.

Eighth Article: Whether We Ought to Love More Those Who Are Connected with Us By Ties of Blood?

We proceed thus to the Eighth Article:—

Objection 1. It would seem that we ought not to love more those who are more closely united to us by ties of blood. For it is written

(Prov. xviii. 24): *A man amiable in society, shall be more friendly than a brother.* Again, Valerius Maximus says (*Fact. et Dict. Memor.* iv. 7): *The ties of friendship are most strong and in no way yield to the ties of blood. Moreover it is quite certain and undeniable, that as to the latter, the lot of birth is fortuitous, whereas we contract the former by an untrammelled will, and a solid pledge.* Therefore we ought not to love more than others those who are united to us by ties of blood.

Obj. 2. Further, Ambrose says (*De Officiis* i. 7): *I love not less you whom I have begotten in the Gospel, than if I had begotten you in wedlock, for nature is no more eager to love than grace. Surely we ought to love those whom we expect to be with us for ever more than those who will be with us only in this world.* Therefore we should not love our kindred more than those who are otherwise connected with us.

Obj. 3. Further, *Love is proved by deeds,* as Gregory states (*Hom. in Ev.* xxx). Now we are bound to do acts of love to others than our kindred: thus in the army a man must obey his officer rather than his father. Therefore we are not bound to love our kindred most of all.

On the contrary, The commandments of the decalogue contain a special precept about the honor due to our parents (Exod. xx. 12). Therefore we ought to love more specially those who are united to us by ties of blood.

I answer that, As stated above (A. 7), we ought out of charity to love those who are more closely united to us more, both because our love for them is more intense, and because there are more reasons for loving them. Now intensity of love arises from the union of lover and beloved: and therefore we should measure the love of different persons according to the different kinds of union, so that a man is more loved in matters touching that particular union in respect of which he is loved. And, again, in comparing love to love we should compare one union with another.

Accordingly we must say that friendship among blood relations is based upon their connection by natural origin, the friendship of fellow-citizens on their civic fellowship, and the friendship of those who are fighting side by side on the comradeship of battle. Wherefore in matters pertaining to nature we should love our kindred most, in matters concerning relations between citizens, we should prefer our fellow-citizens, and on the battlefield our fellow-soldiers. Hence the Philosopher says (*Ethic.* ix 2) that *it is our duty to render to each class of people such respect as is natural and appropriate. This is in fact the principle upon which we seem to act, for we invite our relations to a wedding. . . . It would seem to be a special duty to afford our parents the means of living . . . and to honor them.*

The same applies to other kinds of friendship.

If however we compare union with union, it is evident that the union arising from natural origin is prior to, and more stable than, all others, because it is something affecting the very substance, whereas other unions supervene and may cease altogether. Therefore the friendship of kindred is more stable, while other friendships may be stronger in respect of that which is proper to each of them.

Reply Obj. 1. In as much as the friendship of comrades originates through their own choice, love of this kind takes precedence of the love of kindred in matters where we are free to do as we choose, for instance in matters of action. Yet the friendship of kindred is more stable, since it is more natural, and preponderates over others in matters touching nature; consequently we are more beholden to them in the providing of necessaries.

Reply Obj. 2. Ambrose is speaking of love with regard to favors respecting the fellowship of grace, namely, moral instruction. For in this matter, a man ought to provide for his spiritual children whom he has begotten spiritually, more than for the sons of his body, whom he is bound to support in bodily sustenance.

Reply Obj. 3. The fact that in the battle a man obeys his officer rather than his father proves, that he loves his father less, not simply relatively, i.e. as regards the love which is based on fellowship in battle.

Question 26: Of the Order of Charity

Second Article: Whether to Love Considered As an Act of Charity Is the Same As Goodwill?

We proceed thus to the Second Article:—

Objection 1. It would seem that to love, considered as an act of charity, is nothing else than goodwill. For the Philosopher says (*Rhet.* ii. 4) that *to love is to wish a person well;* and this is goodwill. Therefore the act of charity is nothing but goodwill.

Obj. 2. Further, the act belongs to the same subject as the habit. Now the habit of charity is in the power of the will, as stated above (Q. 24, A. 1). Therefore the act of charity is also an act of the will. But it tends to good only, and this is goodwill. Therefore the act of charity is nothing else than goodwill.

Obj. 3. Further, the Philosopher reckons five things pertaining to friendship (*Ethic.* ix. 4), the first of which is that a man should wish his friend well; the second, that he should wish him to be and to live; the third, that he should take pleasure in his company; the fourth, that he should make choice of the same things; the fifth, that he should grieve and rejoice with him. Now the first two pertain to goodwill. Therefore goodwill is the first act of charity.

On the contrary, The Philosopher says (*ibid.*, 5) that *good-will is neither friendship nor love, but the beginning of friendship.* Now charity is friendship, as stated above (Q. 23, A. 1). Therefore goodwill is not the same as to love considered as an act of charity.

I answer that, Goodwill properly speaking is that act of the will whereby we wish well to another. Now this act of the will differs from actual love, considered not only as being in the sensitive appetite but also as being in the intellective appetite or will. For the love which is in the sensitive appetite is a passion. Now every passion seeks its object with a certain eagerness. And the passion of love is not aroused suddenly, but is born of an earnest consideration of the object loved; wherefore the Philosopher, showing the difference between goodwill and the love which is a passion, says (*Ethic.* ix 5) that *goodwill does not imply impetuosity or desire,* that is to say, has not an eager inclination, because it is by the sole judgement of his reason that one man wishes another well. Again such like love arises from previous acquaintance, whereas goodwill sometimes arises suddenly, as happens to us if we look on at a boxing-match, and we wish one of the boxers to win. But the love, which is in the intellective appetite, also differs from goodwill, because it denotes a certain union of affections between the lover and the beloved, in as much as the lover deems the beloved as somewhat united to him, or belonging to him, and so tends towards him. On the other hand, goodwill is a simple act of the will, whereby we wish a person well, even without presupposing the aforesaid union of the affections with him.

Accordingly, to love, considered as an act of charity, includes goodwill, but such dilection or love adds union of affections, wherefore the Philosopher says (*ibid.*) that *goodwill is a beginning of friendship.*

Reply Obj. 1. The Philosopher, by thus defining *to love,* does not describe it fully, but mentions only that part of its definition in which the act of love is chiefly manifested.

Reply Obj. 2. To love is indeed an act of the will tending to the good, but it adds a certain union with the beloved, which union is not denoted by goodwill.

Reply Obj. 3. These things mentioned by the Philosopher belong to friendship because they arise from a man's love for himself, as he says in the same passage, in so far as a man does all these things in respect of his friend, even as he does them to himself: and this belongs to the aforesaid union of the affections.

Seventh Article: Whether It Is More Meritorious to Love an Enemy Than to Love a Friend?

We proceed thus to the Seventh Article:—

Objection 1. It would seem more meritorious to love an enemy than to love a friend. For it is written (Matth. v. 46): *If you love them that love you, what reward shall you have?* Therefore it is not deserving of reward to love one's friend: whereas, as the same passage proves, to love one's enemy is deserving of a reward. Therefore it is more meritorious to love one's enemy than to love one's friend.

Obj. 2. Further, an act is the more meritorious through proceeding from a greater charity. But it belongs to the perfect children of God to love their enemies, whereas those also who have imperfect charity love their friends. Therefore it is more meritorious to love one's enemy than to love one's friend.

Obj. 3. Further, where there is more effort for good, there seems to be more merit, since *every man shall receive his own reward according to his own labor* (1 Cor. iii. 8). Now a man has to make a greater effort to love his enemy than to love his friend, because it is more difficult. Therefore it seems more meritorious to love one's enemy than to love one's friend.

On the contrary, The better an action is, the more meritorious it is. Now it is better to love one's friend, since it is better to love a better man, and the friend who loves you is better than the enemy who hates you. Therefore it is more meritorious to love one's friend than to love one's enemy.

I answer that, God is the reason for our loving our neighbor out of charity, as stated above (Q. 25, A. 1). When therefore it is asked which is better or more meritorious, to love one's friend or one's enemy, these two loves may be compared in two ways, first, on the part of our neighbor whom we love, secondly, on the part of the reason for which we love him.

In the first way, love of one's friend surpasses love of one's enemy, because a friend is both better and more closely united to us, so that he is a more suitable matter of love, and consequently the act of love that passes over this matter, is better, and therefore its opposite is worse, for it is worse to hate a friend than an enemy.

In the second way, however, it is better to love one's enemy than one's friend, and this for two reasons. First, because it is possible to love one's friend for another reason than God, whereas God is the only reason for loving one's enemy. Secondly, because if we suppose that both are loved for God, our love for God is proved to be all the stronger through carrying a man's affections to things which are furthest from him, namely, to the love of his enemies, even as the power of a furnace is proved to be the stronger, according as it throws its heat to more distant objects. Hence our love for God is proved to be so much the stronger, as the more difficult are the things we accomplish for its sake, just as the power of fire is so much the stronger, as it is able to set fire to a less inflammable matter.

Yet just as the same fire acts with greater force on what is near than on what is distant, so too, charity loves with greater fervor those who are united to us than those who are far removed; and in this respect the love of friends, considered in itself, is more ardent and better than the love of one's enemy.

Reply Obj. 1. The words of Our Lord must be taken in their strict sense: because the love of one's friends is not meritorious in God's sight when we love them merely because they are our friends: and this would seem to be the case when we love our friends in such a way that we love not our enemies. On the other hand the love of our friends is meritorious, if we love them for God's sake, and not merely because they are our friends.

The *Reply* to the other *Objections* is evident from what has been said in the article, because the two arguments that follow consider the reason for loving, while the last considers the question on the part of those who are loved.

Chapter 12

Montaigne, *Of Friendship* (*Essays*)

Michel de Montaigne (1533-1591) was a French essayist and skeptical philosopher who has been called, among other things, "the most learned man who ever wrote a book," "the wisest Frenchman who ever lived," and the "journalist of the 16th century." Born near Bordeaux, he was raised on a wealthy estate where his father, an important merchant, saw that he received a special education. He was awakened every morning by music and was allowed to hear or speak no other language but Latin until he was six. At that time he was sent to the Collège de Guyenne at Bordeaux, where he studied under some of the leading humanists of the time. Still later Montaigne studied law, apparently at the University of Toulouse, a leading center of humanism, and he served for over a decade as a member of the **parlement** *of Bordeaux (one of the higher courts in France).*

After the death of his best friend in 1563, and of his father in 1568, Montaigne retired from public life in order to devote himself to a quiet life of reading and writing at his country estate. The following year he began writing his **Essays,** *informal discussions of various topics, in which self-portrait often became a study in human nature. The first two books of his* **Essays** *were published in 1580; the third appeared in 1588. The earliest of his* **Essays** *tended to reflect the rigid Stoicism of Seneca, while the later ones tended more towards the skepticism of Sextus Empiricus, whose maxims he had carved into the rafter beams of his study, adopting as his own motto, "What do I know?"*

Montaigne lived during a period of profound upheaval and conflict through the aftermath of the Reformation, the wars between Protestants and Catholics, and the bloody massacre of Saint

Bartholomew's Day in which 8,000 Protestants were slaughtered by order of Catherine de Medici in France. He was personally torn by divided loyalties, yet retained a spirit of toleration such that he was respected equally by both sides. His own tolerant disposition was doubtless influenced in no small part by the fact that his own family members represented a plurality of religious commitments. His mother, a Spanish Jewess by descent, was a Protestant, along with a brother and a sister; he himself, his father, three brothers and two sisters were Catholics.

The death of his best friend in 1563, the stoic humanist and poet, Étienne de La Boétie, left an indelible impression on Montaigne. By his own account, the four short years of their friendship meant more to Montaigne than any others during his lifetime. In 1570 he published a book of La Boétie's poetry, to which he appended a letter commemorating his friend's death, his own first significant piece of writing. The same friendship is commemorated in our selection, "Of Friendship," originally published as Chapter 28 of Book I in his **Essays** *(1580) and followed, in Chapter 29, by twenty-nine sonnets of La Boétie.*

Of Friendship

There is nothing to which nature seems to have inclined us more than to society. And Aristotle says that good legislators have had more care for friendship than for justice. Now the ultimate point in the perfection of society is this. For in general, all associations that are forged and nourished by pleasure or profit, by public or private needs, are less beautiful, noble, and so much the less friendships, in so far as they mix into friendship another cause and object and reward than friendship itself. Nor do the four ancient types—natural, social, hospitable, venerian—come up to real friendship, either separately or together.

From children toward fathers, it is rather respect. Friendship feeds on communication, which cannot exist between them because of their too great inequality, and might perhaps interfere with the duties of nature. For neither can all the secret thoughts of fathers be communicated to children, lest this beget an unbecoming intimacy, nor could the admonitions and corrections, which are one of the chief duties of friendship, be administered by children to fathers. There have been nations where by custom the children killed their fathers, and others where the fathers killed their children, to avoid the mutual interference that can sometimes arise; and by nature the one depends on the destruction of the other. There have been philosophers who disdained this natural tie, witness Aristippus: when pressed about the affection he owed his children for having come out of him, he began to spit, saying that that had come out of him just as much, and that we also bred lice and worms. And that other, whom Plutarch wanted to reconcile with his brother, said: *I don't think any more of him for having come out of the same hole.*

Truly the name of brother is a beautiful name and full of affection, and for that reason we made our alliance a brotherhood. But that confusion of ownership, the dividing, and the fact that the richness of one is the poverty of the other, wonderfully softens and loosens the solder of brotherhood. Brothers having to guide the progress of their advancement along the same path and at the same rate, it is inevitable that they often jostle and clash with each other. Furthermore, why should the harmony and kinship which begets these true and perfect friendships be found in them? Father and son may be of entirely different dispositions, and brothers also. He is my son, he is my kinsman, but he is an unsociable man, a knave, or a fool. And then, the more they are friendships which law and natural obligation impose on us, the less of our choice and free will there is in them. And our free will has no product more properly its own than affection and friendship. Not that I have not experienced all the friendship that can exist in that situation, having had the best father that ever was, and the most indulgent, even in his extreme old age, and being of a family famous and exemplary, from father to son, in this matter of brotherly concord: *Known to others for fatherly affection toward my brothers* [Horace].

As for comparing with it affection for women, though this is born of our choice, we cannot do it, nor can we put it in this class. Its fire, I confess, *Of us that goddess is not unaware who blends a bitter sweetness with her care* [Catullus], is more active, more scorching and more intense. But it is an impetuous and fickle flame, wavering and variable, a fever flame, subject to fits and lulls, that holds us only by one corner. In friendship it is a general and universal warmth, all gentleness and smoothness, with nothing bitter and stinging about it. What is more, in love there is nothing but a frantic desire for what flees from us: *Just as a huntsman will pursue a hare o'er hill and dale, in weather cold or fair; the captured hare is worthless in his sight; he only hastens after things in flight* [Ariosto].

As soon as it enters the boundaries of friendship, that is to say harmony of wills, it grows faint and languid. Enjoyment destroys it, as having a fleshly end, subject to satiety. Friendship, on the contrary, is enjoyed according as it is desired; it is bred, nourished, and increased only in enjoyment, since it is spiritual, and the soul grows refined by practice. During the reign of this perfect friendship those fleeting affections once found a place in me, not to speak of my friend, who confesses only too many of them in these verses. Thus these two passions within me have come to be known to each other, but to be compared, never; the first keeping its course in proud and lofty flight, and disdainfully watching the other making its way far, far beneath it.

As for marriage, besides its being a bargain to which only the entrance is free, its continuance being constrained and forced, depending otherwise than on our will, and a bargain ordinarily made for other ends, there supervene a thousand foreign tangles to unravel, enough to break the thread and trouble the course of a lively affection; whereas in friendship there are no dealings or business except with itself. Besides, to tell the truth, the ordinary capacity of women is inadequate for that communion and fellowship which is the nurse of this sacred bond; nor does their soul seem firm enough to endure the strain of so tight and durable a knot. And indeed, but for that, if such a familiarity, free and voluntary, could be built up, in which not only would the souls have this complete enjoyment, but the bodies would also share in the alliance; in which the entire man would be engaged, it is certain that the friendship would be fuller and more complete. But this sex in no ir/stance has yet succeeded in attaining it, and by the common agreement of the ancient schools is excluded from it.

And that other Greek license is justly abhorred by our morality. Since this involved, moreover, according to their practice, such a necessary disparity in age and such a difference in the lovers' obligations, it did not correspond closely enough with the perfect union and harmony that we require here: *For what is this love of friendship? Why does no one love either an ugly youth, or a handsome old man?* [Cicero]   For even the picture the Academy paints of it will not contradict me, I think, if I say this about it: that this first frenzy which the son of Venus inspired in the lover's heart at the sight of the flower of tender youth, in which they allow all the insolent and passionate acts that unrestrained ardor can produce, was simply founded on external beauty, the false image of corporeal generation. For it could not be founded on the spirit, the signs of which were still hidden, which was only at its birth and before the age of budding. If this frenzy seized a base heart, the means of his courtship were riches, presents, favor in advancement to dignities, and other such base merchandise, which they condemn. If it fell on a nobler heart, the medium was also noble:

philosophical instruction, precepts to revere religion, obey the laws, die for the good of the country; examples of valor, prudence, justice; the lover studying to make himself acceptable by the grace and beauty of his soul, that of his body being long since faded, and hoping by this mental fellowship to establish a firmer and more lasting pact.

When this courtship attained its effect in due season (for whereas they do not require of the lover that he use leisure and discretion in his enterprise, they strictly require it of the loved one, because he had to judge an inner beauty, difficult to know and hidden from discovery), there was born in the loved one the desire of spiritual conception through the medium of spiritual beauty. This was the main thing here, and corporeal beauty accidental and secondary; quite the opposite of the lover. For this reason they prefer the loved one, and prove that the gods also prefer him, and strongly rebuke the poet Aeschylus for having, in the love of Achilles and Patroclus, given the lover's part to Achilles, who was in the first beardless bloom of his youth, and the handsomest of all the Greeks.

After this general communion is established, the stronger and worthier partner in it exercising his functions and predominating, they say that there resulted from it fruits very useful personally and to the public; that it constituted the strength of the countries which accepted the practice, and the principal defense of equity and liberty: witness the salutary loves of Harmodius and Aristogeiton. Therefore they call it sacred and divine. And, by their reckoning, only the violence of tyrants and the cowardice of the common people are hostile to it. In short, all that can be said in favor of the Academy is that it was a love ending in friendship; which corresponds pretty well to the Stoic definition of love: *Love is the attempt to form a friendship inspired by beauty.* [Cicero]

I return to my description of a more equitable and more equable kind of friendship. *Only those are to be judged friendships in which the characters have been strengthened and matured by age.* [Cicero]

For the rest, what we ordinarily call friends and friendships are nothing but acquaintanceships and familiarities formed by some chance or convenience, by means of which our souls are bound to each other. In the friendship I speak of, our souls mingle and blend with each other so completely that they efface the seam that joined them, and cannot find it again. If you press me to tell why I loved him, I feel that this cannot be expressed, except by answering: Because it was he, because it was I.

Beyond all my understanding, beyond what I can say about this in particular, there was I know not what inexplicable and fateful force that was the mediator of this union. We sought each other before we met because of the reports we heard of each other, which had more effect on our affection than such reports would reasonably have; I think it was by some ordinance from heaven. We embraced each other's names. And at our first meeting, which by chance came at a great feast and gathering in the city, we found ourselves so taken with each other, so well acquainted, so bound together, that from that time on nothing was so close to us as each other. He wrote an excellent Latin satire, which is published, in which he condones and explains the precipitancy of our mutual understanding, so promptly grown to its perfection. Having so little time to last, and having begun so late, for we were both grown men, and he some years older than I, it could not lose time and conform to the pattern of mild and regular friendships, which need so many precautions in the form of long preliminary association. Our friendship has no other model than itself, and can be compared only with itself. It is not one special consideration, nor two, nor three, nor four, nor a thousand: it is I know not what quintessence of all this mixture, which, having seized my whole will, led it to plunge and lose itself in his; which, having seized his whole will, led it to plunge and lose itself in mine, with equal hunger, equal rivalry. I say lose, in truth, for neither of us reserved anything for himself, nor was anything either his or mine.

When Laelius, in the presence of the Roman consuls, who, after condemning Tiberius Gracchus, prosecuted all those who had been in his confidence, came to ask Caius Blossius, who was his best friend, how much he would have been willing to do for him, he answered: "Everything." 'What, everything?' pursued Laelius. "And what if he had commanded you to set fire to our temples?" "He would never have commanded me to do that," replied Blossius. "But what if he had?" Laelius insisted. "I would have obeyed," he replied. If he was such a perfect friend to Gracchus as the histories say, he did not need to offend the consuls by this last bold confession, and he should not have abandoned the assurance he had of Gracchus' disposition. But nevertheless, those who charge that this answer is seditious do not fully understand this mystery, and fail to assume first what is true, that he had Gracchus' will up his sleeve, both by power over him and by knowledge of him. They were friends more than citizens, friends more than friends or enemies of their country or friends of ambition and disturbance. Having committed themselves absolutely to each other, they held absolutely the reins of each other's inclination; and if you assume that this team was guided by the strength and leadership of reason, as indeed it is quite impossible to harness it without that, Blossius' answer is as it should have been. If their actions went astray, they were by my measure neither friends to each other, nor friends to themselves.

For that matter, this answer has no better ring than would mine if someone questioned me in this fashion: "If your will commanded you to kill your daughter, would you kill her?" and I said yes. For that does not bear witness to any consent to do so, because I have no doubt at all about my will, and just as little about that of such a friend. It is not in the power of all the arguments in the world to dislodge me from the certainty I have of the intentions and judgments of my friend. Not one of his actions could be presented to me, whatever appearance it might have, that I could not immediately find the motive for it. Our souls pulled together in such unison, they regarded each other with such ardent affection, and with a like affection revealed themselves to each other to the very depths of our hearts, that not only did I know his soul as well as mine, but I should certainly have trusted myself to him more readily than to myself.

Let not these other, common friendships be placed in this rank. I have as much knowledge of them as another, and of the most perfect of their type, but I advise you not to confuse the rules of the two; you would make a mistake. You must walk in those other friendships bridle in hand, with prudence and precaution; the knot is not so well tied that there is no cause to mistrust it. *Love him*, Chilo used to say, *as if you have to hate him some day; hate him as if you have to love him.* This precept, which is so abominable in this sovereign and masterful friendship, is healthy in the practice of common and customary friendships, in regard to which we must use the remark that Aristotle so often repeated: *O my friends, there is no friend.*

In this noble relationship, services and benefits, on which other friendships feed, do not even deserve to be taken into account; the reason for this is the complete blending of our wills. For as the friendship I feel for myself receives no increase from the help I give myself in time of need, whatever the Stoics say, and as I feel no gratitude to myself for the service I do myself; so the union of such friends, being truly perfect, makes them lose the sense of such duties, and hate and banish from between them these words implying separation and distinction: benefit, obligation, gratitude, request, thanks, and the like. Everything actually being in common between them—wills, thoughts, judgments, goods, wives, children, honor, and life—and their relationship being that of one soul in two bodies, according to Aristotle's very apt definition, they can neither lend nor give anything to each other. That is why the lawmakers, to honor marriage with some imaginary resemblance to this divine union, forbid gifts between husband and wife, wishing thus to imply that everything should belong to each of them and that they have nothing to divide and split up between them.

If, in the friendship I speak of, one could give to the other, it would be the one who received the benefit who would oblige his friend. For, each of them seeking above all things to benefit the other, the one who provides the matter and the occasion is the liberal one, giving his friend the satisfaction of doing for him what he most wants to do. When the philosopher Diogenes was short of money, he used to say that he asked it back of his friends, not that he asked for it. And to show how this works in practice, I will tell you an ancient example that is singular.

Eudamidas of Corinth had two friends, Charixenus, a Sicyonian, and Aretheus, a Corinthian. When he came to die, being poor, and his two friends rich, he made his will thus: *I leave this to Aretheus, to feed my mother and support her in her old age; this to Charixenus, to see my daughter married and give her the biggest dowry he can; and in case one of them should chance to die, I substitute the survivor in his place.* Those who first saw this will laughed at it; but his heirs, having been informed of it, accepted it with singular satisfaction. And one of them, Charixenus, dying five days later, and the place of substitute being open to Aretheus, he supported the mother with great care, and of five talents he had in his possession, he gave two and a half to his only daughter for her marriage, and two and a half for the marriage of the daughter of Eudamidas, holding their weddings on the same day.

This example is quite complete except for one circumstance, which is the plurality of friends. For this perfect friendship I speak of is indivisible: each one gives himself so wholly to his friend that he has nothing left to distribute elsewhere; on the contrary, he is sorry that he is not double, triple, or quadruple, and that he has not several souls and several wills, to confer them all on this one object. Common friendships can be divided up: one may love in one man his beauty, in another his easygoing ways, in another liberality, in one paternal love, in another brotherly love, and so forth; but this friendship that possesses the soul and rules it with absolute sovereignty cannot possibly be double. If two called for help at the same time, which one would you run to? If they demanded conflicting services of you, how would you arrange it? If one confided to your silence a thing that would be useful for the other to know, how would you extricate yourself? A single dominant friendship dissolves all other obligations. The secret I have sworn to reveal to no other man, I can impart without perjury to the one who is not another man, he is myself. It is a great enough miracle to be doubled, and those who talk of tripling themselves do not know the height of it: nothing is superlative if it has an equal. And he who supposes that of two men I love one just as much as the other, and that they love each other and me just as much as I love them, multiplies into a brotherhood the most single and unified of all things, of which even a single one is the rarest thing in the world to find.

The rest of this story fits in very well with what I was saying, for Eudamidas grants his friends, as a kindness and a favor, to use them for his need. He leaves them heirs to this liberality of his, which consists of putting into their hands a chance to do him good. And without doubt the strength of friendship is shown much more richly in his action than in that of Aretheus.

In short, these are actions inconceivable to anyone who has not tasted friendship, and which make me honor wonderfully the answer of that young soldier to Cyrus, who asked him for how much he would sell a horse with which he had just won the prize in a race, and whether he would exchange him for a kingdom: "No indeed, Sire, but I would most willingly let him go to gain a friend, if I found a man worthy of such an alliance." That was not badly spoken, "if I found one"; for it is easy to find men fit for a superficial acquaintance. But for this kind, in which we act from the very bottom of our hearts, which holds nothing back, truly it is necessary that all the springs of action be perfectly clean and true.

In the relationships which bind us only by one small part, we need look out only for the imperfections that particularly concern that part. The religion of my doctor or my lawyer does not matter. That consideration has nothing in common with the functions of the friendship they owe me. And in the domestic relationship between me and those who serve me, the same is true. And I scarcely inquire of a lackey whether he is chaste; I try to find out whether he is diligent. And I am not as much afraid of a gambling mule driver as of a stupid one, or a profane cook as an ignorant one. I do not take it upon myself to tell the world what it should do—enough others do that—but what I do in it. *That is my practice: do as you see fit* [Terence]. For the familiarity of the table I look for wit, not prudence; for the bed, beauty before goodness; in the association of conversation, competence, even without uprightness. Likewise in other matters.

Just as the man who was found astride a stick, playing with his children, asked the man who surprised him thus to say nothing about it until he was a father himself, in the belief that the passion which would then be born in his soul would make him an equitable judge of such an act, so I should like to talk to people who have experienced what I tell. But knowing how far from common usage and how rare such a friendship is, I do not expect to find any good judge of it. For the very discourses that antiquity has left us on this subject seem to me weak compared with the feeling I have. And in this particular the facts surpass even the precepts of philosophy: *Nothing shall I, while sane, compare with a dear friend* [Horace].

The ancient Menander declared that man happy who had been able to meet even the shadow of a friend. He was certainly right to say so, especially if he spoke from experience. For in truth, if I compare all the rest of my life—though by the grace of God I have spent it pleasantly, comfortably, and, except for the loss of such a friend, free from any grievous affliction, and full of tranquillity of mind, having accepted my natural and original advantages without seeking other ones—if I compare it all, I say, with the four years which were granted me to enjoy the sweet company and society of that man, it is nothing but smoke, nothing but dark and dreary night. Since the day I lost him, *Which evermore I shall recall with pain, with reverence—thus, Gods, did you ordain*—[Virgil] I only drag on a weary life; and the very pleasures that come my way, instead of consoling me, redouble my grief for his loss. We went halves in everything; it seems to me that I am robbing him of his share, *Nor is it right for me to taste of pleasures here alone,—So I resolved—as long as he who shared my life is gone* [Terence]. I was already so formed and accustomed to being double everywhere that only half of me seems to be alive now.

> *Since an untimely blow has snatched away*
> *Part of my soul, why then do I delay,*
> *I the remaining part, less dear than he,*
> *And not entire surviving? The same day*
> *Brought ruin equally to him and me.* [Horace]

There is no action or thought in which I do not miss him, as indeed he would have missed me. For just as he surpassed me infinitely in every other ability and virtue, so he did in the duty of friendship.

> *Why should I be ashamed or exercise control*
> *When I mourn so dear a soul?* [Horace]

> *Brother, your death has left me sad and lone;*
> *Since you departed all our joys have gone,*
> *Which while you lived your sweet affection fed;*
> *My pleasures all lie shattered, with you dead.*
> *Our soul lies in the tomb, with yours entwined;*
> *And since then I have banished from my mind*
> *My studies, and my spirit's dearest joys.*
> *Shall I ne'er speak to you, or hear your voice?*
> *Or see your face, more dear than life to me?*
> *At least I'll love you to eternity.* [Catullus]

But let us listen a while to this boy of sixteen.

Because I have found that this work has since been brought to light, and with evil intent, by those who seek to disturb and change the state of our government without worrying whether they will improve it, and because they have mixed his work up with some of their own concoctions, I have changed my mind about putting it in here. And so that the memory of the author may not be damaged in the eyes of those who could not know his opinions and actions at close hand, I beg to advise them that this subject was treated by him in his boyhood, only by way of an exercise, as a common theme hashed over in a thousand places in books. I have no doubt that he believed what he wrote, for he was so conscientious as not to lie even in jest. And I know further that if he had had the choice, he would rather have been born in Venice than in Sarlac, and with reason. But he had another maxim sovereignly imprinted in his soul, to obey and submit most religiously to the laws under which he was born. There never was a better citizen, or one more devoted to the tranquillity of his country, or more hostile to the commotions and innovations of his time. He would much rather have used his ability to suppress them than to give them material that would excite them further. His mind was molded in the pattern of other ages than this.

Now, in exchange for this serious work, I shall substitute another, produced in that same season of his life, gayer and more jovial.[1]

Notes

[1] In his original collection of essays, Montaigne had originally inserted twenty-nine sonnets of La Boétie immediately following his essay on friendship.

Chapter 13

Francis Bacon, *OF FRIENDSHIP* (*ESSAYS*)

Francis Bacon (1561-1626), a contemporary of Shakespeare and Queen Elizabeth I, is remembered primarily as the founding father of modern science in England. A versatile man, he was also a statesman and distinguished himself in politics, law, literature, philosophy, and science—a true "Renaissance man."

Politically, Bacon was born well-connected. His father, Sir Nicholas Bacon, was Lord Keeper of the Great Seal and Lord Chancellor under Queen Elizabeth. His uncle, Sir William Cecil, was Secretary of State. In 1603 Bacon was knighted by James I and appointed Learned Counsel. In 1607 he was appointed Solicitor General; in 1613, Attorney General; in 1617, Lord Keeper of the Great Seal; and in 1618 he attained the high office of Lord Chancellor and the title of Baron Verulam. This rise to success was cut short, however, when he was impeached for accepting bribes in cases being tried before him in the Court of Chancery. He died in disgrace.

Although Bacon's public service career was cut short, this adversity had its compensations: it provided him leisure to write. His **New Organon** *(1620) was part of a major philosophical project and represents a rejection of the deductive methods of Aristotle and their replacement by the inductive, empirical methods of modern science. His reputation as a philosopher of science rests on his insistence on direct observation of nature as the only way to know truth. He also wrote* **Essays**, *which won him fame, dealing with diverse phases of human life—politics, economy, religion, marriage, friendship, education, and the like. These were published in three editions (1597, 1612, and 1625), each expanding upon the former. Despite his revolt* *against medieval traditions, many of his pages are littered with Latin quotations from ancient writers. But his style is clear, simple, and brilliant, inviting comparisons to Shakespeare.*

Our selection, "Of Friendship," is taken from Gordon S. Haight's edition of the 1625 edition of Bacon's **Essays** *in which the Latin quotations have been translated in the text and reproduced in the original in the notes.*

Of Friendship

It had been hard for him that spake it[1] to have put more truth and untruth together in few words than in that speech: *Whosoever is delighted in solitude, is either a wild beast or a god*: for it is most true that a natural and secret hatred and aversion towards society in any man hath somewhat of the savage beast; but it is most untrue that it should have any character at all of the divine nature, except it proceed, not out of a pleasure in solitude, but out of a love and desire to sequester a man's self for a higher conversation; such as is found to have been falsely and feignedly in some of the heathen; as Epimenides, the Candian; Numa, the Roman; Empedocles, the Sicilian; and Apollonius, of Tyana;[2] truly and really in divers of the ancient hermits and holy fathers of the church. But little do men perceive what solitude is and how far it extendeth; for a crowd is not company, and faces are but a gallery of pictures, and talk but a tinkling cymbal, where there is no love. The Latin adage meeteth with it a little, *A great city is a great solitude*;[3] because in a great town friends are scattered, so that there is not that fellowship, for the most part, which is in less neighborhoods: but we may go further, and affirm most truly, that it is a mere and miserable solitude to want true friends, without which the world is but a wilderness; and even in this sense also of solitude, whosoever in the frame of his nature and affections is unfit for friendship, he taketh it of the beasts, and not from humanity.

A principal fruit of friendship is the ease and discharge of the fullness and swellings of the heart, which passions of all kinds do cause and induce. We know diseases of stoppings and suffocations are the most dangerous in the body, and it is not much otherwise in the mind. You may take sarza[4] to open the liver, steel to open the spleen, flower of sulphur for the lungs, castoreum[5] for the brain, but no receipt openeth the heart but a true friend, to whom you may impart griefs, joys, fears, hopes, suspicions, counsels, and whatsoever lieth upon the heart to oppress it, in a kind of civil shrift or confession.

It is a strange thing to observe how high a rate great kings and monarchs do set upon this fruit of friendship whereof we speak; so great, as they purchase it many times at the hazard of their own safety and greatness; for princes, in regard of the distance of their fortune from that of their subjects and servants, cannot gather this fruit, except (to make themselves capable thereof) they raise some persons to be as it were companions and almost equals to themselves, which many times sorteth to inconvenience. The modern languages give unto such persons the name of favorites, or privadoes, as if it were matter of grace or conversation; but the Roman name attaineth the true use and cause thereof, naming them *Sharers of troubles;*[6] for it is that which tieth the knot. And we see plainly that this hath been done, not by weak and passionate princes only, but by the wisest and most politic that ever reigned, who have oftentimes joined to themselves some of their servants, whom both themselves have called friends, and allowed others likewise to call them in the same manner, using the word received between private men.

L. Sulla, when he commanded Rome, raised Pompey (after surnamed the Great) to that height, that Pompey vaunted himself for Sulla's overmatch; for when he had carried the consulship for a friend of his, against the pursuit of Sulla, and that Sulla did a little resent thereat, and began to speak great, Pompey turned upon him again, and, in effect, bade him be quiet; for that more men adored the sun rising than the sun setting. With Julius Caesar, Decimus Brutus had obtained that interest, as he set him down in his testament for heir in remainder after his nephew; and this was the man that had power with him to draw him forth to his death; for when Caesar would have discharged the senate, in regard of some ill presages, and specially a dream of Calpurnia, this man lifted him gently by the arm out of his chair, telling him he hoped he would not dismiss the senate till his wife had dreamt a better dream;[7] and it seemeth his favor was so great, as Antonius, in a letter which is recited verbatim in one of Cicero's Philippics, calleth him *venefica, witch,* as if he had enchanted Caesar. Augustus raised Agrippa (though of mean birth) to that height, as, when he consulted with Maecenas about the marriage of his daughter Julia, Maecenas took the liberty to tell him that he must either marry his daughter to Agrippa, or take away his life; there was no third way, he had made him so great. With Tiberius Caesar, Sejanus had ascended to that height, as they two were termed and reckoned as a pair of friends. Tiberius, in a letter to him, saith, *Because of our friendship, I have not concealed these things from you.*[8] And the whole senate dedicated an altar to Friendship, as to a goddess, in respect of the great dearness of friendship between them two. The like, or more, was between Septimius Severus and Plautianus; for he forced his eldest son to marry the daughter of Plautianus, and would often maintain Plautianus in doing affronts to his son; and did write also in a letter to the senate, by these words: *I love the man so well, as I wish he may over-live me.*[9] Now if these princes had been as a Trajan, or a Marcus Aurelius, a man might have thought that this had proceeded of an abundant goodness of nature; but being men so wise, of such strength and severity of mind, and so extreme lovers of themselves, as all these were, it proveth most plainly that they found their own felicity (though as great as ever happened to mortal men) but as an half-piece, except they might have a friend to make it entire; and yet, which is more, they were princes that had wives, sons, nephews; and yet all these could not supply the comfort of friendship.

It is not to be forgotten what Comineus[10] observeth of his first master, Duke Charles the Hardy,[11] namely, that he would communicate his secrets with none, and, least of all, those secrets which troubled him most. Whereupon he goeth on, and saith, that towards his latter time that closeness did impair and a little perish his understanding. Surely, Comineus might have made the same judgment, also, if it had pleased him, of his second master, Louis the Eleventh, whose closeness was indeed his tormentor. The parable of Pythagoras is dark, but true: *Cor ne edito, Eat not the heart.* Certainly, if a man would give it a hard phrase, those that want friends to open themselves unto are cannibals of their own hearts; but one thing is most admirable (wherewith I will conclude this first fruit of friendship), which is, that this communicating of a man's self to his friend works two contrary effects, for it redoubleth joys and cutteth griefs in halves; for there is no man that imparteth his joys to his friend, but he joyeth the more; and no man that imparteth his griefs to his friend, but he grieveth the less. So that it is, in truth, of operation upon a man's mind of like virtue as the alchemists used to attribute to their stone for man's body, that it worketh all contrary effects, but still to the good and benefit of nature. But yet, without praying in aid[12] of alchemists, there is a manifest image of this in the ordinary course of nature; for in bodies union strengtheneth and cherisheth any natural action; and on the other side weakeneth and dulleth any violent impression; and even so it is of minds.

The second fruit of friendship is healthful and sovereign for the understanding, as the first is for the affections; for friendship maketh indeed a fair day in the affections from storm and tempests, but it maketh daylight in the understanding, out of darkness and confusion of thoughts. Neither is this to be understood only of faithful counsel, which a man receiveth from his friend; but before you come to that, certain it is, that whosoever hath his mind fraught with many thoughts, his wits and understanding do clarify and break up in the communicating and discoursing with another; he tosseth his thoughts more easily; he marshalleth them more orderly, he seeth how they look when they are turned into words; finally, he waxeth wiser than himself; and that more by an hour's discourse than by a day's meditation. It was well said by Themistocles to the king of Persia: *That speech was like cloth of Arras, opened and put abroad, whereby the imagery doth appear in figure; whereas in thoughts they lie but as in packs.*[13] Neither is this second fruit of friendship, in opening the understanding, restrained only to such friends as are able to give a man counsel (they indeed are best), but even without that a man learneth of himself, and bringeth his own thoughts to light, and whetteth his wits as against a stone, which itself cuts not. In a word, a man were better relate himself to a statue or picture, than to suffer his thoughts to pass in smother.

Add now, to make this second fruit of friendship complete, that other point which lieth more open and falleth within vulgar observation; which is counsel; faithful counsel from a friend. Heraclitus[14] saith well, one of his enigmas, *Dry light is ever the best*; and certain it is that the light that a man receiveth by counsel from another is drier and purer than that which cometh from his own understanding and judgment, which is ever infused and drenched in his affections and customs. So, as there is as much difference between the counsel that a friend giveth, and that a man giveth himself, as there is between the counsel of a friend and of a flatterer; for there is no such flatterer as is a man's self, and there is no such remedy against flattery of a man's self, as the liberty of a friend. Counsel is of two sorts, the one concerning manners, the other concerning business; for the first, the best preservative to keep the mind in health is the faithful admonition of a friend. The calling of a man's self to a strict account is a medicine sometimes too piercing and corrosive; reading good books of morality is a little flat and dead; observing our faults in others is sometimes improper for our case; but the best receipt (best, I say, to work, and best to take) is the admonition of a friend. It is a strange thing to behold what gross errors and extreme absurdities many (especially of the greater sort) do commit for want of a friend to tell them of them, to the great damage both of their fame and fortune; for, as St. James saith, they are as men *that look sometimes into a glass, and presently forget their own shape and favor.*[15] As for business, a man may think, if he will, that two eyes see no more than one; or, that a gamester seeth always more than a looker-on; or, that a man in anger is as wise as he that has said over the four and twenty letters, or, that a musket may be shot off as well upon the arm as upon a rest; and such other fond and high imaginations, to think himself all in all; but when all is done, the help of good counsel is that which setteth business straight. And if any man think that he will take counsel, but it shall be by pieces, asking counsel in one business of one man, and in another business of another man; it is well (that is to say, better, perhaps, than if he asked none at all); but he runneth two dangers: one, that he shall not be faithfully counselled; for it is a rare thing, except it be from a perfect and entire friend, to have counsel given, but such as shall be bowed and crooked to some ends which he hath that given it; the other that he shall have counsel given, hurtful and unsafe (though with good meaning), and mixed partly of mischief and partly of remedy; even as if you would call a physician that is thought good for the cure of the disease you complain of, but is unacquainted with your body; and therefore, may put you in a way for a present cure, but overthroweth your health in some other kind, and so cure the disease and kill the patient. But a friend, wholly acquainted with a man's estate, will beware, by furthering present business, how he dasheth upon other inconvenience. And therefore, rest not upon scattered counsels; they will rather distract and mislead, than settle and direct.

After these two noble fruits of friendship (peace in the affections and support of the judgment), followeth the last fruit, which is like the pomegranate, full of many kernels; I mean aid, and bearing a part in all actions and occasions. Here the best way to represent to life the manifold use of friendship is to cast and see how many things there are which a man cannot do himself; and then it will appear that it was a sparing speech of the ancients to say, *that a friend is another himself,* for that a friend is far more than himself. Men have their time, and die many times in desire of some things which they principally take to heart; the bestowing of a child, the finishing of a work, or the like. If a man have a true friend, he may rest almost secure that the care of those things will continue after him; so that a man hath, as it were, two lives in his desires. A man hath a body, and that body is confined to a place; but where friendship is, all offices of life are, as it were, granted to him and his deputy, for he may exercise them by his friend. How many things are there, which a man cannot, with any face or comeliness, say or do himself? A man can scarce allege his own merits with modesty, much less extol them; a man cannot sometimes brook to supplicate, or beg, and a number of the like; but all these things are graceful in a friend's mouth, which are blushing in a man's own. So, again, a man's person hath many proper[16] relations which he cannot put off. A man cannot speak to his son but as a father; to his wife but as a husband; to his enemy but upon terms; whereas a friend may speak as the case requires, and not as it sorteth with[17] the person. But to enumerate these things were endless. I have given the rule, where a man cannot fitly play his own part: if he have not a friend, he may quit the stage.

Notes

[1] Aristotle, *Politics*, I, 2.

[2] Epimenides, a poet of Crete, is said by Pliny to have fallen into a sleep which lasted 57 years. Numa, legendary Roman King, pretended that he was instructed in the art of legislation by the divine nymph Egeria, who dwelt in the Arician grove. Empedocles, the Sicilian philosopher, is said to have thrown himself into the crater of Mount Aetna so that his disappearance might make people think him a god. Apollonius of Tyana, the Pythagorean philosopher, pretended to miraculous powers.

[3] *Magna civitas, magna solitudo.*

[4] Sarsaparilla.

[5] A medicinal substance obtained from the beaver.

[6] *Participes curarum.*

[7] Plutarch, *Lives*, V, 65.

[8] *Haec pro amicitiâ nostrâ non occultavi.* Tacitus, *Annals*, IV, 40.

[9] Dion Cassius, LXXV, 6.

[10] Philip de Comines, a noted French historian and statesman.

[11] Charles the Bold, Duke of Burgundy.

[12] Becoming an advocate.

[13] Plutarch, Lives, I, 315.

[14] Heraclitus, a celebrated Greek philosopher.

[15] James, I:23.

[16] Personal, private.

[17] Suits.

Chapter 14

Benedict de Spinoza, *Ethics*

Benedict de Spinoza (1632-1677) was an unorthodox Jewish philosopher and rationalist metaphysician. Born in Amsterdam to Portuguese Jewish parents who had emigrated to escape religious persecution, Spinoza was first trained to be a rabbi, receiving education not only in the traditional Hebrew and Arabic literature, but also in Latin. Under the tutorship of Van Den Ende, a German of independent views, he was introduced to the philosophy of Descartes and unorthodox religious ideas. When his own views were later discovered by the Dutch Jewish establishment to have developed in a heretical, pantheistic direction, Spinoza was formally excommunicated and expelled from the Amsterdam synagogue in 1656.

Changing his given name from the Hebrew "Baruch" to the Latin equivalent, "Benedict," Spinoza left Amsterdam and took up lodging, first, with a Mennonite family, then a widow, and later an artist's family, in various parts of Holland. Earning his living by grinding and polishing lenses, he devoted his leisure to discussing philosophical questions with a few loyal friends, both in conversation and in correspondence. The German philosopher Leibniz was among the many notable figures of his time with whom he had personal contact. Despite his maverick status, Spinoza was offered a chair at Heidelberg in 1673, which he nevertheless refused, because of his fear that it would cost him his independence and lead to more controversy. He died four years later after a running bout with tuberculosis, aggravated by dust from his lens grinding.

Spinoza published only two books during his lifetime, the expositional **Principles of Cartesian Philosophy** *(1663) and the* *anonymously published* **Theologico-Political Treatise** *(1670), whose radical religious and political views raised a storm of controversy when it appeared. Because of the inflammatory effect of his unorthodox ideas, the remainder of his writings were not published until after his death. These included his* **Ethics, Political Treatise, Hebrew Grammar,** *and* **Correspondence.**

Spinoza's philosophy involved a form of pantheism and determinism in which all things were regarded as cohering and residing "in God" in such a way that all events come to pass strictly as a necessary consequence of his essence or nature. Since "God" was thus equated with the Nature or the Universe as a whole, Spinoza naturally rejected the belief that God transcends the universe or performs acts of providence or miraculous intervention in the universe as a free and independent personal agent.

Likewise, in his **Ethics,** *he rejected as illusory the conventional ethical assumptions about human freedom and responsibility, the imputation of praise and blame, "good" and "evil." What people call "good" and "evil," he held, is simply what gives them pleasure or pain; but these predicates express characteristics of those who use them, not of the objects about which they are used. The illusion that such predicates express "objective" properties is reinforced by the conventional assumption that people are free agents and that things could be other than they are. But to suppose this is to fail to see that everything occurs necessarily. It is to introduce an element of contingency and imperfection into the universe, which, for Spinoza, is clearly impossible, because the universe is God, and God is necessarily perfect. It is to see oneself at the mercy of the whims of fate, to be in bondage to irrational emotions that becloud the mind and cause unhappiness.*

What is needed to free the mind from this bondage, according to Spinoza, is to seek understanding of the true causes of things, to rise above the limited perspective of one's individuality and learn to view all things "under the aspect of eternity." Happiness is attained only when one learns that every event has a proper, fixed, and necessary place in the perfect order of the universe. And this is achieved by the striving **(conatus)** *for self-preservation, which, in human beings, is directed towards rational perfection and the intellectual love of God.*

Our selection is taken from the **Ethics,** *Propositions XXVII through LIX. This work, which is organized systematically into definitions, axioms, and propositions with their corresponding proofs, corollaries, and explanatory notes, and whose full title includes the words*

Demonstrated in Geometrical Order, *testifies to the influence of Descartes and his conviction that philosophy should emulate the rigorous methods of mathematics.*

The Ethics

PROP. XXXIII. *When we love a thing similar to ourselves we endeavour, as far as we can, to bring about that it should love us in return.*

Proof.—That which we love we endeavour, as far as we can, to conceive in preference to anything else. If the thing be similar to ourselves, we shall endeavour to affect it pleasurably in preference to anything else. In other words, we shall endeavour, as far as we can, to bring it about, that the thing should be affected with pleasure accompanied by the idea of ourselves, that is, that it should love us in return. *Q.E.D.*

PROP. XXXIV. *The greater the emotion with which we conceive a loved object to be affected towards us, the greater will be our complacency.*

Proof.—We endeavour, as far as we can, to bring about, that what we love should love us in return: in other words, that what we love should be affected with pleasure accompanied by the idea of ourself as cause. Therefore, in proportion as the loved object is more pleasurably affected because of us, our endeavour will be assisted—that is, the greater will be our pleasure. But when we take pleasure in the fact, that we pleasurably affect something similar to ourselves, we regard ourselves with pleasure; therefore the greater the emotion with which we conceive a loved object to be affected, &c. *Q.E.D.*

PROP. XXXV. *If anyone conceives, that an object of his love joins itself to another with closer bonds of friendship than he himself has attained to, he will be affected with hatred towards the loved object and with envy towards his rival.*

Proof.—In proportion as a man thinks, that a loved object is well affected towards him, will be the strength of his self-approval, that is, of his pleasure; he will, therefore, endeavour, as far as he can, to imagine the loved object as most closely bound to him; this endeavour or desire will be increased, if he thinks that someone else has a similar desire. But this endeavour or desire is assumed to be checked by the image of the loved object in conjunction with the image of him whom the loved object has joined to itself; therefore he will for that reason be affected with pain, accompanied by the idea of the loved object as a cause in conjunction with the image of his rival; that is, he will be affected with hatred towards the loved object and also towards his rival, which latter he will envy as enjoying the beloved object. *Q.E.D.*

Note.—This hatred towards an object of love joined with envy is called *Jealousy,* which accordingly is nothing else but a wavering of the disposition arising from combined love and hatred, accompanied by the idea of some rival who is envied. Further, this hatred towards the object of love will be greater, in proportion to the pleasure which the jealous man had been wont to derive from the reciprocated love of the said object; and also in proportion to the feelings he had previously entertained towards his rival. If he had hated him, he will forthwith hate the object of his love, because he conceives it is pleasurably affected by one whom he himself hates: and also because he is compelled to associate the image of his loved one with the image of him whom he hates. This condition generally comes into play in the case of love for a woman: for he who thinks, that a woman whom he loves prostitutes herself to another, will feel pain, not only because his own desire is restrained, but also because, being compelled to associate the image of her he loves with the parts of shame and the excreta of another, he therefore shrinks from her. . . .

PROP. XLII. *He who has conferred a benefit on anyone from motives of love or honour will feel pain, if he sees that the benefit is received without gratitude.*

Proof.—When a man loves something similar to himself, he endeavours, as far as he can, to bring it about that he should be loved thereby in return. Therefore he who has conferred a benefit confers it in obedience to the desire, which he feels of being loved in return; that is from the hope of honour or pleasure; hence he will endeavour, as far as he can, to conceive this cause of honour, or to regard it as actually existing. But, by the hypothesis, he conceives something else, which excludes the existence of the said cause of honour: wherefore he will thereat feel pain. *Q.E.D.*

PROP. XLIII. *Hatred is increased by being reciprocated, and can on the other hand be destroyed by love.*

Proof.—He who conceives, that an object of his hate hates him in return, will thereupon feel a new hatred, while the former hatred (by hypothesis) still remains. But if, on the other hand, he conceives that the object of hate loves him, he will to this extent regard himself with pleasure, and will endeavour to please the cause of his emotion. In other words, he will endeavour not to hate him, and not to affect him painfully; this endeavour will be greater or less in proportion to the emotion from which it arises. Therefore, if it be greater than that which arises from hatred, and through which the man endeavours to affect painfully the thing which he hates, it will get the better of it and banish the hatred from his mind. *Q.E.D.*

PROP. XLIV. *Hatred which is completely vanquished by love passes into love: and love is thereupon greater than if hatred had not preceded it.*

Proof.—The proof proceeds in the same way as Prop. xxxviii. of this Part: for he who begins to love a thing, which he was wont to hate or regard with pain, from the very fact of loving feels pleasure. To this pleasure involved in love is added the pleasure arising from aid given to the endeavour to remove the pain involved in hatred, accompanied by the idea of the former object of hatred as cause.

Note.—Though this be so, no one will endeavour to hate anything, or to be affected with pain, for the sake of enjoying this greater pleasure; that is, no one will desire that he should be injured, in the hope of recovering from the injury, nor long to be ill for the sake of getting well. For everyone will always endeavour to persist in his being, and to ward off pain as far as he can. If the contrary is conceivable, namely, that a man should desire to hate someone, in order that he might love him the more thereafter, he will always desire to hate him. For the strength of the love is in proportion to the strength of the hatred, wherefore the man would desire, that the hatred be continually increased more and more, and, for a similar reason, he would desire to become more and more ill, in order that he might take a greater pleasure in being restored to health: in such a case he would always endeavour to be ill, which is absurd.

PROP. XLV. *If a man conceives, that anyone similar to himself hates anything also similar to himself, which he loves, he will hate that person.*

Proof.—The beloved object feels reciprocal hatred towards him who hates it; therefore, the lover, in conceiving that anyone hates the beloved object, conceives the beloved thing as affected by hatred, in other words, by pain; consequently he is himself affected by pain accompanied by the idea of the hater of the beloved thing as cause; that is, he will hate him who hates anything which he himself loves. *Q.E.D.*

PROP. XLVI. *If a man has been affected pleasurably or painfully by anyone, of a class or nation different from his own, and if the pleasure or pain has been accompanied by the idea of the said stranger as cause, under the general category of the class or nation: the man will feel love or hatred, not only to the individual stranger, but also to the whole class or nation whereto he belongs. . . .*

PROP. XLVII. *Joy arising from the fact, that anything we hate is destroyed, or suffers other injury, is never unaccompanied by a certain pain in us.*

Proof.—This is evident from III. xxvii. For in so far as we conceive a thing similar to ourselves to be affected with pain, we ourselves feel pain.

Note. . . . Whenever we remember anything, even if it does not actually exist, we regard it only as present, and the body is affected in the same manner; wherefore, in so far as the remembrance of the thing is strong, a man is determined to regard it with pain; this determination, while the image of the thing in question lasts, is indeed checked by the remembrance of other things excluding the existence of the aforesaid thing, but is not destroyed: hence, a man only feels pleasure in so far as the said determination is checked: for this reason the joy arising from the injury done to what we hate is repeated, every time we remember that object of hatred. For, as we have said, when the image of the thing in question is aroused, inasmuch as it involves the thing's existence, it determines the man to regard the thing with the same pain as he was wont to do, when it actually did exist. However, since he has joined to the image of the thing other images, which exclude its existence, this determination to pain is forthwith checked, and the man rejoices afresh as often as the repetition takes place. This is the cause of men's pleasure in recalling past evils, and delight in narrating dangers from which they have escaped. For when men conceive a danger, they conceive it as still future, and are determined to fear it; this determination is checked afresh by the idea of freedom, which became associated with the idea of the danger when they escaped therefrom: this renders them secure afresh: therefore they rejoice afresh. . . .

PROP. LVI. *There are as many kinds of pleasure, of pain, of desire, and of every emotion compounded of these, such as vacillations of spirit, or derived from these, such as love, hatred, hope, fear, &c., as there are kinds of objects whereby we are affected.*

Proof.—Pleasure and pain, and consequently the emotions compounded thereof, or derived therefrom, are passions, or passive states; now we are necessarily passive, in so far as we have inadequate ideas; and only in so far as we have such ideas are we passive; that is, we are only necessarily passive, in so far as we conceive, or in so far as we are affected by an emotion, which involves the nature of our own body, and the nature of an external body. Wherefore the nature of every passive state must necessarily be so explained, that the nature of the object whereby we are affected be expressed. Namely, the pleasure, which arises from, say, the object A, involves the nature of that object A, and the pleasure, which arises from the object B, involves the nature of the object B; wherefore these two pleasurable emotions are by nature different, inasmuch as the causes whence they arise are by nature different. So again the emotion of pain, which arises from one object, is by nature different from the pain arising from another object, and, similarly, in the case of love, hatred, hope, fear, vacillation, &c.

Thus, there are necessarily as many kinds of pleasure, pain, love, hatred, &c., as there are kinds of objects whereby we are affected. Now desire is each man's essence or nature, in so far as it is conceived as determined to a particular action by any given modification of itself; therefore, according as a man is affected through external causes by this or that kind of pleasure, pain, love, hatred, &c., in other words, according as his nature is disposed in this or that manner, so will his desire be of one kind or another, and the nature of one desire must necessarily differ from the nature of another desire, as widely as the emotions differ, wherefrom each desire arose. Thus there are as many kinds of desire, as there are kinds of pleasure, pain, love, &c., consequently (by what has been shown) there are as many kinds of desire, as there are kinds of objects whereby we are affected. *Q.E.D.*

Note.—Among the kinds of emotions, which, by the last proposition, must be very numerous, the chief are *luxury, drunkenness, lust, avarice,* and *ambition,* being merely species of love or desire, displaying the nature of those emotions in a manner varying according to the object, with which they are concerned. For by luxury, drunkenness, lust, avarice, ambition, &c., we simply mean the immoderate love of feasting, drinking, venery, riches, and fame. Furthermore, these emotions, in so far as we distinguish them from others merely by the objects wherewith they are concerned, have no contraries. For *temperance, sobriety,* and *chastity,* which we are wont to oppose to luxury, drunkenness, and lust, are not emotions or passive states, but indicate a power of the mind which moderates the last-named emotions. However, I cannot here explain the remaining kinds of emotions (seeing that they are as numerous as the kinds of objects), nor, if I could, would it be necessary. It is sufficient for our purpose, namely, to determine the strength of the emotions, and the mind's power over them, to have a general definition of each emotion. It is sufficient, I repeat, to understand the general properties of the emotions and the mind, to enable us to determine the quality and extent of the mind's power in moderating and checking the emotions. Thus, though there is a great difference between various emotions of love, hatred, or desire, for instance between love felt towards children, and love felt towards a wife, there is no need for us to take cognizance of such differences, or to track out further the nature and origin of the emotions.

PROP. LVII. *Any emotion of a given individual differs from the emotion of another individual, only in so far as the essence of the one individual differs from the essence of the other.*

Proof.—This proposition is evident from Ax. i. (which see after Lemma iii. Prop. xiii. Part ii). Nevertheless, we will prove it from the nature of the three primary emotions.

All emotions are attributable to desire, pleasure, or pain, as their definitions above given show. But desire is each man's nature or essence; therefore desire in one individual differs from desire in another individual, only in so far as the nature or essence of the one differs from the nature or essence of the other. Again, pleasure and pain are passive states or passions, whereby every man's power or endeavour to persist in his being is increased or diminished, helped or hindered. But by the endeavour to persist in its being, in so far as it is attributable to mind and body in conjunction, we mean appetite and desire; therefore pleasure and pain are identical with desire or appetite, in so far as by external causes they are increased or diminished, helped or hindered, in other words, they are every man's nature; wherefore the pleasure and pain felt by one man differ from the pleasure and pain felt by another man, only in so far as the nature or essence of the one man differs from the essence of the other; consequently, any emotion of one individual only differs, &c. *Q.E.D.*

Note.—Hence it follows, that the emotions of the animals which are called irrational (for after learning the origin of mind we cannot doubt that brutes feel) only differ from man's emotions, to the extent that brute nature differs from human nature. Horse and man are alike carried away by the desire of procreation; but the desire of the former is equine, the desire of the latter is human. So also the lusts and appetites of insects, fishes, and birds must needs vary according to the several natures. Thus, although each individual lives content and rejoices in that nature belonging to him wherein he has his being, yet the life, wherein each is content and rejoices, is nothing else but the idea, or soul, of the said individual, and hence the joy of one only differs in nature from the joy of another, to the extent that the essence of one differs from the essence of another. Lastly, it follows from the foregoing proposition, that there is no small difference between the joy which actuates, say, a drunkard, and the joy possessed by a philosopher, as I just mention here by the way. Thus far I have treated of the emotions attributable to man, in so far as he is passive. It remains to add a few words on those attributable to him in so far as he is active.

PROP. LVIII. *Besides pleasure and desire, which are passivities or passions, there are other emotions derived from pleasure and desire, which are attributable to us in so far as we are active.*

Proof.—When the mind conceives itself and its power of activity, it feels pleasure: now the mind necessarily contemplates itself, when it conceives a true or adequate idea. But the mind does conceive certain adequate ideas. Therefore, it feels pleasure in so far as it conceives adequate ideas; that is, in so far as it is active. Again, the mind, both in so far as it has clear and distinct ideas, and in so far as it has confused ideas, endeavours to persist in its own being; but by such an endeavour we mean desire; therefore, desire is also attributable to us, in so far as we understand, or in so far as we are active. *Q.E.D.*

PROP. LIX. *Among all the emotions attributable to the mind as active, there are none which cannot be referred to pleasure or pain.*

Proof.—All emotions can be referred to desire, pleasure, or pain, as their definitions, already given, show. Now by pain we mean that the mind's power of thinking is diminished or checked; therefore, in so far as the mind feels pain, its power of understanding, that is, of activity, is diminished or checked; therefore, no painful emotions can be attributed to the mind in virtue of its being active, but only emotions of pleasure and desire, which are attributable to the mind in that condition. *Q.E.D.*

Note.—All actions following from emotion, which are attributable to the mind in virtue of its understanding, I set down to *strength of character (fortitudo),* which I divide into *courage (animositas)* and *highmindedness (generositas).* By *courage* I mean *the desire whereby every man strives to preserve his own being in accordance solely with the dictates of reason.* By *highmindedness* I mean *the desire whereby every man endeavours, solely under the dictates of reason, to aid other men and to unite them to himself in friendship.* Those actions, therefore, which have regard solely to the good of the agent I set down to courage, those which aim at the good of others I set down to highmindedness. Thus temperance, sobriety, and presence of mind in danger, &c., are varieties of courage; courtesy, mercy, &c., are varieties of highmindedness.

I think I have thus explained, and displayed through their primary causes the principal emotions and vacillations of spirit, which arise from the combination of the three primary emotions, to wit, desire, pleasure, and pain. It is evident from what I have said, that we are in many ways driven about by external causes, and that like waves of the sea driven by contrary winds we toss to and fro unwitting of the issue and of our fate. But I have said, that I have only set forth the chief conflicting emotions, not all that might be given. For, by proceeding in the same way as above, we can easily show that love is united to repentance, scorn, shame, &c. I think everyone will agree from what has been said, that the emotions may be compounded one with another in so many ways, and so many variations may arise therefrom, as to exceed all possibility of computation. However, for my purpose, it is enough to have enumerated the most important; to reckon up the rest which I have omitted would be more curious than profitable. It remains to remark concerning love, that it very often happens that while we are enjoying a thing which we longed for, the body, from the act of enjoyment, acquires a new disposition, whereby it is determined in another way, other images of things are aroused in it, and the mind begins to conceive and desire something fresh. For example, when we conceive something which generally delights us with its flavour, we desire to enjoy, that is, to eat it. But whilst we are thus enjoying it, the stomach is filled and the body is thus otherwise disposed. If, therefore, when the body is thus otherwise disposed, the image of the food which is present be stimulated, and consequently the endeavour or desire to eat it be stimulated also, the new disposition of the body will feel repugnance to the desire or attempt, and consequently the presence of the food which we formerly longed for will become odious. This revulsion of feeling is called *satiety* or weariness. For the rest, I have neglected the outward modifications of the body observable in emotions, such, for instance, as trembling, pallor, sobbing, laughter, &c., for these are attributable to the body only, without any reference to the mind. Lastly, the definitions of the emotions require to be supplemented in a few points; I will therefore repeat them, interpolating such observations as I think should here and there be added.

Chapter 15

Thomas Hobbes, *The Citizen*

Thomas Hobbes (1588-1679), sometimes called the father of modern analytic philosophy, was born prematurely in Malmesbury, Wiltshire, England, when his mother heard of the approach of the Spanish Armada. "Fear and I were born twins," he would later say, adding humor to his conviction that fear of death and the desire for security are the psychological basis both for worldly prudence and civil society itself.

*Hobbes was raised by his uncle after his father, vicar of Westport, was involved in a brawl outside his own church and had to flee to London. His uncle, who took the matter of his education very seriously, sent Hobbes to Magdalen Hall, Oxford, when he was only 14. Hobbes was impressed equally by the strong Puritan tradition of the college and the prevalence there of drunkenness, gaming and other vices. After graduating from Oxford, he managed to become tutor to the young son of William Cavendish, earl of Devonshire, which circumstance introduced him to influential people, a first-rate library, and foreign travel. During the course of his life, he met Francis Bacon, made a pilgrimage to Italy to visit Galileo, debated Descartes, and counted Gassendi among his firmest friends. He fled England during the civil war there, which left an indelible impression on him, and briefly tutored the future Charles II in exile in France. Ceaselessly active, he played tennis until he was 75, wrote his autobiography in Latin verse at 84, published a translation of the **Iliad** and **Odyssey** at 86, and died at the age of 91 after a life of travel, study, controversy, and philosophical and literary activity that established him as a virtual English institution.*

Hobbes is primarily famous for his political philosophy, mainly because of his masterpiece **Leviathan.** *But just as* **Leviathan** *itself is far more than a mere political treatise, being also a treatise on psychology, ethics, theology and a self-contained critique of traditional metaphysics, so too, by implication, it is clear that Hobbes was much more than just a political philosopher. This atomist of a sort, a kind of new Democritus, was also a translator and accomplished physicist.*

Hobbes is usually regarded as famous, or infamous, for his rather cynical view of human nature. The selection below bears out this usual opinion to a considerable degree. Below, one will find a selection from **De Cive** *or* **On the Citizen,** *something of a simplified version of parts of the "political" (in the broad sense of the word) philosophy which Hobbes expounds in greater detail in* **Leviathan.**

At bottom, Hobbes contends, man, "prior" to his contractual relations of all kinds in civil society, is in a "state of nature," a state of natural law devoid of "civil" law. This state of nature constitutes a war of "every man against every man" where the first natural "law" is merely that of the promotion of self-preservation. Some scholars believe that Hobbes' somewhat unpleasant view of human nature stemmed from his observations of the protracted civil war in England during his time.

In such a "state of nature," wherein every human has a natural right even unto the very person of another, it would seem to go without saying that there could be no such thing as friendship in any sense. It would seem, indeed, that the only way in which to arise out of that state of nature is by agreeing implicitly to a "social contract," thanks to which, in this establishment of civil society, one does not have to be plummeted back into a state of nature. Hobbes therefore seems to suggest that all friendships are but mere friendships of utility or "market-friendships" at bottom, though it ;may be seen here and there that Hobbes might allow for the emergence of a few inherently good individuals.

Without qualification, taking **Leviathan** *as the reader's guide, it can be said that the greater part of Hobbes' overall work mounts a comprehensive attack on the Aristotelian and Scholastic world-views (St. Thomas, et. al.). The reader may keep this fact in mind when reading the following selections.*

Philosophical Elements of a True Citizen

Of the State of Men without Civil Society

1. The faculties of human nature may be reduced unto four kinds: bodily strength, experience, reason, passion. Taking the beginning of this following doctrine from these, we will declare, in the first place, what manner of inclinations men who are endued with these faculties bear towards each other, and whether, and by what faculty they are born apt for society, and to preserve themselves against mutual violence; then proceeding, we will show what advice was necessary to be taken for this business, and what are the conditions of society, or of human peace; that is to say (changing the words only), what are the fundamental *laws of nature.*

2. The greatest part of those men who have written aught concerning commonwealths, either suppose, or require us or beg of us to believe, that man is a creature born fit[1] for society. The Greeks call him ζωον πολιτικον, and on this foundation they so build up the doctrine of civil society, as if for the preservation of peace, and the government of mankind, there were nothing else necessary than that men should agree to make certain covenants and conditions together, which themselves should then call laws. Which axiom, though received by most, is yet certainly false; and an error proceeding from our too slight contemplation of human nature. For they who shall more narrowly look into the causes for which men come together, and delight in each other's company, shall easily find that this happens not because naturally it could happen no otherwise, but by accident. For if by nature one man should love another, that is, as man, there could no reason be returned why every man should not equally love every man, as being equally man; or why he should rather frequent those, whose society affords him honour or profit. We do not therefore by nature seek society for its own sake, but that we may receive some honour or profit from it; these we desire primarily, that secondarily. How, by what advice, men do meet, will be best known by observing those things which they do when they are met. For if they meet for traffic, it is plain every man regards not his fellow, but his business; if to discharge some office, a certain market-friendship is begotten, which hath more of jealousy in it than true love, and whence factions sometimes may arise, but good will never; if for pleasure and recreation of mind, every man is wont to please himself most with those things which stir up laughter, whence he may, according to the nature of that

which is ridiculous, by comparison of another man's defects and infirmities, pass the more current in his own opinion. And although this be sometimes innocent and without offense, yet it is manifest they are not so much delighted with the society, as their own vain glory. But for the most part, in these kind of meetings we wound the absent; their whole life, sayings, actions are examined, judged, condemned. Nay, it is very rare but some present receive a fling as soon as they part; so as his reason was not ill, who was wont always at parting to go out last. And these are indeed the true delights of society, unto which we are carried by nature, that is, by those passions which are incident to all creatures, until either by sad experience or good precepts it so fall out, which in many never happens, that the appetite of present matters be dulled with the memory of things past: without which the discourse of most quick and nimble men on this subject, is but cold and hungry.

But if it so happen, that being met they pass their time in relating some stories, and one of them begins to tell one which concerns himself; instantly every one of the rest most greedily desires to speak of himself too; if one relate some wonder, the rest will tell you miracles, if they have them; if not, they will feign them. Lastly, that I may say somewhat of them who pretend to be wiser than others: if they meet to talk of philosophy, look, how many men, so many would be esteemed masters, or else they not only love not their fellows, but even persecute them with hatred. So clear is it by experience to all men who a little more narrowly consider human affairs, that all free congress ariseth either from mutual poverty, or from vain glory, whence the parties met endeavour to carry with them either some benefit, or to leave behind them that same ευδοκιμειν, some esteem and honour with those, with whom they have been conversant. The same is also collected by reason out of the definitions themselves of *will, good, honour, profitable*. For when we voluntarily contract society, in all manner of society we look after the object of the will, that is, that which every one of those who gather together, propounds to himself for good. Now whatsoever seems good, is pleasant, and relates either to the senses, or the mind. But all the mind's pleasure is either glory, (or to have a good opinion of one's self), or refers to glory in the end; the rest are sensual, or conducting to sensuality, which may be all comprehended under the word *conveniences*. All society therefore is either for gain, or for glory; that is, not so much for love of our fellows, as for the love of ourselves. But no society can be great or lasting, which begins from vain glory. Because that glory is like honour; if all men have it no man hath it, for they consist in comparison and precellence. Neither doth the society of others advance any whit the cause of my glorying in myself; for every man must account himself, such as he can make himself without the help of others. But though the benefits of this life may be much furthered by mutual help; since yet those may be better attained to by dominion than by the society of others, I hope no body will doubt, but that men would much more greedily be carried by nature, if all fear were removed, to obtain dominion, than to gain society. We must therefore resolve, that the original of all great and lasting societies consisted not in the mutual good will men had towards each other, but in the mutual fear[2] they had of each other.

3. The cause of mutual fear consists partly in the natural equality of men, partly in their mutual will of hurting: whence it comes to pass, that we can neither expect from others, nor promise to ourselves the least security. For if we look on men full grown, and consider how brittle the frame of our human body is, which perishing, all its strength, vigour, and wisdom itself perisheth with it; and how easy a matter it is, even for the weakest man to kill the strongest: There is no reason why any man, trusting to his own strength, should conceive himself made by nature above others. They are equals, who can do equal things one against the other; but they who can do the greatest things, namely, kill, can do equal things. All men therefore among themselves are by nature equal; the inequality we now discern, hath its spring from the civil law.

4. All men in the state of nature have a desire and will to hurt, but not proceeding from the same cause, neither equally to be condemned. For one man, according to that natural equality which is among us, permits as much to others as he assumes to himself; which is an argument of a temperate man, and one that rightly values his power. Another, supposing himself above others, will have a license to do what he lists, and challenges respect and honour, as due to him before others; which is an argument of a fiery spirit. This man's will to hurt ariseth from vain glory, and the false esteem he hath of his own strength; the other's from the necessity of defending himself, his liberty, and his goods, against this man's violence.

5. Furthermore, since the combat of wits is the fiercest, the greatest discords which are, must necessarily arise from this contention. For in this case it is not only odious to contend against, but also not to consent. For not to approve of what a man saith, is no less than tacitly to accuse him of an error in that thing which he speaketh: as in very many things to dissent, is as much as if you accounted him a fool whom you dissent from. Which may appear hence, that there are no wars so sharply waged as between sects of the same religion, and factions of the

same commonweal, where the contestation is either concerning doctrines or politic prudence. And since all the pleasure and jollity of the mind consists in this, even to get some, with whom comparing, it may find somewhat wherein to triumph and vaunt itself; it is impossible but men must declare sometimes some mutual scorn and contempt, either by laughter, or by words, or by gesture, or some sign or other; than which there is no greater vexation of mind, and than from which there cannot possibly arise a greater desire to do hurt.

6. But the most frequent reason why men desire to hurt each other, ariseth hence, that many men at the same time have an appetite to the same thing; which yet very often they can neither enjoy in common, nor yet divide it; whence it follows that the strongest must have it, and who is strongest must be decided by the sword.

7. Among so many dangers therefore, as the natural lusts of men do daily threaten each other withal, to have a care of one's self is not a matter so scornfully to be looked upon, as if so be there had not been a power and will left in one to have done otherwise. For every man is desirous of what is good for him, and shuns what is evil, but chiefly the chiefest of natural evils, which is death; and this he doth by a certain impulsion of nature, no less than that whereby a stone moves downward. It is therefore neither absurd nor reprehensible, neither against the dictates of true reason, for a man to use all his endeavours to preserve and defend his body and the members thereof from death and sorrows. But that which is not contrary to right reason, that all men account to be done justly, and with right. Neither by the word *right* is anything else signified, than that liberty which every man hath to make use of his natural faculties according to right reason. Therefore the first foundation of natural right is this, that *every man as much as in him lies endeavour to protect his life and members.*

8. But because it is in vain for a man to have a right to the end, if the right to the necessary means be denied him, it follows, that since every man hath a right to preserve himself, he must also be allowed a right *to use all the means, and do all the actions, without which he cannot preserve himself.*

9. Now whether the means which he is about to use, and the action he is performing, be necessary to the preservation of his life and members or not, he himself, by the right of nature, must be judge. For say, another man judge that it is contrary to right reason that I should judge of mine own peril. Why now, because he judgeth of what concerns me, by the same reason, because we are equal by nature, will I judge also of things which do belong to him. Therefore it agrees with

right reason, that is, it is the right of nature that I judge of his opinion, that is, whether it conduce to my preservation or not.

10. Nature hath given to *every one a right to all;* that is, it was lawful for every man, in the bare state of nature[3] or before such time as men had engaged themselves by any covenants or bonds, to do what he would, and against whom he thought fit, and to possess, use, and enjoy all what he would, or could get. Now because whatsoever a man would, it therefore seems good to him because he wills it, and either it really doth, or at least seems to him to contribute towards his preservation (but we have already allowed him to be judge, in the foregoing article, whether it doth or not, insomuch as we are to hold all for necessary whatsoever he shall esteem so), and by the 7th article it appears that by the right of nature those things may be done, and must be had, which necessarily conduce to the protection of life and members, it follows, that in the state of nature, to have all, and do all, is lawful for all. And this is that which is meant by that common saying, *nature hath given all to all.* From whence we understand likewise, that in the state of nature profit is the measure of right.

11. But it was the least benefit for men thus to have a common right to all things. For the effects of this right are the same, almost, as if there had been no right at all. For although any man might say of every thing, *this is mine*, yet could he not enjoy it, by reason of his neighbour, who having equal right and equal power, would pretend the same thing to be his.

12. If now to this natural proclivity of men, to hurt each other, which they derive from their passions, but chiefly from a vain esteem of themselves, you add, the right of all to all, wherewith one by right invades, the other by right resists, and whence arise perpetual jealousies and suspicions on all hands, and how hard a thing it is to provide against an enemy invading us with an intention to oppress and ruin, though he come with a small number, and no great provision; it cannot be denied but that the natural state of men, before they entered into society, was a mere war, and that not simply, but a war of all men against all men. For what is WAR, but that same time in which the will of contesting by force is fully declared, either by words or deeds? The time remaining is termed PEACE.

13. But it is easily judged how disagreeable a thing to the preservation either of mankind, or of each single man, a perpetual war is. But it is perpetual in its own nature; because in regard of the equality of those that strive, it cannot be ended by victory. For in this state the conqueror is subject to so much danger, as it were to be

accounted a miracle, if any, even the most strong, should close up his life with many years and old age. They of America are examples hereof, even in this present age: other nations have been in former ages; which now indeed are become civil and flourishing, but were then few, fierce, short-lived, poor, nasty, and deprived of all that pleasure and beauty of life, which peace and society are wont to bring with them. Whosoever therefore holds, that it had been best to have continued in that state in which all things were lawful for all men, he contradicts himself. For every man by natural necessity desires that which is good for him; nor is there any that esteems a war of all against all, which necessarily adheres to such a state, to be good for him. And so it happens, that through fear of each other we think it fit to rid ourselves of this condition, and to get some fellows; that if there needs must be war, it may not yet be against all men, nor without some helps.

Notes

[1] [*Note by Hobbes*] Since we now see actually a constituted society among men, and none living out of it, since we discern all desirous of congress and mutual correspondence, it may seem a wonderful kind of stupidity, to lay in the very threshold of this doctrine such a stumbling block before the reader, as to deny *man to be born fit for society.* Therefore I must more plainly say, that it is true indeed, that to man by nature, or as man, that is, as soon as he is born, solitude is an enemy; for infants have need of others to help them to live, and those of riper years to help them to live well Wherefore I deny not that men (even nature compelling) desire to come together. But civil societies are not mere meetings, but bonds, to the making whereof faith and compacts are necessary; the virtue whereof to children and fools, and the profit whereof to those who have not yet tasted the miseries which accompany its defects, is altogether unknown; whence it happens, that those, because they know not what society is, cannot enter into it; these, because ignorant of the benefit it brings, care not for it. Manifest therefore it is, that all men, because they are born in infancy, are born unapt for society. Many also, perhaps most men, either through defect of mind or want of education, remain unfit during the whole course of their lives; yet have they, infants as well as those of riper years, a human nature. Wherefore man is made fit for society not by nature, but by education. Furthermore, although man were born in such a condition as to desire it, it follows not, that he therefore were born fit to enter into it. For it is one thing to desire, another to be in capacity fit for what we desire; for even they, who through their pride, will not stoop to equal conditions, without which there can be no society, do yet desire it.

[2] It is objected: it is so improbable that men should grow into civil societies out of fear, that if they had been afraid, they would not have endured each

other's looks. They presume, I believe, that to fear is nothing else than to be affrighted. I comprehend in this word *fear*, a certain foresight of future evil; neither do I conceive flight the sole property of fear, but to distrust, suspect, take heed, provide so that they may not fear, is also incident to the fearful. They who go to sleep, shut their doors; they who travel, carry their swords with them, because they fear thieves. Kingdoms guard their coasts and frontiers with forts and castles; cities are compact with walls; and all for fear of neighbouring kingdoms and towns. Even the strongest armies, and most accomplished for fight, yet sometimes parley for peace, as fearing each other's power, and lest they might be overcome. It is through fear that men secure themselves by flight indeed, and in corners, if they think they cannot escape otherwise; but for the most part, by arms and defensive weapons; whence it happens, that daring to come forth they know each other's spirits. But then if they fight, civil society ariseth from the victory; if they agree, from their agreement. [*Note by Hobbes*]

[3] This is thus to be understood: what any man does in the bare state of nature, is injurious to no man; not that in such a state he cannot offend God, or break the laws of nature; for injustice against men presupposeth human laws, such as in the state of nature there are none. Now the truth of this proposition thus conceived, is sufficiently demonstrated to the mindful reader in the articles immediately foregoing; but because in certain cases the difficulty of the conclusion makes us forget the premises, I will contract this argument, and make it most evident to a single view. Every man hath right to protect himself, as appears by the seventh article. The same man therefore hath a right to use all the means which necessarily conduce to this end, by the eighth article. But those are the necessary means which he shall judge to be such, by the ninth article. He therefore hath a right to make use of, and to do all whatsoever he shall judge requisite for his preservation; wherefore by the judgement of him that doth it, the thing done is either right or wrong, and therefore right. True it is therefore in the bare state of nature, &c. But if any man pretend somewhat to tend necessarily to his preservation, which yet he himself doth not confidently believe so, he may offend against the laws of nature, as in the third chapter of this book is more at large declared. It hath been objected by some: if a son kill his father, doth he him no injury? I have answered, that a son cannot be understood to be at any time in the state of nature, as being under the power and command of them to whom he owes his protection as soon as ever he is born, namely, either his father's or his mother's, or his that nourished him; as is demonstrated in the ninth chapter. [*Note by Hobbes*]

Chapter 16

Nicolas Malebranche, *The Search After Truth*

Nicolas Malebranche (1638-1715) is usually considered a bearer of the principles of the philosophy of Descartes. Indeed, one could say that philosophically Malebranche followed Descartes almost to the detail of his mathematics, natural science, and distinction between soul and body, while theologically he was Augustinian through and through.

Malebranche's first and major work was **De la recherche de la verite** *or* **The Search After Truth,** *from which we find his general accounts on a variety of topics such as matter as extension, the ontological argument for the existence of God, the infallibility of thought proper as distinct from the inevitable confusion of the senses and so forth, almost always expressed in accordance with the epistemological and physical precepts of Descartes. However, Malebranche's presentation of these matters is imbued with rather ingenious arguments expressed more systematically than were several of Descartes' own 'first' arguments on so many of these topics which heralded the beginning of modern Idealism.*

Perhaps the one idea emphasized by Descartes which Malebranche felt compelled to render more elaborate was his view of the utter dependence of man on God, not only for his very being but even for his very thought. This and other theological principles derived primarily from Augustine were formulated at some length in works such as his **Dialogues on Metaphysics,** *a work which became so renowned that it won for Malebranche the nickname "the French Plato."*

The remarkable thing about the following selection is how easily this discourse on friendship fits into the flow of very elaborate arguments on far more difficult topics.   The reader will be able to compare this selection with some ease to those found in Augustine and Descartes and see how their theological, moral, and scientific influences are filtered through even in a disquisition on friendship.

Search After Truth

Book Four

Chapter One

I. Minds must have inclinations as bodies have motions.   II. The only impulse God gives to minds is for Himself.   III. Minds are moved toward individual goods only through their impulse toward the good in general.   IV. The source of the principal natural inclinations, which will be the sections into which this fourth book will be divided.

I. Minds must have inclinations as bodies have motions.

There would be no need to discuss natural inclinations, as we are about to do in this fourth book, or the passions, as we shall do in the following book, in order to discover the causes of men's errors, if the understanding did not depend on the will in our perception of objects. But because it receives its direction from the will, and its attention is directed by the will toward certain objects rather than others, it is absolutely necessary that its inclinations be well understood, in order to penetrate the causes of the errors to which we are subject. . . .

II. God has no other principal end for His action than Himself, and the only impulse God gives to minds is for Himself.

It is an unquestionable truth that God can have no other principal end for His operations than Himself and that He may have many subordinate ends all of which tend toward the preservation of the beings He has created. He can have no other special end than Himself because He cannot err or place His final end in beings that do not contain every sort of good. But He can have as a subordinate end the preservation of created beings, since as they participate in His goodness, they are necessarily good and even, according to Scripture, very good: *valde bona.* [Gen. 1:31] Thus, God loves them, and it is even His love that preserves them because every being subsists only insofar as God loves it. . . .

Since the mind's natural inclinations are undoubtedly the constant impressions of the Will of Him who has created and preserves them, it seems to me that these inclinations must be exactly like those of their Creator and Preserver. By their very nature, then, they can have no other principal end than His glory, nor any secondary end than their own preservation as well as the preservation of others, though always in relation to Him who gives them being. For in short, it seems to me incontrovertible that since God cannot will that the wills He has created should love a lesser good more than a greater good, i.e., that they should love more what is less lovable than what is more lovable, He cannot create a creature without directing it toward Himself and commanding it to love Him more than all things, though He can create it free and with the power of separating itself and turning from Him. . . .

IV. The source of the principal natural inclinations that will be the section of this fourth book.

. . . We today, then, still have the same natural inclinations or the same impressions from the Author of nature that Adam had before his sin; we even have the same inclinations as the blessed in heaven, for God does not create or preserve creatures without endowing them with a love like His own. He loves Himself, He loves us, He loves all His creatures; therefore He creates no mind without inclining it to love Him, to love itself, and to love all creatures. . . .

We have then primarily an inclination for the good in general, the cause of all our natural inclinations, of all our passions, and even of all our soul's voluntary love, because this inclination for the good in general gives us the power of withholding our consent to particular goods, which do not fully satisfy it.

Secondly, we have an inclination for the preservation of our own being.

Thirdly, we all have an inclination toward other creatures useful either to us or to those whom we love. We have many other particular inclinations that depend on these, but I give this division only to provide some order. In this fourth book I intend only to relate the errors of our inclinations to three main ones: our inclination for the good in general, self-love, and love of our neighbor.

Book Four

Chapter Thirteen

I. The third natural inclination, which is our friendship for other men.
II. It inclines us to approve the thoughts of our friends and to deceive
them by false praise.

Of all our inclinations, taken in general and in the sense explained in
the first chapter, there remains only the one we have for those with
whom we live and for all the objects around us, of which I shall say but
little because this concerns morals and politics rather than our present
topic. As this inclination is always joined to the passions, it might be
more appropriate to speak of it only in the following book; but in this,
order is not of such great consequence.

I. The third natural inclination, which is our friendship
for other men.

   In order to understand the cause and the effects of this natural
inclination, we must know that God loves all His works and that He
joins them closely to one another for their mutual preservation. For,
loving the works He produces (since it is His love that produces them),
He also constantly imprints a love for His works in our hearts, because
He constantly produces in our hearts a love similar to His own. And in
order that the natural love we have for ourselves not nullify and weaken
too much that which we have for things external to us but, on the
contrary, that these two loves God has placed in us should uphold and
strengthen one another, He has joined us in such a way with everything
around us, and especially to beings of our own species, that their ills
naturally afflict us, their joy pleases us, and their grandeur, their
abasement, their decline, seem to augment or diminish our own being.
New honors for our relatives and friends, new acquisitions by those
most closely related to us, the conquests and victories of our prince, and
even the recent discoveries of the New World, seem to add something
to our substance. Being tied to all these things, we rejoice in their
grandeur and scope; we would even have this world be unbounded.
The view of certain philosophers, that the stars and vortexes are
infinite, not only seems worthy of God but appears most agreeable to
man, who feels a secret joy in being a part of the infinite, because, as

tiny as he is in himself, it seems to him that he becomes like the infinite by expanding into the infinite beings around him.

It is true that our union with all the bodies turning in these great spaces is not very close. Hence it is not perceptible to most men, and there are those who have so little interest in the discoveries made in the heavens that we might well believe they are not united to them by nature did we not also know that this is either from lack of awareness or because they are too closely tied to other things.

The soul, although united to the body that it animates, does not always sense all the movements occurring in it; or if it senses them, it does not always consider them. Since the passion agitating the soul is often greater than the sensation affecting it, the soul seems to hold more closely to the object of its passion than to its own body; for it is principally through the passions that the soul is directed outside, and feels that it is effectively linked to everything around it. In the same way, it is principally by sensation that it is directed into its body, and recognizes that it is united to all the body's components. But just as we cannot conclude that the soul of an impassioned man is not united to his body because he risks death and is not interested in the preservation of his life, so we should not imagine that we are not naturally linked to all things because there are some things for which we show no concern.

Do you wish, for example, to know whether men are linked to their prince and country? Search out those who know the interests of both, and are not absorbed in their own particular affairs, and you will see how great their ardor is for news, their anxiety over battles, their joy at victories, their sadness at defeats. You will then see clearly that men are closely linked to their prince and to their country.

Similarly, would you like to know whether men are linked to China, Japan, the planets, and the fixed stars? Then search out, or imagine to yourself, some individuals whose country and family enjoy a sound peace, who do not have any particular passions, and who do not really feel the union that attaches them to things closer to us than the heavens, and you will recognize that if they have any awareness of the grandeur and the nature of these stars, they will rejoice should any stars be discovered. They will contemplate them with pleasure; and if they are sufficiently skillful, they will willingly take the trouble to observe them and to calculate their movements.

Those involved in the press of business hardly care whether some comet appears or an eclipse occurs; but those not so closely tied to things near them make a considerable fuss over these sorts of events because, indeed, there is nothing to which we are linked, although we are not always aware of it—just as we are not always aware that our souls are united, I do not say to our arm and hand but to our heart and brain.

The strongest natural union that God has established between us and His works is that which binds us to the people with whom we live. God commanded us to love them as we love ourselves; and in order to strengthen our voluntary love of them, He constantly supports and fortifies it by a natural love He impresses in us. For this reason He has established certain invisible bonds that oblige us as if necessarily to love them, to watch over their preservation as we do our own, and to regard them as necessary parts of the whole that we together compose, and without which we could not subsist.

There is nothing more admirable than these natural relations found among the inclinations of the minds of men, among the movements of their bodies, and between these inclinations and movements. This whole hidden concatenation is a marvel that cannot be sufficiently admired and could never be understood. At the sight of some evil that surprises us, or that seems insurmountable by our own power, we let out a great cry, for example. This cry, often uttered mechanically without thinking, unfailingly reaches the ears of those close enough to give the help we need. The cry penetrates them, and is heeded by people of whatever nation or rank; for this cry belongs to all languages and all conditions, as indeed it should. It agitates the brain, instantly changes the entire bodily disposition of those struck by it, and even makes them run to help without thinking. But it is not long before it acts upon their minds and forces them to want to help and to think of ways to aid him who uttered this natural prayer, always providing that this prayer, or rather this command, is just and in accord with the rules of society. For an improper cry, uttered without cause or from an unjustified fear, produces indignation or mockery instead of compassion in those who would help because, in crying out with no reason, one abuses things established by nature for our preservation. This improper cry naturally produces aversion, and the desire to avenge the wrong done to nature, i.e., to the order of things, if he who uttered it without reason did so voluntarily. But it should produce only the passion of *scorn,* mixed with some compassion, without aversion and without a desire for vengeance, if it is fright, i.e., the false appearance of an urgent need, that caused the cry—for the fearful need *scorn* to reassure and correct them, and the weak need compassion to help them—nothing better ordained can be conceived.

I do not claim to explain by one example which mechanisms [*ressorts*] and relations the Author of nature placed in the brains of men and in all the animals to maintain the harmony and union necessary for their preservation. I merely reflect on these mechanisms so that we might carefully consider and seek them, not how they operate or how their operation is communicated by air, light, and all the tiny bodies around us (for all that is nearly incomprehensible and is not necessary here), but in order that we should at least be able to recognize their effects. Through various observations we can recognize the ties that bind us to each other, but we cannot know with any precision how this occurs. It is not difficult to see that a clock marks the hours, but it takes time to understand the reasons; and there are so many different mechanisms in the brain of the smallest animals that there is nothing like it in the most complex machines.

If it is not possible to understand perfectly the mechanisms of our machine, neither is it absolutely necessary to understand them. But in order to conduct ourselves, it is absolutely necessary to know well the effects these mechanisms are capable of producing in us. It is not necessary to know how a watch is made to use it; but if one wishes to use it to regulate one's time, it is necessary at least to know that it marks the hours. Yet there are people who are so little capable of reflection that we might almost compare them to purely inanimate machines. They do not sense the mechanisms within themselves that are released at the sight of objects; they are often agitated without perceiving their own impulses; they are slaves without being aware of their bonds. In short, they are conducted in a thousand different ways without recognizing the hand of Him who controls them. They think they are the sole authors of all the motion that they undergo and, not distinguishing what happens in them as a result of a free act of their will from what is produced in them by the impressions of bodies around them, they believe that they guide themselves when they are being guided by some other. But this is not the place to explain these things.

The relations that the Author of nature has placed among our natural inclinations in order to unite us with one another seem still more worthy of our study and inquiries than those among bodies, or among minds in relation to bodies. For they are ordered in such a way that the inclinations that seem most opposed to society are the most useful to it when they are slightly moderated.

For example, the desire all men have for grandeur tends by itself toward the dissolution of all societies. Nevertheless, this desire is tempered by the order of nature in such a way that it works to the good of the state much more than other weak and languid inclinations. For it gives rise to emulation, excites to virtue, sustains courage in the service of our country, and we would not win so many victories if soldiers and especially officers did not aspire to glory and command. Thus, all those composing armies, working only for their particular interests, nevertheless procure the good of the entire country. This demonstrates that it is most advantageous for the public good that all men have a secret desire for greatness, provided it be moderated.

But if all the individuals should seem to be what they really are, if they should say frankly to others that they want to be the principal part of the body they compose and never the least, this would not be the means of joining them together. Not all the members of a body can be its head and heart; there must be feet and hands, small as well as great, people who obey as well as those who command. And if each says openly that he wants to command and never obey, as indeed each of them does, it is obvious that every body politic would be destroyed, and that disorder and injustice would reign everywhere.

Therefore, it was necessary for those who are most intelligent and most fitted to become the noble parts of this body and to command others, to be naturally civil, i.e., to be led by a secret inclination to show others, through their manners, their courteous and honorable speech, that they think themselves unworthy of consideration, that they believe those to whom they speak are deserving of all sorts of honors, and that they have great esteem and veneration for them. Finally, in default of charity and love of order, it has been necessary for those who command others to have the art of deceiving them by an imaginary abasement that consists only in civilities and speech, in order that they might enjoy without being envied, that preeminence which is necessary in all bodies. For in this way all men possess in some way the greatness they desire—the great really possess it, and the insignificant and weak possess it only through imagination, being persuaded to some extent by the compliments of others that they are not regarded as what they are, namely the least among men.

From what we have just said, it is easy to conclude in passing that it is a most grievous fault against civility to speak of oneself frequently, especially in a flattering way, even though one has all sorts of good qualities, because it is not permissible to speak to those with whom one is conversing as if one regarded them as beneath oneself, except in special surroundings and when there are external and perceptible signs that elevate one above them. For in the end, contempt is the ultimate insult; it is the one most capable of rupturing society; and naturally we should not hope that a man whom we have made aware that we consider him beneath us can ever be joined to us, because men can never stand being the meanest part of the body they compose.

The inclination that men have for making compliments is therefore quite appropriate for counterbalancing the one they have for esteem and elevation, and for softening the internal pain felt by those who are the meanest parts of the body politic. And it cannot be doubted that the mixture of these two inclinations has good effects in the maintenance of society.

But there is an extreme corruption in these inclinations, as well as in friendship, compassion, good will, and the other inclinations that tend to unite men. What would support civil society is often the cause of its disunity and ruin; and, not to depart from my subject, it is often the cause of the communication and entrenchment of error.

II. This inclination leads us to approve of the thoughts of our friends and to deceive them by false praise.

Of all the inclinations necessary for civil society, those that most throw us into error are friendship, favor, gratitude, and all the inclinations that incline us to speak of others with too much flattery in their presence.

We set no bounds to our love in the person of our friends; together with them we love all the things that pertain to them in any way. And as they normally demonstrate sufficient passion in the defense of their opinions, we are inclined to believe them unthinkingly, to approve them, and even to defend them with greater obstinacy and passion than they do themselves. This is because they would often seem to be ill-mannered in the heated defense of their opinions, whereas we cannot be criticized for defending them. In them, this would be self-love; in us, it is generosity.

We bear affection for other men for several reasons, for they can please and serve us in various ways. The similarity of their temperaments, inclinations, functions, airs, ways, virtues, goods, the affection or esteem they show us, the favors that they have done for us or that we hope they will do for us, and several other particular reasons cause us to love them. Therefore, if it should happen that one of our friends, that is to say, some person who has the same inclinations as we, who is well-rounded, speaks in an agreeable manner, whom we believe to be virtuous or of significant station, who shows affection and esteem for us, who has done for us some favor, or from whom we hope to receive one or finally, who loves us for some other particular reason—if it happens, I say, that this person advances some proposition, we immediately allow ourselves to be persuaded without using our reason. We support his opinion without troubling ourselves about whether it is consistent with the truth, and often even in opposition to our own conscience, according to the obscurity and confusion of our minds, the corruption of our hearts, and according to the advantages we hope to draw from our false generosity.

It is not necessary to provide particular examples of these things here, for one hardly ever finds oneself in a group even for a single hour without noticing several of them if one wishes to reflect a little about it. Approval and laughter, as is commonly said, are only rarely on the side of truth, but almost always on the side of the people one loves. The speaker is obliging and civil; therefore, he is right. If what he says is merely probable, it is regarded as true; and if what he puts forth is absolutely ridiculous and foolish, it will become at least very probable. This is a man who loves me, who esteems me, who has done for me some favor, who has the disposition and power to do so again, who supported my views on other occasions; I would therefore be an ingrate and a fool if I were opposed to him, or even if I failed to applaud him. Thus do we make sport with the truth, making it serve our own interests and embracing each other's false opinions.

An honest man should not find fault with anyone for instructing and enlightening him when it is done according to the rules of civility; and when our friends are shocked when we modestly show them that they are mistaken, they must be permitted to love themselves and their mistakes, since that is what they want and since we do not have the power to command them or to change their minds.

But a true friend ought never to approve the errors of his friend, for in the end we must consider that we cause them to be even more mistaken than we think by defending their opinions indiscriminately. Our applause only inflates their hearts and confirms them in their errors. They become incorrigible; in the end they act and make decisions as though they were infallible.

Why is it that the richest, noblest, most powerful, and generally all those who are raised above others, quite often believe themselves to be infallible, and comport themselves as though they were much more reasonable than those of a low or mediocre station, unless it is because we indifferently and loosely approve all their thoughts? Thus, the approbation we tender our friends gradually makes them believe that they are more intelligent than others, which makes them vain, bold, imprudent, and capable of falling into the grossest errors without being aware of it.

This is why our enemies often do us better service and enlighten our minds much more through their opposition than do our friends through their approval, because our enemies force us to be on guard, and pay attention to the things we put forth, which alone suffices to make us recognize our aberrations. But our friends merely lull us to sleep, giving us false confidence that makes us vain and ignorant. Men should therefore never admire their friends and yield to their opinions through friendship, and likewise they should never oppose those of their enemies because of enmity. But they should get rid of their tendencies toward flattery and contradiction in order to become sincere, and to approve clarity and truth wherever they find it.

We should also bear in mind that most men are inclined toward flattery, or toward paying us compliments, because of a sort of natural inclination to appear witty, to draw the good will of others toward themselves, and because they hope for some reward in return, or finally, because of a kind of malice and mockery. And we should never permit ourselves to be confused by anything they say to us: do we not see every day that people who do not know one another nevertheless praise each other to the skies the first time they meet and talk? And what is more common than seeing people give grandiloquent praise and express admiration by extraordinary gestures for a person who has just spoken in public, even in the presence of those with whom they have just mocked that person? No matter how many times someone cries out, pales with admiration, or is astonished at the things he hears, it is not a sound proof that the speaker utters marvels, but rather that he speaks to flatter, that he has friends, or perhaps enemies, who are diverting themselves with him. It is because he speaks in an engaging manner, or is rich or powerful; or, if you will, it is a sufficiently good proof that what he says is based upon the confused and obscure notions of the senses, [which are nonetheless] quite affective and agreeable—or because he has a lively imagination, since praise is given to friendship, riches, honors, to what seems to be true, and very rarely to the truth.

One might expect that having treated the inclinations of minds in general, I should now descend into the exact details of all the particular impulses they feel upon the perception of good and evil; i.e., that I should explain the nature of love, hatred, joy, sadness, and all the intellectual passions, whether general or particular, simple or complex. But I am not engaged in explaining all the various impulses of which minds are capable.

I am quite willing to have it known that my principal design in all I have written to date about the search after truth has been to show men their weakness and ignorance, and that we are all subject to error and sin. I have said it, and I say it again, so it may be remembered; I never planned to treat the basic nature of the mind. But I have been obliged to say something about it in order to explain errors at their source, to explain them in an orderly way; in a word, to make myself intelligible. And if I have crossed the boundaries I set myself, it is because I had, it seemed to me, new things to say that seemed consequential to me, which I even believed might be read with pleasure. Perhaps I was mistaken, but I had to have this presupposition in order to have the courage to write them; for what is the point of speaking with no hope of being heard? It is true that I have said many things that seem to belong less to the subject I am treating than to that of the soul's particular impulses. I admit this, but I do not consider myself obliged to anything when I set up an order for myself. I established an order to guide myself, but I hold that I am allowed to turn my head as I walk, if I find something that deserves to be considered. I even hold that it allows me to rest in certain places along the way, provided I do not lose sight of the road I must follow. Those who do not wish to pause with me are free to pass on; they are allowed to do so; they need only turn the page. But, should they be annoyed, let them know that many people find that the resting places I choose make the road smoother and more pleasant.

Chapter 17

David Hume, *An Enquiry Concerning the Principles of Morals*

David Hume (1711-1776) was a radical empiricist and skeptic, who is known chiefly for the formidable challenges he was the first in modern times to pose for philosophical and theological claims to certainty. Born in Scotland, he attended the University of Edinburgh where he was exposed to the new empiricism of John Locke. In 1734 he moved to France where, living on a shoestring budget, he began his literary career with the writing of his first major work, **Treatise of Human Nature.** *Much to his disappointment, the book "fell dead born from the press," when it was published three years later, failing to attract any significant recognition. But the radical nature of his ideas were sufficiently understood to prevent him from securing an appointment to the chair of moral philosophy at the University of Edinburgh in 1744 and the chair of logic at Glasgow University in 1751.*

Over the course of his life, Hume worked as a tutor to the virtually insane Marquis of Annandale; as the personal secretary to General St. Clair during his abortive attempt to invade the coast of France and during his subsequent tenure as military ambassador to Vienna and Turin; as librarian of the Faculty of Law in Edinburgh; as Secretary to the British Embassy in Paris; and as Undersecretary of State for Great Britain. During no time in his life, however, did he achieve more than a modest reputation as a philosopher, even though he won the respect of eminent men such as Adam Smith and the French philosophe, Diderot.

Nevertheless, Hume was philosophically very productive during his middle years. Among his most important books were **An Enquiry**

Concerning Human Understanding *(1748) and* **Enquiry Concerning the Principles of Morals** *(1751), polished revisions of the first and third books of his earlier* **Treatise.** *Another important work,* **Dialogues Concerning Natural Religion** *was written in the early 1750s but published only posthumously due to its controversial agnostic leanings. Even among his writings, however, it was not for his philosophical works that he was best known during his lifetime, but for his literary and historical works, such as his six-volume* **History of England** *(1754-1762).*

Like John Locke, Hume held that all our knowledge is confined to what we can learn from our senses. But unlike Locke, he pushed the logic of this position to the point of complete skepticism. Especially well known are his claims that our common-sense convictions about the self, the external world, and the future have no empirical legitimacy—claims that still pose a challenge to the very foundations of scientific knowledge.

At best, our judgments about matters of fact are not necessarily *true, according to Hume, but based on habit. Likewise, our moral judgments about "good" and "evil" are based, not on any fixed, unalterable standard in the nature of things, but on habitual associations of certain actions with feelings of approval or disapproval. Nevertheless, since all people have a similar psycho-logical constitution, Hume assumes, their moral judgments generally will be similar.*

It is in this context that Hume's view of friendship emerges. Hume defends the authenticity of friendship along with benevolence and other social virtues. He denies the egoistic hypothesis that all forms of altruism are merely facades of self-love. Nevertheless, if Hume's ethics leads one to wonder whether morality reduces to a mere matter of taste and psychological disposition, one may also wonder what sort of a friend his theory, if consistently applied, would produce.

An Enquiry Concerning the Principles of Morals

Of Self-love

There is a principle, supposed to prevail among many, which is utterly incompatible with all virtue or moral sentiment; and as it can proceed from nothing but the most depraved disposition, so in its turn it tends still further to encourage that depravity. This principle is, that all *benevolence* is mere hypocrisy, friendship a cheat, public spirit a farce, fidelity a snare to procure trust and confidence; and that, while all of us, at bottom, pursue only our private interest, we wear these fair disguises, in order to put others off their guard, and expose them the more to our wiles and machinations. What heart one must be possessed of who professes such principles, and who feels no internal sentiment that belies so pernicious a theory, it is easy to imagine: And also, what degree of affection and benevolence he can bear to a species, whom he represents under such odious colours, and supposes so little susceptible of gratitude or any return of affection. Or if we should not ascribe these principles wholly to a corrupted heart, we must, at least, account for them from the most careless and precipitate examination. Superficial reasoners, indeed, observing many false pretences among mankind, and feeling, perhaps, no very strong restraint in their own disposition, might draw a general and a hasty conclusion, that all is equally corrupted, and that men, different from all other animals, and indeed from all other species of existences, admit of no degrees of good or bad, but are, in every instance, the same creatures under different disguises and appearances.

There is another principle, somewhat resembling the former; which has been much insisted on by philosophers, and has been the foundation of many a system; that, whatever affection one may feel, or imagine he feels for others, no passion is, or can be disinterested; that the most generous friendship, however sincere, is a modification of self-love; and that, even unknown to ourselves, we seek only our own gratification, while we appear the most deeply engaged in schemes for the liberty and happiness of mankind. By a turn of imagination, by a refinement of reflection, by an enthusiasm of passion, we seem to take part in the interests of others, and imagine ourselves divested of all selfish considerations: But, at bottom, the most generous patriot and most niggardly miser, the bravest hero and most abject coward, have, in every action, an equal regard to their own happiness and welfare.

Whoever concludes from the seeming tendency of this opinion, that those, who make profession of it, cannot possibly feel the true sentiments of benevolence, or have any regard for genuine virtue, will often find himself, in practice, very much mistaken. Probity and honour were no strangers to EPICURUS and his sect. ATTICUS and HORACE seem to have enjoyed from nature, and cultivated by reflection, as generous and friendly dispositions as any disciple of the austerer schools. And among the modern, HOBBES and LOCKE, who maintained the selfish system of morals, lived irreproachable lives; though the former lay not under any restraint of religion, which might supply the defects of his philosophy.

An EPICUREAN or a HOBBIST readily allows, that there is such a thing as friendship in the world, without hypocrisy or disguise; though he may attempt, by a philosophical chemistry, to resolve the elements of this passion, if I may so speak, into those of another, and explain every affection to be self-love, twisted and molded, by a particular turn of imagination, into a variety of appearances. But as the same turn of imagination prevails not in every man, nor gives the same direction to the original passion; this is sufficient, even according to the selfish system, to make the widest difference in human characters, and denominate one man virtuous and humane, another vicious and meanly interested. I esteem the man, whose self-love, by whatever means, is so directed as to give him a concern for others, and render him serviceable to society: As I hate or despise him, who has no regard to any thing beyond his own gratifications and enjoyments. In vain would you suggest, that these characters, though seemingly opposite, are, at bottom, the same, and that a very inconsiderable turn of thought forms the whole difference between them. Each character, notwithstanding these inconsiderable differences, appears to me, in practice, pretty durable and untransmutable. And I find not in this more than in other subjects, that the natural sentiments, arising from the general appearances of things, are easily destroyed by subtle reflections concerning the minute origin of these appearances. Does not the lively, cheerful colour of a countenance inspire me with complacency and pleasure; even though I learn from philosophy, that all difference of complexion arises from the most minute differences of thickness, in the most minute parts of the skin; by means of which a superficies is qualified to reflect one of the original colours of light, and absorb the others?

But though the question, concerning the universal or partial selfishness of man be not so material, as is usually imagined, to morality and practice, it is certainly of consequence in the speculative science of human nature, and is a proper object of curiosity and inquiry. It may not, therefore, be unsuitable, in this place, to bestow a few reflections upon it.[1]

The most obvious objection to the selfish hypothesis, is that, as it is contrary to common feeling and our most unprejudiced notions, there is required the highest stretch of philosophy to establish so extraordinary a paradox. To the most careless observer, there appear to be such dispositions as benevolence and generosity; such affections as love, friendship, compassion, gratitude. These sentiments have their causes, effects, objects, and operations, marked by common language and observation, and plainly distinguished from those of the selfish passions. And as this is the obvious appearance of things, it must be admitted; till some hypothesis be discovered, which, by penetrating deeper into human nature, may prove the former affections to be nothing but modifications of the latter. All attempts of this kind have hitherto proved fruitless, and seem to have proceeded entirely, from that love of *simplicity,* which has been the source of much false reasoning in philosophy. I shall not here enter into any detail on the present subject. Many able philosophers have shown the insufficiency of these systems. And I shall take for granted what, I believe, the smallest reflection will make evident to every impartial inquirer.

But the nature of the subject furnishes the strongest presumption, that no better system will ever, for the future, be invented, in order to account for the origin of the benevolent from the selfish affections, and reduce all the various emotions of the human mind to a perfect simplicity. The case is not the same in this species of philosophy as in physics. Many an hypothesis in nature, contrary to first appearances, has been found, on more accurate scrutiny, solid and satisfactory. Instances of this kind are so frequent, that a judicious, as well as witty philosopher,[2] has ventured to affirm, if there be more than one way, in which any phenomenon may be produced, that there is a general presumption for its arising from the causes, which are the least obvious and familiar. But the presumption always lies on the other side, in all inquiries concerning the origin of our passions, and of the internal operations of the human mind. The simplest and most obvious cause, which can there be assigned for any phenomenon, is probably the true one. When a philosopher, in the explication of his system, is obliged to have recourse to some very intricate and refined reflections, and to suppose them essential to the production of any passion or emotion, we have reason to be extremely on our guard against so fallacious an hypothesis. The affections are not susceptible of any impression from the refinements of reason or imagination; and it is always found, that a vigorous exertion of the latter faculties, necessarily, from the narrow capacity of the human mind, destroys all activity in the former. Our predominant motive or intention is, indeed, frequently concealed from ourselves, when it is mingled and confounded with other motives, which the mind, from vanity or self-conceit, is desirous of supposing more prevalent: But there is no instance, that a concealment of this nature has ever arisen from the abstruseness and intricacy of the motive. A man, that has lost a friend and patron, may flatter himself, that all his grief arises from generous sentiments, without any mixture of narrow or interested considerations: But a man, that grieves for a valuable friend, who needed his patronage and protection; how can we suppose, that his passionate tenderness arises from some metaphysical regards to a self-interest, which has no foundation or reality? We may as well imagine, that minute wheels and springs, like those of a watch, give motion to a loaded wagon, as account for the origin of passion from such abstruse reflections.

Animals are found susceptible of kindness, both to their own species and to ours; nor is there, in this case, the least suspicion of disguise or artifice. Shall we account for all *their* sentiments too, from refined deductions of self-interest? Or if we admit a disinterested benevolence in the inferior species, by what rule of analogy can we refuse it in the superior?

Love between the sexes begets a complacency and good-will, very distinct from the gratification of an appetite. Tenderness to their offspring, in all sensible beings, is commonly able alone to counterbalance the strongest motives of self-love, and has no manner of dependence on that affection. What interest can a fond mother have in view, who loses her health by assiduous attendance on her sick child, and afterwards languishes and dies of grief, when freed, by its death, from the slavery of that attendance?

Is gratitude no affection of the human breast, or is that a word merely, without any meaning or reality? Have we no satisfaction in one man's company above another's, and no desire of the welfare of our friend, even though absence or death should prevent us from all participation in it? Or what is it commonly, that gives us any participation in it, even while alive and present, but our affection and regard to him?

These and a thousand other instances are marks of a general benevolence in human nature, where no *real* interests binds us to the object. And how an *imaginary* interest, known and avowed for such, can be the origin of any passion or emotion, seems difficult to explain. No satisfactory hypothesis of this kind has yet been discovered; nor is there the smallest probability, that the future industry of men will ever be attended with more favourable success.

But farther, if we consider rightly of the matter, we shall find, that the hypothesis, which allows of a disinterested benevolence, distinct from self-love, has really more *simplicity* in it, and is more conformable to the analogy of nature, than that which pretends to resolve all friendship and humanity into this latter principle. There are bodily wants or appetites, acknowledged by every one, which necessarily precede all sensual enjoyment, and carry us directly to seek possession of the object. Thus, hunger and thirst have eating and drinking for their end; and from the gratification of these primary appetites arises a pleasure, which may become the object of another species of desire or inclination, that is secondary and interested. In the same manner, there are mental passions, by which we are impelled immediately to seek particular objects, such as fame, or power, or vengeance, without any regard to interest; and when these objects are attained, a pleasing enjoyment ensues, as the consequence of our indulged affections. Nature must, by the internal frame and constitution of the mind, give an original propensity to fame, ere we can reap any pleasure from that acquisition, or pursue it from motives of self-love, and a desire of happiness. If I have no vanity, I take no delight in praise: If I be void of ambition, power gives me no enjoyment: If I be not angry, the punishment of an adversary is totally indifferent to me. In all these cases, there is a passion, which points immediately to the object, and constitutes it our good or happiness; as there are other secondary passions, which afterwards arise, and pursue it as a part of our happiness, when once it is constituted such by our original affections. Were there no appetite of any kind antecedent to self-love, that propensity could scarcely ever exert itself; because we should, in that case, have felt few and slender pains or pleasures, and have little misery or happiness to avoid or to pursue.

Now where is the difficulty in conceiving, that this may likewise be the case with benevolence and friendship and that, from the original frame of our temper, we may feel a desire of another's happiness or good, which, by means of that affection, becomes our own good, and is afterwards pursued, from the combined motives of benevolence and self-enjoyment? Who sees not that vengeance, from the force alone of passion, may be so eagerly pursued, as to make us knowingly neglect every consideration of ease, interest, or safety; and, like some vindictive animals, infuse our very souls into the wounds we give an enemy?[3] And what a malignant philosophy must it be, that will not allow, to humanity and friendship, the same privileges, which are undisputably granted to the darker passions of enmity and resentment? Such a philosophy is more like a satyr than a true delineation or description of human nature; and may be a good foundation for paradoxical wit and raillery, but is a very bad one for any serious argument or reasoning.

Notes

[1] Benevolence naturally divides into two kinds, the *general* and the *particular*. The first is, where we have no friendship or connection or esteem for the person, but feel only a general sympathy with him or a compassion for his pains, and a congratulation with his pleasures. The other species of benevolence is founded on an opinion of virtue, on services done us, or on some particular connections. Both these sentiments must be allowed real in human nature; but whether they will resolve into some nice considerations of self-love, is a question more curious than important. The former sentiment, to wit, that of general benevolence, or humanity, or sympathy, we shall have occasion frequently to treat of in the course of this inquiry; and I assume it as real, from general experience, without any other proof.

[2] Mons. FONTENELLE.

[3] Animasque in vulnere ponunt [... and put their souls in the wounds.] Virg. Geor. 4, 238. Dum alteri noceat, sui negligens [... careless of itself, as long as it can hurt another.], says SENECA of Anger. De Ira. l. I, l.

Chapter 18

Immanuel Kant, *The Doctrine of Virtue*

Immanuel Kant (1724-1804) was one of the most important and influential philosophers of modern times. Born and raised in East Prussia, he never set foot outside of his native province and lived a singularly uneventful professorial life. Although he enjoyed the company of friends, he never married, but remained a classic desk scholar—a man of such regular habits that the fabled housewives of Königsberg (contemporary Kaliningrad) are said to have set their clocks by his punctual daily walks. Raised in a devoutly religious environment, he rejected orthodox Christianity but retained entirely the pathos of his childhood Pietism in his emphasis on moral earnestness and the strength and purity of an indomitable good will.

Despite his geographical provincialism and academic detachment, Kant was well versed in the geography and culture of distant places and followed with interest the French Revolution and other political and social events of his day. His interest ranged with amazing breadth, taking in everything from lunar volcanoes to theology, but he always remained concerned preeminently with the critical, metaphysical and epistemological questions of foundation underlying those other interests.

Like Aristotle and Aquinas, Kant was a great builder of a philosophical system. Those who know him only from his great and imposing **Critiques** *and their formidable language and page-long sentences often are surprised to find* **The Doctrine of Virtue** *so readable and entertaining. Here they find, to their delight, the Kant of Herder's recollections from his days as a student under Kant: "Speech, the richest in thought, flowed from his lips. Playfulness, wit,*

*and humor were at his command. His lectures were the most
entertaining talks."*

*Those used to thinking of Kant's ethics as a system of abstract
formalism are often surprised to find in his* **The Doctrine of Virtue** *a
detailed treatment of a great diversity of specific kinds of (often very
interesting) behavior. Far from being concerned with only the "empty
form" of morality, Kant is here seen to be concerned with showing what
specific kinds of actions may be regarded as morally good and, hence,
as one's duties.*

The Doctrine of Virtue *is divided into two major parts, the first
entitled "Duties to Oneself," the second entitled "Duties of Virtue to
Other Men." In the first part, Kant offers an analysis of duties involved
in the moral perfection of ourselves, distinguishing between duties to
oneself as a rational-moral being and as a natural-animal being. The
former require exercising rational freedom and avoiding the vices of
lying, avarice, and servility; the latter involve the duty of self-
preservation and the avoidance of suicide, sexual perversion, and
gluttony.*

*In the second part, Kant offers an analysis of duties relating to the
happiness of others, distinguishing between our duties as they involve
love and respect of others. The former include the duties of
beneficence, gratitude, and sympathy (and the avoidance of their
corresponding vices—envy, ingratitude, and malicious joy); the latter
include the duty of moderation in one's demands and avoiding the vices
of pride, calumny, and mockery. Love and respect are viewed by Kant
as coinciding in friendship.*

*Our selection, "Duties of Virtue to Other Men," is taken from the
second part of* **The Doctrine of Virtue.**

The Doctrine of Virtue

On the Intimate Union of Love and Respect in Friendship

§ 46

Friendship (considered in its perfection) is the union of two persons
through equal and mutual love and respect. —It is easy to see that
[perfect friendship] is an ideal of the emotional and practical concern
which each of the friends united through a morally good will takes in
the other's welfare; and even if friendship does not produce the

complete happiness of life, the adoption of this ideal in men's attitude to one another contains their worthiness to be happy. Hence men have a duty of friendship. —The striving for perfect friendship (as the maximum good in the attitude of friends to each other) is a duty imposed by reason—not, indeed, an ordinary duty but a duty of honour. Yet it is easy to see that [perfect] friendship is a mere Idea (although a practically necessary one), which cannot be achieved in practice. For in his relations with his neighbour how can a man ascertain whether one of the attitudes essential to this duty (*e.g.* mutual benevolence) is *equal* on the part of both friends? Or, still more important, how can he be sure what relation exists, in the same person, between the feeling connected with the one duty and that connected with the other (*e.g.* between the feeling connected with benevolence and that connected with respect)? And how can he be sure that if one of the friends [469] is more ardent in his *love* he may not, just because of this, forfeit something of the other's *respect?* Does not all this mean that love and respect on the part of both friends can hardly be brought subjectively into that balanced proportion which is yet necessary for friendship? — For we can regard love as attraction and respect as repulsion, and if the principle of love commands friends to come together, the principle of respect requires them to keep each other at a proper distance. This limitation upon intimacy, which is expressed in the rule that even the best of friends should not make themselves *too familiar* with each other, contains a maxim which holds not only for the superior in relation to the inferior but also vice-versa. For if the superior suddenly feels his pride wounded, he may want the inferior's respect to be put aside for the moment, but not abolished. But once respect is violated, its presence within is irrevocably lost, even though the outward marks of it (manners) are brought back to their former course.

Friendship conceived as attainable in its purity or completeness (between Orestes and Pylades, Theseus and Pirithous) is the hobby horse of writers of romance. On the other hand Aristotle says: My dear friends, there is no such thing as a friend! The following remarks may point up the difficulties in perfect friendship.

From a moral point of view it is, of course, a duty for one of the friends to point out the other's faults to him; this is in the other's best interests and is therefore a duty of love. But his *alter ego* sees in this a lack of the respect which he expected from his friend and thinks either that he has already lost something of his friend's respect or that, since he is observed and secretly criticized, he is in constant danger of losing it; and even the fact that his friend observes him and finds fault with him will seem in itself an insult.

How we wish for a friend in need—one who is, of course, an active friend, ready to help us at his own expense! But still it is also a heavy burden to feel chained to another's fate and encumbered with his needs. —Hence friendship cannot be a union aimed at mutual advantage: the union must rather be a pure moral one, and the help that each of the two may count on from the other in case of need must not be regarded as the end and motive of friendship—for in that case he would lose the other's respect—but only as the [470] outward manifestation of an inner heartfelt benevolence, which should not be put to the test since this is always dangerous. Each friend is generously concerned with sparing the other his burden and bearing it all by himself, even concealing it altogether from his friend, while yet he can always flatter himself that in case of need he could confidently count on the other's help. But if one of them accepts a *favour* from the other, then he may well be able to count on equality in love, but not in respect; for he sees himself obviously a step lower in so far as he is under obligation without being able reciprocally to impose obligation. —It is sweet to feel a mutual possession that approximates to a fusion into one person. Yet friendship is something so *delicate (teneritas amicitiae)* that it is never for a moment safe from *interruptions* if it is allowed to rest on feelings and if this mutual sympathy and self-surrender are not subjected to principles or rules preventing excessive familiarity and limiting mutual love by the requirements of respect. Such interruptions are common among uncultivated people, although they do not always result in a *split* (for the rabble fight and make up). These people cannot part with each other, and yet they cannot come to terms with each other since they need quarrels in order to savour the sweetness of being united in reconciliation. —But in any case the love in friendship cannot be an *agitation* [*Affekt*]: for this is blind in its choice, and after a while it goes up in smoke.

§ 47

Moral friendship (as distinguished from emotional friendship) is the complete confidence of two persons in revealing their secret thoughts and feelings to each other, in so far as such disclosures are consistent with mutual respect for each other.

Man is a being meant for society (though he is also an unsociable one), and in cultivating social intercourse he feels strongly the need to reveal himself to others (even with no ulterior purpose). But on the other hand, hemmed in and cautioned by fear of the misuse others may make of this disclosure of his thoughts, he finds himself constrained [471] to *lock up* in himself a good part of his opinions (especially those about other people). He would like to discuss with someone his opinions about his associates, the government, religion and so forth, but he cannot risk it—partly because the other person, while prudently keeping back his own opinions, might use this to harm him, and partly because, if he revealed his failings while the other person concealed his own, he would lose something of the other's respect by presenting himself quite candidly to him.

If he finds someone understanding—someone who, moreover, shares his general outlook on things—with whom he need not be anxious about this danger but can reveal himself with complete confidence, he can then air his views. He is not completely *alone* with his thoughts, as in a prison, but enjoys a freedom denied to him with the rank and file, with whom he must shut himself up in himself. Every man has his secrets and dare not confide blindly in others, partly because most men have a base disposition to use these secrets to his prejudice and partly because many people are indiscreet or incapable of judging and distinguishing what may or may not be repeated. The necessary combination of qualities is seldom found in one person (*rara avis in terris, nigroque simillima cygno*), especially since the closest friendship requires that this understanding and trusted friend be also bound not to share the secrets entrusted to him with anyone else, no matter how reliable he thinks him, without explicit permission to do so....

Appendix

§ 48: *On the Virtues of Social Intercourse* (virtutes homileticae)

It is a duty both to ourselves and to others not to *isolate* ourselves (*separatistam agere*) but to bring our moral perfection into social intercourse (*officium commercii, sociabilitas*); while we should make ourselves a fixed center of our principles, we should regard the circle thus drawn around us as one that also forms a part of the all-inclusive circle of those who, in their attitude, are citizens of the world. The end in this duty is not to promote the highest good of the world but only the means that lead indirectly to this end—means such as pleasantness in our relations with others, good-naturedness, mutual love and respect (affability and propriety, *humanitas aesthetica et decorum*). By this we associate virtue with the graces, and to effect this is in itself a duty of virtue.

These are, indeed, only *outworks* or by-products (*parerga*), which present a fair illusion of something like virtue, an illusion which also deceives no one, since everyone knows how to take it. *Affability, sociability, courtesy, hospitality,* and *gentleness* (in disagreeing without quarreling) are, indeed, only small change; yet they promote the feeling for virtue itself by [arousing] a striving to bring this illusion as near as possible to the truth. All of these, [473] like the mere manners of social intercourse, manifest what is obligatory and also bind others to it; and in so doing they work toward a virtuous attitude in so far as they at least make virtue *fashionable*.

But the question arises here whether we may also keep company with the vicious. We cannot avoid meeting them, unless we leave the world; and besides, our judgment about them is not competent. —But if the vice is a scandal—that is, a publicly given example of contempt for the strict laws of duty, which therefore brings infamy with it—then even if the laws of the country do not punish the vice, we must break off the existing association or avoid it as much as possible. For the further continuation of it does away with all the honour of virtue and puts it up for sale to anyone who is rich enough to bribe parasites with the pleasures of luxury. [474]

Chapter 19

G.W.F. Hegel, *Early Theological Writings*

George Wilhelm Friedrich Hegel (1770-1831), considered by some to be the greatest philosopher of all time, both because of his systematic rigor and encyclopedic brilliance, was born in Stuttgart. After a studious childhood, the young Hegel entered the famed theological seminary at the University of Tübingen. A roommate of the philosopher Schelling and the poet Hölderlin, Hegel's astonishing brilliance did not become manifest in any universally recognized way until he had the opportunity to add the finishing touches to his dialectical system while professor at Heidelberg and later at Berlin. In the years between his rather unspectacular days as a student and his ascent to the pinnacle of the philosophic world on the Continent, Hegel served as a private tutor and as both a journal and newspaper editor.

There was hardly an intellectual discipline which Hegel had not either nearly mastered or transformed by his philosophic insight. His major works, **The Phenomenology of Spirit, The Science of Logic, The Philosophy of Nature,** *and the* **Encyclopaedia of the Philosophical Sciences in Outline,** *present the essentials of his dialectical system, a system built on the principle that the world in its every manifestation, be it in nature, history, revelation or reason is immanently knowable, for according to Hegel the mind is not finite and merely grasping at ever-elusive scientific or theological straws; rather, mind (or spirit) contains the infinite within it, such that the allegedly finite self must merely 'raise itself up to the infinite' by the recognition (primarily through 'the phenomenology of spirit') that the Infinite, indeed the very being of God Himself, is immanently*

*knowable   through   rigorous   self-consciousness,   systematically
comprehended.*

*While Hegel wrote no 'separate' treatise on ethics or on the topic of
friendship in particular, the following selection, drawn from his* **Early
Theological Writings,** *does offer a description rich in its implications
for the subject in the form of an account of the formation of the early
Christian community, beginning with the twelve disciples of Christ and
proceeding to the transformation of the emergent religious society into
a state.*

The Positivity of the Christian Religion[1]

[§ 9.] Miracles

. . . It was not Jesus himself who elevated his religious doctrine into
a peculiar sect distinguished by practices of its own; this result
depended on the zeal of his friends, on the manner in which they
construed his doctrine, on the form in which they preached and
propagated it, on the claims they made for it, and on the arguments by
which they sought to uphold it. Here then arises the question: What
were the character and abilities of Jesus' disciples, and what was the
manner of their connection with Jesus which resulted in turning his
teaching into a positive sectarianism?

[§ 10.] The Positive Element Derived from the Disciples

While we have few details about the character of most of Jesus'
pupils, this much at least seems certain-that they were remarkable for
their honesty, humility, and friendliness, for their pluck and constancy
in avowing their master's teaching, but they were accustomed to a
restricted sphere of activity and had learned and plied their trades in the
usual way as craftsmen. They were distinguished neither as generals
nor as profound statesmen; on the contrary, they made it a point of
honor not to be so. This was their spirit when they made Jesus'
acquaintance and became his scholars. He broadened their horizon a
little, but not beyond every Jewish idea and prejudice.[2] Lacking any
great store of spiritual energy of their own, they had found the basis of
their conviction about the teaching of Jesus principally in their
friendship with him and dependence on him. They had not attained
truth and freedom by their own exertions; only by laborious learning

had they acquired a dim sense of them and certain formulas about them. Their ambition was (163) to grasp and keep this doctrine faithfully and to transmit it equally faithfully to others without any addition, without letting it acquire any variations in detail by working on it themselves. And it could not have been otherwise if the Christian religion was to be maintained, if it was to be established as a public religion and handed on as such to prosperity. If a comparison may be permitted here between the fates of Socrates' philosophy and Jesus' teaching, then in the difference between the pupils of the two sages we find one reason among others why the Socratic philosophy did not grow into a public religion either in Greece or anywhere else.

[§ 11.] The Disciples Contrasted with the Pupils of Socrates

The disciples of Jesus had sacrificed all their other interests, though to be sure these were restricted and their renunciation was not difficult; they had forsaken everything to become followers of Jesus. They had no political interest like that which a citizen of a free republic takes in his native land; their whole interest was confined to the person of Jesus.

From their youth up, the friends of Socrates had developed their powers in many directions. They had absorbed that democratic spirit which gives an individual a greater measure of independence and makes it impossible for any tolerably good head to depend wholly and absolutely on one person. In their state it was worth while to have a political interest, and an interest of that kind can never be sacrificed. Most of them had already been pupils of other philosophers and other teachers. They loved Socrates because of his virtue and his philosophy, not virtue and his philosophy because of him. Just as Socrates had fought for his native land, had fulfilled all the duties of a free citizen as a brave soldier in war and a just judge in peace, so too all his friends were something more than mere inactive philosophers, than mere pupils of Socrates. Moreover, they had the capacity to work in their own heads on what they had learned and to give it the stamp of their own originality. Many of them founded schools of their own in their own right they were men as great as Socrates.

[§ 12.] The Number of Disciples Fixed at Twelve

Jesus had thought fit to fix the number of his trusted friends at twelve, and to these as his messengers and successors he gave a wide authority after his resurrection. Every man has full authority for the diffusion of virtue, and there is no sacrosanct number of the men who feel called to undertake the founding of God's kingdom on earth. Socrates did not have seven disciples, or three times three; any friend of virtue was welcome. In a civil polity, it is appropriate and necessary to fix the number of the members of the representative bodies and the law courts and to maintain it firmly; (164) but a virtue religion cannot adopt forms of that kind drawn from constitutional law. The result of restricting the highest standing to a specific number of men was the ascription of high standing to certain individuals, and this became something continually more essential in the later constitution of the Christian church, the wider the church spread. It made possible Councils which made pronouncements about true doctrine in accordance with a majority vote and imposed their decrees on the world as a norm of faith.

[§ 13.] The Disciples Sent Forth on their Mission

Another striking event in the story of Jesus is his dispatch of his friends and pupils (once in larger and on another occasion in smaller numbers) into districts which he had no opportunity of visiting and enlightening himself. On both occasions they seem to have been absent from him for a few days only. In the short time which they could devote on these journeys to the education and betterment of men, it was impossible to achieve much. At best they could draw the people's attention to themselves and their teacher and spread the story of his wonderful deeds; but they could not make any great conquests for virtue. This method of spreading a religion can suit a positive faith alone. As a method of extirpating Jewish superstition and disseminating morality, it could have no proceeds, because Jesus himself did not carry his most trusted friends very far in this direction even after years of effort and association with them.

[§ 14.] The Resurrection and the Commands Given Thereafter

In this connection we must also notice the command which Jesus gives to his disciples after his resurrection to spread his doctrine and his name. This command (especially as worded in Mark xvi. 15-18)[3] characterizes the teacher of a positive religion just as markedly as the touching form of his parting words before his death characterizes the teacher of virtue:[4] with a voice full of the tenderest friendship, with an inspiring feeling for the worth of religion and morality, at the most important hour of his life he spends his few remaining minutes in commending love and toleration to his friends and in impressing on them that they are to be indifferent to the dangers into which virtue and truth may bring them. Instead of "Go ye," etc., a teacher of virtue would perhaps have said: "Let every man do as much good as possible in the sphere of activity assigned to him by nature and Providence." In his valediction the teacher of virtue places all value in doing; but in the one in Mark all value is placed in believing. Moreover, Jesus sets an external sign, baptism, as a distinguishing mark, makes these two positive things, belief and baptism, the condition of salvation, and condemns the unbeliever. However far you elevate the belief in question into a living belief, active in works of (165) mercy and philanthropy, and however far you lower the unbelief to an obstinate refusal, against one's better knowledge and conscience, to recognize the truth of the Gospel, and even if you then grant that it is only belief and unbelief of this kind that is meant, though that is not exactly stated in plain words, nevertheless a positive element still persistently and essentially clings to the faith and is so attached to the dignity of morality as to be as good as inseparable from it; salvation and damnation are bound up with this element. That it is this positive element which is principally meant in this command to the disciples is clear also from what follows, where the gifts and attributes to be assigned to believers are recited, namely, "to cast out devils in his name, to speak with new tongues, to take up serpents without danger, to drink any poisoned draught without hurt, and to heal the sick through laying on of hands." There is a striking contrast between the attributes here ascribed to men who are well-pleasing to God and what is said in Matthew vii. 22: ["Many will say unto me in that day, Lord, Lord, have we not prophesied in thy name? And in thy name have cast out devils? . . . And then I will profess unto them, I never knew you; depart from me, ye that work iniquity"]. In the latter passage precisely the same traits are sketched, namely, casting out devils in the name of Jesus, speaking in his name in the language of prophets,[5] and performing many other wonderful works, and yet a man with all these attributes may be of such a character that the judgment of condemnation will be pronounced on him by the judge of the world. These words (Mark xvi. 15-18) are possible only on the lips of a teacher of a positive religion, not on those of a teacher of virtue. . . .

[§ 18.] Equality

Equality was a principle with the early Christians; the slave was the brother of his owner; humility, the principle of not elevating one's self above anyone else, the sense of one's own unworthiness, was the first law of a Christian; men were to be valued not by honors or dignity, not by talents or other brilliant qualities, but by the strength of their faith. This theory, to be sure, has been retained in all its comprehensiveness, but with the clever addition that it is in the eyes of Heaven that all men are equal in this sense. For this reason, it receives no further notice in this earthly life. A simple-minded man may hear his bishop or superintendent preaching with touching eloquence about these principles of humility, about the abhorrence of all pride and all vanity, and he may see the edified expressions with which the lords and ladies in the congregation listen to this; but if, when the sermon is over, he approaches his prelate and the gentry with the hope of finding them humble brothers and friends, he will soon read in their laughing or contemptuous faces that all this is not to be taken *au pied de la lettre* and that only in Heaven will it find its literal application. And if even today eminent Christian prelates annually wash the feet of a number of the poor, this is little more than a comedy which leaves things as they are and which has also lost much of its meaning, because washing the feet is in our social life no longer what it was with the Jews, namely, a daily action and a courtesy to guests, performed as a rule only by slaves or servants. On the other hand, while the Chinese emperor's annual turn at the plow may equally have sunk to the level of a comedy, it has yet retained a greater and a more direct significance for every onlooker, because plowing must always be one of the chief occupations of his subjects.

[§ 19.] The Lord's Supper

So too another action which had one form on the lips and in the eyes of the teacher of virtue, Jesus himself, acquired quite a different one for the restricted group of early Christians, and a different one again for the sect when it became universal. Anyone whose talent for interpretation has not been whetted by the concepts of dogmatic theology and who reads the story of the last evening or the last few evenings which Jesus spent in the bosom of his trusted friends will find truly sublime the conversation which he had with his disciples about submission to his fate, about the way the virtuous man's consciousness of duty raised him above sorrows and injustices, about the love for all mankind by which alone obedience to God (169) could be evinced. Equally touching and humane is the way in which Jesus celebrates the Jewish Passover with them for the last time and exhorts them when, their duties done, they refresh themselves with a friendly meal, whether religious or other, to remember him, their true friend and teacher who will then be no longer in their midst; whenever they enjoyed bread and wine, they were to be reminded of his body sacrificed, and his blood shed, for the truth. This sensuous symbol in which he imaginatively conjoined his memory with the serving of the meal they would enjoy in the future was very easily apprehended from the things on the table in front of them; but if it is regarded purely aesthetically, it may seem something of a play on words. Nonetheless, it is more pleasing in itself than the persistent use of the words "blood and flesh," "food and drink" (John vi. 47 ff.), in a metaphysical sense, which even theologians have pronounced to be rather harsh.

This human request of a friend in taking leave of his friends was soon transformed by the Christians, once they had become a sect, into a command equivalent to a divine ordinance. The duty of respecting a teacher's memory, a duty voluntarily arising from friendship, was transformed into a religious duty, and the whole thing became a mysterious act of worship and a substitute for the Jewish and Roman sacrificial feasts. The free-will offerings of the rich put the poor into a position to fulfill this duty which thus became agreeable to them, for otherwise they would have discharged it inadequately or with difficulty. In honor of Christ there was soon ascribed to such feasts an effect independent of and over and above the power that any ordinary healthy meal has on the body, or that unrestrained relaxation has on cheerfulness, or, in this special instance, that pious conversation has on edification.

But as Christianity became more general there arose among the Christians a greater inequality of rank which, to be sure, was rejected in theory but retained in practice, and the result was a cessation of this fraternization. In early times the complaint was occasionally made that the spiritual love-feasts degenerated into occasions and scenes of fleshly love; but gradually there was less and less ground for this complaint, because bodily satisfaction became less and less prominent, while the spiritual and mystical element was valued all the more highly, and other more trifling feelings, which were there at the start in friendly conversation, social intercourse, mutual opening and stimulation of hearts, are no longer considered as of any account in such a sublime enjoyment. . . .

[§ 21.] How a Moral or Religious Society Grows into a State

. . . Jesus aimed at reawakening the moral sense, at influencing the attitude of mind. For this reason, in parables and otherwise, he adduced examples of righteous modes of action, particularly in contrast with what, e.g., a purely legal-minded Levite might regard himself as bound to do, and he left it to his hearers' feelings to decide whether the Levite's action was sufficient. In particular, he showed them how what morality required contrasted with what was required by the civil laws and by those religious commands which had become civil laws (he did this especially in the Sermon on the Mount, where he spoke of the moral disposition as the *complementum*[6] of the laws). He tried to show them how little the observance of these commands constituted the essence of virtue, since that essence is the spirit of acting from respect for duty, first, because it is a duty, and, secondly, because it is also a divine command; i.e., it was religion in the true sense of the word that he tried to instill into them. Despite all their religious feeling, they could only be citizens of the Jewish state; only a few of them were citizens of the Kingdom of God. Once unfettered by the positive commands which were supposed to usurp the place of morality, their reason would have attained freedom and would now have been able to follow its own commands. But it was too immature, too unpracticed in following commands of its own; it was unacquainted with the enjoyment of a self-won freedom, and consequently it was subjected once more to the yoke of formalism.

The early Christians were united by the bond of a common faith, but in addition they formed a society whose members encouraged one another in their progress toward goodness and a firm faith, instructed one another in matters of faith and other duties, dissolved each other's doubts, strengthened waverers, pointed out their neighbors' faults, confessed their own, poured out their repentance and their confession in the bosom of the society, promised obedience to it and to those intrusted with its supervision, and agreed to acquiesce in any punishment which these might impose. Simply by adopting the Christian faith a man entered this society (177), assumed duties toward it, and ceded to it rights against him. To adopt the Christian faith without at the same time submitting to the Christian society and to its claims against proselytes and every Christian would have been contradictory, and the Christian's greater or lesser degree of piety was measured, especially at the start, by the degree of his loyalty or obedience to the society.

On this point too there is a distinction between a positive sect and a philosophical one. It is by the recognition and conviction of the teachings of a philosophical system, or, in practical matters, by virtue, that a man becomes an adherent of a philosophical sect or a citizen of the moral realm, i.e., of the invisible church. In doing so, he adopts no duties except the one imposed by himself, and he gives his society no rights over him except the one that he himself concedes, namely, the duty of acting righteously, and the right to claim such action from him. On the other hand, by entering the society of the "positive" Christian sect, he has assumed the duty of obeying its statutes, not because he has himself taken something for obligatory, good, and useful, but because he has left the society to decide these matters and recognized something as duty simply and solely at another's command and on another's judgment. He has accepted the duty of believing something and regarding it as true because the society has commanded belief in it, whereas, if I am convinced of a philosophical system, I reserve the right to change my conviction if reason so requires. By entering the Christian society the proselyte has transferred to it the right of settling the truth for him and assumed the duty of accepting this truth independently, and even in contradiction, of reason. He has adopted the duty, as in the social contract, of subjecting his private will to a majority vote, i.e., to the general will. Fear clutches at the heart if one imagines one's self in such a situation; the outlook is sadder still if we re-reflect on what the issue of such a pedantry might be; and the most lamentable spectacle of all is what we actually see in history, namely, the miserable sort of culture mankind has adopted by every man's renouncing, for himself and his posterity, all right to decide for himself what is true, good, and right in the most important matters of our faith and knowledge and in all other departments of life.

The ideal of perfection which the Christian sect sought to realize in its members differed at different times, and in the main it was at all times extremely confused and defective. This may be guessed from the very way in which it was to be realized, i.e., by the extinction of all freedom of will and reason (i.e., of (178) both practical and theoretical reason); and we may judge from the champions in whom the church has found its ideal realized how the sort of holy will which it has demanded of its ideal [adherents] is produced by unifying into a single concept what truly pious men have in common with vagrants, lunatics, and scoundrels.

Since an ideal of moral perfection cannot be the aim of civil legislation, and since the Christian ideal could least of all be the aim of Jewish and heathen governments, the Christian sect attempted to influence the attitude of mind and to take that as a standard for determining men's worth and their deserts, whether reward or punishment. The virtues which it approved and rewarded were of the kind which the state cannot reward, and similarly the faults it punished were not the object of the church's vengeance because they conflicted with the civil laws but because they were sins against the divine commands. These faults were of three types: (a) vices and trespasses which, though immoral, could not fall within the competence of civil courts; (b) offenses which were liable to civil punishments but which at the same time contravened morality, or the church's morality, and could be punished by the church only as such contraventions; (c) offenses against purely external ecclesiastical ordinances. The church did not put itself in the state's place or administer the state's jurisdiction: the two jurisdictions were quite distinct. What it did often enough try to do was to withdraw from the arm of the law anyone guilty of a civil offense who had acted in the spirit of the sect.

A common purpose and common means of attaining it, namely, the furtherance of morality by means of mutual encouragement, admonition, and reward, may unite a small society without detriment to the rights of any individual or the state. Respect for a friend's moral qualities and confidence in his love for me must first have awakened my trust in him before I can be assured that the shame with which I confess my faults will not be received with contempt or mortifying laughter; that, if I trust him with my secrets, I shall not have to fear betrayal; and that, in advising me for my good, for my highest good, his motive will be an interest in my well-being and a respect rather for the right than for my material advantage. In short, before men can be united in this way, they must be friends.

This condition necessarily restricts a society of this kind to a few members. If it expands, then I am compelled to take as witnesses of my shame men whose feelings toward me I do not know, as my counselors men of whose wisdom I have no experience, as guides to my duties men whose (179) virtue I cannot yet estimate: an unfair demand. In a small society of friends I can vow obedience, and it can demand obedience from me, only in so far as it has convinced me that a certain way of acting is my duty; I can promise faith and it can demand it only if I have fully made up my mind that there are good reasons why the faith is true. A society of this kind I can leave if I think I need it no more, i.e., when I think I have reached my majority, or if its character appears to be such that I can no longer give it my confidence, that I can no longer regard it as fulfilling its purpose, or that I propose to renounce my aim of making moral progress (an aim which virtue may demand of me though no man may), whether I renounce it altogether or only renounce the sort of progress which the society desires. While I remain in the society I must be left free to choose the means even if I still will the society's end, and my choice must either be made on the basis of my judgement that it is good or else be adopted out of confidence in my friends.

This compact, which is actually found in any friendship based on mutual respect or a common will for the good, may readily become irksome and petty if it is extended to cover trifles and if it meddles with things which properly must always be left to individual choice.

The early Christians were friends in this sense. They were made so, or their previous acquaintanceship was strengthened, by what they had in common, namely, their oppressed situation and their doctrine. Comfort, instruction, support of every kind, each found in the other. Their aim was not a free search for the truth (since the truth was already given) so much as the removal of doubt, the consolidation of faith, and the advance in Christian perfection which was most intimately connected with these. As the faith became more widely disseminated, every Christian should have found in every other, the Egyptian in the Briton, wherever he might chance to meet him, a friend and a brother like those he might expect to find in his household or among his neighbors. But this bond became continually looser, and friendship between Christians went so little below the surface that it was often a friendship between members of a community who, though separated from one another by vanity and clashing interests, did act to outward appearance and by profession in accordance with Christian love, but who regarded their petty envy, their dogmatism, and their arrogance as zeal for Christian virtue and passed them off for such or who could readily put actual animosity down to some dissimilarity in doctrine or insincerity in behavior.

Entry into the society was regarded as every man's duty, his most sacrosanct duty to God; exit from it as entry into (180) hell. But although the sect hated and persecuted anyone who resigned from its fellowship, resignation did not entail the loss of civil rights any more than not joining it at all did. Moreover, by entering the society a man acquired neither those rights nor even the qualification for acquiring them.

A fundamental condition of entry into the Christian society, a condition which differentiates it *in toto* from a philosophical group, was the unconditional obedience in faith and action which had to be vowed to the society. Since everyone was left free either to join the society or not, and since membership had no bearing on civil rights, this condition entailed no injustice.

All these traits which are found in a circle of trusted friends, united for the purpose of truth-seeking or moral improvement, are also found in the society of the Christian sects whose bond is the furtherance of Christian perfection and fortification in Christian truth. These same traits are met later on a large scale in the Christian church once it has become universal; but because this church has become a church which is universal throughout a state, their essence is disfigured, they have become contradictory and unjust, and the church is now a state in itself.

While the Christian church was still in its beginnings, each congregation had the right to choose its own deacons, presbyters, and bishops. When the church expanded and became a state, this right was lost. Just as in the temporal state an individual corporation resigns to the sovereign (whose will is regarded as expressing the will of all) its right of choosing its officials and tax-collectors and fixing its own taxes, so too every Christian congregation has lost the right of choosing its pastor and resigns it to the spiritual state.

Public confessors were appointed as counselors in matters of conscience. Originally, everyone was free to choose a friend whom he respected and to make him the confidant of his secrets and faults, but instead of this the rulers of the spiritual state now arranged that these confessors should be officials to whom everyone had to have recourse.

Confession of one's faults was originally voluntary, but now it is the duty of every citizen of the spiritual state, a duty over whose transgression the church has pronounced its supreme punishment, eternal damnation.

(181) Surveillance of Christian morality is the chief aim of this spiritual state, and therefore even thoughts, as well as those vices and sinful impulses whose punishment is outside the scope of the state proper, are objects of legislation and punishment by the spiritual state. A crime against the temporal state (which as such is punished by that state) is punished over again as a sin by the spiritual state which also punishes as sins all crimes which cannot be the object of civil

legislation. The result is that the list of punishments in canon law is endless.

No society can be denied the right to exclude those who refuse to submit to its laws, because everyone is free in his choice to enter it, to assume the duties of membership, and thereby to acquire a right to its benefits. Just as this right is granted to every guild and corporation, so too the church has the right to exclude from its fellowship those people who decline to accept the conditions imposed, namely, faith and the other modes of behavior. But since the scope of this [spiritual] state is now the same as that of the temporal state, a man excluded from the spiritual state is thereby deprived of his civil rights as well. This did not happen while the church was still circumscribed, still not dominant, and hence it is only now that these two kinds of state come into collision with one another. . . .

Notes

[1] The notes in this chapter are Hegel's and are reproduced as they appear in the Knox edition cited on the acknowledgements page (above, p. xiii). The use of square brackets in the text indicates that what they enclose has been added by the translator.

[2] For an instance see Acts [xii.11], where Peter, the most fervent of them all, says: "Now I know for a surety [that the Lord hath sent his angel]." Cf. also the vessel with the different animals [Acts x. 9 ff.], and the incidents cited above [p. 70, note].

[3] ["Go ye into all the world and preach the gospel to every creature. He that believeth and is baptized shall be saved; but he that believeth not shall be damned. And these signs shall follow them that believe: In my name shall they cast out devils; they shall speak with new tongues; they shall take up serpents; and if they drink any deadly thing it shall not hurt them; they shall lay hands on the sick and they shall recover."]

[4] [Hegel is contrasting the command (whose authenticity he clearly doubts) with John's account of the discourses after the Last Supper. See below, the first paragraph of §19 and also pp. 276-77.]

[5] It is common knowledge that this means more than just prophesying; it approximates rather, or is at least akin to καιναις γλωσσαις λαλειν [speaking with new tongues, Mark xvi. 17.].

[6] [I.e., "fulfillment" (see *The Spirit of Christianity and Its Fate*, §ii).]

Chapter 20

Arthur Schopenhauer, *The World as Will and Representation*

Arthur Schopenhauer (1788-1860) has come to be labeled the philosopher of **pessimism.** *Schopenhauer took his starting point in philosophy from Kant's work, yet conceived of a world-view which Kant most certainly would have rejected, both in principle and in its particulars.*

For Kant, the only good thing in the world, without qualification, is a good will. For Schopenhauer, one might say, though at the risk of oversimplification, the only thing in the world is the Will. Indeed, the world itself is nothing but a universal Will, a will-to-life which by implication must destroy something in its very being. Thus, the world as Will is nothing but a universally destructive Will, of which the human will is but a particular manifestation. This is not at all "the best of all possible worlds," as it was for Leibniz, the predecessor to Kant; rather, for Schopenhauer, this is probably the worst of all possible worlds, since the Universal Will emerges in individual will (thus Schopenhauer's emphasis on the **principium individuationis,** *the principle of individuation), wills divided from the rest by the very nature of their being. Such a will, which can only at bottom will its particularity, must therefore be destructive to a degree in its very nature. Therefore, for Schopenhauer, the only way in which to approximate a "good" life is by living a life of asceticism.*

Needless to say, Schopenhauer had reservations about friendship, as the following selections from **The World as Will and Representation** *show. And, for what it is worth, Schopenhauer lived a*

233

life relatively true to his principle. The son of a very successful businessman and of a mother who was a "popular" novelist, Schopenhauer inherited a considerable sum of money and lived a life removed from the busier world around him.

The World as Will and Representation

Vol. I: Fourth Book: The World as Will: Second Aspect

§ 66

Morality without argumentation and reasoning, that is, mere moralizing, cannot have any effect, because it does not motivate. But a morality that *does* motivate can do so only by acting on self-love. Now what springs from this has no moral worth. From this it follows that no genuine virtue can be brought about through morality and abstract knowledge in general, but that such virtue must spring from the intuitive knowledge that recognizes in another's individuality the same inner nature as in one's own.

For virtue does indeed result from knowledge, but not from abstract knowledge communicable through words. If this were so, virtue could be taught, and by expressing here in the abstract its real nature and the knowledge at its foundation, we should have ethically improved everyone who comprehended this. But this is by no means the case. On the contrary, we are as little able to produce a virtuous person by ethical discourses or sermons as all the systems of aesthetics from Aristotle's downwards have ever been able to produce a poet. For the concept is unfruitful for the real inner nature of virtue, just as it is for art; and only in a wholly subordinate position can it serve as an instrument in elaborating and preserving what has been ascertained and inferred in other ways. *Velle non discit*ur.[1] In fact, abstract dogmas are without influence on virtue, i.e., on goodness of disposition; false dogmas do not disturb it, and true ones hardly support it. Actually it would be a bad business if the principal thing in a man's life, his ethical worth that counts for eternity, depended on something whose attainment was so very much subject to chance as are dogmas, religious teachings, and philosophical arguments. For morality dogmas have merely the value that the man who is virtuous from another kind of knowledge shortly to be discussed has in them a scheme or formula. According to this, he renders to his own faculty of reason an account, for the most part only fictitious, of his non-egoistical actions, the nature of which it, in other words he himself, does not *comprehend.* With such an account he has been accustomed to rest content. . . .

Genuine goodness of disposition, disinterested virtue, and pure nobleness of mind, therefore, do not come from abstract knowledge; yet they do come from knowledge. But it is a direct and intuitive knowledge that cannot be reasoned away or arrived at by reasoning; a knowledge that, just because it is not abstract, cannot be communicated, but must dawn on each of us. It therefore finds its real and adequate expression not in words, but simply and solely in deeds, in conduct, in the course of a man's life. We who are here looking for the theory of virtue, and who thus have to express in abstract terms the inner nature of the knowledge lying at its foundation, shall nevertheless be unable to furnish that knowledge itself in this expression, but only the concept of that knowledge. We thus always start from conduct, in which alone it becomes visible, and refer to such conduct as its only adequate expression. We only interpret and explain this expression, in other words, express in the abstract what really takes place in it.

Now before we speak of the *good* proper, in contrast to the *bad* that has been described, we must touch on the mere negation of the bad as an intermediate stage; this is *justice.* We have adequately explained above what right and wrong are; therefore we can briefly say here that the man who voluntarily recognizes and accepts that merely moral boundary between wrong and right, even where no State or other authority guarantees it, and who consequently, according to our explanation, never in the affirmation of his own will goes to the length of denying the will that manifests itself in another individual, is *just.* Therefore, in order to increase his own well-being, he will not inflict suffering on others; that is to say, he will not commit any crime; he will respect the rights and property of everyone. We now see that for such a just man the *principium individuationis* is no longer an absolute partition as it is for the bad; that he does not, like the bad man, affirm merely his own phenomenon of will and deny all others; that others are not for him mere masks, whose inner nature is quite different from his. On the contrary, he shows by his way of acting that he *again recognizes* his own inner being, namely the will-to-live as thing-in-itself, in the phenomenon of another given to him merely as representation. Thus he finds himself again in that phenomenon up to a certain degree, namely that of doing no wrong, i.e., of not injuring. Now in precisely this degree he sees through the *principium individuationis*, the veil of Maya.

To this extent he treats the inner being outside himself like his own; he does not injure it.

If we examine the innermost nature of this justice, there is to be found in it the intention not to go so far in the affirmation of one's own will as to deny the phenomena of will in others by compelling them to serve one's own will. We shall therefore want to provide for others just as much as we benefit from them. The highest degree of this justice of disposition, which, however, is always associated with goodness proper, the character of this last being no longer merely negative, extends so far that a person questions his right to inherited property, desires to support his body only by his own powers, mental and physical, feels every service rendered by others, every luxury, as a reproach, and finally resorts to voluntary poverty. Thus we see how Pascal would not allow the performance of any more services when he turned to asceticism, although he had servants enough. In spite of his constant bad health, he made his own bed, fetched his own food from the kitchen, and so on. (*Vie de Pascal,* by his sister, p. 19) Quite in keeping with this, it is reported that many Hindus, even rajas, with great wealth, use it merely to support and maintain their families, their courts, and their establishment of servants, and follow with strict scrupulousness the maxim of eating nothing but what they have sown and reaped with their own hands. Yet at the bottom of this there lies a certain misunderstanding, for just because the individual is rich and powerful, he is able to render such important services to the whole of human society that they counterbalance inherited wealth, for the security of which he is indebted to society. In reality, that excessive justice of such Hindus is more than justice, indeed actual renunciation, denial of the will-to-live, asceticism, about which we shall speak last of all. On the other hand, pure idleness and living through the exertions of others with inherited property, without achieving anything, can indeed be regarded as morally wrong, even though it must remain right according to positive laws.

We have found that voluntary justice has its innermost origin in a certain degree of seeing through the *principium individuationis,* while the unjust man remains entirely involved in this principle. This seeing through can take place not only in the degree required for justice, but also in the higher degree that urges a man to positive benevolence and well-doing, to philanthropy. Moreover, this can happen however strong and energetic the will that appears in such an individual may be in itself. Knowledge can always counterbalance it, can teach a man to resist the temptation to do wrong, and can even produce every degree of goodness, indeed of resignation. Therefore the good man is in no way to be regarded as an originally weaker phenomenon of will than the bad, but it is knowledge that masters in him the blind craving of will. Certainly there are individuals who merely seem to be good-natured on account of the weakness of the will that appears in them; but what they are soon shows itself in the fact that they are not capable of any considerable self-conquest, in order to perform a just or good deed.

Now if, as a rare exception, we come across a man who possesses a considerable income, but uses only a little of it for himself, and gives all the rest to persons in distress, whilst he himself forgoes many pleasures and comforts, and we try to make clear to ourselves the action of this man, we shall find, quite apart from the dogmas by which he himself will make his action intelligible to his faculty of reason, the simplest general expression and the essential character of his way of acting to be that he *makes less distinction than is usually made between himself and others.* This very distinction is in the eyes of many so great, that the suffering of another is a direct pleasure for the wicked, and a welcome means to their own well-being for the unjust. The merely just person is content not to cause it; and generally most people know and are acquainted with innumerable sufferings of others in their vicinity, but do not decide to alleviate them, because to do so they would have to undergo some privation. Thus a strong distinction seems to prevail in each of all these between his own ego and another's. On the other hand, to the noble person, whom we have in mind, this distinction is not so significant. The *principium individuationis,* the form of the phenomenon, no longer holds him so firmly in its grasp, but the suffering he sees in others touches him almost as closely as does his own. He therefore tries to strike a balance between the two, denies himself pleasures, undergoes privations, in order to alleviate another's suffering. He perceives that the distinction between himself and others, which to the wicked man is so great a gulf, belongs only to a fleeting, deceptive phenomenon. He recognizes immediately, and without reasons or arguments, that the in-itself of his own phenomenon is also that of others, namely that will-to-live which constitutes the inner nature of everything, and lives in all; in fact, he recognizes that this extends even to the animals and to the whole of nature; he will therefore not cause suffering even to an animal.[2]

He is now just as little able to let others starve, while he himself has enough and to spare, as anyone would one day be on short commons, in order on the following day to have more than he can enjoy. For the veil of Maya has become transparent for the person who performs works of love, and the deception of the *principium individuationis* has left him. Himself, his will, he recognizes in every creature, and hence in the sufferer also. He is free from the perversity with which the will-to-live, failing to recognize itself, here in one individual enjoys fleeting and delusive pleasures, and there in another individual suffers and starves in return for these. Thus this will inflicts misery and endures misery, not knowing that, like Thyestes, it is eagerly devouring its own flesh. Then it here laments its unmerited suffering, and there commits an outrage without the least fear of Nemesis, always merely because it fails to recognize itself in the phenomenon of another, and thus does not perceive eternal justice, involved as it is in the *principium individuationis*, and so generally in that kind of knowledge which is governed by the principle of sufficient reason. To be cured of this delusion and deception of Maya and to do works of love are one and the same thing; but the latter is the inevitable and infallible symptom of that knowledge. . . .

§ 67

. . . Selfishness is ερως, sympathy or compassion is αγαπη. Combinations of the two occur frequently; even genuine friendship is always a mixture of selfishness and sympathy. Selfishness lies in the pleasure in the presence of the friend, whose individuality corresponds to our own, and it almost invariably constitutes the greatest part; sympathy shows itself in a sincere participation in the friend's weal and woe, and in the disinterested sacrifices made for the latter. Even Spinoza says: *Benevolentia nihil aliud est, quam cupiditas ex commiseratione orta*[3] (*Ethics*, iii, pr. 27, cor. 3 schol.). As confirmation of our paradoxical sentence, it may be observed that the tone and words of the language and the caresses of pure love entirely coincide with the tone of sympathy or compassion. Incidentally, it may be observed also that sympathy and pure love are expressed in Italian by the same word, *pietà*. . . .

Vol. II: Ch. XIX: On the Primacy of the Will in Self-Consciousness

. . . Everywhere those who promote the appearance of any piece of work appeal, in the event of its turning out unsatisfactorily, to their good will, of which there was no lack. In this way they believe they safeguard the essential, that for which they are properly responsible, and their true self. The inadequacy of their faculties, on the other hand, is regarded by them as the want of a suitable tool.

If a person is *stupid,* we excuse him by saying that he cannot help it; but if we attempted to excuse in precisely the same way the person who is bad, we should be laughed at. And yet the one quality, like the other, is inborn. This proves that the will is the man proper, the intellect its mere tool.

Therefore it is always only our *willing* that is regarded as dependent on us, in other words, the expression of our real inner nature, for which we are therefore made responsible. For this reason it is absurd and unjust when anyone tries to take us to task for our beliefs, and so for our knowledge; for we are obliged to regard this as something that, although it rules within us, is as little within our power as are the events of the external world. Therefore here also it is clear that the *will* alone is man's own inner nature; that the *intellect,* on the other hand, with its operations which occur regularly like the external world, is related to the will as something external, as a mere tool.

High intellectual faculties have always been regarded as a *gift* of nature or of the gods; thus they have been called *Gaben, Begabung, ingenii dotes,* gifts (a man highly gifted), and have been regarded as something different from man himself, as something that has fallen to his lot by favour. On the other hand, no one has ever taken the same view with regard to moral excellences, though they too are inborn; on the contrary, these have always been regarded as something coming from the man himself, belonging to him essentially, in fact constituting his own true self. Now it follows from this that the will is man's real inner nature, while the intellect, on the other hand, is secondary, a tool, an endowment.

In accordance with this, all religions promise a reward beyond this life in eternity for excellences of the *will* or of the heart, but none for excellences of the head, of the understanding. Virtue expects its reward in the next world; prudence hopes for it in this; genius neither in this world nor in the next; for it is its own reward. Accordingly the will is the external part, the intellect the temporal.

Association, community, intercourse between persons is based as a rule on relations concerning the *will,* rarely on such as concern the *intellect.* The first kind of community may be called the *material,* the other the *formal.* Of the former kind are the bonds of family and relationship, as well as all connections and associations that rest on any common aim or interest, such as that of trade, profession, social position, a corporation, party, faction, and so on. With these it is a question merely of the disposition, the intention, and there may exist the greatest diversity of intellectual faculties and of their development. Therefore everyone can not only live with everyone else in peace and harmony, but cooperate with him and be allied to him for the common good of both. Marriage also is a union of hearts, not of heads. Matters are different, however, with merely *formal* community that aims only at an exchange of ideas; this requires a certain equality of intellectual faculties and of culture. Great differences in this respect place an impassable gulf between one man and another; such a gulf lies, for example, between a great mind and a blockhead, a scholar and a peasant, a courtier and a sailor. Therefore such heterogeneous beings have difficulty in making themselves understood, so long as it is a question of communicating ideas, notions, and views. Nevertheless, close *material* friendship can exist between them, and they can be faithful allies, conspirators, and persons under a pledge. For in all that concerns the *will* alone, which includes friendship, enmity, honesty, fidelity, falseness, and treachery, they are quite homogeneous, formed of the same clay, and neither mind nor culture makes any difference to this; in fact, in this respect the uncultured man often puts the scholar to shame, and the sailor the courtier. For in spite of the most varied degrees of culture there exist the same virtues and vices, emotions and passions; and although somewhat modified in their expression, they very soon recognize one another, even in the most heterogeneous individuals, whereupon those who are like-minded come together, and those of contrary opinion show enmity to one another.

Brilliant qualities of the mind earn admiration, not affection; that is reserved for moral qualities, qualities of character. Everyone will much rather choose as his friend the honest, the kind-hearted, and even the complaisant, easy-going person who readily concurs, than one who is merely witty or clever. Many a man will be preferred to one who is clever, even through insignificant, accidental, and external qualities that are exactly in keeping with the inclinations of someone else. Only the man who himself possesses great intellect will want a clever man for his companion; on the other hand, his friendship will depend on moral qualities, for on these rests his real estimation of a person, in which a single good trait of character covers up and effaces great defects of understanding. The known goodness of a character makes us patient and accommodating to weaknesses of understanding as well as to the obtuseness and childishness of old age. A decidedly noble character, in spite of a complete lack of intellectual merits and culture, stands out as one that lacks nothing; on the other hand, the greatest mind, if tainted by strong moral defects, will nevertheless always seem blameworthy. For just as torches and fireworks become pale and insignificant in the presence of the sun, so intellect, even genius, and beauty likewise, are outshone and eclipsed by goodness of heart. Where such goodness appears in a high degree, it can compensate for the lack of those qualities to such an extent that we are ashamed of having regretted their absence. Even the most limited understanding and grotesque ugliness, whenever extraordinary goodness of heart has proclaimed itself as their accompaniment, become transfigured, as it were, enwrapped in rays of a beauty of a more exalted kind, since now a wisdom speaks out of them in whose presence all other wisdom must be reduced to silence. For goodness of heart is a transcendent quality; it belongs to an order of things reaching beyond this life, and is incommensurable with any other perfection. Where it is present in a high degree, it makes the heart so large that this embraces the world, so that everything now lies within it, no longer outside. For goodness of heart identifies all beings with its own nature. It then extends to others the boundless indulgence that everyone ordinarily bestows only on himself. Such a man is not capable of becoming angry; even when his own intellectual or physical defects have provoked the malicious sneers and jeers of others, in his heart he reproaches himself alone for having been the occasion of such expressions. He therefore continues, without imposing restrictions on himself, to treat those persons in the kindest manner, confidently hoping that they will turn from their error in his regard, and will recognize themselves also in him. What are wit and genius in comparison with this? What is Bacon?

A consideration of the estimation of our own selves leads also to the same result that we have here obtained from considering our estimation of others. How fundamentally different is the self-satisfaction which occurs in a moral respect from that which occurs in an intellectual! The former arises from our looking back on our conduct and seeing that we have practiced fidelity and honesty with heavy sacrifices, that we have helped many, forgiven many, have been better to others than they have been to us, so that we can say with King Lear: "I am a man more sinn'd against than sinning"; and it arises to the fullest extent when possibly even some noble deed shines in our memory. A profound seriousness will accompany the peaceful bliss that such an examination affords us; and if we see others inferior to us in this respect, this will not cause us any rejoicing; on the contrary, we shall deplore it and sincerely wish that they were as we are. How entirely differently, on the other hand, does the knowledge of our intellectual superiority affect us! Its ground-bass is really the above-quoted saying of Hobbes: *Omnis animi voluptas, omnisque alacritas in eo sita est, quod quis habeat, quibuscum conferens se, possit magnifice sentire de se ipso.*[4] Arrogant, triumphant vanity, a proud, scornful, contemptuous disdain of others, inordinate delight in the consciousness of decided and considerable superiority, akin to pride of physical advantages—this is the result here. This contrast between the two kinds of self-satisfaction shows that the one concerns our true inner and eternal nature, the other a more external, merely temporal, indeed scarcely more than a mere physical advantage. In fact, the *intellect* is a mere function of the brain; the *will*, on the contrary, is that whose function is the whole man, according to his being and inner nature.

Notes

[1] "Willing cannot be taught." [*Tr.*]

[2] Man's right over the life and power of animals rests on the fact that, since with the enhanced clearness of consciousness suffering increases in like measure, the pain that the animal suffers through death or work is still not so great as that which man would suffer through merely being deprived of the animal's flesh or strength. Therefore in the affirmation of his own existence, man can go so far as to deny the existence of the animal. In this way, the will-go-live as a whole endures less suffering than if the opposite course were adopted. At the same time, this determines the extent to which man may, without wrong, make use of the powers of animals. This limit, however, is often exceeded, especially in the case of beasts of burden, and of hounds used in hunting. The activities of societies for the prevention of cruelty to animals are therefore directed especially against these. In my opinion, that right does not extend to vivisection, particularly of the higher animals. On the other hand, the insect does not suffer through its death as much as man suffers through its sting. The Hindus do not see this. [*Note by Schopenhauer*]

[3] "Benevolence is nothing but a desire sprung from compassion." [*Tr.*]

[4] "All the delights of the heart and every cheerful frame of mind depend on our having someone with whom we can compare ourselves and think highly of ourselves." [*Tr.*]

Chapter 21

Søren Kierkegaard, *Either/Or*

Søren Aabye Kierkegaard (1813-1855) was a Danish philosopher and religious thinker and is frequently regarded as the father of existentialism. A melancholy, hunchbacked, and delightfully witty bachelor, he attacked the provincial Danish literary and ecclesiastical establishments of his time for their passionless intellectual conformism. Calling himself "that Individual," he directed his brilliant sarcasm and irony at their collective contempt for the individual. He rejected both the grand Hegelian system of philosophy he encountered at the University of Copenhagen and the organized liberal Lutheranism of the state church, because neither supplied what he wanted—"a truth which is true *for me, to find* the idea for which I can live and die" (**Journal**, Aug. 1, 1835).*

While his maverick psychological and spiritual probings and new, anti-rationalistic, introspective way of philosophizing without a "system" alienated the press, the church, and the philosophical establishment of his age, Kierkegaard's writings wielded an enormous influence on "depth psychology," the "neo-orthodox theology" of Karl Barth and others, and the work of twentieth-century existentialists such as Heidegger, Jaspers, and Sartre.

In the twelve year period preceding his premature death at the age of forty-two, Kierkegaard produced twenty-one extraordinary books, and his unpublished papers extended in print to over eight thousand pages. Not only was Kierkegaard a prolific writer; his work is of exceptional literary quality and bears the mark of a brilliant philosopher-theologian, a shrewd social analyst, and master psychologist, making for unusually interesting reading.

Kierkegaard deals with three levels or stages of existence in his writings—the aesthetic, ethical and religious—and the first two of these were the focus of his first major work, **Either/Or** *(1843). This book, like many of his books published pseudonymously, claims to contain the manuscripts of two men—the two halves, "Either" and "Or," which constitute the whole work. One is a young romantic who, in delightfully witty essays, such as "Rotation Method" and the famous "Diary of a Seducer," presents the pleasures of the* aesthetic *life. The other is an older man named Judge William, who writes letters discussing marriage, friendship and human nature (such as the "Aesthetic Validity of Marriage" and "Equilibrium") in which he tries to convince his young friend of the superiority of the* ethical *life.*

Either/Or, *then, confronts us with two alternative life-styles: the "aesthete's" life of pleasure, self-indulgence and personal taste (championed by the young, Don Juan figure who is the anonymous author of* **Either**); *and the ethical life of moral principle and duty (championed by Judge William). How the issue of friendship is regarded and dealt with from each perspective is of paramount interest. Kierkegaard offers no "objective" assessment of the two alternative views from the position of a detached, impartial observer; for, of course, he rejects the very possibility of such a position. Within the context of* **Either/Or** *he may seem to be encouraging the choice of the ethical life; yet within the context of his larger philosophy, his intention is rather to show the inadequacy of both positions in order to clear the way for the emergence of the category of the religious. This element of "paradox" is a recurring theme in existentialism.*

Our selections, from "The Rotation Method" and "Equilibrium," are taken respectively from Volumes I and II of **Either/Or**.

Vol. I: The Rotation Method

Starting from a principle is affirmed by people of experience to be a very reasonable procedure; I am willing to humor them, and so begin with the principle that all men are bores. Surely no one will prove himself so great a bore as to contradict me in this.... Boredom is the root of all evil. Strange that boredom, in itself so staid and stolid, should have such power to set in motion. The influence it exerts is altogether magical, except that it is not the influence of attraction, but of repulsion.

In the case of children, the ruinous character of boredom is universally acknowledged. Children are always well-behaved as long as they are enjoying themselves.... What wonder, then, that the world goes from bad to worse, and that its evils increase more and more, as boredom increases, and boredom is the root of all evil.

The history of this can be traced from the very beginning of the world. The gods were bored, and so they created man. Adam was bored because he was alone, and so Eve was created. Thus boredom entered the world, and increased in proportion to the increase of population. Adam was bored alone; then Adam and Eve were bored together; then Adam and Eve and Cain and Abel were bored *en famille*; then the population of the world increased, and the peoples were bored *en masse*. To divert themselves they conceived the idea of constructing a tower high enough to reach the heavens. This idea is itself as boring as the tower was high, and constitutes a terrible proof of how boredom gained the upper hand....

All men are bores. The word itself suggests the possibility of a subdivision. It may just as well indicate a man who bores others as one who bores himself. Those who bore others are the mob, the crowd, the infinite multitude of men in general. Those who bore themselves are the elect, the aristocracy; and it is a curious fact that those who do not bore themselves usually bore others, while those who bore themselves entertain others. Those who do not bore themselves are generally people who, in one way or another, keep themselves extremely busy; these people are precisely on this account the most tiresome, the most utterly unendurable....

Now since boredom as shown above is the root of all evil, what can be more natural than the effort to overcome it?...

My own dissent from the ordinary view is sufficiently expressed in the use I make of the word, "rotation." This word might seem to conceal an ambiguity, and if I wished to use it so as to find room in it for the ordinary method, I should have to define it as a change of field. But the farmer does not use the word in this sense. I shall, however, adopt this meaning for a moment, in order to speak of the rotation which depends on change in its boundless infinity, its extensive dimension, so to speak.

This is the vulgar and inartistic method, and needs to be supported by illusion. One tires of living in the country, and moves to the city; one tires of one's native land, and travels abroad; one is *europamüde*,[1] and goes to, and so on; finally one indulges in a sentimental hope of endless journeyings from star to star. Or the movement is different but still extensive. One tires of porcelain dishes and eats on silver; one tires of silver and turns to gold; one burns half of to get an idea of the burning of. This method defeats itself; it is plain endlessness. And what did Nero gain by it? Antonine was wiser; he says: "It is in your power to review your life, to look at things you saw before, from another point of view."[2]

My method does not consist in change of field, but resembles the true rotation method in changing the crop and the mode of cultivation. Here we have at once the principle of limitation, the only saving principle in the world. The more you limit yourself, the more fertile you become in invention. A prisoner in solitary confinement for life becomes very inventive, and a spider may furnish him with much entertainment. One need only hark back to one's schooldays. We were at an age when aesthetic considerations were ignored in the choice of one's instructors, most of whom were for that reason very tiresome; how fertile in invention one then proved to be! How entertaining to catch a fly and hold it imprisoned under a nut shell and to watch how it pushed the shell around; what pleasure from cutting a hole in the desk, putting a fly in it, and then peeping down at it through a piece of paper! How entertaining sometimes to listen to the monotonous drip of water from the roof! How close an observer one becomes under such circumstances, when not the least noise nor movement escapes one's attention! Here we have the extreme application of the method which seeks to achieve results intensively, not extensively.

One must guard against *friendship*. How is a friend defined? He is not what philosophy calls the necessary other, but the superfluous third. What are friendship's ceremonies? You drink each other's health, you open an artery and mingle your blood with that of the friend. It is difficult to say when the proper moment for this arrives, but it announces itself mysteriously; you feel some way that you can no longer address one another formally. When once you have had this feeling, then it can never appear that you have made a mistake, like Geert Vestphaler, who discovered that he had been drinking to friendship with the public hangman.[3] What are the infallible marks of friendship? Let antiquity answer: *idem velle, idem nolle, ea demum firma amicitia,*[4] and also extremely tiresome. What are the infallible marks of friendship? Mutual assistance in word and deed. Two friends form a close association in order to be everything to one another, and that although it is impossible for one human being to be anything to another human being except to be in his way. To be sure one may help him with money, assist him in and out of his coat, be his humble servant, and tender him congratulations on New Year's Day, on the day of his wedding, on the birth of a child, on the occasion of a funeral.

But because you abstain from friendship it does not follow that you abstain from social contacts. On the contrary, these social relationships may at times be permitted to take on a deeper character, provided you always have so much more momentum in yourself that you can sheer off at will, in spite of sharing for a time in the momentum of the common movement. It is believed that such conduct leaves unpleasant memories, the unpleasantness being due to the fact that a relationship which has meant something now vanishes and becomes as nothing. But this is a misunderstanding. The unpleasant is merely a piquant ingredient in the sullenness of life. Besides, it is possible for the same relationship again to play a significant role, though in another manner. The essential thing is never to stick fast, and for this it is necessary to have oblivion back of one. The experienced farmer lets his land lie fallow now and then, and the theory of social prudence recommends the same. Everything will doubtless return, though in a different form; that which has once been present in the rotation will remain in it, but the mode of cultivation will be varied. You therefore quite consistently hope to meet your friends and acquaintances in a better world, but you do not share the fear of the crowd that they will be altered so that you cannot recognize them; your fear is rather lest they be wholly unaltered. It is remarkable how much significance even the most insignificant person can gain from a rational mode of cultivation.

One must never enter into the relation of *marriage*. Husband and wife promise to love one another for eternity. This is all very fine, but it does not mean very much; for if their love comes to an end in time, it will surely be ended in eternity. If, instead of promising forever, the parties would say: until Easter, or until May-day comes, there might be some meaning in what they say; for then they would have said something definite, and also something that they might be able to keep. And how does a marriage usually work out? In a little while one party begins to perceive that there is something wrong, then the other party complains, and cries to heaven: faithless! faithless! A little later the second party reaches the same standpoint, and a neutrality is established in which the mutual faithlessness is mutually canceled, to the satisfaction and contentment of both parties. But it is now too late, for there are great difficulties connected with divorce.

Such being the case with marriage, it is not surprising that the attempt should be made in so many ways to bolster it up with moral supports. When a man seeks separation from his wife, the cry is at once raised that he is depraved, a scoundrel, etc. How silly, and what an indirect attack upon marriage! If marriage has reality, then he is sufficiently punished by forfeiting this happiness; if it has no reality, it is absurd to abuse him because he is wiser than the rest. When a man grows tired of his money and throws it out of the window, we do not call him a scoundrel; for either money has reality, and so he is sufficiently punished by depriving himself of it, or it has none, and then he is, of course, a wise man.

One must always take care not to enter into any relationship in which there is a possibility of many members. For this reason friendship is dangerous, to say nothing of marriage. Husband and wife are indeed said to become one, but this is a very dark and mystic saying. When you are one of several, then you have lost your freedom; you cannot send for your traveling boots whenever you wish, you cannot move aimlessly about in the world. If you have a wife it is difficult; if you have a wife and perhaps a child, it is troublesome; if you have a wife and children, it is impossible. True, it has happened that a gypsy woman has carried her husband through life on her back, but for one thing this is very rare, and for another, it is likely to be tiresome in the long run—for the husband. Marriage brings one into fatal connection with custom and tradition, and traditions and customs are like the wind and weather, altogether incalculable. In Japan, I have been told, it is the custom for husbands to lie in childbed. Who knows but the time will come when the customs of foreign countries will obtain a foothold in Europe?

Friendship is dangerous, marriage still more so; for woman is and ever will be the ruin of a man, as soon as he contracts a permanent relation with her. Take a young man who is fiery as an Arabian courser, let him marry, he is lost. Woman is first proud, then is she weak, then she swoons, then he swoons, then the whole family swoons. A woman's love is nothing but dissimulation and weakness.

But because a man does not marry, it does not follow that his life need be wholly deprived of the erotic element. And the erotic ought also to have infinitude; but poetic infinitude, which can just as well be limited to an hour as to a month. When two beings fall in love with one another and begin to suspect that they were made for each other, it is time to have the courage to break it off; for by going on they have everything to lose and nothing to gain. This seems a paradox, and it is so for the feeling, but not for the understanding. In this sphere it is particularly necessary that one should make use of one's moods; through them one may realize an inexhaustible variety of combinations.

One should never accept appointment to an official position. If you do, you will become a mere Richard Roe, a tiny little cog in the machinery of the body politic; you even cease to be master of your own conduct, and in that case your theories are of little help. You receive a title, and this brings in its train every sin and evil. The law under which you have become a slave is equally tiresome, whether your advancement is fast or slow. A title can never be got rid of except by the commission of some crime which draws down on you a public whipping; even then you are not certain, for you may have it restored to you by royal pardon.

Even if one abstains from involvement in official business, one ought not to be inactive, but should pursue such occupations as are compatible with a sort of leisure; one should engage in all sorts of breadless arts. In this connection the self-development should be intensive rather than extensive, and one should, in spite of mature years, be able to prove the truth of the proverb that children are pleased with a rattle and tickled with a straw.

If one now, according to the theory of social jurisprudence, varies the soil—for if he had contact with one person only, the rotation method would fail as badly as if a farmer had only one acre of land, which would make it impossible for him to fallow, something which is of extreme importance—then one must also constantly vary himself, and this is the essential secret. For this purpose one must necessarily have control over one's moods. To control them in the sense of producing them at will is impossible, but prudence teaches how to utilize the moment. As an experienced sailor always looks out over the water and sees a squall coming from far away, so one ought always to see the mood a little in advance. One should know how the mood affects one's own mind and the mind of others, before putting it on. You first strike a note or two to evoke pure tones, and see what there is in a man; the intermediate tones follow later. The more experience you have, the more readily you will be convinced that there is often much in a man which is not suspected. When sentimental people, who as such are extremely tiresome, become angry, they are often very entertaining. Badgering a man is a particularly effective method of exploration.

The whole secret lies in arbitrariness. People usually think it easy to be arbitrary, but it requires much study to succeed in being arbitrary so as not to lose oneself in it, but so as to derive satisfaction from it. One does not enjoy the immediate but something quite different which he arbitrarily imports into it. You go to see the middle of a play, you read the third part of a book. By this means you insure yourself a very different kind of enjoyment from that which the author has been so kind as to plan for you. You enjoy something entirely accidental; you consider the whole of existence from this standpoint; let its reality be stranded thereon. I will cite an example. There was a man whose chatter certain circumstances made it necessary for me to listen to. At every opportunity he was ready with a little philosophical lecture, a very tiresome harangue. Almost in despair, I suddenly discovered that he perspired copiously when talking. I saw the pearls of sweat gather on his brow, unite to form a stream, glide down his nose, and hang at the extreme point of his nose in a drop-shaped body. From the moment of making this discovery, all was changed. I even took pleasure in inciting him to begin his philosophical instruction, merely to observe the perspiration on his brow and at the end of his nose.

The poet Baggesen says somewhere of someone that he was doubtless a good man, but that there was one insuperable objection against him, that there was no word that rhymed with his name. It is extremely wholesome thus to let the realities of life split upon an arbitrary interest. You transform something accidental into the absolute, and, as such, into the object of your admiration. This has an excellent effect, especially when one is excited. This method is an excellent stimulus for many persons. You look at everything in life from the standpoint of a wager, and so forth. The more rigidly consistent you are in holding fast to your arbitrariness, the more amusing the ensuing combinations will be. The degree of consistency shows whether you are an artist or a bungler; for to a certain extent all men do the same. The eye with which you look at reality must constantly be changed. The Neo-Platonists assumed that human beings who had been less perfect on earth became after death more or less perfect animals, all according to their deserts. For example, those who had exercised the civic virtues on a lower scale (retail dealers) were transformed into busy animals, like bees. Such a view of life, which here in this world sees all men transformed into animals or plants (Plotinus also thought that some would become plants), suggests rich and varied possibilities. The painter Tischbein sought to idealize every human being into an animal. His method has the fault of being too serious, in that it endeavors to discover a real resemblance.

The arbitrariness in oneself corresponds to the accidental in the external world. One should therefore always have an eye open for the accidental, always be *expeditus*,[5] if anything should offer. The so-called social pleasures for which we prepare a week or two in advance amount to so little; on the other hand, even the most insignificant thing may accidentally offer rich material for amusement. It is impossible here to go into detail, for no theory can adequately embrace the concrete. Even the most completely developed theory is poverty-stricken compared with the fullness which the man of genius easily discovers in his ubiquity.

Vol. II: Equilibrium Between the Aesthetical an the Ethical in the Composition of Personality

... You are an observer, you will therefore concede the justice of my observation that marked individual difference in character is indicated by considering whether the season of friendship falls in the period of very early youth or emerges only at a later age. Volatile natures have no difficulty in adjusting themselves to themselves, their self is from the very beginning current coin; so then trade begins at once. It is not so easy for the deeper natures to find themselves, and until they have found their self they cannot wish that anyone should offer them a friendship they cannot requite. Such natures are commonly absorbed in themselves, and they are observers—but an observer is no friend. So the situation might be explained if such were the case with my friend. However, he has been married. Now the question is whether there is something abnormal in the fact that friendship only appeared after this—for in the foregoing discussion we agreed that it was proper for friendship to come about in later years, but we did not speak of its relation to marriage. Let us here make use again of our common observation. We must now take into consideration a man's relation to the other sex. To those who at a very early age seek the relation of friendship it not rarely happens that when love begins to assert itself friendship fades completely. They discover that friendship was an imperfect form, break off the earlier relationship and concentrate their whole soul exclusively upon love. Others have the opposite experience. Those who too early tasted the sweetness of love, relishing its joys in the intoxication of youth, acquired perhaps an erroneous impression of the other sex. They became perhaps unjust towards the other sex. By their frivolity they purchased perhaps costly experiences, perhaps believed in feelings within themselves which proved not to be durable, or they believed in feelings on the part of others which vanished like a dream. So they gave up love; it was both too little and too much for them, for they had encountered the dialectical difficulty in love without being able to solve it. They then chose friendship. Both of these formations may be regarded as abnormal. My friend is in neither of these situations. He had not made a youthful trial of friendship before he learned to know love, but neither had he harmed himself by enjoying too early the unripe fruit of love. In his love he found the deepest and most complete satisfaction, but precisely because he was thus absolutely set at rest, there now was opened up to him the possibility of a different relationship which in another way might acquire for him a profound and beautiful significance, for whosoever hath, to him shall be given, and he shall have more abundance. *A propos* of this he often remembers that there are trees which bear flowers after the fruit, so that both flowers and fruit are contemporary. With such a tree he compares his life.

But precisely because it was by and with his marriage he learned to see the beauty in having a friend or friends, he has not been for an instant perplexed as to how he ought to regard friendship, or in doubt that it loses its significance if one does not regard it ethically. The many experiences of his life had pretty much destroyed his faith in the aestheticists, but marriage had entirely eradicated every trace of this from his soul. So he felt no inclination to let himself be infatuated by aesthetical jugglery but acquiesced in the view of the ethicists.

In case my friend had not been of such a mind I might have found pleasure in referring him to you, for what you have to say on this topic is confused to such a degree that presumably he would have become completely perplexed at listening to you. You treat friendship as you do everything else. Your soul lacks ethical concentration to such a degree that one can get from you opposite explanations about the same thing, and you are in the highest degree a proof of the thesis that sentimentality and heartlessness are one and the same. Your view of friendship can best be likened to a witch's letter, and he who is willing to adopt this view must become crazy, as to a certain degree the one who propounds it must be assumed to be. If when you are incited to it one hears you propounding the divinity of love for young men, the beauty of encountering a kindred soul, one may be almost tempted to fear that your sentimentality will cost you your young life. At other times you talk in such a way that one would almost think you were an old practitioner who had become sufficiently acquainted with the emptiness and inanity of the world. "A friend," you say, "is an enigmatical thing; like fog he can be seen only at a distance, for only when one has become unfortunate does one remark that one *has had* a friend." It is easy to see that at the bottom of such a judgement upon friendship there lies a different requirement from that which you previously made. Previously you were talking about intellectual friendship, about the beauty of a spiritual erotic with a common enthusiasm for ideas; now you talk about a practical friendship on a business basis, about mutual assistance in the difficulties of earthly life. There is something true in both requirements, but if one cannot find for them a point of unity, it is doubtless best to conclude with your final result, that friendship is nonsense, a result which you deduce from each of your theses and from both in their reciprocal contradiction.

The absolute condition for friendship is agreement in a life view. If one has that, one will not be tempted to found one's friendship upon obscure feelings or upon inexplicable sympathies. Consequently, one will not experience these ludicrous reversals of one day having a friend and the next day having none. One will not fail to appreciate the importance of the inexplicable sympathies, for one is not in a stricter sense a friend of everybody who shares the same life view, but it is not alone upon the enigmatic factor of sympathy one has to count. A true friendship always requires consciousness of its motives and is thereby saved from being a vain enthusiasm.

The moral view in which friends are united must be a positive view. Thus my friend and I have a positive view in common. Therefore, when we look at one another we do not laugh like those augurs of the Roman story, on the contrary, we become serious. It was quite natural for the augurs to laugh, for their view of life was a negative one. You understand that very well, for it is one of your romantic wishes "to find a kindred soul with whom one could laugh at the whole thing." And you say that "the dreadful thing about life, the thing that almost terrifies one, is that hardly anybody notices how miserable it is, and of these few there is only a rare exception who knows how to retain his good humor and laugh at it all." If this longing of yours for a kindred soul is not satisfied, you know how to make the best of it, "for it is in conformity with the idea that there can only be one who laughs; such a one is the true pessimist; if there were more of that kind, it would be proof in fact that the world was not entirely miserable." Now your thought is in full swing and knows no limit. So you express the opinion that "even laughter is only an imperfect expression of the derision the world deserves. If it is to be perfect, one ought properly to be serious. It would be the most perfect mockery of the world if one who propounded the deepest truth was not an enthusiastic believer but a doubter. And this would not be unthinkable, for no one can propound positive truth so admirably as a doubter, the only drawback is that he doesn't believe it. If he were a hypocrite, the mockery would rebound upon him; if he were a doubter, wishing perhaps to believe what he propounded, the mockery would be entirely objective, existence would be mocking itself through him; he propounded a doctrine which could explain everything, the whole race could repose in it securely, but this doctrine could not explain the founder of it. If a man were so shrewd as to be able to conceal the fact that he was mad, he would be able to make the whole world mad." Having such a notion of life, it is difficult to find a friend with a common moral view. Or have you perhaps found such a friend in the mystical society of *Symparanekromenoi* you sometimes talk about?[6] Are you perhaps an association of friends who mutually regard one another as so shrewd that you know how to conceal your madness?

There lived in Greece a wise man; he enjoys the singular honor of being reckoned among the seven wise men if it is assumed that this number was fourteen. If my memory is not very much at fault, his name was Myson. An ancient author relates that he was a misanthrope. This author tells his story very briefly: "It is related of Myson that he was a misanthrope and that he laughed when he was alone. When someone asked why he did so, he replied, 'Just because I am alone.'" You see that you have a predecessor; you will aspire in vain to be admitted into the number of the seven wise men, even though this were defined as twenty-one, for Myson stands in your way. This, however, is of minor importance; but you yourself will perceive that he who laughs when he is alone cannot possibly have a friend, and that for two reasons: first, because he doesn't get a chance to laugh so long as the friend is present; secondly, because the friend must be afraid that he is only waiting for him to go in order that he may have a chance to laugh at him. Therefore, behold, the devil must be your friend! I might almost be tempted to beg you to take this literally, for it is said also of the devil that he laughs when he is alone. It appears to me that there is something very disconsolate in such an isolation, and I cannot help thinking how dreadful it is when a man awakes to another life on the Day of Judgment and again stands there quite alone.

So then friendship requires a positive view of life. But a positive life view cannot be conceived unless it has in it an ethical factor. To be sure, in our age one often enough encounters people who have a system in which there is no place for the ethical.[7] Let them have ten times a system, a life view they have not. In our age such a phenomenon can be explained readily; for as our age is preposterous in so many ways, so it is also in the fact that one is initiated into the greater mysteries before being initiated into the lesser ones. The ethical factor in the life view is thus the starting-point for friendship, and only when one regards friendship in this way does it acquire significance and beauty. If one stops with the sympathetic, the mysterious, then friendship will find its most perfect expression in the relation which exists between the social birds, the so-called lovebirds, whose solidarity is so heartfelt that the death of one is also the death of the other. Although in nature such a relation is beautiful, it is unseemly in the world of spirit. Agreement in a moral view is the constituent factor in friendship. If this is present, the friendship endures even though the friend dies, for the transfigured friend lives on in the other; if this ceases to be, friendship is over even though the friend goes on living.

If one regards friendship thus, one regards it ethically and therefore with a view to its beauty. It thus acquires both significance and beauty. Do I have to cite an authority on my side against you? Very well, then! How did Aristotle interpret friendship? Did he not make this the starting-point for his whole ethical view of life? For with friendship, he says, the concepts of justice are so broadened that they coalesce with it. He bases the concept of justice upon the idea of friendship.[8] His category is thus in a certain sense more perfect than the modern view which bases justice upon duty, the abstract categorical—he bases it upon the social sense. One easily sees from this that for Aristotle the idea of the state becomes the highest idea—but this in turn is the imperfection in his category.

However, I shall not venture to enter into such investigations as the relation between the Aristotelian and the Kantian interpretation of the ethical. I cited Aristotle only to remind you that he too perceived that friendship contributes to help one ethically in gaining reality.

He who regards friendship ethically sees it as a duty. I might therefore say that it is every man's duty to have a friend. However, I prefer to use another expression which exhibits the ethical element in friendship and in everything else which was dealt with in the foregoing discussion, and at the same time emphasizes sharply the difference between the ethical and the aesthetical: I say that it is every man's duty to become revealed. The Scripture teaches that every man must die, and then comes the Judgement when everything shall be revealed. Ethics says that it is the significance of life and of reality that every man become revealed. So if he is not, the revelation will appear as a punishment. The aestheticist, on the contrary, will not attribute significance to reality, he remains constantly concealed, because, however frequently and however much he gives himself up to the world, he never does it totally, there always remains something that he keeps back; if he were to do it totally, he would be doing it ethically. But this thing of playing hide and seek always avenges itself, and of course it does so by the fact that one becomes enigmatical to oneself. Hence it is that all mystics, when they do not recognize the claim of reality upon every man that he become revealed, stumble upon difficulties and terrors which no one else knows of. It is as though they discovered an entirely different world, as though their nature was reduplicated in itself. He who will not contend with realities gets phantoms to fight with.

Herewith I am through for the present. To propound a doctrine of morals was never my intention. What I wanted to do was to show how the ethical, in the regions which border on the aesthetical, is so far from depriving life of its beauty that it bestows beauty upon it. It affords peace, assurance, and security, for it calls to us constantly: *quod petis, hic est.*[9] It saves from every vain enthusiasm which would enfeeble the soul and bestows upon it health and strength. It teaches one not to overvalue the adventitious or to deify fortune. It teaches one to be joyful in good fortune (and even this the aestheticist is not able to do), for good fortune merely as such is an endless relativity; it teaches one to be joyful in misfortune....

Notes

[1] *Europamüde*, or "tired of Europe," was a literary catchword around 1840.

[2] The Emperor Marcus Aurelius (Antoninus Philosophus), in his *Meditations*, VII, 2, says: "To recover thy life is in thy power. Look at things again as thou didst use to look at them; for in this consists the recovery of thy life" (trans. By G. Long). In the rough draft Kierkegaard translated it: "Look at things you saw before from another point of view." In this it would appear S.K. was following the German translation of J.M. Schultz. Kierkegaard reads the translation but cites the original, apparently without taking notice of the real meaning of the latter.

[3] See Holberg's comedy of that name.

[4] To will the same and not to will the same makes for a firm friendship (Sallust, *Catilina*, 20).

[5] Prepared, ready to march.

[6] Part 3 of Vol. I is an essay on tragedy delivered before this society fantastically named "All-dead-together."

[7] This was S.K.'s constant complaint against the Hegelian system.

[8] *Nicomachean Ethics* VIII, 9 and 11.

[9] Horace, *Letters*, I, 11, 29: "What you seek is here."

Chapter 22

Ralph Waldo Emerson, Of Friendship
(Essays)

Ralph Waldo Emerson (1803-1882) was a lapsed minister, a leading spirit of New England Transcendentalism and one of the greatest of America's original thinkers. Born in Boston into the family of a long line of ministers, he managed, despite the death of his father in his youth, to pay his way through Harvard by running errands and waiting on tables. Subsequently he attended Harvard Divinity School and, upon graduation, became, like his father, a pastor of a prominent Unitarian church in Boston and chaplain of the state senate.

The liberal, deistic Unitarian faith that prevailed in New England during Emerson's time was a far cry from the trinitarian of its founders. Nevertheless, Emerson soon found even this too limiting. He began to conceive of God as an impersonal moral force, capable of being perceived only by a direct intuition that transcended the powers of sensation or reason. Eventually finding himself at odds with the more precise doctrines of the Unitarians, he resigned from the ministry in 1832.

Settling in Concord, Emerson remarried after the death of his first wife, and began a new career as a writer and lecturer, publishing his first book, Nature, in 1836. But it was not until his second trip to Great Britain in 1847, when the great Scottish-born man of letters, Thomas Carlyle, called attention to his work, that Emerson achieved wide fame and recognition. This event brought success not only to his numerous publications, but to his lecture circuit, which was eventually expanded from coast to coast by the growing Union Pacific railway. By 1866, his reputation was sufficient enough that the trustees of

Harvard felt obliged to forgive and forget a scandal, which his unorthodox theological views had created in an address to the divinity school in 1838, and awarded him the LL.D. degree; and shortly thereafter it made him a member of the Board of Overseers.

Emerson's philosophy may be classified as a species of American Transcendentalism associated with the famous Concord group, which included Henry David Thoreau. Perhaps under the indirect influence of post-Kantian idealism, he regarded the universe as consisting of the "Me" and "Not-Me," or the Soul and Nature—conceived as appearances of a more ultimate reality: the divine "Over-Soul," or Universal Being. By submitting to the influence of Nature, the individual can enter into a kind of mystical union Being (God as);with the divine spirit: "Standing on the bare ground—my head bathed by the blithe air, and uplifted into infinite space—all mean egotism vanishes. I become a transparent eyeball; I am nothing; I see all; the currents of the Universal Being circulate through me; I am part or parcel of God."

This quasi-pantheistic metaphysic was supplemented by a prophetic sense that a progressive "new age" was dawning, an outlook of disdain for traditions from the European past, and a preference for the immediate and experiential—all of which may remind us somewhat of the New Age "philosophy" of our own day. In any case, Emerson's thought, like that of Mark Twain, bore a quintessentially American stamp. This was due in large measure to the emphasis he placed on the themes of individualism, self-reliance, and a down-to-earth regard for the significance of the "man in the street" (Emerson's expression) and his opposition to passive, collective dependence upon any central authority such as the state. In this sense, Emerson embodied the ideals of classic liberalism, tempered by an American love for the common and mundane.

Emerson's best known books include his two series of **Essays** *(1841, 1844),* **Poems** *(1847),* **Representative Men** *(1850), and* **English Traits** *(1856). Our selection, "Friendship," is taken from his* **Essays** *of 1841. Of particular interest is how his view of friendship fits within his overall "Transcendental" metaphysic—his view of the relation of the individual to the Universal Being, of the human Soul to Nature and to the "Over-Soul."*

Of Friendship

"Friendship"

A ruddy drop of manly blood
The surging sea outweighs;
The world uncertain comes and goes,
The lover rooted stays.
I fancied he was fled,
And, after many a year,
Glowed unexhausted kindliness
Like daily sunrise there.
My careful heart was free again,—
O friend, my bosom said,
Through thee alone the sky is arched,
Through thee the rose is red,
All things through thee take nobler form
And look beyond the earth,
The mill-round of our fate appears
A sun-path in thy worth.
Me too thy nobleness has taught
To master my despair;
The fountains of my hidden life
Are through thy friendship fair.

We have a great deal more kindness than is ever spoken. Maugre all the selfishness that chills like east winds the world, the whole human family is bathed with an element of love like a fine ether. How many persons we meet in houses, whom we scarcely speak to, whom yet we honor and who honor us! How many we see in the street, or sit with in church, whom, though silently, we warmly rejoice to be with! Read the language of these wandering eye-beams. The heart knoweth.

The effect of the indulgence of this human affection is a certain cordial exhilaration. In poetry and in common speech the emotions of benevolence and complacency which are felt towards others are likened to the material effects of fire; so swift, or much more swift, more active, more cheering, are these fine inward irradiations. From the highest degree of passionate love to the lowest degree of good will, they make the sweetness of life.

Our intellectual and active powers increase with our affection. The scholar sits down to write, and all his years of meditation do not furnish him with one good thought or happy expression; but it is necessary to write a letter to a friend—and forthwith troops of gentle thoughts invest themselves, on every hand, with chosen words. See, in any house where virtue and self-respect abide, the palpitation which the approach of a stranger causes. A commended stranger is expected and announced, and an uneasiness betwixt pleasure and pain invades all the hearts of a household. His arrival almost brings fear to the good hearts that would welcome him. The house is dusted, all things fly into their places, the old coat is exchanged for the new, and they must get up a dinner if they can. Of a commended stranger, only the good report is told by others, only the good and new is heard by us. He stands to us for humanity. He is what we wish. Having imagined and invested him, we ask how we should stand related in conversation and action with such a man, and are uneasy with fear. The same idea exalts conversation with him. We talk better than we are wont. We have the nimblest fancy, a richer memory, and our dumb devil has taken leave for the time. For long hours we can continue a series of sincere, graceful, rich communications drawn from the oldest, secretest experience, so that they who sit by, of our own kinsfolk and acquaintance, shall feel a lively surprise at our unusual powers. But as soon as the stranger begins to intrude his partialities, his definitions, his defects into the conversation, it is all over. He has heard the first, the last, and best he will ever hear from us. He is no stranger now. Vulgarity, ignorance, misapprehension are old acquaintances. Now, when he comes, he may get the order, the dress and the dinner, but the throbbing of the heart and the communications of the soul, no more.

What is so pleasant as these jets of affection which make a young world for me again? What so delicious as a just and firm encounter of two, in a thought, in a feeling? How beautiful, on their approach to this beating heart, the steps and forms of the gifted and the true! The moment we indulge our affections, the earth is metamorphosed; there is no winter and no night; all tragedies, all ennuis[1] vanish—all duties even; nothing fills the proceeding eternity but the forms all radiant of beloved persons. Let the soul be assured that somewhere in the universe it should rejoin its friend, and it would be content and cheerful alone for a thousand years.

I awoke this morning with devout thanksgiving for my friends, the old and the new. Shall I not call God the Beautiful, who daily showeth himself so to me in his gifts? I chide society, I embrace solitude, and yet I am not so ungrateful as not to see the wise, the lovely and the noble-minded, as from time to time they pass my gate. Who hears me, who understands me, becomes mine, a possession for all time. Nor is Nature so poor but she gives me this joy several times, and thus we weave social threads of our own, a new web of relations and, as many thoughts in succession substantiate themselves, we shall by and by stand in a new world of our own creation, and no longer strangers and pilgrims in a traditionary globe. My friends have come to me unsought. The great God gave them to me. By oldest right, by the divine affinity of virtue with itself, I find them, or rather not I, but the Deity in me and in them derides and cancels the thick walls of individual character, relation, age, sex, circumstance, at which he usually connives, and now makes many one. High thanks I owe you, excellent lovers, who carry out the world for me to new and noble depths and enlarge the meaning of all my thoughts. These are new poetry of the first Bard—poetry without stop—hymn, ode, and epic, poetry still flowing, and the chanting still. Will these too separate themselves from me again, or some of them? I know not, but I fear it not; for my relation to them is so pure that we hold by simple affinity, and the Genius of my life being thus social, the same affinity will exert its energy on whomsoever is as noble as these men and women, wherever I may be.

I confess to an extreme tenderness of nature on this point. It is almost dangerous to me to "crush the sweet poison of misused wine"[2] of the affections. A new person is to me a great event and hinders me from sleep. I have often had fine fancies about persons which have given me delicious hours; but the joy ends in the day; it yields no fruit. Thought is not born of it; my action is very little modified. I must feel pride in my friend's accomplishments as if they were mine, and a property in his virtues. I feel as warmly when he is praised as the lover when he hears applause of his engaged maiden. We overestimate the conscience of our friend. His goodness seems better than our goodness, his nature finer, his temptations less. Everything that is his, his name, his form, his dress, books and instruments, fancy enhances. Our own thought sounds new and larger from his mouth.

Yet the systole and diastole of the heart are not without their analogy in the ebb and flow of love. Friendship, like the immortality of the soul, is too good to be believed. The lover, beholding his maiden, half knows that she is not verity that which he worships; and in the golden hour of friendship we are surprised with shades of suspicion and unbelief. We doubt that we bestow on our hero the virtues in which he shines and afterwards worship the form to which we have ascribed this divine inhabitation. In strictness, the soul does not respect men as it respects itself. In strict science all persons underlie the same condition of an infinite remoteness. Shall we fear to cool our love by mining for the metaphysical foundation of this Elysian temple? Shall I not be as real as the things I see? If I am, I shall not fear to know them for what they are. Their essence is not less beautiful than their appearance, though it needs finer organs for its apprehension. The root of the plant is not unsightly to science, though for chaplets and festoons we cut the stem short. And I must hazard the production of the bald fact amidst these pleasing reveries, though it should prove an Egyptian skull at our banquet. A man who stands united with his thought conceives magnificently of himself. He is conscious of a universal success, even though bought by uniform particular failures. No advantages, no powers, no gold or force, can be any match for him. I cannot choose but rely on my own poverty more than on your wealth. I cannot make your consciousness tantamount to mine. Only the star dazzles; the planet has a faint, moonlike ray. I hear what you say of the admirable parts and tried temper of the party you praise, but I see well that, for all his purple cloaks, I shall not like him unless he is at least a poor Greek like me. I cannot deny it, O friend, that the vast shadow of the Phenomenal includes thee also in its pied and painted immensity—thee also, compared with whom all else is shadow. Thou art not Being, as Truth is, as Justice is—thou art not my soul, but a picture and effigy of that. Thou hast come to me lately and already thou art seizing thy hat and cloak. Is it not that the soul puts forth friends as the tree puts forth leaves, and presently, by the germination of new buds, extrudes the old leaf? The law of nature is alternation forevermore. Each electrical state superinduces the opposite. The soul environs itself with friends that it may enter into a grander self-acquaintance or solitude; and it goes alone for a season that it may exalt its conversation or society. This method betrays itself along the whole history of our personal relations. The instinct of affection revives the hope of union with our mates, and the returning sense of insulation recalls us from the chase. Thus every man passes his life in the search after friendship, and if he should record his true sentiment, he might write a letter like this to each new candidate for his love:

Dear Friend,

If I was sure of thee, sure of thy capacity, sure to match my mood with thine, I should never think again of trifles in relation to thy comings and goings. I am not very wise; my moods are quite attainable, and I respect thy genius; it is to me as yet unfathomed; yet dare I not presume in thee a perfect intelligence of me, and so thou art to me a delicious torment. Thine ever, or never.

Yet these uneasy pleasures and fine pains are for curiosity and not for life. They are not to be indulged. This is to weave cobweb, and not cloth. Our friendships hurry to short and poor conclusions, because we have made them a texture of wine and dreams instead of the tough fiber of the human heart. The laws of friendship are austere and eternal, of one web with the laws of nature and of morals. But we have aimed at a swift and petty benefit, to suck a sudden sweetness. We snatch at the slowest fruit in the whole garden of God, which many summers and many winters must ripen. We seek our friend not sacredly, but with an adulterate passion which would appropriate him to ourselves. In vain. We are armed all over with subtle antagonisms which, as soon as we meet, begin to play, and translate all poetry into stale prose. Almost all people descend to meet. All association must be a compromise, and, what is worst, the very flower and aroma of the flower of each of the beautiful natures disappears as they approach each other. What a perpetual disappointment is actual society, even of the virtuous and gifted! After interviews have been compassed with long foresight we must be tormented presently by baffled blows, by sudden, unseasonable apathies, by epilepsies of wit and of animal spirits, in the heyday of friendship and thought. Our faculties do not play us true, and both parties are relieved by solitude.

I ought to be equal to every relation. It makes no difference how many friends I have and what content I can find in conversing with each if there be one to whom I am not equal. If I have shrunk unequal from one contest, the joy I find in all the rest becomes mean and cowardly. I should hate myself if then I made my other friends my asylum:

> The valiant warrior famousèd for fight,
> After a hundred victories, once foiled,
> Is from the book of honor razèd quite
> And all the rest forgot for which he toiled.[3]

Our impatience is thus sharply rebuked. Bashfulness and apathy are a tough husk in which a delicate organization is protected from premature ripening. It would be lost if it knew itself before any of the best souls were yet ripe enough to know and own it. Respect the *Naturlangsamkeit*[4] which hardens the ruby in a million years and works in duration in which Alps and Andes come and go as rainbows. The good spirit of our life has no heaven which is the price of rashness. Love, which is the essence of God, is not for levity, but for the total worth of man. Let us not have this childish luxury in our regards but the austerest worth; let us approach our friend with an audacious trust in the truth of his heart, in the breadth, impossible to be overturned, of his foundations.

The attractions of this subject are not to be resisted, and I leave, for the time, all account of subordinate social benefit, to speak of that select and sacred relation which is a kind of absolute and which even leaves the language of love suspicious and common, so much is this purer, and nothing is so much divine.

I do not wish to treat friendships daintily, but with roughest courage. When they are real, they are not glass threads or frostwork, but the solidest thing we know. For now, after so many ages of experience, what do we know of nature or of ourselves? Not one step has man taken toward the solution of the problem of his destiny. In one condemnation of folly stand the whole universe of men. But the sweet sincerity of joy and peace which I draw from this alliance with my brother's soul is the nut itself whereof all nature and all thought is but the husk and shell. Happy is the house that shelters a friend! It might well be built, like a festal bower or arch, to entertain him a single day. Happier, if he know the solemnity of that relation and honor its law! He who offers himself a candidate for that covenant comes up, like an Olympian, to the great games where the first-born of the world are the competitors. He proposes himself for contests where Time, Want, Danger are in the lists, and he alone is victor who has truth enough in his constitution to preserve the delicacy of his beauty from the wear and tear of all these. The gifts of fortune may be present or absent, but all the speed in that contest depends on intrinsic nobleness and the contempt of trifles. There are two elements that go to the composition of friendship, each so sovereign that I can detect no superiority in either, no reason why either should be first named. One is truth. A friend is a person with whom I may be sincere. Before him I may think aloud. I am arrived at last in the presence of a man so real and equal that I may drop even those undermost garments of dissimulation, courtesy, and second thought, which men never put off, and may deal with him with the simplicity and wholeness with which one chemical atom meets another. Sincerity is the luxury allowed, like diadems and authority, only to the highest rank; *that* being permitted to speak truth, as having none above it to court or conform unto. Every man alone is sincere. At the entrance of a second person, hypocrisy begins. We parry and fend the approach of our fellow man by compliments, by gossip, by amusements, by affairs. We cover up our thought from him under a hundred folds. I knew a man who under a certain religious frenzy cast off this drapery, and omitting all compliment and commonplace, spoke to the conscience of every person he encountered, and that with great insight and beauty. At first he was resisted, and all men agreed he was mad. But persisting—as indeed he could not help doing—for some time in this course, he attained to the advantage of bringing every man of his acquaintance into true relations with him. No man would think of speaking falsely with him, or of putting him off with any chat of markets or reading-rooms. But every man was constrained by so much sincerity to the like plain dealing, and what love of nature, what poetry, what symbol of truth he had, he did certainly show him.[5] But to most of us society shows not its face and eye, but its side and its back. To stand in true relations with men in a false age is worth a fit of insanity, is it not? We can seldom go erect. Almost every man we meet requires some civility—requires to be humored; he has some fame, some talent, some whim of religion or philanthropy in his head that is not to be questioned and which spoils all conversation with him. But a friend is a sane man who exercises not my ingenuity but me. My friend gives me entertainment without requiring any stipulation on my part. A friend therefore is a sort of paradox in nature. I who alone am, I who see nothing in nature whose existence I can affirm with equal evidence to my own, behold now the semblance of my being in all its height, variety, and curiosity, reiterated in a foreign form; so that a friend may well be reckoned the masterpiece of nature.

The other element of friendship is tenderness. We are holden to men by every sort of tie, by blood, by pride, by fear, by hope, by lucre, by lust, by hate, by admiration, by every circumstance and badge and trifle—but we can scarce believe that so much character can subsist in another as to draw us by love. Can another be so blessed and we so pure that we can offer him tenderness? When a man becomes dear to me I have touched the goal of fortune. I find very little written directly to the heart of this matter in books. And yet I have one text which I cannot choose but remember. My author[6] says, "I offer myself faintly and bluntly to those whose I effectually am, and tender myself least to him to whom I am the most devoted." I wish that friendship should have feet as well as eyes and eloquence. It must plant itself on the ground before it vaults over the moon. I wish it to be a little of a citizen before it is quite a cherub. We chide the citizen because he makes love a commodity. It is an exchange of gifts, of useful loans; it is good neighborhood; it watches with the sick; it holds the pall at the funeral; and quite loses sight of the delicacies and nobility of the relation. But though we cannot find the god under this disguise of a sutler, yet on the other hand we cannot forgive the poet if he spins his thread too fine and does not substantiate his romance by the municipal virtues of justice, punctuality, fidelity, and pity. I hate the prostitution of the name of friendship to signify modish and worldly alliances. I much prefer the company of plough-boys and tin-peddlers to the silken and perfumed amity which celebrates its days of encounter by a frivolous display, by rides in a curricle[7] and dinners at the best taverns. The end of friendship is a commerce the most strict and homely that can be joined; more strict than any of which we have experience. It is for aid and comfort through all the relations and passages of life and death. It is fit for serene days and graceful gifts and country rambles, but also for rough roads and hard fare, shipwreck, poverty, and persecution. It keeps company with the sallies of the wit and the trances of religion. We are to dignify to each other the daily needs and offices of man's life and embellish it by courage, wisdom, and unity. It should never fall into something usual and settled, but should be alert and inventive and add rhyme and reason to what was drudgery.

Friendship may be said to require natures so rare and costly, each so well tempered and so happily adapted, and withal so circumstanced (for even in that particular, a poet says, love demands that the parties be altogether paired), that its satisfaction can very seldom be assured. It cannot subsist in its perfection, say some of those who are learned in this warm lore of the heart, betwixt more than two. I am not quite so strict in my terms, perhaps because I have never known so high a fellowship as others. I please my imagination more with a circle of godlike men and women variously related to each other and between whom subsists a lofty intelligence. But I find this law of *one to one* peremptory for conversation, which is the practice and consummation of friendship. Do not mix waters too much. The best mix as ill as good and bad. You shall have very useful and cheering discourse at several times with two several men, but let all three of you come together and you shall not have one new and hearty word. Two may talk and one may hear, but three cannot take part in a conversation of the most sincere and searching sort. In good company there is never such discourse between two, across the table, as takes place when you leave them alone. In good company the individuals merge their egotism into a social soul exactly coextensive with the several consciousnesses there present. No partialities of friend to friend, no fondnesses of brother to sister, of wife to husband, are there pertinent, but quite otherwise. Only he may then speak who can sail on the common thought of the party and not poorly limited to his own. Now this convention, which good sense demands, destroys the high freedom of great conversation, which requires an absolute running of two souls into one.

No two men but being left alone with each other enter into simpler relations. Yet it is affinity that determines *which* two shall converse. Unrelated men give little joy to each other, will never suspect the latent powers of each. We talk sometimes of a great talent for conversation, as if it were a permanent property in some individuals. Conversation is an evanescent relation—no more. A man is reputed to have thought and eloquence; he cannot, for all that, say a word to his cousin or his uncle. They accuse his silence with as much reason as they would blame the insignificance of a dial in the shade. In the sun it will mark the hour. Among those who enjoy his thought he will regain his tongue.

Friendship requires that rare mean betwixt likeness and unlikeness that piques each with the presence of power and of consent in the other party. Let me be alone to the end of the world, rather than that my friend should overstep, by a word or a look, his real sympathy. I am equally balked by antagonism and by compliance. Let him not cease an instant to be himself. The only joy I have in his being mine is that the *not mine* is *mine.* I hate, where I looked for a manly furtherance or at least a manly resistance, to find a mush of concession. Better be a nettle in the side of your friend than his echo. The condition which high friendship demands is ability to do without it. That high office requires great and sublime parts. There must be very two before there can be very one. Let it be an alliance of two large, formidable natures, mutually beheld, mutually feared, before yet they recognize the deep identity which, beneath these disparities, unites them.

He only is fit for this society who is magnanimous; who is sure that greatness and goodness are always economy; who is not swift to intermeddle with his fortunes. Let him not intermeddle with this. Leave to the diamond its ages to grow, nor expect to accelerate the births of the eternal. Friendship demands a religious treatment. We talk of choosing our friends, but friends are self-elected. Reverence is a great part of it. Treat your friend as a spectacle. Of course he has merits that are not yours and that you cannot honor if you must needs hold him close to your person. Stand aside; give those merits room; let them mount and expand. Are you the friend of your friend's buttons or of his thought? To a great heart he will still be a stranger in a thousand particulars, that he may come near in the holiest ground. Leave it to girls and boys to regard a friend as property, and to suck a short and all-confounding pleasure instead of the noblest benefit.

Let us buy our entrance to this guild by a long probation. Why should we desecrate noble and beautiful souls by intruding on them? Why insist on rash personal relations with your friend? Why go to his house, or know his mother and brother and sisters? Why be visited by him at your own? Are these things material to our covenant? Leave this touching and clawing. Let him be to me a spirit. A message, a thought, a sincerity, a glance from him, I want, but not news, nor pottage. I can get politics and chat and neighborly conveniences from cheaper companions. Should not the society of my friend be to me poetic, pure, universal, and great as nature itself? Ought I to feel that our tie is profane in comparison with yonder bar of cloud that sleeps on the horizon or that clump of waving grass that divides the brook? Let us not vilify, but raise it to that standard. That great defying eye, that scornful beauty of his mien and action, do not pique yourself on reducing, but rather fortify and enhance. Worship his superiorities; wish him not less by a thought, but hoard and tell them all. Guard him as thy counterpart. Let him be to thee forever a sort of beautiful enemy, untamable, devoutly revered, and not a trivial conveniency to be soon outgrown and cast aside. The hues of the opal, the light of the diamond, are not to be seen if the eye is too near. To my friend I write a letter and from him I receive a letter. That seems to you a little. It suffices me. It is a spiritual gift, worthy of him to give and of me to receive. It profanes nobody. In these warm lines the heart will trust itself, as it will not to the tongue, and pour out the prophecy of a godlier existence than all the annals of heroism have yet made good.

Respect so far the holy laws of this fellowship as not to prejudice its perfect flower by your impatience for its opening. We must be our own before we can be another's. There is at least this satisfaction in crime, according to the Latin proverb—you can speak to your accomplice on even terms. *Crimen quos inquinat, aequat.*[8] To those whom we admire and love, at first we cannot. Yet the least defect of self-possession vitiates, in my judgement, the entire relation. There can never be deep peace between two spirits, never mutual respect, until in their dialogue each stands for the whole world.

What is so great as friendship, let us carry with what grandeur of spirit we can. Let us be silent—so we may hear the whisper of the gods. Let us not interfere. Who set you to cast about what you should say to the select souls or how to say anything to such? No matter how ingenious, no matter how graceful and bland. There are innumerable degrees of folly and wisdom, and for you to say aught is to be frivolous. Wait, and thy heart shall speak. Wait until the necessary and everlasting overpowers you, until day and night avail themselves of your lips. The only reward of virtue is virtue; the only way to have a friend is to be one. You shall not come nearer a man by getting into his house. If unlike, his soul only flees the faster from you, and you shall never catch a true glance of his eye. We see the noble afar off and they repel us, why should we intrude? Late, very late, we perceive that no arrangements, no introductions, no consuetudes[9] or habits of society would be of any avail to establish us in such relations with them as we desire, but solely the uprise of nature in us to the same degree it is in them; then shall we meet as water with water; and if we should not meet them then, we shall not want them, for we are already they. In the last analysis, love is only the reflection of a man's own worthiness from other men. Men have sometimes exchanged names with their friends, as if they would signify that in their friend each loved his own soul.

The higher the style we demand of friendship, of course the less easy to establish it with flesh and blood. We walk alone in the world. Friends such as we desire are dreams and fables. But a sublime hope cheers ever the faithful heart that elsewhere, in other regions of the universal power, souls are now acting, enduring, and daring which can love us and which we can love. We may congratulate ourselves that the period of nonage, of follies, of blunders and of shame, is passed in solitude, and when we are finished men we shall grasp heroic hands in heroic hands. Only be admonished by what you already see not to strike leagues of friendship with cheap persons, where no friendship can be. Our impatience betrays us into rash and foolish alliances which no god attends. By persisting in your path though you forfeit the little you gain the great. You demonstrate yourself, so as to put yourself out of the reach of false relations, and you draw to you the first-born of the world—those rare pilgrims whereof only one or two wander in nature at once and before whom the vulgar great show as specters and shadows merely.

It is foolish to be afraid of making our ties too spiritual, as if so we could lose any genuine love. Whatever correction of our popular views we make from insight, nature will be sure to bear us out and, though it seem to rob us of some joy, will repay us with a greater. Let us feel if we will the absolute insulation of man. We are sure that we have all in us. We go to Europe, or we pursue persons, or we read books, in the instinctive faith that these will call it out and reveal us to ourselves. Beggars all. The persons are such as we; the Europe, an old faded garment of dead persons; the books, their ghosts. Let us drop this idolatry. Let us give over this mendicancy. Let us even bid our dearest friends farewell, and defy them, saying, "Who are you? Unhand me: I will be dependent no more. " Ah! seest thou not, O brother, that thus we part only to meet again on a higher platform and only be more each other's because we are more our own? A friend is Janus-faced; he looks to the past and the future. He is the child of all my foregoing hours, the prophet of those to come, and the harbinger of a greater friend.

I do then with my friends as I do with my books. I would have them where I can find them, but I seldom use them. We must have society on our own terms and admit or exclude it on the slightest cause. I cannot afford to speak much with my friend. If he is great he makes me so great that I cannot descend to converse. In the great days, presentiments hover before me in the firmament. I ought then to dedicate myself to them. I go in that I may seize them, I go out that I may seize them. I fear only that I may lose them receding into the sky in which now they are only a patch of brighter light. Then, though I prize my friends, I cannot afford to talk with them and study their visions, lest I lose my own. It would indeed give me a certain household joy to quit this lofty seeking, this spiritual astronomy or search of stars, and come down to warm sympathies with you; but then I know well I shall mourn always the vanishing of my mighty gods. It is true, next week I shall have languid moods when I can well afford to occupy myself with foreign objects; then I shall regret the lost literature of your mind and wish you were by my side again. But if you come, perhaps you will fill my mind only with new visions; not with yourself but with your lusters,[10] and I shall not be able any more than now to converse with you. So I will owe to my friends this evanescent intercourse. I will receive from them not what they have but what they are. They shall give me that which properly they cannot give but which emanates from them. But they shall not hold me by any relations less subtle and pure. We will meet as though we met not, and part as though we parted not.

It has seemed to me lately more possible than I knew to carry on a friendship greatly, on one side, without due correspondence on the other. Why should I cumber myself with regrets that the receiver is not capacious? It never troubles the sun that some of his rays fall wide and vain into ungrateful space and only a small part on the reflecting planet. Let your greatness educate the crude and cold companion. If he is unequal, he will presently pass away; but thou art enlarged by thy own shining and, no longer a mate for frogs and worms, dost soar and burn with the gods of the empyrean. It is thought a disgrace to love unrequited. But the great will see that true love cannot be unrequited. True love transcends the unworthy object and dwells and broods on the eternal, and when the poor interposed mask crumbles, it is not sad, but feels rid of so much earth and feels its independency the surer. Yet these things may hardly be said without a sort of treachery to the relation. The essence of friendship is entireness, a total magnanimity and trust. It must not surmise or provide for infirmity. It treats its object as a god, that it may deify both.

Notes

¹ Listlessness and dissatisfaction; boredom.

² Milton, *Comus,* line 47.

³ Shakespeare, Sonnet 25. It reads "The *painful* warrior" and "After a *thousand* victories."

⁴ Slowness or deliberateness of nature.

⁵ This passage alludes to Jones Very (1813-1880, poet and religious mystic, whose belief that all his actions were prompted by God led many of his friends to consider him insane.

⁶ Montaigne, *Essays,* I, xxxix, "A Consideration upon Cicero."

⁷ A light, open two-wheeled carriage, drawn by two horses abreast.

⁸ Crime makes equal those whom it corrupts.

⁹ Customs.

¹⁰ Bright-colored surfaces.

Chapter 23

Friedrich Nietzsche, *Human, All-Too-Human* and *The Joyful Wisdom*

Friedrich Nietzsche (1844-1900) is perhaps the most controversial figure in the history of modern philosophy. Few thinkers have been so often quoted and misquoted, and misunderstood. Nietzsche's postulations of the "Overman" and the "Eternal Return" have made him the subject of not only philosophers in particular but political thinkers and theologians as well.

Many of Nietzsche's critics, and there are many, accuse him of fostering proto-Nazism by way of his distinction between a "master morality" and a "slave morality," while other critics accuse him of being the atheist par excellence *who would too hastily "re-evalu-ate all values." Many, however, are also defenders of Nietzsche, defenders who say simply that if one looks at* all *of Nietzsche's writings, and overlooks his aphoristic style, which by its very nature is intended to shock the reader, then one finds a Nietzsche who is anything but a proto-Nazi or a superficial atheist.*

On the surface, Nietzsche would seem to care little for morality, or for humanity for that matter. However, as he once wrote, his was an ethic which contained "a more severe morality" than was to be found anywhere else, in any other philosopher or in any religion. This seeming contradiction stems from the fact that Nietzsche had lost all patience with those political institutions and religious institutions of his time which would claim to be "moral" through and through, namely democracy and socialism, wherein everyone was to be seen as equal, and Christianity which preached what he regarded as a rather pathetic sympathy for sufferers. In contradistinction from these "moralizers"

who would "level all of humanity" into an unfree, joyless mass,
Nietzsche expounded the notion of "master morality," to be taken up by
the individual, in order that one live a life by the highest of standards.

Though born in Germany, Nietzsche disliked much of German
culture. Even the philosophy, he said, had "too much beer in it."
Nietzsche spent the greater part of his adult life outside of Germany. At
an early age he became professor of classical philology at the
University of Basel. Only a few years thereafter, due to bad health
which had plagued him even in his childhood, Nietzsche retired to Italy,
where he spent his most productive years. His death in 1900 seems
almost symbolic, as both his critics and admirers alike agree that he
seems to have been something of a prophet of the ills of the twentieth
century in particular.

Human, All-Too-Human

46. Sympathy Stronger than Suffering.—There are cases when
sympathy is stronger than actual suffering. For instance, we are more
pained when one of our friends is guilty of something shameful than
when we do it ourselves. For one thing, we have more faith in the
purity of his character than he has himself; then our love for him,
probably on account of this very faith, is stronger than his love for
himself. And even if his egoism suffers more thereby than our egoism,
inasmuch as it has to bear more of the bad consequences of his fault,
the un-egoistic in us—this word is not to be taken too seriously, but
only as a modification of the expression—is more deeply wounded by
his guilt than is the un-egoistic in him. . . .

49. Goodwill.—Amongst the small, but countlessly frequent and
therefore very effective, things to which science should pay more
attention than to the great, rare things, is to be reckoned goodwill; I
mean that exhibition of a friendly disposition in intercourse, that
smiling eye, that clasp of the hand, that cheerfulness with which almost
all human actions are usually accompanied. Every teacher, every
official, adds this to whatever is his duty; it is the perpetual occupation
of humanity, and at the same time the waves of its light, in which
everything grows; in the narrowest circle, namely, within the family,
life blooms and flourishes only through that goodwill. Kindliness,
friendliness, the courtesy of the heart, are ever-flowing streams of un-
egoistic impulses, and have given far more powerful assistance to

egoistic impulses, and have given far more powerful assistance to culture than even those much more famous demonstrations which are called pity, mercy, and self-sacrifice. But they are thought little of, and, as a matter of fact, there is not much that is un-egoistic in them. The *sum* of these small doses is nevertheless mighty, their united force is amongst the strongest forces. Thus one finds much more happiness in the world than sad eyes see, if one only reckons rightly, and does not forget all those moments of comfort in which every day is rich, even in the most harried of human lives. . . .

51. *How Appearance Becomes Actuality.*—The actor finally reaches such a point that even in the deepest sorrow he cannot cease from thinking about the impression made by his own person and the general scenic effect; for instance, even at the funeral of his child, he will weep over his own sorrow and its expression like one of his own audience. The hypocrite, who always plays one and the same part, ceases at last to be a hypocrite; for instance, priests, who as young men are generally conscious or unconscious hypocrites, become at last natural, and are then really without any affectation, just priests; or if the father does not succeed so far, perhaps the son does, who makes use of his father's progress and inherits his habits. If any one long and obstinately desires to *appear* something, he finds it difficult at last to *be* anything else. The profession of almost every individual, even of the artist, begins with hypocrisy, with an imitating from without, with a copying of the effective. He who always wears the mask of a friendly expression must eventually obtain a power over well-meaning dispositions without which the expression of friendliness is not to be compelled,—and finally, these, again, obtain a power over him: he *is* well-meaning. . . .

58. *What One May Promise.*—One may promise actions, but no sentiments, for these are involuntary. Whoever promises to love or hate a person, or be faithful to him for ever, promises something which is not within his power; he can certainly promise such actions as are usually the results of love, hate, or fidelity, but which may also spring from other motives; for many ways and motives lead to one and the same action. The promise to love some one for ever is, therefore, really: So long as I love you I will act towards you in a loving way; if I cease to love you, you will still receive the same treatment from me, although inspired by other motives, so that our fellow-men will still be deluded into the belief that our love is unchanged and ever the same.

One promises, therefore, the continuation of the semblance of love, when, without deception, one speaks vows of eternal love.

59. *Intellect and Morality.*—One must have a good memory to be able to keep a given promise. One must have a strong power of imagination to be able to feel pity. So closely is morality bound to the goodness of the intellect. . . .

368. *The Talent for Friendship.*—Two types are distinguished amongst people who have a special faculty for friendship. The one is ever on the ascent, and for every phase of his development he finds a friend exactly suited to him. The series of friends which he thus acquires is seldom a consistent one, and is sometimes at variance and in contradiction, entirely in accordance with the fact that the later phases of his development neutralize or prejudice the earlier phases. Such a man may jestingly be called a *ladder*. The other type is represented by him who exercises an attractive influence on very different characters and endowments, so that he wins a whole circle of friends; these, however, are thereby brought voluntarily into friendly relations with one another in spite of all differences. Such a man may be called a *circle*, for this homogeneousness of such different temperaments and natures must somehow be typified in him. Furthermore, the faculty for having good friends is greater in many people than the faculty for being a good friend. . . .

376. *Of Friends.*—Just consider with thyself how different are the feelings, how divided are the opinions of even the nearest acquaintances; how even the same opinions in thy friend's mind have quite a different aspect and strength from what they have in thine own; and how manifold are the occasions which arise for misunderstanding and hostile severance. After all this thou wilt say to thyself, "How insecure is the ground upon which all our alliances and friendships rest, how liable to cold downpours and bad weather, how lonely is every creature!" When a person recognizes this fact, and, in addition, that all opinions and the nature and strength of them in his fellow-men are just as necessary and irresponsible as their actions; when his eye learns to see this internal necessity of opinions, owing to the indissoluble interweaving of character, occupation, talent, and environment,—he will perhaps get rid of the bitterness and sharpness of the feeling with which the sage exclaimed, "Friends, there are no friends!" Much rather will he make the confession to himself:—Yes, there are friends, but they were drawn towards thee by error and deception concerning thy character; and they must have learnt to be silent in order to remain thy friends; for such human relationships almost always rest on the fact that some few things are never said, are never, indeed, alluded to; but if these pebbles are set rolling friendship follows afterwards and is broken. Are there any who would not be mortally injured if they were to learn what their most intimate friends really knew about them? By getting a knowledge of ourselves, and by looking upon our nature as a changing sphere of opinions and moods, and thereby learning to despise ourselves a little, we recover once more our equilibrium with the rest of mankind. It is true that we have good reason to despise each of our acquaintances, even the greatest of them; but just as good reason to turn this feeling against ourselves. And so we will bear with each other, since we bear with ourselves; and perhaps there will come to each a happier hour, when he will exclaim:

> "Friends, there are really no friends!" thus cried
> th' expiring old sophist;
> "Foes, there is really no foe!"—thus shout I,
> the incarnate fool.

241. *Good Friendship.*—A good friendship arises when the one man deeply respects the other, more even than himself; loves him also, though not so much as himself; and finally, to facilitate intercourse, knows how to add the delicate bloom and veneer of intimacy, but at the same time wisely refrains from a true, real intimacy, from the confounding of *meum* and *tuum*.

242. *Friends as Ghosts.*—If we change ourselves vitally, our friends, who have not changed, become ghosts of our own past: their voice sounds shadowy and dreadful to us, as if we heard our own voice speaking, but younger, harder, less mellow. . . .

260. *Making Friends only with the Industrious.*—The man of leisure is dangerous to his friends, for, having nothing to do, he talks of what his friends are doing or not doing, interferes, and finally makes himself a nuisance. The clever man will only make friends with the industrious. . . .

263. *Demonstrating One's Vanity to Friends and Foe.*—Many a man, from vanity, maltreats even his friends, when in the presence of witnesses to whom he wishes to make his own preponderance clear. Others exaggerate the merits of their enemies, in order to point proudly to the fact that they are worthy of such foes. . . .

333. Intercourse as an Enjoyment.—If a man renounces the world and intentionally lives in solitude, he may come to regard intercourse with others, which he enjoys but seldom, as a special delicacy. . . .

The Joyful Wisdom

279. Stellar Friendship.—We were friends, and have become strangers to each other. But this is as it ought to be, and we do not want either to conceal or obscure the fact, as if we had to be ashamed of it. We are two ships, each of which has its goal and its course; we may, to be sure, cross one another in our paths, and celebrate a feast together as we did before,—and then the gallant ships lay quietly in one harbour and in one sunshine, so that it might have been thought they were already at their goal, and that they had had one goal. But then the almighty strength of our tasks forced us apart once more into different seas and into different zones, and perhaps we shall never see one another again,—or perhaps we may see one another, but not know one another again; the different seas and suns have altered us! That we had to become strangers to one another is the law to which we are *subject:* just by that shall we become more sacred to one another! Just by that shall the thought of our former friendship become holier! There is probably some immense, invisible curve and stellar orbit in which our courses and goals, so widely different, may be *comprehended* as small stages of the way,—let us raise ourselves to this thought! But our life is too short, and our power of vision too limited for us to be more than friends in the sense of that sublime possibility.—And so we will *believe* in our stellar friendship, though we should have to be terrestrial enemies to one another. . . .

329. Leisure and Idleness.—There is an Indian savagery, a savagery peculiar to the Indian blood, in the manner in which the Americans strive after gold: and the breathless hurry of their work—the characteristic vice of the New World—already begins to infect old Europe, and makes it savage also, spreading over it a strange lack of intellectuality. One is now ashamed of repose: even long reflection almost causes remorse of conscience. Thinking is done with a stopwatch, as dining is done with the eyes fixed on the financial newspaper; we live like men who are continually "afraid of letting opportunities slip." "Better do anything whatever, than nothing"—this principle also is a noose with which all culture and all higher taste may be strangled. And just as all form obviously disappears in this hurry of workers, so the sense for form itself, the ear and the eye for the melody of movement, also disappear. The proof of this is the *clumsy perspicuity* which is now everywhere demanded in all positions where a person would like to be sincere with his fellows, in intercourse with friends, women, relatives, children, teachers, pupils, leaders and princes,—one has no longer either time or energy for ceremonies, for roundabout courtesies, for any *esprit* in conversation, or for any *otium* whatever. For life in the hunt for gain continually compels a person to consume his intellect, even to exhaustion, in constant dissimulation, overreaching, or forestalling: the real virtue nowadays is to do something in a shorter time than another person. And so there are only rare hours of sincere intercourse *permitted:* in them, however, people are tired, and would not only like "to let themselves go," but *to stretch their legs* out wide in awkward style. The way people write their *letters* nowadays is quite in keeping with the age; their style and spirit will always be the true "sign of the times." If there be still enjoyment in society and in art, it is enjoyment such as over-worked slaves provide for themselves. Oh, this moderation in "joy" of our cultured and uncultured classes! Oh, this increasing suspiciousness of all enjoyment! *Work* is winning over more and more the good conscience to its side: the desire for enjoyment already calls itself "need of recreation," and even begins to be ashamed of itself. "One owes it to one's health," people say, when they are caught at a picnic. Indeed, it might soon go so far that one could not yield to the desire of the *vita contemplativa* (that is to say, excursions with thoughts and friends), without self-contempt and a bad conscience.—Well! Formerly it was the very reverse: it was "action" that suffered from a bad conscience. A man of good family *concealed* his work when need compelled him to labour. The slave laboured under the weight of the feeling that he did something contemptible:—the "doing" itself was something contemptible. "Only in *otium* and *bellum* is there nobility and honour": so rang the voice of ancient prejudice!

Chapter 24

George Santayana, *The Life of Reason*

George Santayana (1863-1952) is almost always generally regarded as an American philosopher, though in fact he was born in Madrid, Spain, spent many years in England and France, and finally settled in Rome. He graduated from Harvard in 1886 and taught on the Harvard faculty until 1912.

In general, Santayana is primarily noted from his work in aesthetics. His **The Sense of Beauty** *was his first major work and constituted as much a critique of ethics as it did an evaluation of aesthetic principles. Therein, Santayana suggests that aesthetic value alone is "positive," while moral judgments, designed primarily for the avoidance of pain and suffering of some kind, inevitably bear a more "negative" character.*

The selection below is drawn from one of Santayana's more significant works, **The Life of Reason.** *Eschewing the preoccupations with philosophical* method *which he considered one of the things that both Continental and analytic philosophers, for all of their differences otherwise, oddly had in common, Santayana argues rather prosaically in the tradition of idealism that mind, though acknowledged to be entrenched in the evolutionary biological process, was yet prior to the natural domain proper, insofar as it could, most importantly, lend leading ideals and aesthetic judgments to the varieties of phenomenal experience. Indeed, Santayana almost defiantly avoids the question of philosophic method in this work as he tries to re-evaluate what he thought were rather extreme idealistic tendencies in rationalism and idealism. The reader will see that Santayana's prose, no matter what his subject, remains both vitally personal and accessible.*

Free Society (from *The Life of Reason*)

NATURAL SOCIETY unites beings in time and it fixes affection on those creatures on which we depend and to which our action must be adapted. Natural society begins at home and radiates over the world, as more and more things become tributary to our personal being. In marriage and the family, in industry, government, and war, attention is riveted on temporal existence, on the fortunes of particular bodies, natural or corporate. There is then a primacy of nature over spirit in social life; and this primacy, in a certain sense, endures to the end, since all spirit must be the spirit of something, and reason could not exist or be conceived at all unless a material organism, personal or social, lay beneath to give thought an occasion and a point of view, and to give preference a direction. Things could not be near or far, worse or better, unless a definite life were taken as a standard, a life lodged somewhere in space and time. Reason is a principle of order appearing in a subject-matter which in its subsistence and quantity must be an irrational datum. Reason expresses purpose, purpose expresses impulse, and impulse expresses a natural body with self-equilibrating powers.

At the same time, natural growths may be called achievements only because, when formed, they support a joyful and liberal experience. Nature's works first acquire a meaning in the commentaries they provoke; material processes have interesting climaxes only from the point of view of the life that expresses them, in which their ebb and flow grows impassioned and vehement. Nature's values are imputed to her retroactively by spirit, which in its material dependence has a logical and moral primacy of its own. In themselves events are perfectly automatic, steady, and fluid, not stopping where we see a goal nor avoiding what we call failures. And so they would always have remained in crude experience, if no cumulative reflection, no art, and no science had come to dominate and foreshorten that equable flow of substance, arresting it ideally in behalf of some rational interest. . . .

Free society differs from that which is natural and legal precisely in this, that it does not cultivate relations which in the last analysis are experienced and material, but turns exclusively to unanimities in meanings, to collaborations in an ideal world. The basis of free society is of course natural, as we said, but free society has ideal goals. Spirits cannot touch save by becoming unanimous. At the same time public opinion, reputation, and impersonal sympathy reinforce only very general feelings, and reinforce them vaguely; and as the inner play of sentiment becomes precise, it craves more specific points of support or comparison. It is in creatures of our own species that we chiefly scent the aroma of inward sympathy, because it is they that are visibly moved on the same occasions as ourselves; and it is to those among our fellow-men who share our special haunts and habits that we feel more precise affinities. Though the ground for such feeling is animal contact and contagion, its deliverance does not revert to those natural accidents, but concerns a represented sympathy in represented souls. Friendship, springing from accidental association, terminates in a consciousness of ideal and essential agreement.

Comradeship is a form of friendship still akin to general sociability and gregariousness. When men are "in the same boat together," when a common anxiety, occupation, or sport unites them, they feel their human kinship in an intensified form without any greater personal affinity subsisting between them. The same effect is produced by a common estrangement from the rest of society. For this reason comradeship lasts no longer than the circumstances that bring it about. Its constancy is proportionate to the monotony of people's lives and minds. There is a lasting bond among school-fellows because no one can become a boy again and have a new set of playmates. There is a persistent comradeship with one's countrymen, especially abroad, because seldom is a man pliable and polyglot enough to be at home among foreigners, or really to understand them. There is an inevitable comradeship with men of the same breeding or profession, however bad these may be, because habits soon monopolize the man. Nevertheless a greater buoyancy, a longer youth, a richer experience, would break down all these limits of fellowship. Such clingings to the familiar are three parts dread of the unfamiliar and want of resource in its presence, for one part in them of genuine loyalty. Plasticity loves new moulds because it can fill them, but for a man of sluggish mind and bad manners there is decidedly no place like home.

Though comradeship is an accidental bond, it is a condition of ideal friendship, for the ideal, in all spheres, is nothing but the accidental confirming itself and generating its own standard. Men must meet to love, and many other accidents besides conjunction must conspire to make a true friendship possible. In order that friendship may fulfill the conditions even of comradeship, it is requisite that the friends have the same social status, so that they may live at ease together and have congenial tastes. They must further have enough community of occupation and gifts to give each an appreciation of the other's faculty; for qualities are not complementary unless they are qualities of the same substance. Nothing must be actual in either friend that is not potential in the other.

For this reason, among others, friends are generally of the same sex, for when men and women agree, it is only in their conclusions; their reasons are always different. So that while intellectual harmony between men and women is easily possible, its delightful and magic quality lies precisely in the fact that it does not arise from mutual understanding, but is a conspiracy of alien essences and a kissing, as it were, in the dark. As man's body differs from woman's in sex and strength, so his mind differs from hers in quality and function: they can cooperate but can never fuse. The human race, in its intellectual life, is organized like the bees: the masculine soul is a worker, sexually atrophied, and essentially dedicated to impersonal and universal arts; the feminine is a queen, infinitely fertile, omnipresent in its brooding industry, but passive and abounding in intuitions without method and passions without justice. Friendship with a woman is therefore apt to be more or less than friendship: less, because there is no intellectual parity; more, because (even when the relation remains wholly dispassionate, as in respect to old ladies) there is something mysterious and oracular about a woman's mind which inspires a certain instinctive deference and puts it out of the question to judge what she says by masculine standards. She has a kind of sibylline intuition and the right to be irrationally *à propos*. There is a gallantry of the mind which pervades all conversation with a lady, as there is a natural courtesy towards children and mystics; but such a habit of respectful concession, marking as it does an intellectual alienation as profound as that which separates us from the dumb animals, is radically incompatible with friendship.

Friends, moreover, should have been young together. Much difference in age defeats equality and forbids frankness on many a fundamental subject; it confronts two minds of unlike focus: one near-sighted and without perspective, the other seeing only the background of present things. While comparisons in these respects may be interesting and borrowings sometimes possible, lending the older mind life and the younger mind wisdom, such intercourse has hardly the value of spontaneous sympathy, in which the spark of mutual intelligence flies, as it should, almost without words. Contagion is the only source of valid mind-reading: you must imitate to understand, and where the plasticity of two minds is not similar their mutual interpretations are necessarily false. They idealize in their friends whatever they do not invent or ignore, and the friendship which should has lived on energies conspiring spontaneously together dies into conscious appreciation.

All these are merely permissive conditions for friendship; its positive essence is yet to find. How, we may ask, does the vision of the general *socius*, humanity, become specific in the vision of a particular friend without losing its ideality or reverting to practical values? Of course, individuals might be singled out for the special benefits they may have conferred; but a friend's only gift is himself, and friendship is not friendship, it is not a form of free or liberal society, if it does not terminate in an ideal possession, in an object loved for its own sake. Such objects can be ideas only, not forces, for forces are subterranean and instrumental things, having only such value as they borrow from their ulterior effects and manifestations. To praise the utility of friendship, as the ancients so often did, and to regard it as a political institution justified, like victory or government, by its material results, is to lose one's moral bearings. The value of victory or good government is rather to be found in the fact that, among other things, it might render friendship possible. We are not to look now for what makes friendship useful, but for whatever may be found in friendship that may lend utility to life.

The first note that gives sociability a personal quality and raises the comrade into an incipient friend is doubtless sensuous affinity. Whatever reaction we may eventually make on an impression, after it has had time to soak in and to merge in some practical or intellectual habit, its first assault is always on the senses, and no sense is an indifferent organ. Each has, so to speak, its congenial rate of vibration and gives its stimuli a varying welcome. Little as we may attend to these instinctive hospitalities of sense, they betray themselves in unjustified likes and dislikes felt for casual persons and things, in the *je ne sais quoi* that makes instinctive sympathy. Voice, manner, aspect, hints of congenial tastes and judgments, a jest in the right key, a gesture marking the right aversions, all these trifles leave behind a pervasive impression. We reject a vision we find indigestible and without congruity to our inner dream; we accept and incorporate another into our private pantheon, where it becomes a legitimate figure, however dumb and subsidiary it may remain.

In a refined nature these sensuous premonitions of sympathy are seldom misleading. Liking cannot, of course, grow into friendship over night as it might into love; the pleasing impression, even if retained, will lie perfectly passive and harmless in the mind, until new and different impressions follow to deepen the interest at first evoked and to remove its centre of gravity altogether from the senses. In love, if the field is clear, a single glimpse may, like Tristan's potion, produce a violent and irresistible passion; but in friendship the result remains more proportionate to the incidental causes, discrimination is preserved, jealousy and exclusiveness are avoided.   That vigilant, besetting, insatiable affection, so full of doubts and torments, with which the lover follows his object, is out of place here; for the friend has no property in his friend's body or leisure or residual ties; he accepts what is offered and what is acceptable, and the rest he leaves in peace. He is distinctly not his brother's keeper, for the society of friends is free.

Friendship may indeed come to exist without sensuous liking or comradeship to pave the way; but unless intellectual sympathy and moral appreciation are powerful enough to react on natural instinct and to produce in the end the personal affection which at first was wanting, friendship does not arise. Recognition given to a man's talent or virtue is not properly friendship.   Friends must desire to live as much as possible together and to share their work, thoughts, and pleasures. Good-fellowship and sensuous affinity are indispensable to give spiritual communion a personal accent; otherwise men would be indifferent vehicles for such thoughts and powers as emanated from them, and attention would not be in any way arrested or refracted by the human medium through which it beheld the good.

No natural vehicle, however, is indifferent; no natural organ is or should be transparent.   Transparency is a virtue only in artificial instruments, organs in which no blood flows and whose intrinsic operation is not itself a portion of human life.   In looking through a field-glass I do not wish to perceive the lenses nor to see rainbows about their rim; yet I should not wish the eye itself to lose its pigments and add no dyes to the bulks it discerns. The sense for colour is a vital endowment and an ingredient in human happiness; but no vitality is added by the intervention of further media which are not themselves living organs.

A man is sometimes a coloured and sometimes a clear medium for the energies he exerts. When a thought conveyed or a work done enters alone into the observer's experience, no friendship is possible. This is always the case when the master is dead; for if his reconstructed personality retains any charm, it is only as an explanation or conceived nexus for the work he performed. In a philosopher or artist, too, personality is merely instrumental, for, although in a sense pervasive, a creative personality evaporates into its expression, and whatever part of it may not have been translated into ideas is completely negligible from the public point of view. That portion of a man's soul which he has not alienated and objectified is open only to those who know him otherwise than by his works and do not estimate him by his public attributions. Such persons are his friends. Into their lives he has entered not merely through an idea with which his name may be associated, nor through the fame of some feat he may have performed, but by awakening an inexpressible animal sympathy by the contagion of emotions felt before the same objects. Estimation has been partly arrested at its medium and personal relations have added their homely accent to universal discourse. Friendship might thus be called ideal sympathy refracted by a human medium, or comradeship and sensuous affinity colouring a spiritual light.

The tie that in contemporary society most nearly resembles the ancient ideal of friendship is a well-assorted marriage. In spite of intellectual disparity and of divergence in occupation, man and wife are bound together by a common dwelling, common friends, common affection for children, and, what is of great importance, common financial interests. These bonds often suffice for substantial and lasting unanimity, even when no ideal passion preceded; so that what is called a marriage of reason, if it is truly reasonable, may give a fair promise of happiness, since a normal married life can produce the sympathies it requires.

When the common ideal interest needed to give friendship a noble strain become altogether predominant, so that comradeship and personal liking may be dispensed with, friendship passes into more and more political fellowships. Discipleship is a union of this kind. Without claiming any share in the master's private life, perhaps without having ever seen him, we may enjoy communion with his mind and feel his support and guidance in following the ideal which links us together. Hero-worship is an imaginative passion in which latent ideals assume picturesque shapes and take actual persons for their symbols. Such companionship, perhaps wholly imaginary, is a very clear and simple example of ideal society. The unconscious hero, to be sure, happens to exist, but his existence is irrelevant to his function, provided only he be present to the idealizing mind. There is or need be no comradeship, no actual force or influence transmitted from him. Certain capacities and tendencies in the worshipper are brought to a focus by the hero's image, who is thereby first discovered and deputed to be a hero. He is an unmoved mover, like Aristotle's God and like every ideal to which thought or action is directed.

The symbol, however, is ambiguous in hero-worship, being in one sense ideal, the representation of an inner demand, and in another sense a sensible experience, the representative of an external reality. Accordingly the symbol, when highly prized and long contemplated, may easily become an idol; that in it which is not ideal nor representative of the worshipper's demand may be imported confusedly into the total adored, and may thus receive a senseless worship. The devotion which was, in its origin, an ideal tendency grown conscious and expressed in fancy may thus become a mechanical force vitiating that ideal. For this reason it is very important that the first objects to fix the soul's admiration should be really admirable, for otherwise their accidental blemishes will corrupt the mind to which they appear *sub specie boni*.

Discipleship and hero-worship are not stable relations. Since the meaning they embody is ideal and radiates from within outward, and since the image to which that meaning is attributed is controlled by a real external object, meaning and image, as time goes on, will necessarily fall apart. The idol will be discredited. An ideal, ideally conceived and known to be an ideal, a spirit worshipped in spirit and in truth, will take the place of the pleasing phenomenon; and in regard to every actual being, however noble, discipleship will yield to emulation, and worship to an admiration more or less selective and critical.

A disembodied ideal, however, is unmanageable and vague; it cannot exercise the natural and material suasion proper to a model we are expected to imitate. The more fruitful procedure is accordingly to idealize some historical figure or natural force, to ignore or minimize in it what does not seem acceptable, and to retain at the same time all the unobjectionable personal colour and all the graphic traits that can help to give that model a persuasive vitality. This poetic process is all the more successful for being automatic. It is in this way that heroes and gods have been created. A legend or fable lying in the mind and continually repeated gained insensibly at each recurrence some new eloquence, some fresh congruity with the emotion it had already awakened, and was destined to awake again. To measure the importance of this truth the reader need only conceive the distance traversed from the Achilles that may have existed to the hero in Homer, or from Jesus as he might have been in real life, or even as he is in the gospels, to Christ in the Church.

Chapter 25

C.S. Lewis, *The Four Loves*

Clive Staples Lewis (1898-1963), born in Belfast, Northern Ireland, was originally trained as a philosopher at Oxford, where he was appointed lecturer in philosophy upon his graduation in 1924. The following year he was elected a fellow of Magdalen College, Oxford, where he served as tutor in English literature from 1925 to 1954. He became Professor of Renaissance and Medieval Literature at Cambridge University from 1955 to 1963.

A prolific writer, Lewis produced over 40 volumes of philosophy, theology, literary history and criticism, poetry, letters, essays, fantasy, science fiction, a historical novel, an autobiography, allegory, biblical studies, sermons, a spiritual diary, short stories, and children's novels (the now classic **Chronicles of Narnia**).

Perhaps the most influential and winsome Christian apologist of our century, Lewis combined his literary scholarship and his fiction with clear and persuasive argumentation for traditional Christianity. Along with some of his works of fiction, many of his religious works continue to be best sellers; and even his non-philosophical writing contains much that is directly or indirectly of philosophical interest.

In **The Four Loves** *(1960), Lewis compares classical, Christian, and contemporary views of several varieties of love. In his Introduction, Lewis differentiates between gift-love, need-love and appreciative love. Gift-love is always Divine or God-like; need-love is ordinarily more than mere selfishness, since even human love for God is a form of need-love; appreciative love neither gives nor needs but simply takes pleasure in beauty.*

Opening his work with a discussion of "Likings and Loves for the

*Sub-Human," such as love of nature and love of country, Lewis
proceeds to distinguish and analyze four loves represented in his title:
(1) Affection, (2) Friendship, (3) Eros, and (4) Charity. "The highest,"
he says, quoting Thomas à Kempis, "does not stand without the
lowest." His principal thesis is that natural loves have a certain
irreducibility and are important, but are not self-sufficient.
Accordingly, he concludes his Introduction to his own work with the
following words:*

> It follows from what has been said that we must join neither the
> idolaters nor the "debunkers" of human love. Idolatry both of erotic
> love and of "the domestic affections" was the great error of
> nineteenth-century literature. Browning, Kingsley, and Patmore
> sometimes talk as if they thought that falling in love was the same
> thing as sanctification; the novelists habitually oppose to "the
> World" not the Kingdom of Heaven but the home. We live in the
> reaction against this. The debunkers stigmatise as slush and
> sentimentality a very great deal of what their fathers said in praise of
> love. They are always pulling up and exposing the grubby roots of
> our natural loves. But I take it we must listen neither "to the over-
> wise nor to the over-foolish giant." The highest does not stand
> without the lowest. A plant must have roots below as well as sunlight
> above and roots must be grubby. Much of the grubbiness is clean
> dirt if only you will leave it in the garden and not keep on sprinkling
> it over the library table. The human loves can be glorious images of
> Divine love. No less than that: but also no more—proximities of
> likeness which in one instance may help, and in another may hinder,
> proximity of approach. Sometimes perhaps they have not very much
> to do with it either way.

*Lewis's deeply religious understanding of how all loves (including
friendship) are connected to the highest of loves (charity), through
which they find their ultimate meaning and purpose, is communicated
eloquently in the following passage from "The Weight of Glory":*

> . . . It is a serious thing to live in a society of possible gods and
> goddesses, to remember that the dullest and most uninteresting person
> you talk to may one day be a creature which, if you saw it now, you
> would be strongly tempted to worship, or else a horror and a
> corruption such as you now meet, if at all, only in a nightmare. All
> day long we are, in some degree, helping each other to one or other of
> these destinations. It is in light of these overwhelming possibilities, it
> is with the awe and circumspection proper to them, that we should
> conduct all our dealings with one another, all friendships, all loves, all

play, all politics. There are no ordinary people. You never talked to a mere mortal. Nations, cultures, arts, civilizations—these are mortal, and their life is to ours as the life of a gnat. But it is immortals whom we joke with, work with, marry, snub, and exploit—immortal horrors or everlasting splendors. . . .

Friendship

When either Affection or Eros is one's theme, one finds a prepared audience. The importance and beauty of both have been stressed and almost exaggerated again and again. Even those who would debunk them are in conscious reaction against this laudatory tradition and, to that extent, influenced by it. But very few modern people think Friendship a love of comparable value or even a love at all. I cannot remember that any poem since *In Memoriam*, or any novel, has celebrated it. Tristan and Isolde, Antony and Cleopatra, Romeo and Juliet, have innumerable counterparts in modern literature: David and Jonathan, Pylades and Orestes, Roland and Oliver, Amis and Amile, have not. To the Ancients, Friendship seemed the happiest and most fully human of all loves; the crown of life and the school of virtue. The modern world, in comparison, ignores it. We admit of course that besides a wife and family a man needs a few "friends." But the very tone of the admission, and the sort of acquaintanceships which those who make it would describe as "friendships," show clearly that what they are talking about has very little to do with that *Philia* which Aristotle classified among the virtues or that *Amicitia* on which Cicero wrote a book. It is something quite marginal; not a main course in life's banquet; a diversion; something that fills up the chinks of one's time. How has this come about?

The first and most obvious answer is that few value it because few experience it. And the possibility of going through life without the experience is rooted in that fact which separates Friendship so sharply from both the other loves. Friendship is—in a sense not at all derogatory to it—the least *natural* of loves; the least instinctive, organic, biological, gregarious and necessary. It has least commerce with our nerves; there is nothing throaty about it; nothing that quickens the pulse or turns you red and pale. It is essentially between individuals; the moment two men are friends they have in some degree drawn apart together from the herd. Without Eros none of us would have been begotten and without Affection none of us would have been reared; but we can live and breed without Friendship. The species, biologically considered, has no need of it. The pack or herd—the community—may even dislike and distrust it. Its leaders very often do. Headmasters and Headmistresses and Heads of religious communities, colonels and ships' captains, can feel uneasy when close and strong friendships arise between little knots of their subjects.

This (so to call it) "non-natural" quality in Friendship goes far to explain why it was exalted in ancient and medieval times and has come to be made light of in our own. The deepest and most permanent thought of those ages was ascetic and world-renouncing. Nature and emotion and the body were feared as dangers to our souls, or despised as degradations of our human status. Inevitably that sort of love was most prized which seemed most independent, or even defiant, of mere nature. Affection and Eros were too obviously connected with our nerves, too obviously shared with the brutes. You could feel these tugging at your guts and fluttering in your diaphragm. But in Friendship—in that luminous, tranquil, rational world of relationship freely chosen—you got away from all that. This alone, of all the loves, seemed to raise you to the level of gods or angels.

But then came Romanticism and "tearful comedy" and the "return to nature" and the exaltation of Sentiment; and in their train all that great wallow of emotion which, though often criticised, has lasted ever since. Finally, the exaltation of instinct, the dark gods in the blood; whose hierophants may be incapable of male friendship. Under this new dispensation all that had once commended this love now began to work against it. It had not tearful smiles and keepsakes and baby-talk enough to please the sentimentalists. There was not blood and guts enough about it to attract the primitivists. It looked thin and etiolated; a sort of vegetarian substitute for the more organic loves.

Other causes have contributed. To those—and they are now the majority—who see human life merely as a development and complication of animal life all forms of behaviour which cannot produce certificates of an animal origin and of survival value are suspect. Friendship's certificates are not very satisfactory. Again, that outlook which values the collective above the individual necessarily disparages Friendship; it is a relation between men at their highest level of individuality. It withdraws men from collective "togetherness" as surely as solitude itself could do; and more dangerously, for it withdraws them by two's and three's. Some forms of democratic sentiment are naturally hostile to it because it is selective and an affair of the few. To say "These are my friends" implies "Those are not."

For all these reasons if a man believes (as I do) that the old estimate of Friendship was the correct one, he can hardly write a chapter on it except as a rehabilitation.

This imposes on me at the outset a very tiresome bit of demolition. It has actually become necessary in our time to rebut the theory that every firm and serious friendship is really homosexual.

The dangerous word *really* is here important. To say that every Friendship is consciously and explicitly homosexual would be too obviously false; the wiseacres take refuge in the less palpable charge that it is *really*—unconsciously, cryptically, in some Pickwickian sense—homosexual. And this, though it cannot be proved, can never of course be refuted. The fact that no positive evidence of homosexuality can be discovered in the behaviour of two Friends does not disconcert the wiseacres at all: "That," they say gravely, "is just what we should expect." The very lack of evidence is thus treated as evidence; the absence of smoke proves that the fire is very carefully hidden. Yes—if it exists at all. But we must first prove its existence. Otherwise we are arguing like a man who should say "If there were an invisible cat in that chair, the chair would look empty; but the chair does look empty; therefore there is an invisible cat in it."

A belief in invisible cats cannot perhaps be logically disproved, but it tells us a good deal about those who hold it. Those who cannot conceive Friendship as a substantive love but only as a disguise or elaboration of Eros betray the fact that they have never had a Friend. The rest of us know that though we can have erotic love and friendship for the same person yet in some ways nothing is less like a Friendship than a love-affair. Lovers are always talking to one another about their love; Friends hardly ever about their Friendship. Lovers are normally face to face, absorbed in each other; Friends, side by side, absorbed in some common interest. Above all, Eros (while it lasts) is necessarily between two only. But two, far from being the necessary number for Friendship, is not even the best. And the reason for this is important.

Lamb says somewhere that if, of three friends (A, B, and C), A should die, then B loses not only A but "A's part in C," while C loses not only A but "A's part in B." In each of my friends there is something that only some other friend can fully bring out. By myself I am not large enough to call the whole man into activity; I want other lights than my own to show all his facets. Now that Charles is dead, I shall never again see Ronald's reaction to a specifically Caroline joke. Far from having more of Ronald, having him "to myself" now that Charles is away, I have less of Ronald. Hence true Friendship is the least jealous of loves. Two friends delight to be joined by a third, and three by a fourth, if only the newcomer is qualified to become a real friend. They can then say, as the blessed souls say in Dante, "Here comes one who will augment our loves." For in this love "to divide is not to take away." Of course the scarcity of kindred souls—not to mention practical considerations about the size of rooms and the audibility of voices—set limits to the enlargement of the circle; but within those limits we possess each friend not less but more as the number of those with whom we share him increases. In this, Friendship exhibits a glorious "nearness by resemblance" to Heaven itself where the very multitude of the blessed (which no man can number) increases the fruition which each has of God. For every soul, seeing Him in her own way, doubtless communicates that unique vision to all the rest. That, says an old author, is why the Seraphim in Isaiah's vision are crying "Holy, Holy, Holy" *to one another* (Isaiah VI, 3). The more we thus share the Heavenly Bread between us, the more we shall all have.

The homosexual theory therefore seems to me not even plausible. This is not to say that Friendship and abnormal Eros have never been combined. Certain cultures at certain periods seem to have tended to the contamination. In war-like societies it was, I think, especially likely to creep into the relation between the mature Brave and his young armor-bearer or squire. The absence of the women while you were on the war-path had no doubt something to do with it. In deciding, if we think we need or can decide, where it crept in and where it did not, it must surely be guided by the evidence (when there is any) and not by an *a priori* theory. Kisses, tears and embraces are not in themselves evidence of homosexuality. The implications would be, if nothing else, too comic. Hrothgar embracing Beowulf, Johnson embracing Boswell (a pretty flagrantly heterosexual couple) and all those hairy old toughs of centurions in Tacitus, clinging to one another and begging for last kisses when the legion was broken up . . . all pansies? If you can believe that you can believe anything. On a broad historical view it is, of course, not the demonstrative gestures of Friendship among our ancestors but the absence of such gestures in our own society that calls for some special explanation. We, not they, are out of step.

I have said that Friendship is the least biological of our loves. Both the individual and the community can survive without it. But there is something else, often confused with Friendship, which the community does need; something which, though not Friendship, is the matrix of Friendship.

In the early communities the cooperation of the males as hunters or fighters was no less necessary than the begetting and rearing of children. A tribe where there was no taste for the one would die no less surely than a tribe where there was no taste for the other. Long before history began we men have got together apart from the women and done things. We had to. And to like doing what must be done is a characteristic that has survival value. We not only had to do the things, we had to talk about them. We had to plan the hunt and the battle. When they were over we had to hold a *post mortem* and draw conclusions for future use. We liked this even better. We ridiculed or punished the cowards and bunglers, we praised the star-performers. We revelled in technicalities. ("He might have known he'd never get near the brute, not with the wind that way" . . . "You see, I had a lighter arrowhead; that's what did it" ... "What I always say is——" ... "stuck him just like that, see? Just the way I'm holding this stick" ...) In fact, we talked shop. We enjoyed one another's society greatly: we Braves, we hunters, all bound together by shared skill, shared dangers and hardships, esoteric jokes—away from the women and children. As some wag has said, palaeolithic man may or may not have had a club on his shoulder but he certainly had a club of the other sort. It was probably part of his religion; like that sacred smoking-club where the savages in Melville's *Typee* were "famously snug" every evening of their lives.

What were the women doing meanwhile? How should I know? I am a man and never spied on the mysteries of the Bona Dea. They certainly often had rituals from which men were excluded. When, as sometimes happened, agriculture was in their hands, they must, like the men, have had common skills, toils and triumphs. Yet perhaps their world was never as emphatically feminine as that of their menfolk was masculine. The children were with them; perhaps the old men were there too. But I am only guessing. I can trace the pre-history of Friendship only in the male line.

This pleasure in cooperation, in talking shop, in the mutual respect and understanding of men who daily see one another tested, is biologically valuable. You may, if you like, regard it as a product of the "gregarious instinct." To me that seems a roundabout way of getting at something which we all understand far better already than anyone has ever understood the word *instinct*—something which is going on at this moment in dozen of ward-rooms, bar-rooms, common-rooms, messes and golf-clubs. I prefer to call it Companionship—or Clubbableness.

This Companionship is, however, only the matrix of Friendship. It is often called Friendship, and many people when they speak of their "friends" mean only their companions. But it is not Friendship in the sense I give to the word. By saying this I do not at all intend to disparage the merely Clubbable relation. We do not disparage silver by distinguishing it from gold.

Friendship arises out of mere Companionship when two or more of the companions discover that they have in common some insight or interest or even taste which the others do not share and which, till that moment, each believed to be his own unique treasure (or burden). The typical expression of opening Friendship would be something like, "What? You too? I thought I was the only one." We can imagine that among those early hunters and warriors single individuals—one in a century? one in a thousand years?—saw what others did not; saw that the deer was beautiful as well as edible, that hunting was fun as well as necessary, dreamed that his gods might be not only powerful but holy. But as long as each of these percipient persons dies without finding a kindred soul, nothing (I suspect) will come of it; art or sport or spiritual religion will not be born. It is when two such persons discover one another, when, whether with immense difficulties and semi-articulate fumblings or with what would seem to us amazing and elliptical speed, they share their vision—it is then that Friendship is born. And instantly they stand together in an immense solitude.

Lovers seek for privacy. Friends find this solitude about them, this barrier between them and the herd, whether they want it or not. They would be glad to reduce it. The first two would be glad to find a third.

In our own time Friendship arises in the same way. For us of course the shared activity and therefore the companionship on which Friendship supervenes will not often be a bodily one like hunting or fighting. It may be a common religion, common studies, a common profession, even a common recreation. All who share it will be our companions; but one or two or three who share something more will be our Friends. In this kind of love, as Emerson said, *Do you love me?* means *Do you see the same truth?*—Or at least, "Do you *care about* the same truth?" The man who agrees with us that some question, little regarded by others, is of great importance can be our Friend. He need not agree with us about the answer.

Notice that Friendship thus repeats on a more individual and less socially necessary level the character of the Companionship which was its matrix. The Companionship was between people who were doing something together—hunting, studying, painting or what you will. The

Friends will still be doing something together, but something more inward, less widely shared and less easily defined; still hunters, but of some immaterial quarry; still collaborating, but in some work the world does not, or not yet, take account of; still travelling companions, but on a different kind of journey. Hence we picture lovers face to face but Friends side by side; their eyes look ahead.

That is why those pathetic people who simply "want friends" can never make any. The very condition of having Friends is that we should want something else besides Friends. Where the truthful answer to the question *Do you see the same truth?* would be "I see nothing and I don't care about the truth; I only want a Friend," no Friendship can arise—though Affection of course may. There would be nothing for the Friendship to be *about*; and Friendship must be about something, even if it were only an enthusiasm for dominoes or white mice. Those who have nothing can share nothing; those who are going nowhere can have no fellow-travellers.

When the two people who thus discover that they are on the same secret road are of different sexes, the friendship which arises between them will very easily pass—may pass in the first half-hour—into erotic love. Indeed, unless they are physically repulsive to each other or unless one or both already loves elsewhere, it is almost certain to do so sooner or later. And conversely, erotic love may lead to Friendship between the lovers. But this, so far from obliterating the distinction between the two loves, puts it in a clearer light. If one who was first, in the deep and full sense, your Friend, is then gradually or suddenly revealed as also your lover you will certainly not want to share the Beloved's erotic love with any third. But you will have no jealousy at all about sharing the Friendship. Nothing so enriches an erotic love as the discovery that the Beloved can deeply, truly and spontaneously enter into Friendship with the Friends you already had: to feel that not only are we two united by erotic love but we three or four or five are all travellers on the same quest, have all a common vision.

The coexistence of Friendship and Eros may also help some moderns to realise that Friendship is in reality a love, and even as great a love as Eros. Suppose you are fortunate enough to have "fallen in love with" and married your Friend. And now suppose it possible that you were offered the choice of two futures: "*Either* you two will cease to be lovers but remain forever joint seekers of the same God, the same beauty, the same truth, *or else*, losing all that, you will retain as long as you live the raptures and ardours, all the wonder and the wild desire of

Eros. Choose which you please." Which should we choose? Which choice should we not regret after we had made it?

I have stressed the "unnecessary" character of Friendship, and this of course requires more justification than I have yet given it.

It could be argued that Friendships are of practical value to the Community. Every civilised religion began in a small group of friends. Mathematics effectively began when a few Greek friends got together to talk about numbers and lines and angles. What is now the Royal Society was originally a few gentlemen meeting in their spare time to discuss things which they (and not many others) had a fancy for. What we now call "the Romantic Movement" once *was* Mr. Wordsworth and Mr. Coleridge talking incessantly (at least Mr. Coleridge was) about a secret vision of their own. Communism, Tractarianism, Methodism, the movement against slavery, the Reformation, the Renaissance, might perhaps be said, without much exaggeration, to have begun in the same way.

There is something in this. But nearly every reader would probably think some of these movements good for society and some bad. The whole list, if accepted, would tend to show, at best, that Friendship is both a possible benefactor and a possible danger to the community. And even as a benefactor it would have, not so much survival value, as what we may call "civilisation-value"; would be something (in Aristotelian phrase) which helps the community not to live but to live well. Survival value and civilisation value coincide at some periods and in some circumstances, but not in all. What at any rate seems certain is that when Friendship bears fruit which the community can use it has to do so accidentally, as a by-product. Religions devised for a social purpose, like Roman emperor-worship or modern attempts to "sell" Christianity as a means of "saving civilisation," do not come to much. The little knots of Friends who turn their backs on the "World" are those who really transform it. Egyptian and Babylonian Mathematics were practical and social, pursued in the service of Agriculture and Magic. But the free Greek Mathematics, pursued by Friends as a leisure occupation, have mattered to us more.

Others again would say that Friendship is extremely useful, perhaps necessary for survival, to the individual. They could produce plenty of authority: "bare is back without brother behind it" and "there is a friend that sticketh closer than a brother." But when we speak thus we are using *friend* to mean "ally." In ordinary usage *friend* means, or should mean, more than that. A friend will, to be sure, prove himself to be also an ally when alliance becomes necessary; will lend or give when we are in need, nurse us in sickness, stand up for us among our enemies, do what he can for our widows and orphans. But such good offices are not the stuff of Friendship. The occasions for them are almost interruptions. They are in one way relevant to it, in another not. Relevant, because you would be a false friend if you would not do them when the need arose; irrelevant, because the role of benefactor always remains accidental, even a little alien, to that of Friend. It is almost embarrassing. For Friendship is utterly free from Affection's need to be needed. We are sorry that any gift or loan or night-watching should have been necessary—and now, for heaven's sake, let us forget all about it and go back to the things we really want to do or talk of together. Even gratitude is no enrichment to this love. The stereotyped "Don't mention it" here expresses what we really feel. The mark of perfect Friendship is not that help will be given when the pinch comes (of course it will) but that, having been given, it makes no difference at all. It was a distraction, an anomaly. It was a horrible waste of the time, always too short, that we had together. Perhaps we had only a couple of hours in which to talk and, God bless us, twenty minutes of it has had to be devoted to *affairs!*

For of course we do not want to know our Friend's affairs at all. Friendship, unlike Eros, is uninquisitive. You become a man's Friend without knowing or caring whether he is married or single or how he earns his living. What have all these "unconcerning things, matters of fact" to do with the real question, *Do you see the same truth?* In a circle of true Friends each man is simply what he is: stands for nothing but himself. No one cares twopence about any one else's family, profession, class, income, race, or previous history. Of course you will get to know about most of these in the end. But casually. They will come out bit by bit, to furnish an illustration or an analogy, to serve as pegs for an anecdote; never for their own sake. That is the kingliness of Friendship. We meet like sovereign princes of independent states, abroad, on neutral ground, freed from our contexts. This love (essentially) ignores not only our physical bodies but that whole embodiment which consists of our family, job, past and connections. At home, besides being Peter or Jane, we also bear a general character; husband or wife, brother or sister, chief, colleague or subordinate. Not among our Friends. It is an affair of disentangled, or stripped, minds. Eros will have naked bodies; Friendship naked personalities.

Hence (if you will not misunderstand me) the exquisite arbitrariness and irresponsibility of this love. I have no duty to be anyone's Friend and no man in the world has a duty to be mine. No claims, no shadow of necessity. Friendship is unnecessary, like philosophy, like art, like the universe itself (for God did not need to create). It has no survival value; rather it is one of those things which give value to survival.

When I spoke of Friends as side by side or shoulder to shoulder I was pointing a necessary contrast between their posture and that of the lovers whom we picture face to face. Beyond that contrast I do not want the image pressed. The common quest or vision which unites Friends does not absorb them in such a way that they remain ignorant or oblivious of one another. On the contrary it is the very medium in which their mutual love and knowledge exist. One knows nobody so well as one's "fellow." Every step of the common journey tests his metal; and the tests are tests we fully understand because we are undergoing them ourselves. Hence, as he rings true time after time, our reliance, our respect and our admiration blossom into an Appreciative love of a singularly robust and well-informed kind. If, at the outset, we had attended more to him and less to the thing our Friendship is "about," we should not have come to know or love him so well. You will not find the warrior, the poet, the philosopher or the Christian by staring in his eyes as if he were your mistress: better fight beside him, read with him, argue with him, pray with him.

In a perfect Friendship this Appreciative love is, I think, often so great and so firmly based that each member of the circle feels, in his secret heart, humbled before all the rest. Sometimes he wonders what he is doing there among his betters. He is lucky beyond desert to be in such company. Especially when the whole group is together, each bringing out all that is best, wisest, or funniest in all the others. Those are the golden sessions; when four or five of us after a hard day's walking have come to our inn; when our slippers are on, our feet spread out towards the blaze and our drinks at our elbows; when the whole world, and something beyond the world, opens itself to our minds as we talk; and no one has any claim on or any responsibility for another, but all are freemen and equals as if we had first met an hour ago, while at the same time an Affection mellowed by the years enfolds us. Life—natural life—has no better gift to give. Who could have deserved it?

From what has been said it will be clear that in most societies at most periods Friendships will be between men and men or between women and women. The sexes will have met one another in Affection and in Eros but not in this love. For they will seldom have had with each other the companionship in common activities which is the matrix of Friendship. Where men are educated and women not, where one sex works and the other is idle, or where they do totally different work, they will usually have nothing to be Friends about. But we can easily see that it is this lack, rather than anything in their natures, which excludes Friendship; for where they can be companions they can also become Friends. Hence in a profession (like my own) where men and women work side by side, or in the mission field, or among authors and artists, such Friendship is common. To be sure, what is offered as Friendship on one side may be mistaken for Eros on the other, with painful and embarrassing results. Or what begins as Friendship in both may become also Eros. But to say that something can be mistaken for, or turn into, something else is not to deny the difference between them. Rather it implies it; we should not otherwise speak of "turning into" or being "mistaken for."

In one respect our own society is unfortunate. A world where men and women never have common work or a common education can probably get along comfortably enough. In it men turn to each other, and only to each other, for Friendship, and they enjoy it very much. I hope the women enjoy their feminine Friends equally. Again, a world where all men and women had sufficient common ground for this relationship could also be comfortable. At present, however, we fall between two stools. The necessary common ground, the matrix, exists between the sexes in some groups but not in others. It is notably lacking in many residential suburbs. In a plutocratic neighbourhood where the men have spent their whole lives in acquiring money some at least of the women have used their leisure to develop an intellectual life—have become musical or literary. In such places the men appear among the women as barbarians among civilised people. In another neighbourhood you will find the situation reversed. Both sexes have, indeed, "been to school." But since then the men have had a much more serious education; they have become doctors, lawyers, clergymen, architects, engineers, or men of letters. The women are to them as children to adults. In neither neighbourhood is real Friendship between the sexes at all probable. But this, though an impoverishment, would be tolerable if it were admitted and accepted. The peculiar trouble of our own age is that men and women in this situation, haunted by rumours and glimpses of happier groups where no such chasm between the sexes exists, and bedevilled by the egalitarian idea that what is possible for some ought to be (and therefore is) possible to all, refuse to acquiesce in it. Hence, on the one hand, we get the wife as school-marm, the "cultivated" woman who is always trying to bring her husband "up to her level." She drags him to concerts and would like him to learn morris-dancing and invites "cultivated" people to the house. It often does surprisingly little harm. The middle-aged male has great powers of passive resistance and (if she but knew) of indulgence; "women will have their fads." Something much more painful happens when it is the men who are civilised and the women not, and when all the women, and many of the men too, simply refuse to recognise the fact.

When this happens we get a kind, polite, laborious and pitiful pretence. The women are "deemed" (as lawyers say) to be full members of the male circle. The fact—in itself not important—that they now smoke and drink like the men seems to simple-minded people a proof that they really are. No stag-parties are allowed. Wherever the men meet, the women must come too. The men have learned to live among ideas. They know what discussion, proof and illustration mean. A woman who has had merely school lessons and has abandoned soon after marriage whatever tinge of "culture" they gave her—whose reading is the Women's Magazines and whose general conversation is almost wholly narrative—cannot really enter such a circle. She can be locally and physically present with it in the same room. What of that? If the men are ruthless, she sits bored and silent through a conversation which means nothing to her. If they are better bred, of course, they try to bring her in. Things are explained to her: people try to sublimate her irrelevant and blundering observations into some kind of sense. But the efforts soon fail and, for manners' sake, what might have been a real discussion is deliberately diluted and peters out in gossip, anecdotes, and jokes. Her presence has thus destroyed the very thing she was brought to share. She can never really enter the circle because the circle ceases to be itself when she enters it—as the horizon ceases to be the horizon when you get there. By learning to drink and smoke and perhaps to tell *risqué* stories, she has not, for this purpose, drawn an inch nearer to the men than her grandmother. But her grandmother was far happier and more realistic. She was at home talking real women's talk to other women and perhaps doing so with great charm, sense and even wit. She herself might be able to do the same. She may be quite as clever as the men whose evening she has spoiled, or cleverer. But she is not really interested in the same things, nor mistress of the same methods. (We all appear as dunces when feigning an interest in things we care nothing about.)

The presence of such women, thousands strong, helps to account for the modern disparagement of Friendship. They are often completely victorious. They banish male companionship, and therefore male Friendship, from whole neighbourhoods. In the only world they know, an endless prattling "Jolly" replaces the intercourse of minds. All the men they meet talk like women while women are present.

This victory over Friendship is often unconscious. There is, however, a more militant type of woman who plans it. I have heard one say "Never let two men sit together or they'll get talking about some *subject* and then there'll be no fun." Her point could not have been more accurately made. Talk, by all means; the more of it the better; unceasing cascades of the human voice; but not, please, a subject. The talk must not be about anything.

This gay lady—this lively, accomplished, "charming," unendurable bore—was seeking only each evening's amusement, making the meeting "go." But the conscious war against Friendship may be fought on a deeper level. There are women who regard it with hatred, envy and fear as the enemy of Eros and, perhaps even more, of Affection. A woman of that sort has a hundred arts to break up her husband's Friendships. She will quarrel with his Friends herself or, better still, with their wives. She will sneer, obstruct and lie. She does not realise that the husband whom she succeeds in isolating from his own kind will not be very well worth having; she has emasculated him. She will grow to be ashamed of him herself. Nor does she remember how much of his life lies in places where she cannot watch him. New Friendships will break out, but this time they will be secret. Lucky for her, and lucky beyond her deserts, if there are not soon other secrets as well.

All these, of course, are silly women. The sensible women who, if they wanted, would certainly be able to qualify themselves for the world of discussion and ideas, are precisely those who, if they are not qualified, never try to enter it or to destroy it. They have other fish to fry. At a mixed party they gravitate to one end of the room and talk women's talk to one another. They don't want us, for this sort of purpose, any more than we want them. It is only the riff-raff of each sex that wants to be incessantly hanging on the other. Live and let live. They laugh at us a good deal. That is just as it should be. Where the sexes, having no real shared activities, can meet only in Affection and Eros—cannot be Friends—it is healthy that each should have a lively sense of the other's absurdity. Indeed it is always healthy. No one ever really appreciated the other sex—just as no one really appreciates children or animals—without at times feeling them to be funny. For both sexes are. Humanity is tragi-comical; but the division into sexes enables each to see in the other the joke that often escapes it in itself—and the pathos too.

I gave warning that this chapter would be largely a rehabilitation. The preceding pages have, I hope, made clear why to me at least it seems no wonder if our ancestors regarded Friendship as something that raised us almost above humanity. This love, free from instinct, free from all duties but those which love has freely assumed, almost wholly free from jealousy, and free without qualification from the need to be needed, is eminently spiritual. It is the sort of love one can imagine between angels. Have we here found a natural love which is Love itself?

Before we rush to any such conclusion let us beware of the ambiguity in the word *spiritual.* There are many New Testament contexts in which it means "pertaining to the (Holy) Spirit," and in such contexts the spiritual is, by definition, good. But when *spiritual* is used simply as the opposite of corporeal, or instinctive, or animal, this is not so. There is spiritual evil as well as spiritual good. There are unholy, as well as holy, angels. The worst sins of men are spiritual. We must not think that in finding Friendship to be *spiritual* we have found it to be in itself holy or inerrant. . . .

Perhaps we may now hazard a guess why Scripture uses Friendship so rarely as an image of the highest love. It is already, in actual fact, too spiritual to be a good symbol of Spiritual things. The highest does not stand without the lowest. God can safely represent Himself to us as Father and Husband because only a lunatic would think that He is physically our sire or that His marriage with the Church is other than mystical. But if Friendship were used for this purpose we might mistake the symbol for the thing symbolised. The danger inherent in it would be aggravated. We might be further encouraged to mistake that nearness (by resemblance) to the heavenly life which Friendship certainly displays for a nearness of approach.

Chapter 26

Jean-Paul Sartre, *Situations*

Jean-Paul Sartre (1905-1980) was a philosopher whose name has become synonymous with existentialism. Of those thinkers who are usually associated with "existentialism," for example, Kierkegaard, Nietzsche, Heidegger, Camus, Marcel, et al., he is the only one who really uses the term to denote his particular world-view. In view of his famous words, "existence precedes essence," the Sartrean claim, perhaps at the risk of oversimplifying matters, is that man, both as an individual and as a species, is not a "ready made" entity, either as a natural, political, or theological phenomenon. Rather, man, Sartre suggests, must "make himself" what he is and what he wants to be, without resorting to a pre-ordained view of man, God or nature.

*Sartre, the second cousin of the famous Albert Schweitzer, was an avowed atheist, though he was familiar with the Christian existentialist Gabriel Marcel, and with another famous fellow Frenchman, Albert Camus, who was said to have been returning to his Catholic background before he was killed in a car crash. Most of all, Sartre was very familiar with the French phenomenologist, Maurice Merleau-Ponty, with whom Sartre edited the journal, **Les Temps Moderns.***

*Sartre was a prolific writer. His major philosophical works are **Being and Nothingness** and **Critique of Dialectical Materialism**. But most people know of his name and of his work from his plays and novels. Sartre was awarded the Nobel prize for literature in 1964, though he refused to accept it.*

There are several scattered references to friendship in books about Sartre and in books in which he discusses his personal friendships with a friend, Simone de Beauvoir. But the only conscious account of friendship as such which Sartre goes out of his way to deliver in some orderly way may be found in his book **Situations**, *in which he gives a first-hand account of his sometimes stormy friendship with Merleau-Ponty, as both men find themselves in the middle of a rather confused setting in post-war France.*

In this selection, Sartre actually discusses friendship on a variety of levels as he simultaneously deals with the foibles of friendship on a variety of levels. Both he and Merleau-Ponty were members of the French Resistance; both were aware of their rather staid bourgeois upbringing, and the both of them wrestled with that upbringing together. Internally and externally, both wrestled with the desire to preserve the bourgeois culture that promoted liberal learning, while also trying to deal with the revolutionary forces of the East. Thus, the chronicle of Sartre's friendship with Merleau-Ponty in this sometimes friendly, sometimes unfriendly, "situation."

Merleau-Ponty (from *Situations*)

I have lost so many friends who are still alive. No one was to blame. It was they. It was myself. Events made us, brought us together, separated us. And I know that Merleau-Ponty said the same thing when he thought of the people who haunted, and then left his life. But he never lost me, and he had to die for me to lose him. We were equals, friends, but not brothers. We understood this immediately, and at first, our differences amused us. And then, about 1950, the barometer fell: fair wind for Europe and the world, but as for us, a gale knocked our heads together, and a moment later, it tossed each of us at opposite poles of the other. Our ties, often strained, were never broken. If I were asked why, I would say that we had a great deal of luck, and sometimes even virtue, on our side. We each tried to remain true to ourselves and to one another, and we nearly succeeded. Merleau is still too much alive for anyone to be able to describe him. Perhaps he will be more easily approached—to my way of thinking, in any case—if I tell the story of that quarrel which never took place, our friendship.

At the École Normale, we knew each other without being friends. He was a day student, I was a boarder. Each of these states took itself for a chivalric order, in which the other was the foot soldier. When we were drafted, I was an enlisted man, and he became a second lieutenant. Thus he was a knight twice over.[1] We lost sight of each other. He had a teaching post in Beauvais, I think, while I taught in Le Havre. Each of us, nevertheless, was preparing himself, without knowing it, for an encounter with the other. Each of us was trying to understand the world insofar as he could, and with the means at his disposal. And we had the same means—then called Husserl and Heidegger—since we were similarly disposed.

One day in 1947, Merleau told me that he had never recovered from an incomparable childhood. He had known that private world of happiness from which only age drives us. Pascalian from adolescence, without even having read Pascal, he experienced his singular selfhood as the singularity of an adventure. To be someone, is something which happens and unhappens, but not without first tracing the ribs of a future, always new and always begun anew. What was he, if not this paradise lost, a wild and undeserved piece of luck, a gratuitous gift transformed, after the fall, into adversity, depopulating the world and disenchanting him in advance? This story is both extraordinary and commonplace. Our capacity for happiness is dependent upon a certain equilibrium between what we refuse and concede to our childhood. Completely deprived or completely endowed, we are lost. Thus, there are an infinite number of lots we can draw. His was to have won too soon. He had to live, nonetheless. To the end, it remained for him to make himself as the event had made him. That way and other ways. Seeking the golden age, and with that as his point of departure he forged his myths and what he has since called his "style of life." It established his preferences—choosing, at the same time, the traditions which recalled the rituals of childhood, and the "spontaneity" which evoked childhood's superintended liberty. This naïveté, by starting from *what has happened*, also discovered the meaning of *what is happening*, and finally, it made a prophecy based on this inventory and its evaluation. This is what he felt as a young man, without as yet being able to express it. Through these detours, he finally arrived at philosophy. He wondered—nothing more. Everything is played out from the beginning, and we continue in spite of this. Why? Why do we lead a life which is disqualified by its absences? And what does it mean to live?

Futile and serious, our teachers were ignorant of. They replied that these were questions which shouldn't be asked, or that were badly expressed, or (and this was a tic of every teacher at that time) that "the answers were to be found in the questions." To think is to weigh, said one of them, who did neither. And all of them said: man and nature form the object of universal concepts, which was precisely what Merleau-Ponty refused to accept. Tormented by the archaic secrets of his own prehistory, he was infuriated by these well-meaning souls who, taking themselves for small airplanes, indulged in "high-altitude" thinking, and forgot that we are grounded from birth. They pride themselves, he was to later say, on looking the world in the face. Don't they know that it envelops and produces us? . . .

Philosophy, as we know, has no direct efficacity. It took the war to bring us close together. In 1941, intellectuals, more or less throughout the country, formed groups which claimed to be resisting the conquering enemy. I belonged to one of these groups, "Socialism and Liberty." Merleau joined us. This encounter was not the result of chance. Each of us had come from a *petit bourgeois* background. Our tastes, our tradition and our professional conscience moved both of us to defend freedom of the pen. Through this freedom, we discovered all the others. But aside from that, we were simpletons. Born of enthusiasm, our little group caught a fever and died a year later, of not knowing what to do. The other groups in the Occupied Zone met the same fate, and doubtless for the same reason. In 1942, only one of them remained. A little later Gaullism and the *Front National* reclaimed these first-hour Resistants. As for the two of us, in spite of our failure, "Socialism and Liberty" had at least brought us into contact with one another. The era helped us. There was then, among Frenchmen, an unforgettable transparency of heart, which was the reverse of hatred. Through this national friendship, which approved of each man in advance, provided he hated the Nazis, we recognized each other. . . .

Merleau had believed he would live in peace. A war had made him into a warrior, and he had made war. Suppose this strange merry-go-round were to define for us, both the limits and the scope of historical action? We had to examine it closely. Investigator, witness, defendant, and judge, he turned back and examined, in the light of our defeat, and the future German defeat (of which we were assured after Stalingrad), the false war which he had fought, the false peace in which he had thought he was going to live. And there he was, always, at the juncture of things, the briber bribed, the practical joker hoaxed, victim and accomplice, in spite of a good faith of which there could be no doubt, but which nevertheless had to be questioned.[2] Everything happened in silence. He had no need of a partner to make this new day dawn upon the singularity of his era, upon his own singularity. But we have the proof that he never ceased to reflect upon his era. Even in 1945 he wrote: "In sum, we have learned history, and maintain that we must not forget it."[3] . . .

The intellectual Communists weren't wrong about us. As soon as the calm seas of 1945 were past, they attacked me. My political thinking was confused, my ideas were dangerous. Merleau, on the contrary, seemed close to them. A flirtation began. He often saw Courtade, Hervé, Desanti. His own traditionalism found company in theirs. After all, the Communist Party was a tradition. He preferred its rituals, its tough-mindedness, refined by twenty-five years of History, to the speculations of those without a party.

However, he was not a Marxist. It wasn't the idea which he rejected, but the fact that it was a dogma. He refused to acknowledge that historical materialism is the unique light of History, or that this light emanates from an eternal source, which principle extracts from the vicissitudes of the event. He reproached this intellectualism of objectivity, as he did classical rationalism, for looking the world in the face, and for forgetting that it envelops us. He would have accepted the doctrine if he could only have seen it as phosphorescence, a shawl upon the sea, billowed out, unfurled by the swells, and whose truth depended specifically upon its perpetual participation in the underwater surges. A system of references, yes: on condition that it is altered through the act of referring to it; an explanation, if you wish, but one which is deformed as it is explained. Should we speak here of a "Marxist relativism"? Yes and no. Whatever the doctrine might be, he distrusted it, fearing that it would only be another version of "high altitude thinking." Thus, a relativism, but a relativism of precaution. He believed only in this one absolute: our anchorage, life. In essence, for what did he reproach the Marxist theory of History? Only this—which is capital, and nothing else—that it had not given contingency its rightful place. "Every historical undertaking has something of an adventure about it, as it is never guaranteed by any *absolutely* rational structure of things. It always involves a utilization of chance, one must always be cunning with things (and with people), since we must bring forth an order not inherent to them. Thus, there still remains the possibility of an immense compromise, of a corruption of History, or of the class struggle, powerful enough to destroy, but not enough so to construct, and where the guiding lines of History, as they have been drawn in the, will be erased." The contingence of each man and of all men, the contingence of the human venture, and within the womb of the latter, the contingence of the Marxist venture. Here we discover the fundamental experience of Merleau-Ponty. First he reflected upon the singularity of his life, then, turning back to his historical existence, he had discovered that the one and the other were made from the same cloth. . . .

Born of the class struggle, the determines its policy on the basis of this struggle. In capitalist countries, the Party couldn't survive the disappearance of the proletariat. But Merleau-Ponty no longer believed in civil war, and by the same token, even challenged the legitimacy of the Communist organization. The paradox remains that he proposed, at this same moment, that we ally ourselves with the Party.

There was still another paradox. Go find a bishop, and tell him, just to see what he will say: "God is dead. I doubt that he will be resurrected, but, in the meantime, I will go along with you." He will thank you for your gracious proposals, but he won't swallow them. But Merleau's Communist friends took just the reverse attitude. They gave him hell, but nicely, and without driving him away. If we really think about it, this wasn't surprising. The Party came out of the Resistance ahead. It was less strict in the choice of its fellow travelers. But, more than anything else, its intellectuals were in an uncomfortable position. Radical by the order of things, they would have wanted the proletariat to organize their conquests, continuing their march forward. The bourgeoisie, terrorized by the publicity given its betrayals, would have let them do anything. But, instead, the Communists procrastinated. They said: "Let's seize power." And they were answered: "The Anglo-Saxons might intervene at any minute." A new contradiction appeared in the movement of a "flying wedge": in order to save peace and the socialist countries, a revolution required by the masses from within could be countermanded from without. These young men who had come to the Party through the Resistance didn't retract their faith. Far from it. But there were doubts and disputes. After all, France was a bourgeois democracy. What was the C.P. doing in a tripartite government? . . .

What Merleau misunderstood was the fact that his friends had grown roots. He returned to this question fifteen years later in the preface to. There, on the contrary, he insisted upon the status of a militant enveloped, involved, and who, nevertheless, would himself contribute through his fidelity and through his acts to making the party which had made him. This was ambiguous repentance, which led him, above all, to justify his denials. It is easy to laugh when you are serenely judging a policy from the outside. When those who create it from day to day, if only by their acquiescence, discover its meaning, and when they see their own shadow cast upon the wall, there is nothing left for them but to break with it. But the argument can be turned the other way, and I think that he knew it. For those young men who struggled between good faith and sworn faith, by means of acts which they daily assumed, and whose meaning they saw changed in their very hands, for them, more than once, the "high-altitude thinker" was Merleau-Ponty.

They, in turn, misunderstood him. They didn't know the road he had followed. From a few conversations which we had later, I was left with the feeling that before 1939, he had been closer to Marxism than he was ever to be subsequently. What made him withdraw from it? I imagine that it was the Trials. He must have been very upset by them, for he spoke of them at great length, ten years later, in *Humanism and Terror*. After the trials, he could hardly even be disturbed by the German-Soviet Pact. He amused himself by writing rather "Machiavellian" letters to "distribute the blame." Through friends and through the writings of Rosa Luxemburg, he had been converted to the idea of "the spontaneity of the masses," which was close to the general movement of his particular movement. When he saw "Reasons of State" smoldering behind the masses, he turned away.

A at twenty, he ceased to be one because, as he said: "We believe that we believe, but we don't believe." More specifically, he asked that Catholicism reintegrate him in the unity of immanence, and this was precisely what it couldn't do. Christians love each other in God. I wouldn't go so far as to say that he moved from this idea to socialism: this would be too schematic. But the time came when he encountered Marxism and asked what it offered. He found this to be the future unity of a classless society and, in the meantime, the warm comradeship of battle. After 1936, there is no doubt. It was the Communist Party which disturbed him. One of his most constant characteristics was to seek everywhere for lost immanence, to be rejected by this immanence in favor of transcendence, and then, to vanish. Nevertheless, he didn't remain at this level of the original contradiction. From 1950 to 1962 he conceived gradually of a new link between being and intersubjectivity. But if, in 1945, he still dreamed of transcendence, he hadn't yet found it.

In short, he had come a long way, when, in spite of the disgusts he had endured, he proposed this hard-hitting, severe and disillusioned Marxism. And if it was true that he had "learned History" with no taste for it, from a sense of vocation and from obstinacy, it was equally true that he would never forget it. And this is what his Communist friends, more sensitive to unreserved adherence than to specific and limited areas of agreement, didn't see at the time. Solely concerned, as he was, with probing his relation to History, I imagine that their criticisms would have affected him very little, causing him, at most, to persist in his ideas silently, if, by chance, we hadn't started *Les Temps Modernes* just at that time. Now he had the instrument, and he was almost forced to express all the aspects of his thought. . . .

In sum, the prewar period denied the times. When our walls were blown down by a cyclone, we looked among the wreckage for the survivors, and we said to them: "It's nothing, really." The worst of it is that they believed us. Merleau-Ponty "learned history" more quickly than we did, because he took a painful and unqualified pleasure in time as it flowed by. This is what made him our political commentator without his even wanting to be, and without anyone being aware of him as such. . . .

I read, I learned, I ended by becoming an avid reader. He was my guide. It was *Humanism and Terror* which caused me to make an important decision. This small dense book revealed to me the method and object. It gave me the push I had needed to release me from my immobility. We know what a scandal it created everywhere. Communists vomited on it, who today don't see a thing wrong with it. But above all, it caused a fine commotion on our Right. One sentence in particular, which assimilated the opponent to the traitor and inversely, the traitor to the opponent, set off the dynamite. In Merleau's mind, this applied to those disturbed and threatened societies which huddle together around a revolution. This was viewed as a sectarian condemnation of all opposition to Stalin. Within a few days, Merleau became the man with a knife between his teeth. When Simone de Beauvoir visited the editors of the *Partisan Review* in New York, they didn't bother to hide their dismay. We were being manipulated. The hand of Moscow held the pen of our father Joseph. Those poor people! One evening at Boris Vian's apartment, Camus took Merleau aside and reproached him for justifying the Trials. It was most painful. I see them still. Camus, revolted, Merleau-Ponty courteous and firm, somewhat pale, the one indulging himself, the other refusing the delights of violence. Suddenly, Camus turned his back and left. I ran after him, accompanied by Jacques Bost. We found him in the deserted street. I tried as best I could to explain Merleau's ideas, which the latter hadn't deigned to do. With the sole result that we parted estranged. It took six months and a chance meeting to bring us together again. This memory is not a pleasant one for me. What a foolish idea it was to offer my services in this affair. It is true. I was to the Right of Merleau, and to the Left of Camus. What perverse humor prompted me to become the mediator between two friends, both of whom, a little later, were to reproach me for my friendship for the Communists, and who are both dead, unreconciled? . . .

Were we so sure that we could reject the Stalinist regime without rejecting Marxism? I received an indignant letter from Bloch-Michel, which said, in substance: "How can you not understand that the Soviet economy needs manual slave labor, and that it systematically recruits millions of underfed and overexploited workers every year?" If he was right, Marx had thrown us from one barbarism into another. I showed the letter to Merleau, who didn't find it convincing. We found legitimate rage in it, and reasons of the heart, but not of the Reason. No matter. Better thought out, substantiated by proven facts, by arguments, how did we know that it wouldn't have dissolved our loyalty? The problems of industrialization, a period of socialist accumulation, being surrounded on all sides, the resistance of the peasants, the necessity of assuring adequate food production, demographic problems, suspicion, police terror and dictatorship—this combination of facts and consequences amply sufficed to overpower us. But what could we have said, what could we have done, even had it been proven to us that the concentration camp system had been required by the infrastructure? We would have had to know much more about the USSR and its production quotas. Several years later, I was able to acquire this knowledge, and I was liberated from my fears at the very hour when the camps opened their gates. But throughout the winter of 1950 we lived in grim uncertainty. The fact was that we couldn't be disturbed by the power of the Communists without being disturbed about ourselves. However inadmissible may have been their policies, we couldn't disavow them, at least not in the old capitalist countries, without resigning ourselves to a kind of betrayal. And it is the same thing to ask "Just how far can they go," as "How far can I follow them?" There is a morality of politics—a difficult subject, and never clearly treated—and when politics must betray its morality, to choose morality is to betray politics. Now, find your way out of that one! Particularly when the politics has taken as its goal bringing about the reign of the human. At the same moment as Europe discovered the camps, Merleau finally came upon the class struggle unmasked: strikes and repression, the massacres in, the war in Vietnam, McCarthyism and the American Terror, the reawakening of Nazism, the Church in power everywhere, sanctimoniously protecting the rebirth of Fascism with her cloak. How could we not smell the stench of the bourgeois cadaver? And how could we publicly condemn slavery in the East without abandoning, on our side, the exploited to their exploitation? But could we allow ourselves to work with the Party, if this would mean putting France into chains and covering it with barbed wire? What should we do? Should we mercilessly strike those giants to the Left and the Right who wouldn't even feel our blows? This was the solution of despair. Merleau suggested this, for lack of a better one. I saw no other solution either, but I was worried. We hadn't budged an inch, the yes had simply changed to no. In 1945 we said: "Gentlemen, we are everybody's friend, and above all, the friend of our dear C.P." And five years later: "We are the enemies of all, the only privilege of the Party is that it still deserves our severity." Without even speaking of it, we both had the feeling that this "high altitude" objectivity wouldn't take us very far. We hadn't chosen when choice had been imposed upon everyone, and we had been right. Perhaps now, our universal surliness could delay the choice for a few more months. But whether publishers of a daily paper, or a weekly magazine, it was high time that we take the plunge or simply fold. The somewhat confidential character of our review gave us some respite, but our position, at first political, was in danger of gradually becoming moralistic. We never descended to the level of Beautiful Souls, but Fine Sentiments were flowering in our vicinity, at the same time that manuscripts were becoming scarcer. We were slowing down, people no longer wanted to write for us.

Once in China, I was shown the statues of two traitors in the bottom of a ditch. People had spat on them for centuries. They were all shiny, eroded by human saliva. We weren't shiny yet, but erosion had started. We wouldn't be forgiven for refusing Manicheism. On the Right, they hired butchers' boys to insult us. Everything was permitted them. They showed their behinds to the critics, who discovered that this was the "new generation." All of the fairies had been present at their cradle, but one. They disappeared for lack of talent. They lacked a certain zest, nothing more, but it had been denied them at birth. They would be dying of starvation today if they weren't fed by the Algerian War. Crime pays. They made a lot of noise, but did little damage. On the Left, things were more serious. Our friends in the Party hadn't been able to digest the article on the camps. Right was on our side and this was our feast. Their insults didn't bother me in the least: rat, hyena, viper, polecat—I rather liked this bestiary. It took me out of myself. Merleau was more upset by it, still recalling the comradeship of 1945. There were two times of day to be abused: first he was insulted in the early morning news sheets; then, by the end of the evening, he received

the clandestine apologies of his Communist friends. This lasted until it
was found simpler for these same people to take on more work. They
wrote the articles at dawn and apologized at twilight. Merleau suffered
less from being insulted by those close to him, than from the fact of
being no longer able to respect them. Today, I would say that they
were possessed by a violence which was literally mad, born of an
exhausting war which wore them out, which took place elsewhere, but
whose effects made themselves felt even in the depths of our province.
They tried to believe they were others and they couldn't quite succeed.
Merleau, I think, saw their faults and not their disease, this
provincialism. This is conceivable as he knew them in their day-to-day
life. In short, he kept his distance since this was what they wanted.
The Communist Party had tolerated these fringes of critical sympathy
on its edges without liking them. Beginning in 1949, it decided to
annihilate them. Outside friends were kindly requested to keep their
mouths shut. Should one of them make public his reservations, they
would disgust him into becoming an enemy. Thus the Party proved to
every militant (and each militant thought he proved to himself) that
free examination of dogma is the beginning of treason. What
Merleau's friends hated in him was *themselves*. What anguish there
was in all that, and how it exploded after the electric shock of the XX
Congress! Merleau knew the music. Communist tantrums didn't
reduce him to anti-Communism. He took the blows without giving
them. He did the right thing and let them talk. In short, he went on
with his undertaking. No matter. They cut off his oxygen, exiling him
once more to the combustible gas of solitary life. Born of historic
upheaval, the Communist Party with its traditions and restraints, had
formerly seemed to him, even from afar, as a possible society. Now he
had lost it. To be sure, he had numerous friends who weren't
Communists, and who remained loyal to him. But what could he find
in them except the affectionate indifference of the prewar period? They
sat around a common table, eating together, in order to pretend for a
moment that they had a common task. These completely diverse men,
still in a state of shock from the intrusion of History into their private
lives, had nothing in common but a bottle of Scotch and a leg of lamb.
And of course these reunions came to the same thing as death
certificates. The Resistance had crumbled, he finally realized that. But
these apperceptions have no profound truth unless we feel them as a
creeping form of our own death. I saw Merleau often during the winter
and spring. He showed hardly any sign of nerves, but he was extremely
hypersensitive. I felt that, little by little, he was dying. Five years later

he was to write: "The writer knows full well that there is no common denominator between the rumination of his life and what this life might have given his work, making it clearer and more precise." This is true. Everyone ruminates. We mull over insults suffered, disgust swallowed, accusations, recriminations, pleading; and then we try to piece everything together, end to end, fragmented material with neither head nor tail. Merleau, like each of us, was familiar with these tedious repetitions, occasionally pierced by a flash of lightning. But that year, there was neither thunder nor light. He tried to take his bearings, to go back to that crossroads where his own history intersected the history of France and of the world, where the course of his thinking had been born from the course of things. This was what he had tried and succeeded in doing between 1939 and 1945. But in 1950, it was too late and too soon. "I would like," he said to me one day, "to write a novel about myself." I replied: "Why not write an autobiography?" "There are too many unanswered questions. In a novel, I could give them imaginary resolutions." Don't be deceived by this recourse to imagination. Let me remind you here of the role assigned to imagination in phenomenology, within this complex movement which realizes itself through the intuition of an essence. It was nonetheless true that this life was running out, but through meditation, it was discovering shores of shadow, solutions of continuity. In order then, to have launched, in spite of himself, into this conflict with old friends, wouldn't he have to have made a mistake at the very beginning? Or else, wasn't he forced to assume, at the risk of destroying himself, the deviations and digressions of an immense movement which had produced him and yet whose inner mechanism remained out of his reach? Or else—and as he himself had indicated in 1945, as a simple conjecture—hadn't we all fallen, for a time at least, into non-meaning? Perhaps there was nothing else for us to do but *endure,* by holding fast to a few rare values. He kept his office at *Les Temps Modernes* and refused to change any of his activities. But, while it brought him closer to his origins, the "rumination of his life" slowly turned him away from day-to-day politics. This was his good fortune. When someone leaves the marginal zone of the Communist Party, they have to go somewhere. They walk for a while, and suddenly find themselves on the Right. Merleau never committed this treason. When he was dismissed, he took refuge in his inner life.

Summer came. The Koreans had begun fighting among themselves. We were separated from one another when the news reached us, and each of us, by himself, made his own comments on the situation. We met again for a day, in August, in Saint-Raphael. Too late. We were overjoyed to rediscover our respective gestures, voices, all those familiar singularities which all friends throughout the world love in their friends. A single flaw: our thoughts, already formed, were incommunicable. From morning to night, we only talked of war, lying by the water's edge, immobile, then at a table, then at the terrace of a café, surrounded by naked vacationers. We argued while walking, we were still arguing at the station as I waited for my train. Two deaf men—we needn't have bothered. I talked more than he did, I'm afraid, and not without vehemence. He replied calmly, briefly. His flickering, thin smile with its childlike malice, made me hope that he still hesitated. But no. He had never trumpeted his decisions. I was forced to recognize that he had made up his mind. He repeated quietly: "The only thing left for us is silence."

"Who is 'us'?" I said, pretending not to understand.

"Well, us *Les Temps Modernes*."

"You mean, you want us to put the key under the door?"

"No, not that. But I don't want us to breathe another word of politics."

"But why not?"

"They're fighting."

"Well, all right, in Korea."

"Tomorrow they'll be fighting everywhere."

"And even if they were fighting here, why should we be quiet?"

"Because brute force will decide the outcome. Why speak to what has no ears?"

I leaned out of the window and waved, as one should. I saw that he waved back, but I remained in a state of shock until the journey's end. . . .

But I had other *rendez-vous* with him, and I don't want to lie about our relationship, nor end on a note of lofty optimism. I still see his last melancholy expression—as we parted, at the rue Claude Bernard—disappointed, suddenly closed. He remains inside me, a painful sore, infected by sorrow, remorse and some bitterness. Changed from within, our friendship is there summed up forever. I neither accord any privilege to its last moments, nor do I believe that these moments contain the truth about a lifetime. Yet in that life, everything had been gathered up: all the silences with which, starting in 1950, he opposed me, are frozen in that silent expression, and reciprocally, I still feel to this day the eternity of his absence as a deliberate mutism. It is clear to me that our final misunderstanding—which would have been nothing had I seen him alive again—was made of the same fabric as all the others. It compromised nothing, revealing our mutual affection, our common desire not to spoil anything between us, but it also showed our lives were out-of-phase, causing our initiatives to be out-of-step; and then joined later by adversity, which suspended our dealings without violence, but forever. Death is an incarnation like birth. His death was non-meaning, full of a meaning which remained obscure, but fulfilled in all that concerned us, the contingency and necessity of a friendship without joy. Nevertheless, there had been something for which to strive. With our good qualities and our failings, the public violence of the one and the secret outrage of the other, we weren't so badly suited after all. And what did we do with it? Nothing, except avoid total estrangement. Each of you may blame whom he will. In any case, we weren't really very guilty, so little, in fact, that sometimes all I can see in our adventure was its necessity. That is the way men live in our time. That is the way they love. Badly. This is true, but it is also true that it was us, we two, who loved each other badly. There is nothing to be concluded from this except that this long friendship, neither done nor undone, obliterated when it was about to be reborn, or broken, remains inside me, an ever-open wound.

Notes

[1] I don't know whether he regretted, in 1939, when he came into contact with what his chiefs referred to as "the men," that he hadn't enlisted as a simple soldier. But I know that when I saw my officers, those incompetents, I regretted, for my part, my prewar anarchy. Since we had to fight, we were wrong to have left leadership in the hands of these conceited imbeciles. In any case, we know that Merleau remained an officer after the brief period of Resistance, which accounts for some of the difficulties between us. [*This and the following notes are by Sartre*]

[2] Not as I did, in 1942, by the eidetic imagery of bad faith, but by the empirical study of our historical fidelities, and of the inhuman forces which pervert them.

[3] Merleau-Ponty, "La guerre a eu lieu," in *Les Temps Modernes,* October, 1945.

Chapter 27

J. Glenn Gray, *The Warriors: Reflections on Men in Battle*

J. Glenn Gray (1933-1977) was an American philosopher who, while not as prolific as some philosophers, has nevertheless written one distinctly unforgettable memoir, **The Warriors: Reflections on Men in Battle** *(1959). This work chronicles Gray's varied and intense war experience.*

Gray was raised in Pennsylvania where he was educated at Juniata College, and at the University of Pittsburgh, where he received his master's degree in 1938. From there he went on to earn his doctorate at Columbia University in 1941. He taught at Juniata College in Huntingdon, Pennsylvania, from 1936-1938, at Swarthmore College and the University of Pennsylvania from 1945-1946, Haverford College from 1947-1948, and received an appointment as associate professor of philosophy at Colorado College, Colorado Springs, where he remained until his death.

The following selection is a fascinating and riveting description of the various differences Gray observes between friendship and sexual love, and between friendship and "preservative love," especially as these manifest themselves in the dramatic experiences of war. Ultimately, Gray draws a fine distinction also between true friendship and mere comradeship, the latter of which apparently might occur in any of several circumstances, while the former, true friendship, appears to be able to blossom under only one condition: peace.

An accomplished translator and Hegel scholar, Gray has also written at length on the topic of problems of American education, both in its theory and practice. He was also general editor of Martin

Heidegger's works in English translation published by Harper and Row
from 1966-1977. Gray was a personal friend of Hannah Arendt, who
wrote an introduction to the second, revised edition of his **Warriors** *in*
1967. Their friendship continued throughout their lives.

Gray was one of those rare individuals who could act ably and
honorably on his philosophical principles, and not only live to tell
about it, but also tell about it passionately and eloquently. Gray's life
changed drastically on May 8, 1941, a day on which he was not only
awarded his Ph.D. in Philosophy from Columbia University, but also a
day on which he received his "greetings from the President" inducting
him into the Army for service in the war. Gray served nobly in both his
military and professional calling, the combination of which served to
generate the following powerful reflections.

Love: War's Ally and Foe

... I have observed three distinct kinds of love operating during war.
They are erotic love between the sexes, preservative love, which is
independent of sex distinctions, and the love called friendship. These
loves are, of course, not unknown to peace. But in times of strife they
are sometimes more clearly defined, and the ornamentations in which
love abounds are more likely to be stripped away. War has its own
conventions, to be sure, and it quickly camouflages true relations and
original impulses among human creatures. Yet there are moments of
lucidity, even terrible clarity, which can be enlightening when we
succeed in re-creating them in memory without distortion.

For many soldiers of World War II, love between the sexes
appeared to be nothing else than an outlet in the purely physical sense,
which physiologists of love are fond of describing. There was an
unmistakable similarity in it to eating and drinking, a devouring of the
woman as object. Even the appetite seemed to recur with the same
regularity as do hunger and thirst. To these soldiers it did not much
matter who the woman was they used to satisfy themselves. Their
claims on her were only on her external features, so that prostitutes
gave such soldiers as much as any other girl could, and were usually
much more in accord with military needs. It is not at all surprising that
many army commanders have over the centuries sought to organize
love by providing legal brothels for soldiers. From a narrow military

standpoint, these establishments have always appeared to limit the dangers of physical love and insure efficiency of soldiering.

It is not easy to grasp the full coarseness of this gross physical love. Those who are repelled by the descriptions of it some soldiers like to give are accustomed to class it as bestial and animalistic without reflecting upon it further. In the memories and imaginations of these soldiers, women were reduced not only to objects, but to sexual organs which they could manipulate to their complete satisfaction. There was little or no tenderness in their passion, and gentleness in its expression was a thing unknown. The sexual need of these soldiers appeared to lie so near the surface as to be associated with only one part of their being. To put it more exactly, the need appeared to be separable as a passion that shook them from without and at intervals only. Such soldiers could not be called sensualists, for they knew little about the real pleasures of physical love. Their passion was too external and superficial for that....

I do not need to furnish any further description of this level of erotic love. Any veteran who reads these lines will have a thousand memories of it, personal or vicarious. Even those who escaped much contact with such love know well enough its appeal and realize that we are not separated from it by any absolute barrier. Fastidiousness, moral restraint, or the habit of treating the opposite sex as human beings may prohibit sympathy for soldiers such as these. But there is enough of the rapist in every man to give him insight into the grossest manifestations of sexual passion. Hence it is presumptuous for any of us to scorn the practitioners of this lowest kind of passion as beings with whom we have no kinship.

Surely this kind of love is intimately associated with the impersonal violence of war. Ares and Aphrodite here attract one another as true mates. Copulation under such circumstances is an act of aggression; the girl is the victim and her conquest the victor's triumph. Preliminary resistance on her part always increases his satisfaction, since victory is more intoxicating the harder the winning may be. It is not without significance that the language of physical love and the language of battle have a large correspondence, and the phrase "the war of the sexes" can be rich in connotation. Love like this can be as cruel as battle, because it arises from one part of the human being only, a part that is sundered from the whole.

That we can respond with only one aspect of our total selves is the frightening quality of our human life. Far from being weaker, this abstract response is usually more virulent and violent than response by the whole person. It seems hardly necessary to remark that such degradation is not possible for other than the human species. The animal cannot transform his mate into an object because it does not regard itself as a subject. A human being who thus deserts his humanity does not become like an animal, but, in the expressive German term, an *Untier* (an "unanimal"), in an exact sense, a creature without parallel in nature. . . .

For other soldiers at war, the erotic appeal is evidently in contrast with the ugly realities of combat. Ares and Aphrodite attract as opposites and not as soul mates. Such soldiers long for the gentleness and affection that only women can bring into the very male character of martial existence. Physical need might well be a basis of this love, and sensuous excitement its very breath, but its sweetness and beauty make it memorable and worthy. A soldier who feels this may not know what it is that stirs him so profoundly about a girl's presence, but he surmises dimly that it is her presence itself and not merely her body that moves him. It is the feminine quality of being that he unconsciously wants to fulfill him. Physical and spiritual elements are so fused in his desire that they are indistinguishable.

In the battle areas of World War II, there was something indescribably poignant about many such love liaisons. Plain and commonplace as the women might be under normal circumstances, they appeared as angels of beauty and tenderness to combat soldiers starved for these qualities. More often than not, the soldier and his newly found sweetheart understood little or nothing of each other's language. But the inability to communicate and the strangeness of different customs appeared to heighten the joy of discovery for them. The brevity and often stolen character of their love gave every incident a special imprint on the memory. Those tingling guarded memories of tenderness and beauty were frequently sufficient to preserve the courage of the soldier and strengthen him for the return to battle. To have a yielding, caressing girl in his arms after hideous or nondescript days and nights in battle was to have impossibly much when he had got used to so little.

Here the physical relationship was frequently veiled by an all-encompassing tenderness, and came to seem, in their need of each other, an incident only. Almost of necessity there was much illusion in this love. The soldier who returned after the war to marry his sweetheart of a night or two often found heartache and disillusion, as the statistics of such marriages reveal, for the attraction on both sides was too obviously a product of the immediate situation and the war. Another soldier or another girl under similar conditions might have satisfied as well the need for affection and physical love. For the soldier who did not return, his memories remain unsullied and inextinguishable. . . .

Still other soldiers find in war erotic love that goes deeper than the appeals of tenderness and beauty, love that fills them completely and is painfully specific and individual, painfully, because such love is exposed to the arbitrariness of bullets and bombs in a cruel way and painfully, too, because this love is no respecter of persons and frequently chooses archenemies as its unhappy principals. How often in recent wars has the tragedy of Romeo and Juliet been re-enacted, without benefit of Shakespeare's lyric music to moderate the agony! To the lovers, their love appears to be independent of and unrelated to the war and all its madness. Their love is written in the stars and not in the march orders and manipulations of a military headquarters. They would have met and found each other had the war never been. If in fact their attachment is not so dissevered from the abysses of war as they think, the principals are quite certain that its issue is all that really matters. Their passionate recognition that they belong together causes them to disregard every claim to their allegiance that conflicts with their love. Loyalty to country and comrades, to family and to established habits of life, cannot withstand the demands and claims of such a relationship. . . .

Few of us can comprehend the mystery of this love. We see Ares and Aphrodite mated and so well mated that their child might well be named Harmonia. At the same time the world lies in ruins around them, not only physically but morally, too, for their union tears apart the firmest beliefs in the worth of family, nation, and the whole complex of inherited tradition.

Yet we may well ask whether this love of a man and a woman for each other in which both have their whole being is really a mating of love and war. Is not war in this case an absurd accompaniment only? What can war and tragedy give this love that it would not have in time of peace? Certainly such love takes place in peace and among fellow countrymen more commonly than among members of opposed nations. Hence it does not require perverse outer circumstances for its fulfillment. Nevertheless, the presence of danger and the threat of separation do add something in the way of perfection or completeness, perhaps the realization of good fortune in having found the true love.

Too many of us as yet are so constituted that we cannot gain under peaceful skies an awareness of our own nature and the possibility of its union with another. When death and deprivation lurk near at hand, and only then, can many of us summon the necessary seriousness and wisdom, the necessary joy, to recognize love's true form. Genuine love can hardly actualize itself in Utopia, and certainly cannot there produce an awareness of its nature. The infinite uncertainty of outer fate is required, I fear, for profounder lovers to become fully conscious of inner certainty. We express this often in the familiar phrase: Lovers must know heartbreak in their love before it is secure.

The most necessary insight, however, that such tragic love can bring to participants and observers alike is that it has its being beyond the physiological and psychological, that it is indeed a cosmic force. When we see lovers assert the unity of their being in the face of desolation and destruction, a being in the midst of, but also above, conflict, we are forced to acknowledge the transcendent character of love. The lovers exemplify it, they do not create it; they are caught up in it rather than possess it. Love's very nature is to be ecstatic, to draw single units out of themselves and into a higher unity. Its roots are in the widest reaches of being itself, uniting the human entity to the rest of creation. When we confront a love of this tragic kind, we are nearly forced to say, foolishly wise: This is the way the world is. Though we may forget tomorrow what it teaches us today, we are dimly aware that other dimensions of reality exist than are disclosed to everyday moods.

That such love is inexorably wedded to war, we may justly doubt, but that war has often enabled lovers to understand the true fount and origin of their love is also beyond dispute. It is, of all the forms of erotic love, the least wedded to violence. Clearly, the reason is that it is the most integral, uniting, as it does, not only two individuals to each other, but two individuals to the wider realms of being. That even this does not always bring them peace is an indication that the world substance itself, whatever it may be, is not harmonious, complete, or single. True lovers hate war with all their heart, since it demonstrates too well that others have not found the secret of life that they know. But perhaps even they may sometimes admit that they learned the secret only when suspended over the abyss of death. We human beings are not very creative, otherwise we should have discovered other extreme situations that could serve better than war to teach us what we need to know, and without war's loss and unintelligibility.

It is my belief that there is no higher form of love than this total involvement of a man and a woman in each other. No other kind can grant us deeper glimpses into the nature of man or the world he inhabits. Christian love or Greek friendship, so often declared superior, are simply different, but not more limitless or rewarding. That this is a faith for which I cannot adduce evidence, I freely confess. My reason for holding it is simply the belief that no love has a deeper base in nature or, perhaps, a higher reach in the spirit. Its blindness to values that other loves know how to cherish is a limitation to which all forces in human life are subject. The Greeks were surely wise to deify Aphrodite and to make Eros a child of her union with Ares.

The threat to life and limb and to all man-created things in time of war calls up in some men a sentiment of love not closely related to the erotic, but extending beyond the human sphere. It might best be designated as an impersonal passion to preserve and succor that which is threatened, or to hold back from annihilation as much life and material as possible. This love is protective and maternal in kind. Its nature is perhaps best expressed in the old English word "concern." What men are concerned about, as the derivation of the word makes clear, they are implicated in and related to. The urge to preserve from destruction sometimes takes on comical and even absurd aspects. But its presence is deeply reassuring, for it helps to humanize partly the most ferocious battles and to rescue many spirits for the peace that always follows combat. If we do not find it in many men as a dominant motive of character, I think love as concern is widely distributed, and is discoverable frequently in the least likely prospects. Yes, soldier-killers, intent upon the inverted creativeness of destruction, have been known to show more than traces of such love in moments and on occasion.

What is it that men are concerned to preserve and to care for in battle? The most obvious answer is self-preservation, taking care of their own lives. This is true in a different sense from the common biological teaching of self-preservation as a basic instinct that men share with other animals. It is also true in a different sense from the egoistic psychology that traces all motivation to self-interest. He who has seen men throw away their lives in battle when caught up in communal passion or expose themselves recklessly and carelessly to mortal danger will be cured forever of such easy interpretations of human motivation. Nothing is clearer than that men can act contrary to the alleged basic instinct of self-preservation and against all motives of self-interest and egoism. Were it not so, the history of warfare in our civilization would be completely different from what it has been.

Nevertheless, self-preservation is a dependable and pervasive feature of human existence in a deeper sense than egoistic theories suppose. The philosopher Spinoza called it the striving to persevere in our own being, and the phrase is exact. Though striving to persevere in our own being is not absolute (for men may deliberately choose suicide) and not merely biological selfishness (since men are capable of dying for others), it is a power that lies both in and beyond the conscious, rational life. Many a soldier has been surprised to discover the desire to continue in being as a final hold and support, after superhuman exertion and mental strain had robbed him of conscious will, and any religious faith he may have possessed had ceased to be meaningful. The literature of war is full of the accounts of armies, beaten and bled, starved and weakened, yet tenaciously staying alive and rescuing a remnant of their strength and numbers. The account of the ancient Greek in the *Anabasis* may be taken as a classic example of this survival power in soldiers. Hardly a major war since Xenophon's time has been without similar feats of endurance, though few have had a chronicler such as he.

What is the relation of possessions to this self-preservative love? Can men in extreme peril separate the rescue of their naked lives from the preservation of their nearest possessions? Possessions are for the combat soldier his only assurance of protection against a threatening world. He cares for them, often with more attention than he pays to his own body. His weapons are in this category, and also some articles of dress and precious souvenirs. The intimate relation of the soldier to his weapons involves more than any love of possessions. Often the vehicles and implements of war come to be a replacement for home. This appears to be the crucial relation of possessions to the impulse of self-preservation. Such possessions are not only an extension of the soldier's own power, but they are his link with past and future. In one of the letters in the volume *Letzte Briefe aus Stalingrad*, we read of a hardened German tank soldier sobbing irresistibly because his tank had been destroyed. Its loss meant more to him than did the loss of his comrades. Why? I think it was because the tank had become an imaginative equivalent of the home he had left. It was a second skin, a protective layer against the harsh outer world. . . .

In cases of extreme exposure, nevertheless, the majority of soldiers seem able to grasp the difference between life and possessions, and will commonly sacrifice all they have to preserve their own being. As prisoners of war, or on long forced marches, or in campaigns of extreme hazard, soldiers learn more often than civilians ever do that everything external is replaceable, while life is not. When a soldier has had to face death often enough, something like a rough hierarchy of values develops in even the simplest mind, and life is nearly always ahead of possessions in the scale. Selfish, egotistical natures prove in such situations to possess less of the genuine love of self-preservation than do others who on the surface are not so eager for life. I suppose the shallow nature is not easily able to view his naked existence, since part of his being is having. Hence soldiers like this often lose their lives in the effort to hold on to some treasured possession.

One would think that learning to do without possessions, experiencing the loss of external holdings, might produce a peculiar blessing for the soldier in his future life as a civilian. But in fact most soldiers quickly forget their wartime order of values when they return to the security of peace, as most of us forget the blessings of health when we are no longer ill. Property comes to be once more an inseparable part of the drive to persevere in our own being. Pure awareness of the struggle to preserve ourselves is not granted to us often in life, just as the imminence of death at any moment of our lives is commonly concealed from us by unconscious suppression.

Preservative love, or concern, is clearly observed in combat in a soldier's care for life other than his own. There is something endlessly instructive in the spectacle of doctors and nurses fighting stubbornly to preserve life and minimal health amid chaos. And the medical corpsman whose duty it is to recover the wounded from front lines often overcomes his fear of death and frightful weariness in performing his work. Sympathy and tenderheartedness are not notably present in such people; they quickly grow callused to suffering. The motive that drives them forward, more than any other, I believe, is an impersonal passion for protecting and conserving life itself.

This impulse is not restricted at all to those whose official duty it is to preserve; it sometimes becomes a general passion and finds a place in the majority of soldiers. Waifs and orphans and lost pets have a peculiar claim on the affections of combat soldiers, who lavish upon them unusual care and tenderness. For the most part, there is little affinity between protector and protected in these cases. The soldiers are moved by the impersonal compassion that the fragility and helplessness of mortal creatures can call up in most of us. This frequently extends to the enemy wounded. Medical men will risk their lives on occasion to rescue wounded enemy soldiers, and doctors in field hospitals will fight as obstinately for the one as the other. The distinction between friend and foe has here been erased by the recognition of the helplessness of a creature whose life is threatened with extinction. . . .

Again, as in the highest form of erotic love, this kind of love produces a kind of awareness that is lacking in normal life. Our deeper powers lie dormant and undeveloped unless we are pushed to the abyss. Perhaps those philosophers of history are right who read civilization in terms of alternating periods of conservation and destruction, and hold that both are necessary for any real progress. For them, the delight in destruction and preservative love are necessary powers in human history, in some manner complementing each other. The exclusive interest in conserving the already existent would lead to stagnation were it not balanced by destructive forces which periodically sweep away ossified forms as a means of renewal. Love as concern for preserving in being is only meaningful, these philosophers would hold, when it is pitted against revolutionary forces of destruction. I do not know. At all events, I have never again in my life been so aware of the beneficent character of concern as during the war years.

There is another kind of love, with no relation to destruction, that men sometimes experience in war in the most crucial way. It is the love we call friendship. Now friendship has often enough been defined in our tradition as that relationship between human beings in which each dispassionately seeks the welfare of the other. Friendship is thus thought to be the most unselfish form of love, since in the pure state it devotes itself without reserve to the interests of the other. Accordingly, many societies have exalted friendship as the noblest of all relationships, and even the founder of Christianity, to whom another form of love took precedence, is declared to have said: "Greater love has no man than this, that a man lay down his life for his friends."

What meaning has friendship for warriors? How can a young man endure battle when the fear of death is doubled, when not only his own life but that of his friend is at stake? Is the quality of this relationship heightened or reduced by the dread strain of war? Before trying to answer these questions, I must first attempt to make clear a basic difference between friends and comrades. Only those men or women can be friends, I believe, who possess an intellectual and emotional affinity for each other. They must be predetermined for each other, as it were, and then must discover each other, something that happens rarely enough in peace or war.

Though many men never have a friend, and even the most fortunate of us can have few, comradeship is fortunately within reach of the vast majority. Suffering and danger cannot create friendship, but they make all the difference in comradeship. Men who have lived through hard and dangerous experiences together are frequently deceived about their relationship. Comrades love one another like brothers, and under the influence of shared experience commonly vow to remain true friends for the rest of their lives. But when other experiences intervene and common memories dim, they gradually become strangers. At veterans' conventions they can usually regain the old feelings only with the aid of alcoholic stimulation. The false heartiness and sentimentality of such encounters are oppressive and pathetic. Men who once knew genuine closeness to each other through hazardous experience have lost one another forever. And since most men rarely attain anything closer to friendship than this, the loss of comradeship cannot be taken lightly. When veterans try to feel for their old buddies what they felt in battle and fail, they frequently cherish somewhere in their secret memories the unsentimental original passion.

The essential difference between comradeship and friendship consists, it seems to me, in a heightened awareness of the self in friendship and in the suppression of self-awareness in comradeship. Friends do not seek to lose their identity, as comrades and erotic lovers do. On the contrary, friends find themselves in each other and thereby gain greater self-knowledge and self-possession. They discover in their own breasts, as a consequence of their friendship, hitherto unknown potentialities for joy and understanding. This fact does not make friendship a higher form of selfishness, as some misguided people have thought, for we do not seek such advantages in friendship for ourselves. Our concern, insofar as we are genuine friends, is for the friend. That we ourselves also benefit so greatly reveals one of the hidden laws of human affinity. While comrade-ship wants to break down the walls of self, friendship seeks to expand these walls and keep them intact. The one relationship is ecstatic, the other is wholly individual. Most of us are not capable of meeting the demands on self that friendship brings, whereas comradeship is in most respects an easing of these demands. Comrades are content to be what they are and to rest in their emotional bliss. Friends must always explore and probe each other, in the attempt to make each one complete through drawing out the secrets of another's being. Yet each recognizes that the inner fountain of the other is inexhaustible. Friends are not satiable, as comrades so often are when danger is past.

"That a man lay down his life for his friends" is indeed a hard saying and testifies to a supreme act of fortitude. Friends live for each other and possess no desire whatsoever for self-sacrifice. When a man dies for his friend, he does it deliberately and not in an ecstasy of emotion. Dying for one's comrades, on the other hand, is a phenomenon occurring in every war, which can hardly be thought of as an act of superhuman courage. The impulse to self-sacrifice is an intrinsic element in the association of organized men in pursuit of a dangerous and difficult goal.

For friends, however, dying is terribly hard, even for each other; both have so much to lose. The natural fear of dying is not so hard for them to overcome. What is hard is the loss or diminution of companionship through death. Friends know—I am tempted to say, only friends know—what they are giving up through self-sacrifice. It is said, to be sure, that they can communicate with one another even beyond death, but the loss is nevertheless cruel and final. Too often at moments of greatest need, when one's friend is dead, communication is broken off and one's dialogue becomes monologue. Friends can hardly escape the recognition of death as unmitigated evil and the most formidable opponent of their highest value.

War and battle create for this love both a peculiar kind of security and a kind of exposure, which other forms of love seldom know. The security arises from the insulation that friendship affords against the hatreds and the hopelessness that combat often brings. Even though one friend may be in safety at home, the friend who fights knows that somewhere the other is participating in his life. Through letters he can communicate his deepest feelings and his explorations of the evil experiences through which he is passing. Even when letters are cut off, friends can communicate in their memories of each other, each explaining in imagination to the other and having the assurance of being understood. There is joy in having a person who understands completely and whom you understand. It insulates the soldier's heart without closing his mind to the experiences he is undergoing. The German poet Goethe put nearly perfectly the situation of friends even in wartime. The English translation is by J. S. Dwight.

> Selig, wer sich vor der Welt
> Ohne Hass verschliesst,
> Einen Freund am Busen hält
> Und mit dem geniesst,
>
> Was, von Menschen nicht gewusst
> Oder nicht bedacht,
> Durch das Labyrinth der Brust
> Wandelt in der Nacht.

Happy he who, hating none,
Leaves the world's dull noise,
And with trusty friend alone,
Quietly enjoys

What, forever unexpressed,
Hid from common sight,
Through the mazes of the breast
Softly steals by night!

Friends can indeed close themselves without hatred from the world and draw from the labyrinth of each other's being inexhaustible wealth. They can thus endure much of war's horror without losing the zest for life. More than that, they can discover meaning in experiences of the most gruesome sort which others do not see. Friendship opens up the world to us by insulating us against passions that narrow our sympathies. It gives us an assurance that we belong in the world and helps to prevent the sense of strangeness and lostness that afflicts sensitive people in an atmosphere of hatred and destruction. When we have a friend, we do not feel so much accidents of creation, impotent and foredoomed. The assurance of friendship has been enough to help soldiers over many dreadful things without harm to their integrity.

But friendship makes life doubly dear, and war is always a harvest of death. Hence friends are exposed to an anxiety even greater than that of other lovers. There is no destructive dynamic in friendship, no love of death or sacrifice. Because friends supplement each other, they cannot face the prospect of the other's death without shuddering. Comforts can be easily abjured, dangers easily borne, if death is not the issue. The unendurable fear that grips friends on the battlefield is at the farthest remove from the recklessness of the soldier-killer. Among friends war's ultimate horror is experienced without much counterbalancing compensation. Like love as concern, it is directed toward preservation of being.

In every slain man on the battlefield, one can recognize a possible friend of someone. His fate makes all too clear the horrible arbitrariness of the violence to which my friend is exposed. Therefore, in love as friendship we have the most dependable enemy of war. The possible peaks of intensity and earlier maturity which war may bring to friendship are as nothing compared with the threats of loss it holds.

The feelings and the affinities that are the core of friendship are the true opposites of the hostile disposition that underlies all warfare. That the one disposition can so easily destroy the other tempts every man who knows friendship to despair and hopelessness.

When death comes to one's friend in the natural course, his loss is cruel enough, reducing the possibility of comprehending events. But friends in time can grow resigned to the finitude of existence, and old age, with its infirmities, helps to reconcile most of us to death. Friendship cut off in its flower by war's arbitrariness is likely to seem the height of unreason and madness. What earlier had been luminous, ordered, and purposeful in experience becomes suddenly emptied of meaning. Unlike other loves, the preciousness of friendship has no connection with its precariousness. Hence no ultimate consolation is possible for the loss of a friend. Love as concern can find new being to preserve and care for; its affection is not individualized. Erotic love can usually, though not always, find itself renewed when time has passed. The companionship of a lost friend is not replaceable.

I do not mean to assert that erotic love, in which the whole person is involved, and love as concern for preservation are less inimical to war than is love as friendship. Analysis of the distinctive forms of love should not betray us into forgetting their blood relationship. These three forms alike stand to lose in battle what makes life dear to them. Love in all three forms stands clearly in opposition to Ares and carries the hope of ultimate freedom from his reign. We do well to remember that love is a genus with many species, and there is little danger of exhausting the inner relations of the species. Those psychologists who find erotic elements in friendship and in maternal love are hardly wrong. And I have intimated already that there is a close affinity between love as concern and love as friendship.

What has become clear to me, however, as I have meditated on love and war, is that battle offers a very different exercise field for these different forms of love. Insofar as Eros is physical passion and sensual impulse, war has been from of old its true mate and bedfellow, as the ancient myth makes clear. And erotic love of the fuller sort can find a dwelling place in the violence of war that forever astounds us and remains inexplicable. Here Ares and Aphrodite meet as opposites who have a powerful attraction for each other. Love as concern can achieve at times its greatest satisfaction and triumph in struggling to preserve what Ares is intent on destroying. Though deeply opposed to conflict, this love is not as exposed or helpless as is friendship. In the exercise of its ancient rights, preservative love sanctifies even the battlefield by its presence and holds men back from being delivered over wholly to the lustful powers of destruction. But love as friendship, despite its insulation, must subsist haphazardly and as best it may in the midst of war. Its true domain is peace, only peace.

Chapter 28

Hannah Arendt, *On Humanity in Dark Times: Thoughts about Lessing*

Hanna Arendt (1906-1975) was a German-born American philosopher and political scientist known for her critical writing on Jewish affairs and her study of totalitarianism. Born in Hanover, Germany, she studied at the universities of Marburg and Freiburg, receiving her doctorate in philosophy from the University of Heidelberg in 1928. In 1933 when the Nazis came to power in Germany, she fled to Paris, where she worked for the immigration of Jewish refugee children into Palestine. In 1940 she married Heinrich Bluecher, a professor of philosophy, and in 1941 came to the United States, where she became a citizen in 1951.

In New York City, she served as Research Director of the Conference on Jewish Relations, chief editor of Schocken Books, Executive Director of Jewish Cultural Reconstruction, which sought to salvage Jewish writings dispersed by the Nazis. She also served as visiting professor at several universities, including California, Princeton, Columbia, and Chicago, and University Professor at the Graduate Faculty of The New School for Social Research. She was awarded a Guggenheim Fellowship in 1952 and won the annual Arts and Letters Grant of the National Institute of Arts and Letters in 1954. In 1967 she received the Sigmund Freud Prize of the German Akademie für Sprache und Dichtung for "scholarly prose."

Her monumental **Origins of Totalitarianism** *(1951), which related the development of totalitarianism to 19th-century anti-Semitism and imperialism, established Arendt as a major political thinker. Her controversial* **Eichmann in Jerusalem** *(1963), based on her reportage of the trial of Adolf Eichmann in 1961, portrayed that Nazi war criminal as merely an ambitious bureaucrat whose routine extermination of Jews exemplified "the fearsome, word-and-thought-defying banality of evil" of that time. Her other books include,* **The**

335

Human Condition *(1958)*, **Between Past and Future** *(1961)*, **On Revolution** *(1963)*, **On Violence** *(1970), and* **Crisis of the Republic** *(1972).*

The present essay is taken from her **Men in Dark Times** *(1968), a collection of essays on various individuals (mostly from the first half of the twentieth century) written over a period of twelve years. The reference to "dark times" in the title is borrowed from Brecht's famous poem "To Posterity," which mentions the disorder, hunger, massacres, slaughterers, the outrage over injustice, the despair "when there was only wrong and no outrage," the legitimate hatred that makes one ugly nevertheless, and the well-founded wrath that makes the voice grow hoarse. Even amidst the darkest times, she says, we may find some illumination that comes "from the uncertain, flickering, and often weak light" kindled by certain men and women in their lives and works. It is in the form of such illumination that the humanizing reality of friendship emerges from out of the darkness of the times. This is one of the chief themes of her reflections on Lessing—himself a light amidst the darkness of his times—in the address she delivered on the occasion of receiving the Lessing Prize of the Free City of Hamburg in 1959.*

On Humanity in Dark Times: Thoughts about Lessing

I

The distinction conferred by a free city, and a prize that bears the name of Lessing, are a great honor. I admit that I do not know how I have come to receive it, and also that it has not been altogether easy for me to come to terms with it. In saying this I can ignore entirely the delicate question of merit. In this very respect an honor gives us a forcible lesson in modesty; for it implies that it is not for us to judge our own merits as we judge the merits and accomplishments of others. In awards, the world speaks out, and if we accept the award and express our gratitude for it, we can do so only by ignoring ourselves and acting entirely within the framework of our attitude toward the world, toward a world and public to which we owe the space into which we speak and in which we are heard.

But the honor not only reminds us emphatically of the gratitude we owe the world; it also, to a very high degree, obligates us to it. Since we can always reject the honor, by accepting it we are not only strengthened in our position within the world but are accepting a kind of commitment to it. That a person appears in public at all, and that the public receives and confirms him, is by no means a matter to be taken for granted. Only the genius is driven by his very gifts into public life, and is exempted from any decision of this sort. In his case alone, honors only continue the concord with the world, sound an existing harmony in full publicity, which has arisen independently of all considerations and decisions, independently also of all obligations, as if it were a natural phenomenon erupting into human society. To this phenomenon we can in truth apply what Lessing once said about the man of genius in two of his finest lines of verse:

> *Was ihn bewegt, begegt. Was ihm gefällt, gefällt.*
> *Sein glücklicher Geschmack ist der Geschmack der Welt.*

> (What moves him, moves. What pleases him, pleases.
> His felicitous taste is the world's taste.)

Nothing in our time is more dubious, it seems to me, than our attitude toward the world, nothing less to be taken for granted than that concord with what appears in public which an honor imposes on us, and the existence of which it affirms. In our century even genius has been able to develop only in conflict with the world and the public realm, although it naturally finds, as it always has done, its own peculiar concord with its audience. But the world and the people who inhabit it are not the same. The world lies between people, and this in-between— much more than (as is often thought) men or even man—is today the object of the greatest concern and the most obvious upheaval in almost all the countries of the globe. Even where the world is still halfway in order, or is kept halfway in order, the public realm has lost the power of illumination which was originally part of its very nature. More and more people in the countries of the Western world, which since the decline of the ancient world has regarded freedom from politics as one of the basic freedoms, make use of this freedom and have retreated from the world and their obligations within it. This withdrawal from the world need not harm an individual; he may even cultivate great talents to the point of genius and so by a detour be useful to the world again. But with each such retreat an almost demonstrable loss to the world takes place; what is lost is the specific and usually irreplaceable in-between which should have formed between this individual and his fellow men.

When we thus consider the real meaning of public honors and prizes under present conditions, it may occur to us that the Hamburg Senate found a solution to the problem rather like that of Columbus' egg when it decided to link the city's prize with the name of Lessing. For Lessing never felt at home in the world as it then existed and probably never wanted to, and still after his own fashion he always remained committed to it. Special and unique circumstances governed this relationship. The German public was not prepared for him and as far as I know never honored him in his lifetime. He himself lacked, according to his own judgment, that happy, natural concord with the world, a combination of merit and good fortune, which both he and Goethe considered the sign of genius. Lessing believed he was indebted to criticism for something that "comes very close to genius," but which never quite achieved that natural harmonization with the world in which Fortuna smiles when Virtù appears. All that may have been important enough, but it was not decisive. It almost seems as if at some time he had decided to pay homage to genius, to the man of "felicitous taste," but himself to follow those whom he once half ironically called "the wise men" who "make the pillars of the best-known truths shake wherever they let their eyes fall." His attitude toward the world was neither positive nor negative, but radically critical and, in respect to the public realm of his time, completely revolutionary. But it was also an attitude that remained indebted to the world, never left the solid ground of the world, and never went to the extreme of sentimental utopianism. In Lessing the revolutionary temper was associated with a curious kind of partiality which clung to concrete details with an exaggerated, almost pedantic carefulness, and gave rise to many misunderstandings. One component of Lessing's greatness was the fact that he never allowed supposed objectivity to cause him to lose sight of the real relationship to the world and the real status in the world of the things or men he attacked or praised. That did not help his credit in Germany, where the true nature of criticism is less well understood than elsewhere. It was hard for the Germans to grasp that justice has little to do with objectivity in the ordinary sense.

Lessing never made his peace with the world in which he lived. He enjoyed "challenging prejudices" and "telling the truth to the court minions." Dearly though he paid for these pleasures, they were literally pleasures. Once when he was attempting to explain to himself the source of "tragic pleasure," he said that "all passions, even the most unpleasant, are as passions pleasant" because "they make us ... more conscious of our existence, they make us feel more real." This sentence strikingly recalls the Greek doctrine of passions, which counted anger, for example, among the pleasant emotions but reckoned hope along with fear among the evils. This evaluation rests on differences in reality, exactly as in Lessing; not, however, in the sense that reality is measured by the force with which the passion affects the soul but rather by the amounts of reality the passion transmits to it. In hope, the soul overleaps reality, as in fear it shrinks back from it. But anger, and above all Lessing's kind of anger, reveals and exposes the world just as Lessing's kind of laughter in *Minna von Barnhelm* seeks to bring about reconciliation with the world. Such laughter helps one to find a place in the world, but ironically, which is to say, without selling one's soul to it. Pleasure, which is fundamentally the intensified awareness of reality, springs from a passionate openness to the world and love of it. Not even the knowledge that man may be destroyed by the world detracts from the "tragic pleasure."

If Lessing's aesthetics, in contrast to Aristotle's, sees even fear as a variety of pity, the pity we feel for ourselves, the reason is perhaps that Lessing is trying to strip fear of its escapist aspect in order to save it as a passion, that is to say, as an affect in which we are affected by ourselves just as in the world we are ordinarily affected by other people. Intimately connected with this is the fact that for Lessing the essence of poetry was action and not, as for Herder, a force—"the magic force that affects my soul"—nor, as for Goethe, nature which has been given form. Lessing was not at all concerned with "the perfection of the work of art in itself," which Goethe considered "the eternal, indispensable requirement." Rather—and here he is in agreement with Aristotle—he was concerned with the effect upon the spectator, who as it were represents the world, or rather, that worldly space which has come into being between the artist or writer and his fellow men as a world common to them.

Lessing experienced the world in anger and in laughter, and anger and laughter are by their nature biased. Therefore, he was unable or unwilling to judge a work of art "in itself," independently of its effect in the world, and therefore he could attack or defend in his polemics according to how the matter in question was being judged by the public and quite independently of the degree to which it was true or false. It was not only a form of gallantry when he said that he would "leave in peace those whom all are striking at"; it was also a concern, which had become instinctive with him, for the relative rightness of opinions which for good reasons get the worst of it. Thus even in the dispute over Christianity he did not take up a fixed position. Rather, as he once said with magnificent self-knowledge, he instinctively became dubious of Christianity "the more cogently some tried to prove it to me," and instinctively tried "to preserve it in [his] heart" the more "wantonly and triumphantly others sought to trample it underfoot." But this means that where everyone else was contending over the "truth" of Christianity, he was chiefly defending its position in the world, now anxious that it might again enforce its claim to dominance, now fearing that it might vanish utterly. Lessing was being remarkably farsighted when he saw that the enlightened theology of his time "under the pretext of making us rational Christians is making us extremely irrational philosophers." That insight sprang not only from partisanship in favor of reason. Lessing's primary concern in this whole debate was freedom, which was far more endangered by those who wanted "to compel faith by proofs" than by those who regarded faith as a gift of divine grace. But there was in addition his concern about the world, in which he felt both religion and philosophy should have their placed, but separate laces, so that behind the "partition ... each can go its own way without hindering the other."

Criticism, in Lessing's sense, is always taking sides for the world's sake, understanding and judging everything in terms of its position in the world at any given time. Such a mentality can never give rise to a definite world view which, once adopted, is immune to further experiences in the world because it has hitched itself firmly to one possible perspective. We very much need Lessing to teach us this state of mind, and what makes learning it so hard for us is not our distrust of the Enlightenment or of the eighteenth century's belief in humanity. It is not the eighteenth but the nineteenth century that stands between Lessing and us. The nineteenth century's obsession with history and commitment to ideology still looms so large in the political thinking of or times that we are inclined to regard entirely free thinking, which employs neither history nor coercive logic as crutches, as having no authority over us. To be sure, we are still aware that thinking calls not only for intelligence and profundity but above all for courage. But we are astonished that Lessing's partisanship for the world could go so far that he could even sacrifice to it the axiom of noncontradiction, the claim to self-consistency, which we assume is mandatory to all who write and speak. For he declared in all seriousness: "I am not duty-bound to resolve the difficulties I create. May my ideas always be somewhat disjunct, or even appear to contradict one another, if only they are ideas in which readers will find material that stirs them to think for themselves." He not only wanted no one to coerce him, but he also wanted to coerce no one, either by force or by proofs. He regarded the tyranny of those who attempt to dominate thinking by reasoning and sophistries, by compelling argumentation, as more dangerous to freedom than orthodoxy. Above all he never coerced himself, and instead of fixing his identity in history with a perfectly consistent system, he scattered into the world, as he himself knew, "nothing but *fermenta cognitionis.*"

Thus Lessing's famous *Selbstdenken*—independent thinking for oneself—is by no means an activity pertaining to a closed, integrated organically grown and cultivated individual who then as it were looks around to see where in the world the most favorable place for his development might be, in order to bring himself into harmony with the world by the detour of thought. For Lessing, thought does not arise out of the individual and is not the manifestation of a self. Rather, the individual—whom Lessing would say was created for action, not ratiocination—elects such thought because he discovers in thinking another mode of moving in the world in freedom. Of all the specific liberties which may come into our minds when we hear the word "freedom," freedom of movement is historically the oldest and also the most elementary. Being able to depart for where we will is the prototypal gesture of being free, as limitation of freedom of movement has from time immemorial been the precondition for enslavement. Freedom of movement is also the indispensable condition for action, and it is in action that men primarily experience freedom in the world. When men are deprived of the public space—which is constituted by acting together and then fills of its own accord with the events and stories that develop into history—they retreat into their freedom of thought. That is a very ancient experience, of course. And some such retreat seems to have been forced upon Lessing. When we hear of such a retreat from enslavement in the world to freedom of thought, we naturally remember the Stoic model, because it was historically the most effective. But to be precise, Stoicism represents not so much a retreat from action to thinking as an escape from the world into the self which, it is hoped, will be able to sustain itself in sovereign independence of the outside world. There was nothing of the sort in Lessing's case. Lessing retreated into thought, but not at all into his own self; and if for him a secret link between action and thought did exist (I believe it did, although I cannot prove it by quotations), the link consisted in the fact that both action and thought occur in the form of movement and that, therefore, freedom underlies both: freedom of movement.

Lessing probably never believed that acting can be replaced by thinking, or that freedom of thought can be a substitute for the freedom inherent in action. He knew very well that he was living in what was then the "most slavish country in Europe," even though he was allowed to "offer the public as many idiocies against religion" as he pleased. For it was impossible to raise "a voice for the rights of subjects ... against extortion and despotism," in other words, to act. The secret relationship of his "self-thinking" to action lay in his never binding his thinking to results. In fact, he explicitly renounced the desire for results, insofar as these might mean the final solution of problems which his thought posed for itself; his thinking was not a search for truth, since every truth that is the result of a thought process necessarily puts an end to the movement of thinking. The *fermenta cognitionis* which Lessing scattered into the world were not intended to communicate conclusions, but to stimulate others to independent thought, and this for no other purpose than to bring about a discourse between thinkers. Lessing's thought is not the (Platonic) silent dialogue between me and myself, but an anticipated dialogue with others, and this is the reason that it is essentially polemical. But even if he had succeeded in bringing about his discourse with other independent thinkers and so escaping a solitude which, for him in particular, paralyzed all faculties, he could scarcely have been persuaded that this put everything to rights. For what was wrong, and what no dialogue and no independent thinking ever could right, was the world—namely, the thing that arises between people and in which everything that individuals carry with them innately can become visible and audible. In the two hundred years that separate us from Lessing's lifetime, much has changed in this respect, but little has changed for the better. The "pillars of the best-known truths" (to stay with his metaphor), which at the time were shaken, today lie shattered; we need neither criticism nor wise men to shake them any more. We need only look around to see that we are standing in the midst of a veritable rubble heap of such pillars.

Now in a certain sense this could be an advantage, promoting a new kind of thinking that needs no pillars and props, no standards and traditions to move freely without crutches over unfamiliar terrain. But with the world as it is, it is difficult to enjoy this advantage. For long ago it became apparent that the pillars of the truths have also been the pillars of the political order, and that the world (in contrast to the people who inhabit it and move freely about in it) needs such pillars in order to guarantee continuity and permanence, without which it cannot offer mortal men the relatively secure, relatively imperishable home that they need. To be sure, the very humanity of man loses its vitality to the extent that he abstains from thinking and puts his confidence into old verities or even new truths, throwing them down as if they were coins with which to balance all experiences. And yet, if this is true for man, it is not true for the world. The world becomes inhuman, inhospitable to human needs—which are the needs of mortals—when it is violently wrenched into a movement in which there is no longer any sort of permanence. That is why ever since the great failure of the French Revolution people have repeatedly re-erected the old pillars which were then overthrown, only again and again to see them first quivering, then collapsing anew. The most frightful errors have replaced the "best-known truths," and the error of these doctrines constitutes no proof, no new pillar for the old truths. In the political realm restoration is never a substitute for a new foundation but will be at best an emergency measure that becomes inevitable when the act of foundation, which is called revolution, has failed. But it is likewise inevitable that in such a constellation, especially when it extends over such long spans of time, people's mistrust of the world and all aspects of the public realm should grow steadily. For the fragility of these repeatedly restored props of the public order is bound to become more apparent after every collapse, so that ultimately the public order is based on people's holding as self-evident precisely those "best-known truths" which secretly scarcely anyone still believes in.

II

History knows many periods of dark times in which the public realm has been obscured and the world become so dubious that people have ceased to ask any more of politics than that it show due consideration for their vital interests and personal liberty. Those who have lived in such times and been formed by them have probably always been inclined to despise the world and the public realm, to ignore them as far as possible, or even to overleap them and, as it were, reach behind them—as if the world were only a façade behind which people could conceal themselves—in order to arrive at mutual understandings with their fellow men without regard for the world that lies between them. In such times, if things turn out well, a special kind of humanity develops. In order properly to appreciate its possibilities we need only think of *Nathan the Wise,* whose true theme—"It suffices to be a man"—permeates the play. The appeal: "Be my friend," which runs like a leitmotif through the whole play, corresponds to that theme. We might equally well think of *The Magic Flute,* which likewise has as its theme such a humanity, which is more profound than we generally think when we consider only the eighteenth century's usual theories of a basic human nature underlying the multiplicity of nations, peoples, races, and religions into which the human race is divided. If such a human nature were to exist, it would be a natural phenomenon, and to call behavior in accordance with it "human" would assume that human and natural behavior are one and the same. In the eighteenth century the greatest and historically the most effective advocate of this kind of humanity was Rousseau, for whom the human nature common to all men was manifested not in reason but in compassion, in an innate repugnance, as he put it, to see a fellow human being suffering. With remarkable accord, Lessing also declared that the best person is the most compassionate. But Lessing was troubled by the egalitarian character of compassion—the fact that, as he stressed, we feel "something akin to compassion" for the evildoer also. This did not trouble Rousseau. In the spirit of the French Revolution, which leaned upon his ideas, he saw *fraternité* as the fulfillment of humanity. Lessing, on the other hand, considered friendship—which is as selective as compassion is egalitarian—to be the central phenomenon in which alone true humanity can prove itself.

Before we turn to Lessing's concept of friendship and its political relevance, we must dwell for a moment on fraternity as the eighteenth century understood it. Lessing, too, was well acquainted with it; he spoke of "philanthropic feelings," of a brotherly attachment to other human beings which springs from hatred of the world in which men are treated "inhumanly." For our purposes, however, it is important that humanity manifests itself in such brotherhood most frequently in "dark times." This kind of humanity actually becomes inevitable when the times become so extremely dark for certain groups of people that it is no longer up to them, their insight or choice, to withdraw from the world. Humanity in the form of fraternity invariably appears historically among persecuted peoples and enslaved groups; and in eighteenth-century Europe it must have been quite natural to detect it among the Jews, who then were newcomers in literary circles. This kind of humanity is the great privilege of pariah peoples; it is the advantage that the pariahs of the world always and in all circumstances can have over others. The privilege is dearly bought; it is often accompanied by so radical a loss of the world, so fearful an atrophy of all the organs with which we respond to it—starting with the common sense with which we orient ourselves in a world common to ourselves and others and going on to the sense of beauty, or taste, with which we love the world—that in extreme cases, in which pariahdom has persisted for centuries, we can speak of real worldlessness. And worldlessness, alas, is always a form of barbarism.

In this as it were organically evolved humanity it is as if under the pressure of persecution the persecuted have moved so closely together that the interspace which we have called world (and which of course existed between them before the persecution, keeping them at a distance from one another) has simply disappeared. This produces a warmth of human relationships which may strike those who have had some experience with such groups as an almost physical phenomenon. Of course I do not mean to imply that this warmth of persecuted peoples is not a great thing. In its full development it can breed a kindliness and sheer goodness of which human beings are otherwise scarcely capable. Frequently it is also the source of a vitality, a joy in the simple fact of being alive, rather suggesting that life comes fully into its own only among those who are, in worldly terms, the insulted and injured. But in saying this we must not forget that the charm and intensity of the atmosphere that develops is also due to the fact that the pariahs of this world enjoy the great privilege of being unburdened by care for the world.

Fraternity, which the French Revolution added to the liberty and equality which have always been categories of man's political sphere—that fraternity has its natural place among the repressed and persecuted, the exploited and humiliated, whom the eighteenth century called the unfortunates, *les malheureux,* and the nineteenth century the wretched, *les misrables.* Compassion, which for both Lessing and Rousseau (though in very different contexts) played so extraordinary a part in the discovery and confirmation of a human nature common to all men, for the first time became the central motive of the revolutionary in Robespierre. Ever since, compassion has remained inseparably and unmistakably part of the history of European revolutions. Now compassion is unquestionably a natural, creature affect which involuntarily touches every normal person at the sight of suffering, however alien the sufferer may be, and would therefore seem an ideal basis for a feeling that reaching out to all mankind would establish a society in which men might really become brothers. Through compassion the revolutionary-minded humanitarian of the eighteenth century sought to achieve solidarity with the unfortunate and the miserable—an effort tantamount to penetrating the very domain of brotherhood. But it soon became evident that this kind of humanitarianism, whose purest form is a privilege of the pariah, is not transmissible and cannot be easily acquired by those who do not belong among the pariahs. Neither compassion nor actual sharing of suffering is enough. We cannot discuss here the mischief that compassion has introduced into modern revolutions by attempts to improve the lot of the unfortunate rather than to establish justice for all. But in order to gain a little perspective on ourselves and the modern way of feeling we might recall briefly how the ancient world, so much more experienced in all political matters than ourselves, viewed compassion and the humanitarianism of brotherhood.

Modern times and antiquity agree on one point: both regard compassion as something totally natural, as inescapable to man as, say, fear. It is therefore all the more striking that antiquity took a position wholly at odds with the great esteem for compassion of modern times. Because they so clearly recognized the affective nature of compassion, which can overcome us like fear without our being able to fend it off, the ancients regarded the most compassionate person as no more entitled to be called best than the most fearful. Both emotions, because they are purely passive, make action impossible. This is the reason Aristotle treated compassion and fear together. Yet it would be altogether misguided to reduce compassion to fear—as though the sufferings of others aroused in us fear for ourselves—or fear to compassion—as though in fear we felt only compassion for ourselves. We are even more surprised when we hear (from Cicero in the *Tusculanae Disputationes* III 21) that the Stoics saw compassion and envy in the same terms: "For the man who is pained by another's misfortune is also pained by another's prosperity." Cicero himself comes considerably closer to the heart of the matter when he asks (*ibid.* IV 56): "Why pity rather than give assistance if one can? Or, are we unable to be open-handed without pity?" In other words, should human beings be so shabby that they are incapable of acting humanly unless spurred and as it were compelled by their own pain when they see others suffer?

In judging these affects we can scarcely help raising the question of selflessness, or rather the question of openness to others, which in fact is the precondition for "humanity" in every sense of that word. It seems evident that sharing joy is absolutely superior in this respect to sharing suffering. Gladness, not sadness, is talkative, and truly human dialogue differs from mere talk or even discussion in that it is entirely permeated by pleasure in the other person and what he says. It is tuned to the key of gladness, we might say. What stands in the way of this gladness is envy, which in the sphere of humanity is the worst vice; but the antithesis to compassion is not envy but cruelty, which is an affect no less than compassion, for it is a perversion, a feeling of pleasure where pain would naturally be felt. The decisive factor is that pleasure and pain, like everything instinctual, tend to muteness, and while they may well produce sound, they do not produce speech and certainly not dialogue.

All this is only another way of saying that the humanitarianism of brotherhood scarcely befits those who do not belong among the insulted and the injured and can share in it only through their compassion. The warmth of pariah peoples cannot rightfully extend to those whose different position in the world imposes on them a responsibility for the world and does not allow them to share the cheerful unconcern of the pariah. But it is true that in "dark times" the warmth which is the pariahs' substitute for light exerts a great fascination upon all those who are so ashamed of the world as it is that they would like to take refuge in invisibility. And in invisibility, in that obscurity in which a man who is himself hidden need no longer see the visible world either, only the warmth and fraternity of closely packed human beings can compensate for the weird irreality that human relationships assume wherever they develop in absolute worldlessness, unrelated to a world common to all people. In such a state of worldlessness and irreality it is easy to conclude that the element common to all men is not the world, but "human nature" of such and such a type. What the type is depends on the interpreter; it scarcely matters whether reason, as a property of all men, is emphasized, or a feeling common to all, such as the capacity for compassion. The rationalism and sentimentalism of the eighteenth century are only two aspects of the same thing; both could lead equally to that enthusiastic excess in which individuals feel ties of brotherhood to all men. In any case this rationality and sentimentality were only psychological substitutes, localized in the realm of invisibility, for the loss of the common, visible world.

Now this "human nature" and the feelings of fraternity that accompany it manifest themselves only in darkness, and hence cannot be identified in the world. What is more, in conditions of visibility they dissolve into nothingness like phantoms. The humanity of the insulted and injured has never yet survived the hour of liberation by so much as a minute. This does not mean that it is insignificant, for in fact it makes insult and injury endurable; but it does mean that in political terms it is absolutely irrelevant.

III

These and similar questions of the proper attitude in "dark times" are of course especially familiar to the generation and the group to which I belong. If concord with the world, which is part and parcel of receiving honors, has never been an easy matter in our times and in the circumstances of our world, it is even less so for us. Certainly honors were no part of our birthright, and it would not be surprising if we were no longer capable of the openness and trustfulness that are needed simply to accept grateful openness and trustfulness that are needed simply to accept gratefully what the world offers in good faith. Even those among us who by speaking and writing have ventured into public life have not done so out of any original pleasure in the public scene, and have hardly expected or aspired to receive the stamp of public approval. Even in public they tend to address only their friends or to speak to those unknown, scattered readers and listeners with whom everyone who speaks and writes at all cannot help feeling joined in some rather obscure brotherhood. I am afraid that in their efforts they felt very little responsibility towards the world; these efforts were, rather, guided by their hope of preserving some minimum of humanity in a world grown inhuman while at the same time as far as possible resisting the weird irreality of this worldlessness—each after his own fashion and some few by seeking to the limits of their ability to understand even inhumanity and the intellectual and political monstrosities of a time out of joint.

I so explicitly stress my membership in the group of Jews expelled from Germany at a relatively early age because I wish to anticipate certain misunderstandings which can arise only too easily when one speaks of humanity. In this connection I cannot gloss over the fact that for many years I considered the only adequate reply to the question, Who are you? to be: A Jew. That answer alone took into account the reality of persecution. As for the statement with which Nathan the Wise (in effect, though not in actual wording) countered the command: "Step closer, Jew"—the statement: I am a man—I would have considered as nothing but a grotesque and dangerous evasion of reality.

Let me also quickly clear away another likely misunderstanding. When I use the word "Jew" I do not mean to suggest any special kind of human being, as though the Jewish fate were either representative of or a model for the fate of mankind. (Any such thesis could at best have been advanced with cogency only during the last stage of Nazi domination, when in fact the Jews and anti-Semitism were being exploited solely to unleash and keep in motion the racist program of extermination. For this was an essential part of totalitarian rule. The Nazi movement, to be sure, had from the first tended toward totalitarianism, but the Third Reich was not by any means totalitarian during its early years. By "early years" I mean the first period, which lasted from 1933 to 1938.) In saying, "A Jew," I did not even refer to a reality burdened or marked out for distinction by history. Rather, I was only acknowledging a political fact through which my being a member of this group outweighed all other questions of personal identity or rather had decided them in favor of anonymity, of namelessness. Nowadays such an attitude would seem like a pose. Nowadays, therefore, it is easy to remark that those who react in this way had never got very far in the school of "humanity," had fallen into the trap set by Hitler, and thus had succumbed to the spirit of Hitlerism in their own way. Unfortunately, the basically simple principle in question here is one that is particularly hard to understand in times of defamation and persecution: the principle that one can resist only in terms of the identity that is under attack. Those who reject such identifications on the part of a hostile world may feel wonderfully superior to the world, but their superiority is then truly no longer of this world; it is the superiority of a more or less well-equipped cloud-cuckoo-land.

When I thus bluntly reveal the personal background of my reflections, it may easily sound to those who know the fate of the Jews only from hearsay as if I am taking out of school, a school they have not attended and whose lessons do not concern them. But as it happens, during that selfsame period in Germany there existed the phenomenon known as the "inner emigration," and those who know anything about that experience may well recognize certain questions and conflicts akin to the problems I have mentioned in more than a mere formal and structural sense. As its very name suggests, the "inner emigration" was a curiously ambiguous phenomenon. It signified on the one hand that there were persons inside Germany who behaved as if they no longer belonged to the country, who felt like emigrants; and on the other hand it indicated that they had not in reality emigrated, but had withdrawn to an interior realm, into the invisibility of thinking and feeling. It would be a mistake to imagine that this form of exile, a withdrawal from the world into an interior realm, existed only in Germany, just as it would be a mistake to imagine that such emigration came to an end with then end of the Third Reich. But in that darkest of times, inside and outside Germany the temptation was particularly strong, in the face of a seemingly unendurable reality, to shift from the world and its public space to an interior life, or else simply to ignore that world in favor of an imaginary world "as it ought to be" or as it once upon a time had been.

There has been much discussion of the widespread tendency in Germany to act as though the years from 1933 to 1945 never existed; as though this part of German and European and thus world history could be expunged from the textbooks; as though everything depended on forgetting the "negative" aspect of the past and reducing horror to sentimentality. (The world-wide success of *The Diary of Anne Frank* was clear proof that such tendencies were not confined to Germany.) It was a grotesque state of affairs when German young people were not allowed to learn the facts that every school child a few miles away could not help knowing. Behind all this there was, of course, genuine perplexity. And this very incapacity to face the reality of the past might possibly have been a direct heritage of the inner emigration, as it was undoubtedly to a considerable extent, and even more directly, a consequence of the Hitler regime—that is to say, a consequence of the organized guilt in which the Nazis had involved all inhabitants of the German lands, the inner exiles no less than the stalwart Party members and the vacillating fellow travelers. It was the fact of this guilt which the Allies simply incorporated into the fateful hypothesis of collective guilt. Herein lies the reason for the Germans' profound awkwardness, which strikes every outsider, in any discussion of questions of the past. How difficult it must be to find a reasonable attitude is perhaps more clearly expressed by the cliché that the past is still "unmastered" and in the conviction held particularly by men of good will that the first thing to be done is to set about "mastering" it. Perhaps that cannot be done with any past, but certainly not with the past of Hitler Germany. The best that can be achieved is to know precisely what it was, and to endure this knowledge, and then to wait and see what comes of knowing and enduring.

Perhaps I can best explain this by a less painful example. After the First World War we experienced the "mastering of the past" in a spate of descriptions of the war that varied enormously in kind and quality; naturally, this happened not only in Germany, but in all the affected countries. Nevertheless, nearly thirty years were to pass before a work of art appeared which so transparently displayed the inner truth of the event that it became possible to say: Yes, this is how it was. And in this novel, William Faulkner's *A Fable,* very little is described, still less explained, and nothing at all "mastered"; its end is tears, which the reader also weeps, and what remains beyond that is the "tragic effect" or the "tragic pleasure," the shattering emotion which makes one able to accept the fact that something like this war could have happened at all. I deliberately mention tragedy because it more than the other literary forms represents a process of recognition. The tragic hero becomes knowledgeable by re-experiencing what has been done in the way of suffering, and in this *pathos,* in resuffering the past, the network of individual acts is transformed into an event, a significant whole. The dramatic climax of tragedy occurs when the actor turns into a sufferer; therein lies its peripeteia, the disclosure of the dénouement. But even non-tragic plots become genuine events only when they are experienced a second time in the form of suffering by memory operating retrospectively and perceptively. Such memory can speak only when indignation and just anger, which impel us to action, have been silenced—and that needs time. We can no more master the past than we can undo it. But we can reconcile ourselves to it. The form for this is the lament, which arises out of all recollection. It is, as Goethe has said (in the Dedication to *Faust*):

> *Der Schmerz wird neu, es wiederholt die Klage*
> *Des Lebens labyrinthisch irren Lauf.*

> (Pain arises anew, lament repeats
> Life's labyrinthine, erring course.)

The tragic impact of this repetition in lamentation affects one of the key elements of all action; it establishes its meaning and that permanent significance which then enters into history. In contradistinction to other elements peculiar to action—above all to the preconceived goals, the impelling motives, and the guiding principles, all of which become visible in the course of action—the meaning of a committed act is revealed only when the action itself has come to an end and become a story susceptible to narration. Insofar as any "mastering" of the past is possible, it consists in relating what has happened; but such narration, too, which shapes history, solves no problems and assuages no suffering; it does not master anything once and for all. Rather, as long as the meaning of the events remains alive—and this meaning can persist for very long periods of time—"mastering of the past" can take the form of ever-recurrent narration. The poet in a very general sense and the historian in a very special sense have the task of setting this process of narration in motion and of involving us in it. And we who for the most part are neither poets nor historians are familiar with the nature of this process from our own experience with life, for we too have the need to recall the significant events in our own lives by relating them to ourselves and others. Thus we are constantly preparing the way for "poetry," in the broadest sense, as a human potentiality; we are, so to speak, constantly expecting it to erupt in some human being. When this happens, the telling-over of what took place comes to a halt for the time being and a formed narrative, one more item is added to the world's stock. In reification by the poet of the historian, the narration of history has achieved permanence and persistence. Thus the narrative has been given its place in the world, where it will survive us. There it can live on—one story among many. There is no meaning to these stories that is entirely separable from them—and this, too, we know from our own, non-poetic experience. No philosophy, no analysis, no aphorism, be it ever so profound, can compare in intensity and richness of meaning with a properly narrated story.

I seem to have digressed from my subject. The question is how much reality must be retained even in a world become inhuman if humanity is not to be reduced to an empty phrase or a phantom. Or to put it another way, to what extent do we remain obligated to the world even when we have been expelled from it or have withdrawn from it? For I certainly do not wish to assert that the "inner emigration," the flight from the world to concealment, from public life to anonymity (when that is what it really was and not just a pretext for doing what everyone did with enough inner reservations to salve one's conscience), was not a justified attitude, and in many cases the only possible one. Flight from the world in dark times of impotence can always be justified as long as reality is not ignored, but constantly acknowledged as the thing that must be escaped. When people choose this alternative, private life too can retain a by no means insignificant reality, even though it remains impotent. Only it is essential for them to realize that the realness of this reality consists not in its deeply personal note, any more than it springs from privacy as such, but inheres in the world from which they have escaped. They must remember that they are constantly on the run, and that the world's reality is actually expressed by their escape. Thus, too, the true force of escapism springs from persecution and the personal strength of the fugitives increases as the persecution and danger increase.

At the same time we cannot fail to see the limited political relevance of such an existence, even if it is sustained in purity. Its limits are inherent in the fact that strength and power are not the same; that power arises only where people act together, but not where people grow stronger as individuals. No strength is ever great enough to replace power; wherever strength is confronted by power, strength will always succumb. But even the sheer strength to escape and to resist while fleeing cannot materialize where reality is bypassed or forgotten—as when an individual thinks himself too good and noble to pit himself against such a world, or when he falls to face up to the absolute "negativeness" of prevailing world conditions at a given time. How tempting it was, for example, simply to ignore the intolerably stupid blabber of the Nazis. But seductive though it may be to yield to such temptations and to hole up in the refuge of one's own psyche, the result will always be a loss of humanness along with the forsaking of reality.

Thus, in the case of a friendship between a German and a Jew under the conditions of the Third Reich it would scarcely have been a sign of humanness for the friends to have said: Are we not both human beings? It would have been mere evasion of reality and of the world common to both at that time; they would not have been resisting the world as it was. A law that prohibited the intercourse of Jews and Germans could be evaded but could not be defied by people who denied the reality of the distinction. In keeping with a humanness that had not lost the solid ground of reality, a humanness in the midst of the reality of persecution, they would have had to say to each other: A German and a Jew, and friends. But wherever such a friendship succeeded at that time (of course the situation is completely changed, nowadays) and was maintained in purity, that is to say without false guilt complexes on the one side and false complexes of superiority or inferiority on the other, a bit of humanness in a world become inhuman had been achieved.

IV

The example of friendship, which I had adduced because it seems to me a variety of reasons to be specially pertinent to the question of humanness, brings us back to Lessing again. As is well known, the ancients thought friends indispensable to human life, indeed that a life without friends was not really worth living. In holding this view they gave little consideration to the idea that we need the help of friends in misfortune; on the contrary, they rather thought that there can be no happiness or good fortune for anyone unless a friend shares in the joy of it. Of course there is something to the maxim that only in misfortune do we find out who our true friends are; but those whom we regard as our true friends without such proof are usually those to whom we unhesitatingly reveal happiness and whom we count on to share our rejoicing.

We are wont to see friendship solely as a phenomenon of intimacy, in which the friends open their hearts to each other unmolested by the world and its demands. Rousseau, not Lessing, is the best advocate of this view, which conforms so well to the basic attitude of the modern individual, who is in his alienation from the world can truly reveal himself only in privacy and in the intimacy of face-to-face encounters. Thus it is hard for us to understand the political relevance of friendship. When, for example, we read in Aristotle that *philia,* friendship among citizens, is one of the fundamental requirements for the well-being of the City, we tend to think that he was speaking of no more than the absence of factions and civil war within it. But for the Greeks the essence of friendship consisted in discourse. They held that only the constant interchange of talk united citizens in a *polis.* In discourse the political importance of friendship, and the humanness peculiar to it, were made manifest. This converse (in contrast to the intimate talk in which individuals speak about themselves), permeated though it may be by pleasure in the friend's presence, is concerned with the common world, which remains "inhuman" in a very literal sense unless it is constantly talked about by human beings. For the world is not humane just because it is made by human beings, and it does not become humane just because the human voice sounds in it, but only when it has become the object of discourse. However much we are affected by the things of the world, however deeply they may stir and stimulate us, they become human for us only when we can discuss them with our fellows. Whatever cannot become the object of discourse—the truly sublime, the truly horrible or the uncanny—may find a human voice through which to sound into the world, but it is not exactly human. We humanize what is going on in the world and in ourselves only by speaking of it, and in the course of speaking of it we learn to be human.

The Greeks called this humanness which is achieved in the discourse of friendship *philanthropia,* "love of man," since it manifests itself in a readiness to share the world with other men. Its opposite, misanthropy, means simply that the misanthrope finds no one with whom he cares to share the world, that he regards nobody as worthy of rejoicing with him in the world and nature and the cosmos. Greek philanthropy underwent many a change in become Roman *humanitas.* The most important of these changes corresponded to the political fact that in Rome people of widely different ethnic origins and descent could acquire Roman citizenship and thus enter into the discourse among cultivated Romans, could discuss the world and life with them. And this political background distinguishes Roman *humanitas* from what moderns call humanity, by which they commonly mean a mere effect of education.

That humaneness should be sober and cool rather than sentimental; that humanity is exemplified not in fraternity but in friendship; that friendship is not intimately personal but makes political demands and preserves reference to the world—all this seems to us so exclusively characteristic of classical antiquity that it rather perplexes us when we find quite kindred features in *Nathan the Wise*—which, modern as it is, might with some justice be called the classical drama of friendship. What strikes us as so strange in the play is the "We must, must be friends," with which Nathan turns to the Templar, and in fact to everyone he meets; for this friendship is obviously so much more important to Lessing than the passion of love that he can brusquely cut the love story off short (the lovers, the Templar and Nathan's adopted daughter Recha, turn out to be brother and sister) and transform it into a relationship in which friendship is required and love ruled out. The dramatic tension of the play lies solely in the conflict that arises between friendship and humanity with truth. That fact perhaps strikes modern men as even stranger, but once again it is curiously close to the principles and conflicts which concerned classical antiquity. In the end, after all, Nathan's wisdom consists solely in his readiness to sacrifice truth to friendship.

Lessing had highly unorthodox opinions about truth. He refused to accept any truths whatever, even those presumably handed down by Providence, and he never felt compelled by truth, be it imposed by others' or by his own reasoning processes. If he had been confronted with the Platonic alternative of *doxa* or *aletheia*, of opinion or truth, there is no question how he would have decided. He was glad that—to use his parable—the genuine ring, if it had ever existed, had been lost; he was glad for the sake of the infinite number of opinions that arise when men discuss the affairs of this world. If the genuine ring did exist, that would mean an end to discourse and thus to friendship and thus to humanness. On these same grounds he was content to belong to the race of "limited gods," as he occasionally called men; and he thought that human society was in no way harmed by those "who take more trouble to make clouds than to scatter them," while it incurred "much harm from those who wish to subject all men's ways of thinking to the yoke of their own." This has very little to do with tolerance in the ordinary sense (in fact Lessing himself was by no means an especially tolerant person), but it has a great deal to do with the gift of friendship, with openness to a great deal to do with the gift of friendship, with openness to the world, and finally with genuine love of mankind.

The theme of "limited gods," of the limitations of the human understanding, limitations which speculative reason can point out and thereby transcend, subsequently became the great object of Kant's critiques. But whatever Kant's attitudes may have in common with Lessing's—and in fact they do have much in common—the two thinkers differed on one decisive point. Kant realized that there can be no absolute truth for man, at least not in the theoretical sense. He would certainly have been prepared to sacrifice truth to the possibility of human freedom; for if we possessed truth we could not be free. But he would scarcely have agreed with Lessing that the truth, if it did exist, could be unhesitatingly sacrificed to humanity, to the possibility of friendship and of discourse among men. Kant argued that an absolute exists, the duty of the categorical imperative which stands above men, is decisive in all human affairs, and cannot be infringed even for the sake of humanity in every sense of the word. Critics of the Kantian ethic have frequently denounced this thesis as altogether inhuman and unmerciful. Whatever the merits of their arguments, the inhumanity of Kant's moral philosophy is undeniable. And this is so because the categorical imperative is postulated as absolute and in its absoluteness introduces into the interhuman realm—which by its nature consists of relationships—something that runs counter to its fundamental relativity. The inhumanity which is bound up with the concept of one single truth emerges with particular clarity in Kant's work precisely because he attempted to found truth on practical reason; it is as though he who had so inexorably pointed out man's cognitive limits could not bear to think that in action, too, man cannot behave like a god.

Lessing, however, rejoiced in the very thing that has ever—or at least since Parmenides and Plato—distressed philosophers: that the truth, as soon as it is uttered, is immediately transformed into one opinion among many, is contested, reformulated, reduced to one subject of discourse among others. Lessing's greatness does not merely consist in a theoretical insight that there cannot be one single truth within the human world but in his gladness that it does not exist and that, therefore, the unending discourse among men will never cease so long as there are men at all. A single absolute truth, could there have been one, would have been the death of all those disputes in which this ancestor and master of all polemicism in the German language was so much at home and always took sides with the utmost clarity and definiteness. And this would have spelled the end of humanity.

It is difficult for us today to identify with the dramatic but untragic conflict of *Nathan the Wise* as Lessing intended it. That is partly because in regard to truth it has become a matter of course for us to behave tolerantly, although for reasons that have scarcely any connection with Lessing's reasons. Nowadays someone may still occasionally put the question at least in the style of Lessing's parable of the three rings—as, for example, in Kafka's magnificent pronouncement: "It is difficult to speak the truth, for although there is only one truth, it is alive and therefore has a live and changing face." But here, too, nothing is said of the political point of Lessing's antinomy—that is, the possible antagonism between truth and humanity. Nowadays, moreover, it is rare to meet people who believe they possess the truth; instead, we are constantly confronted by those who are sure that they are right. The distinction is plain; the question of truth was in Lessing's time still a question of philosophy and of religion, whereas our problem of being right arises within the framework of science and is always decided by a mode of thought oriented toward science. In saying this I shall ignore the question of whether this change in ways of thinking has proved to be for our good or ill. The simple fact is that even men who are utterly incapable of judging the specifically scientific aspects of an argument are as fascinated by scientific rightness as men of the eighteenth century were by the question of truth. And strangely enough, modern men are not deflected from their fascination by the attitude of scientists, who as long as they are really proceeding scientifically know quite well that their "truths" are never final but are continually undergoing radical revision by living research.

In spite of the difference between the notions of possessing the truth and being right, these two points of view have one thing in common: those who take one or the other are generally not prepared to sacrifice their view to humanity or friendship in case a conflict should arise. They actually believe that to do so would be to violate a higher duty, the duty of "objectivity"; so that even if they occasionally make such a sacrifice they do not feel they are acting out of conscience but are even ashamed of their humanity and often feel distinctly guilty about it. In terms of the age in which we live, and in terms of the many dogmatic opinions that dominate our thinking, we can translate Lessing's conflict into one closer to our experience, by showing its application to the twelve years and to the dominant ideology of the Third Reich. Let us for the moment set aside the fact that Nazi racial doctrine is in principle unprovable because it contradicts man's "nature." (By the way, it is worth remarking that these "scientific" theories were neither an invention of the Nazis nor even a specifically German invention.) But let us assume for the moment that the racial theories could have been convincingly proved. For it cannot be gainsaid that the practical political conclusions the Nazis drew from these theories were perfectly logical. Suppose that a race could indeed be shown, by indubitable scientific evidence, to be inferior; would that fact justify its extermination? But the answer to this question is still too easy, because we can invoke the "Thou shalt not kill" which in fact has become the fundamental commandment governing legal and moral thinking of the Occident ever since the victory of Christianity over antiquity. But in terms of a way of thinking governed by neither legal nor moral nor religious strictures—and Lessing's thought was as untrammeled, as "live and changing" as that—the question would have to be posed thus: *Would any such doctrine, however convincingly proved, be worth the sacrifice of so much as a single friendship between two men?*

Thus we have come back to my starting point, to the astonishing lack of "objectivity" in Lessing's polemicism, to his forever vigilant partiality, which has nothing whatsoever to do with subjectivity because it is always framed not in terms of the self but in terms of the relationship of men to their world, in terms of their positions and opinions. Lessing would not have found any difficulty in answering the question I have just posed. No insight into the nature of Islam or of Judaism or of Christianity could have kept him from entering into a friendship and the discourse of friendship with a convinced Mohammedan or a pious Jew or a believing Christian. Any doctrine that in principle barred the possibility of friendship between two human beings would have been rejected by his untrammeled and unerring conscience. He would instantly have taken the human side and given short shrift to the learned or unlearned discussion in either camp. That was Lessing's humanity.

This humanity emerged in a politically enslaved world whose foundations, moreover, were already shaken. Lessing, too, was already living in "dark times," and after his own fashion he was destroyed by their darkness. We have seen what a powerful need men have, in such times, to move closer to one another, to seek in the warmth of intimacy the substitute for that light and illumination which only the public realm can cast. But this means that they avoid disputes and try as far as possible to deal only with people with whom they cannot come into conflict. For a man of Lessing's disposition there was little room in such an age and in such a confined world; where people moved together in order to warm one another, they moved away from him. And yet he, who was polemical to the point of contentiousness, could no more endure loneliness than the excessive closeness of a brotherliness that obliterated all distinctions. He was never eager really to fall out with someone with whom he had entered into a dispute; he was concerned solely with humanizing the world by incessant and continual discourse about its affairs and the things in it. He wanted to be the friend of many men, but no man's brother.

He failed to achieve this friendship in the world with people in dispute and discourse, and indeed under the conditions then prevailing in German-speaking lands he could scarcely have succeeded. Sympathy for a man who "was worth more than all his talents" and whose greatness "lay in his individuality" (Friedrich Schlegel) could never really develop in Germany because such sympathy would have to arise out of politics in the deepest sense of the word. Because Lessing was a completely political person, he insisted that truth can exist only where it is humanized by discourse, only where each man says not what just happens to occur to him at the moment, but what he "deems truth." But such speech is virtually impossible in solitude; it belongs to an area in which there are many voices and where the announcement of what each "deems truth" both links and separates men, establishing in fact those distances between men which together comprise the world. Every truth outside this area, no matter whether it brings men good or ill, is inhuman in the literal sense of the word; but not because it might rouse men against one another and separate them. Quite the contrary, it is because it might have the result that all men would suddenly unite in a single opinion, so that out of many opinions one would emerge, as though not men in their infinite plurality but man in the singular, one species and its exemplars, were to inhabit the earth. Should that happen, the world, which can form only in the interspaces between men in all their variety, would vanish altogether. For that reason the most profound thing that has been said about the relationship between truth and humanity is to be found in a sentence of Lessing's which seems to draw from all his works wisdom's last word. The sentence is:

Jeder Sage was ihm Wahrheit Dünkt,
Und die Wahrheit selbst sei Gott empfohlen!

(Let each man say what he deems truth,
and let truth itself be commended unto God!)

Chapter 29

MARY E. HUNT, *Friends and Family Values: A New Old Song*

Mary E. Hunt is cofounder and codirector of the Women's Alliance for Theology, Ethics and Ritual in Silver Spring, Maryland. She received her undergraduate education in philosophy and theology from Marquette University. She earned her Master of Divinity degree at the Jesuit School of Theology in Berkeley, and received her doctorate from the Graduate Theological Union in Berkeley. She has numerous published articles in various journals. She is the editor of **From Woman-Pain to Woman-Vision** *by Anne McGrew Bennett. She is most well-known as the author of* **Fierce Tenderness: A Feminist Theology of Friendship,** *which received the Crossroad Women's Studies Prize for 1990. She is a member of the Board of Directors of Catholics for a Free Choice, and serves on the Editorial Board of the* **Journal of Feminist Studies in Religion.** *The present selection is taken from her contribution to the anthology,* **The Changing Face of Friendship** *(1994), edited by Leroy S. Rouner.*

Friends and Family Values: A New Old Song

SHORTLY AFTER I PUBLISHED *Fierce Tenderness: A Feminist Theology of Friendship*,[1] when some might argue that I said all I have to say about friendship, I dutifully began a new file in order to keep thinking about the topic. The politics of the Reagan-Bush-Quayle era made clear that much of what I had proposed is anathema to the right wing. So-called "traditional family values" do not include the wide expanse of friendship, the deep reach of inclusivity. In fact, much of that rhetoric seems to run counter to anything that would encourage friendship as the primary mode, or even one of several significant relational modes.

Living "inside the Beltway," I may be overly sensitive to such matters, but it seems clear that issues related directly to friendship are making an impact far beyond what any scholars might imagine. I am not suggesting that my work, or the work of other philosophers and theologians on friendship, is enough to sway an election. But concern about the contours of relational life in the cosmos is not disconnected from how "a good society" ought to be shaped in the most concrete ways. To the contrary, we are all deeply involved in the political order, especially my feminist foresisters in the field. Late nineteenth-century feminist theologians were suffrage workers; late twentieth-century feminist/womanist/mujerista theologians struggle for reproductive rights, against racism, and in favor of a wide range of options in human relationships, all because, like the suffrage seekers, we believe that substantive social structural changes require deep shifts in theology, and vice versa.

This essay spells out a renewed understanding of friendship and how it reinforces rather than destroys what is useful about traditional family values. The "new world order" emerging when friendship and not heterosexual marriage holds sway as the dominant paradigm is really an extension of some of the most admirable values—fidelity, nurture, attention, commitment.

My argument has four parts:

1. A brief review of my position on friendship, what I have elsewhere called "fierce tenderness," with emphasis on what a feminist theological perspective offers.

2. Several dangers I perceive with the metaphor and institutionalization of friendship as opposed to heterosexual coupling as the normative relationship. While this is a position I share, I want to suggest some critiques of it, as well as indicate some of my own reservations, as a way of expanding my position.

3. A look at the fallacy of the "traditional family values" debate and why I suspect those who were originally so enthused about it have backed off so rapidly.

4. A concluding comment on why and how friendship can function to ground what George Bush called a "new world order" which we need in order to move into the twenty-first century creatively.

This approach represents several sharp contrasts to my earlier work. *Fierce Tenderness* was based on a look at women's friendships; now I want to look at both women's and men's. That book was essentially a book of feminist theology; this essay is a political philosophy informed by religious feminism. The earlier work was poetic and ideological; this treatment is practical and prophetic at once as the urgency of social change calls out for such reflection.

I. Fierce Tenderness Explored

Friendship remains an infrequently tackled subject in Christian theology (to which I will confine my analysis for sake of brevity and competence). This is an odd situation given that a tenet of that faith includes "Love one's neighbor," "Go and make disciples/friends in all nations," and assorted other exhortations to form relationships of accountability. Further, the majority of the writings which exist are based on an Aristotelian model in which a) only men's experiences of friendship are taken into account, b) friendship is measured quantitatively, not qualitatively (numbers decreasing with increasing intimacy), c) social structures are built on marriage as the fundamental social unit, with friendship (that is, anything other than heterosexual marriage) forming an also-ran category.

The consequences of this method have been predictable in Christian theology, which is in turn the ideological framework that shapes a great deal of Western social mores; namely, analysis of and learning from women's experiences of friendship is either presumed to be the same as men's and therefore ignored on its own terms, or assumed to be so different and/or so trivial as not to merit attention at all.

The model of quantitative thinking as opposed to qualitative thinking about relationships persists, especially in areas of sexual ethics. The questions are how many, how far, how big, how long, rather than qualitative thinking which emphasizes the kind of accountability, generativity, and commitment which characterizes friendship. Rule-based sexual ethics so popular in the Roman Catholic tradition of which I am a part are but a few examples of the limits of such thinking. The current teachings and tenets are constitutionally inadequate for the range of relationships we experience, a sign that change is needed.

This leads to the third conclusion, namely, that social structures which undergird marriage and family life in a patriarchal, normatively heterosexual culture are constructed to prioritize marriage and to relegate friendship to a noble but lesser plane. While not wanting to romanticize friendship, I believe that putting friendship first—and of course permitting, even encouraging, marriage as well—is fundamentally more suited to the complex needs of our society. And that, of course, is why the political struggle over so called "traditional family values" is raging. Note that I do not oppose the family; I simply see it in wider terms than the blood line.

Many people hear such a proposal as an attack on marriage. When it comes from a religious starting point they are sure that "godless communism" has been replaced by "radical feminism" with the end of the world as we know it in sight. Far from being the case, mine is simply an effort to reshape priorities to reflect what we have learned about how people form intimate relationships. Some people partner, some join communities, some remain happily single, some change their partnerships, repartner, and blend families. All these are ways we know good people live which are quite other than Mr. and Mrs. Forever Amen. The job of theology and philosophy is to reflect on these realities and to hint, suggest, cajole, inspire people to live with integrity and concern for the whole community.

It is in this context that I have developed a model of friendship which I call "fierce tenderness," based on women's friendships.! I explored women's friendships primarily because they were my widest and deepest pool of experience, and because they remain virtually unexplored in the theological and theo-ethical traditions. Similarly, I proposed four elements that make up successful friendships: love, power, embodiment, and spirituality. I did not prescribe nor even suggest their proportions. Rather I suggested that when these are in some semblance of harmony in a relationship, the resultant friendship is a rich and productive one.

By contrast, the myriad problems we have all faced in our friendships can be summed up as varying experiences of disharmony in these elements. Put bluntly, when I love you more than you love me; when John uses his power over Susan; when Karen wants to go to bed with Janice but Janice isn't interested; when Paul generally prefers opera to Tad's yen for pool, we can see that these friendships are heading for rocky times. My model is not means to explain away all of the complexities of human loving. Nor is it meant to put therapists and counselors out of business. Rather, it is meant to serve as a starting point for understanding and encouraging friendships since it is my contention that these are the foundation of our social fabric, a tapestry ripped by racism, soiled by sexism, and wrinkled by power differences which translate into privilege and want.

There is much to explore about these dynamics, but my intention is to demonstrate that models are only helpful insofar as they illuminate and nurture real experiences. What is unique about this model is: first, that it emerges not from the Aristotelian notion of scarcity (that is, I only have so much relational energy so it needs to be more focused as I ascend the hierarchy of intimacy), but from a feminist insight into equality. It is not the myth of sameness, which has been used to discredit feminists as unable to distinguish between and among competing claims. Rather, it is the need for treating all that is, persons, animals other aspects of nature, with the same fundamental respect, that is, in the same friendly manner. This does not mean, of course, that I need be equally attentive to my pet as to my lover. But it does mean that the fundamental way of *paying attention* which is the hallmark of friendship, as well as the generativity which comes from our common attention, is something to strive for in every relationship.

Happily, no reviewer of this work has made the reductionistic claim that I urge friendship instead of marriage as normative simply because I wish to make the world safe for people who choose not to marry. However, there would be some, albeit partial, truth to the matter insofar as I have constructed a whole model of friendship based primarily on women's friendships with women. That I include, even encourage, appropriate sexual expression in some same-sex friendships adds to the debate. Moreover, I claim that such friendships, far from being relational also-rans in a marriage-manic society, are in fact equally valid, in some instances more beneficial relationships than many marriages.

It is claims of this sort, wherein friendship *replaces* marriage as the relationship of record, that make right-wing politicians exclaim that "traditional family values" are in the balance. The fact is that in an important way they are correct. Since married people can be friends, but all friends cannot be married, the implication of taking lesbian/gay relationships seriously is to see friendships between persons of the same sex who choose sexual expression in their friendships as in fact the relational equivalent of marriage. Moves in the direction of domestic partnership bills, civil and religious recognition of same-sex relationships, happy, healthy, holy lesbian/gay families, are just what I have in mind.

These exist all over the country now, but the point is that in the absence of legal changes to accommodate, indeed to celebrate and encourage, something as traditional as a stable relational unit and attention to children, philosophical and theological space must be made first to pave the way for legal and attitudinal shifts. That is my job as a theologian, despite the unpopular reaction it may evoke from certain church officials.

Religion, especially certain forms of evangelical Christianity and other fundamentalist faiths, is used in the public forum to negate what I now call the friendship norm. Recall that in and of itself friendship does not preclude or eclipse marriage. It challenges the hegemony of heterosexual marriage as the only way to file joint income taxes, visit a spouse in the hospital, automatically inherit another's goods without a blood tie, and so forth. Sex is but a small part of any relationship. Social supports or lack of them play a large part in how and whether friendships, including heterosexual marriages, deepen, mature, endure.

Longevity is never the ultimate criterion for friendship; that would be a quantitative measure instead of a qualitative one. But duration does provide an opportunity for shared memories as well as shared newness, repetition of good experiences as well as endless novelty, in-depth knowing as opposed to more superficial awareness. Even in the sexual arena, I would argue after a dozen years with the same beloved partner that practice makes perfect. But all of this is condemned by those who oppose homosexuality *per se*, against the social scientific and biological information to the contrary that proves it to be a perfectly healthy lifestyle for upwards of 10 percent of the population, perhaps even an occasional experience for far more than that. While less is known about bisexuality, and even less about heterosexuality without coercion, conservative religious ideology which grounds the efforts of the so-called Religious Right is rooted in the rejection of any relationships but heterosexual monogamy and celibate friendships.

The Roman Catholic Church has codified such demands into a rigid sexual prescription, at least at the official level. While many Catholics ignore the teachings about birth control, masturbation, divorce, and homosexuality yet still consider themselves in full communion, a dangerous trend toward intrusion into the political arena was confirmed by a summer 1992 letter to U.S. Catholic Bishops from the Congregation for the Doctrine of the Faith.[2] The Vatican claimed that "there are areas in which it is not unjust discrimination to take sexual orientation into account, for example, in the placement of children for adoption or foster care, in employment of teachers or athletic coaches, and in military recruitment."[3] While reconciling traditional Christian teachings with any form of discrimination is a theological sleight of hand that is the ethical equivalent of the Wizard of Oz behind the screen, this is indeed what this Vatican Declaration calls for.

The document becomes quite specific on how and by whom discrimination is to be carried out: "Finally, where a matter of the common good is concerned, it is inappropriate for church authorities to remain neutral toward adverse legislation even if it grants exceptions to church organizations and institutions. The church has the responsibility to promote family life and the public morality of the entire civil society on the basis of fundamental moral values, not simply to protect herself (sic) from the application of harmful laws."[4] Catholic bishops are urged to enter the political fray on behalf of monogamous marriage and celibate friendship.

Read through the lens of a friendship norm, such pronouncements reveal a deeply rooted denial of how many of us love and how successful we are at it! Jane Redmont in her book *Generous Lives* names this quality of friendship aptly.[5] Such counterintuitive moves by the bishops in the face of such generosity and the vehemence with which they are made make me wonder why allegedly celibate men in a homosocial hierarchy protest so much. Don't they have any friends? But more substantively, I am persuaded by the contradictory nature of their utterings that *something* important has set them off, and that the something appears to be the obvious success of friendships—many kinds between and among many people—in the face of a 50 percent divorce rate and the crying need for children to be nurtured in responsible constellations of adults who love them regardless of the adults' gender or marital status.

This is why as a theologian I take seriously that the religious foundations of ethics are finally determinative. No other sector of society has as its reason for being specifically a concern with morals. Universities educate as well as shape ethics; businesses make profits as well as shape ethics; medical workers heal as their primary work, with ethical concerns factored in. But religious professionals, especially ethicists and moral theologians, shape the fabric of a society's ethics as a primary responsibility. Hence, when we jump the ship of state, turn state's witness on our co-religionists by urging into being new relational paradigms, in this case friendship over marriage, we can expect problems.

Problems heat up when the divine or God is likened not to Father, Mother, or even Parent, but to Friend. Then the seriousness of the project becomes more obvious. Without wanting to overuse the metaphor, it is this move away from heterosexual family images that underlies the panic. When we recall that equal consternation was expressed by opponents of inclusive language in scripture, it is not hard to imagine the wrath that awaits the explicit move to relational language which evokes equality not hierarchy, mutuality not dominance, and even unpredictability.

A feminist theological approach involves a critical appraisal of metaphors for the divine with a "preferential option" for inclusivity. Insofar as the language and imagery function to limit and exclude, they are left aside; insofar as they illuminate and invite participation in the divine reality they describe, such language and imagery are to be encouraged in worship and common life. It is on the basis of taking such discourse seriously that we reshape laws and other social structures. To the degree that we succeed, feminist theology will have accomplished an important goal, the increased empowerment of women and men.

II. Some Problems with the Friendship Metaphor

Despite my heralding of friendship, which I define as "those voluntary human relationships that are entered into by people who intend one another's well-being, and who intend that their love relationship is part of a justice-seeking community," I am nonetheless critical of it as well.[6] Four problems that I perceive illustrate that my perspective is anything but romantic. I am indebted to the many reviewers of my book for attention to these matters and to Barbara Darling-Smith for her clear perceptions.

I sketch these not to retreat from my claim that friendship and not marriage is the most adequate social framework, but to acknowledge that the transition takes place in a society in the United States which is structurally flawed by racism, sexism, class divisions, and rampant homo-hatred. These are not trivial matters when one undertakes a consciousness shift of the proportions I propose. To the contrary, the very elements which make safety and well-being distant dreams for so many would-be friends in our society need attention if friendship becomes normative. In addition, the same religious foundations which underlie the opposition to a friendship norm also underlie those social elements which will finally subvert it. Hence, my focus on

A. violence
B. racial/ethnic considerations
C. safeguards for the care/nurture of children

D. the coopting of lesbian/gay friendships into couples

A. Violence

Domestic violence statistics stagger the imagination. The American Medical Association, in recognition of the problem, changed the standard of practice so that patients who present symptoms which might be caused by violence must be asked if such were the case. Estimates vary but it is generally agreed that one of eleven boys and one of seven girls suffers incest; that half of all women experience violence (physical and/or psychological) in their marriages. In short, for many people "home sweet home" is really "home dangerous home," with few support systems to change the behaviors and structures literally embedded in many nuclear families.

Of course it is my hope that moving toward a friendship norm is a step in the right direction. If heterosexual marriage is about unequal power relationships in patriarchy, and if "compulsory heterosexuality" as Adrienne Rich describes it forces some people to live in situations which do not express their deepest longings, then it would seem that friendship would take care of the problem. But we are just beginning to learn about violence in same-sex relationships, something that the lesbian and gay communities understandably wish would go away. It is hard to be honest about such matters when the wolf is at the door, that is, when lesbian-gay bashing is on the rise and the AIDS pandemic is decimating our ranks. With regard to violence, we know little about cross-gender friendships which are not marriages. Whether they are more or less prone to violence remains to be researched.

Still, honesty compels me to counter that my worst fear of a friendship norm is that it will not stem the tide of violence much more effectively than the marriage norm has. We are just beginning to understand that violence is deeply woven into the Christian tradition, with some theologians suggesting that the action of a "Father God" giving up "his only begotten Son" for the salvation of the world—the Christian doctrine of the Atonement—functions as a kind of perverse legitimation for child abuse.[7] While this and the resultant deconstruction of Christianity around other issues of violence deserves further attention, the important issue for our consideration is whether such a dynamic is mitigated by friendship.

What about the dictum from the same source to "lay down one's life for one's friends"? Is this any more helpful? Does it invite yet another manifestation of the same dynamic? Is it sage advice for women and persons from racial/ethnic groups which have been discriminated against? This is the kind of feminist theological work in the 1990s which parallels the deconstruction of Christianity on the basis of gender in the 1970s and 1980s. My sense is that the currents of violence may run so deep in the Christian tradition as to mitigate any small changes that a shift from marriage to friendship may produce. Still, I urge the experiment, cognizant of the danger that lurks not in the corners but in the center of our society.

B. Racial/ethnic considerations

The Euro-American middle-class location of my perspective on friendship necessarily raises important questions about its grounding in and/or applicability in other contexts. The frank answer is that I do not know, nor am I persuaded that it needs to be applicable elsewhere in order to be valid in the partial, limited, and contextual situation about which I do make claims. This is a difficult problem, but it illustrates what is in my judgment the most important change in theological thinking in this century, namely, the radical contextualization of all theology.

In short, no position is valid without a clear articulation of its social location—this coming most profoundly from African-American, feminist, and Latin American liberation theologies. Further, no one person or group speaks for the whole, a decided reversal of the universal claims with which theology has been identified. Rather, my frank admission is that the limits of my perspective imply *de facto* limits on the usefulness of my insights. Far from weakening my position because I am not claiming that others must hold it, the resultant theological mix includes an explicit invitation to people from other contexts to consider, weigh, even reject my insight in favor of their own.

This is the nature of contemporary theological work, especially in feminist/womanist/mujerista circles where the survival of women and dependent children and the "hearing each other into speech" demand no less. If I were persuaded that a friendship norm would exacerbate the already hideous racism in this country, I would drop it immediately. But precisely because I am persuaded that it reflects the reality and aids the survival of many people, especially people who are marginalized because they are viciously condemned as single mothers, absent fathers, and boarder babies, I insist on its justice-seeking potential.

C. Safeguards for the care/nurture of children

A third concern which I put to the friendship norm is an explicit concern for how children will fare. It seems so obvious now that one major plus for a marriage norm is the clear concern for having a structure, that is, the nuclear family, in which to care and provide for children. Thus far, most discussion of friendship has passed over this dimension, something that leaves those of us who advance it vulnerable to charges of solipsism and irresponsibility.

While I do not believe that everyone must have and/or nurture children to be a whole adult in our society, I do take the care of children to be a communal and not finally an individual responsibility. Hence, I must advance the theo-ethical concern of how this is done as the paradigm shifts away from marriage. In fact, statistics, from infant mortality to abandonment, from access to early childhood education to latchkey kids, raise this question in a profound way. The current social arrangement is not doing very well. But will a shift away from the legal obligations of parents to their children take place when friendship and not necessarily blood or marital ties apply?

One can only plead ignorance about the question since data are insufficient to answer it. But there are several trends which I find helpful in countering the ghastly images right-wing defenders promote of Mom in the kitchen pulling the apple pie from the oven. One is the effort on the part of unrelated same-sex partners—call them friends for lack of a more precise legal term—to adopt children. This is especially impressive when the children have special needs; for example, friends of mine, two Euro-American women, adopted a child who was HIV-positive.

The communal effort which was extended for his care during five years of living and eventually dying from AIDS-related causes assured me that no heterosexually married couple could have done more. As this phenomenon of Shawn having two moms or Amanda having two dads spreads, we see an enrichment of the single parent pressures that one would think even the most virulent homophobe would applaud. Yet when children's books featuring same-sex parents are introduced into the curriculum, many people frown. Is it that a child could ever get too much nurture?

D. *The cooptation of Lesbian/gay friendships*

This leads to my fourth worry about a friendship norm, namely, the degree to which it can be quickly coopted into yet another form of the same pattern. One might argue that there is really nothing new under the relational sun, that we love one another as we always did whether in same- or different-sex combinations. I am more concerned about the rapid mainstreaming of a certain number of "good" lesbian and gay friends: monogamously committed, prepared to live happily ever after, able to afford and aspire to a marriage license, with a job that has health insurance for a partner—prepared to register their china and silver patterns at the local emporium. While this caricature does not fit most of us anymore, and while everyone has a right to social trappings they desire, I would be remiss if I did not launch a critical warning on this front.

Will the move toward acceptability and assimilation of what have heretofore been different ways of "constructing a life" blunt the real contribution of a friendship norm? Will it mean that the variety, flexibility, and sometimes even changeability that have characterized other than marital relationships in our society will be lost? Will the fight over joint property and custody of the cat, not to mention children, in lesbian-gay divorces be as frequent and as brutal as in the heterosexual counterparts? Perhaps. But the point is that while there is still time, before complete cooptation has taken place, we need to think through the benefits and liabilities of adopting the prevailing customs for all relationships. Instead of moving inexorably toward lesbian-gay marriages, a friendship norm invites moving away from compulsory marriage for heterosexuals, for example, away from coupling and toward community.

III. The Traditional Family Values Debate: A Short Story

The discussion of "traditional family values" tapered off quickly for two major reasons. First, the economic picture in this country and around the world is so grim that most people are content to pay their bills and have no time to speculate on how their neighbors are paying theirs. Jobs and not bedroom behavior are on top of most people's minds. Second, even in those parts of the country where campaigns against reproductive choice and relational choice find their most ardent supporters, most people have by now experienced divorce, homosexuality, and children born and reared outside of a marital relationship. In many instances they have been edified by what has followed their worst fears, namely, that life goes on and even improves when options open up and honesty prevails.

This is the direct, if by some dreaded, consequence of a friendship norm. Of course it is not to be confused with license for promiscuity, the breaking of promises, or a lack of accountability. Rather, it is simply the same old values played to a new tune. I suggest that there is a nascent intuition of this even among those who oppose it deeply.

Some cynical political philosophers may simply attribute the rapid dissipation of the debate to polls which show that lesbian and gay people vote, that unmarried heterosexuals who live together in record numbers vote, and single mothers vote. But I think this is to miss the more interesting shift that is underway, namely, a society which is groping for effective ways to embody, both personally and corporately, friendly values.

Conclusion

Some concrete examples of those values in place in society will hasten their arrival.

1. Friendship and not marriage is the relationship of primary importance. Hence, commitments, not weddings, are encouraged; children live with their adult friends, not only with their biological parents; families are constructed on the basis of choice, not blood line. Surely the outline allows for some falling through the cracks—what if no one chooses me for their family?—but will there be any more loss than we presently experience? I don't know, but are we willing to try? I am not sure. A small step in the direction would be to loosen up restrictions on adoption and foster care by non-married people, something that in most states is still a distant dream.

2. Government programs need to be adjusted accordingly. Tax laws, pension systems, and health care coverage would need to shift from a bias toward those who are legally married to equality for all. For example, inheritance would not pass automatically to one's blood relatives, but to the friends so named by everyone whether married or not. Wider visitation rights in hospitals and explicitly designated power of attorney would replace any such automatic rights that heterosexually married people have over the rest of us. The point is to avoid making unmarried people second-class citizens. To encourage the full range of

relational options by leveling the relational playing field, by making civil rights available to all based on age not marital status, would be a step in the right direction.

3. Religious and ethical changes would include rethinking what it means to live in what Carter Heyward and others deem "right relation." The "good man" of philosophical fame is redefined to resemble the friend, not the father. In this new situation the normatively good person would come in both genders, many races, and endless relational possibilities. His goodness is measured as much by how he loves his pets as his current partner, how she claims power for herself as well as with her co-workers, how he safeguards himself and his sexual partners in the AIDS pandemic, and finally how she names her spiritual commitment to social change as part of her justice-seeking life.

It all begins to sound wonderfully familiar, like an old tune with new lyrics or a new tune with old words. An ethic based on friendship, what I have called "fierce tenderness" and for now simply call relational justice, is rapidly coming into focus. It needs more work, to make it explicit, to smooth out those parts which do not enhance our common well-being. But I trust that it cannot be worse than what currently prevails, and that it probably will be a great deal better in our lifetime and in the times of today's children's children.

Notes

[1] Cf. Mary E. Hunt, *Fierce Tenderness: A Feminist Theology of Friendship* (New York: Crossroad, 1991).

[2] "Some Considerations Concerning the Response to Legislative Proposals on the Non-Discrimination of Homosexual Persons," Congregation for the Doctrine of the Faith, leaked to the press on July 15, 1992, by New ways Ministry and released (with minor revisions) by the Vatican on *July* 23, 1992.

[3] Ibid., par. 11.

[4] Ibid., par. 16.

[5] Jane Redmont, *Generous Lives: American Catholic Women Today* (New York: William Morrow & Co., 1992).

[6] Hunt, *Fierce Tenderness*, p. 29.

[7] Joanne Carlson Brown and Rebecca Parker, "For God so Loved the World?" in *Christianity, Patriarchy, and Abuse*, ed. Brown and Parker (New York: Pilgrim Press, 1989), pp. 1-30.

Chapter 30

Gilbert Meilaender, *When Harry and Sally Read the* Nicomachean Ethics: *Friendship between Men and Women*

Gilbert C. Mailaender, Jr. (b. 1946) holds the Board of Directors Chair in Theological Ethics at Valparaiso University, where he has taught since 1996. Prior to that he was Professor of Religion at Oberlin College, where he taught for eighteen years. Having learned at the age of seventeen that he was unable to hit a curve ball, he says he was moved to do the next best thing: to study theology. He did his undergraduate work at Concordia Senior College in Fort Wayne, Indiana, and received his doctorate at Princeton. He is a member of the editorial boards of several journals in religious ethics. He is a prolific writer, and regularly contributes articles to numerous journals. He is author of five books, including **Faith and Faithfulness: Basic Themes in Christian Ethics; The Limits of Love; The Theory and Practice of Virtue;** *and* **The Taste for the Other: The Social and Ethical Thought of C.S. Lewis** *(1978). Particularly relevant to the present volume is his* **Friendship: A Study in Theological Ethics** *(1981). Meilaender is a member of the American Theological Society and Society of Christian Ethics. He has also taught at the University of Virginia, and served as Assistant Pastor of the Lutheran Church of the Messiah in Princeton, New Jersey, during his graduate studies at Princeton University. The present selection is taken from his contribution to the anthology,* **The Changing Face of Friendship** *(1994), edited by Leroy S. Rouner.*

When Harry and Sally Read the *Nicomachean Ethics:* Friendship between Men and Women

IN XENOPHON's *OECONOMICUS* Socrates and Critobulus are discussing household management, in which the wife plays a major role. The exchange goes this way:

> "Anyhow, Critobulus, you should tell us the truth, for we are all
> friends here. Is there anyone to whom you commit more affairs
> of importance than you commit to your wife?"
> "There is not."
> "Is there anyone with whom you talk less?"
> "There are few or none, I confess."[1]

Friendship between husband and wife is, of course, only one possible kind of friendship between the sexes, though an important one. But most classical thinkers—with the exception of Epicurus—were inclined to think friendship between men and women impossible.

No doubt this can be accounted for in part, perhaps large part, by social and cultural circumstances—differences in education, a public life from which most women were excluded, constant warfare which drew males away from home. In my own view, these circumstances have changed considerably, but not everyone agrees. Thus, for example, writing very recently, Mary Hunt says: "Economic, political, psychological, and other differences between the genders result in the fact that women find it difficult to be friends with men and vice versa."[2] I will suggest that Hunt is in part mistaken about the reasons, but it is true that the relation between the sexes in our society is a tense and often anxious one. It still makes sense to ask the classical question: Is friendship possible between men and women? Or, more modestly put, are there reasons why friendship between men and women may be more difficult to sustain than same-sex friendships?

When we ask this question, the first problem that comes to mind is the one raised by Harry Burns in the 1989 movie *When Harry Met Sally.* In the opening scene, as he and Sally are driving together from Chicago to New York, Harry says: "Men and women can't be friends—because the sex part always gets in the way." Harry has an important point. And, though I do not think it is finally the deepest issue raised by our topic, I shall devote a good bit of attention to it.

Aristotle, whose two books on friendship in the *Nicomachean Ethics* are recognized almost universally as the most important piece of writing on the subject, tends to agree with Harry. Aristotle recognizes, of course, that there is a kind of friendship between husband and wife, but it is one example of what he calls friendship between unequals. In such bonds the equality that friendship always requires can be present only if it is "proportionate" rather than "strict"—only, that is, if "the better and more useful partner . . . [receives] more affection than he gives."[3] Still, of the three types of friendship which Aristotle discusses—based respectively on advantage, pleasure, or character— the highest, based on character, can exist even between unequals as long as this proportion is present. And Aristotle seems to think that such a character friendship, with the necessary proportionate equality, is possible between husband and wife (cf. 8.12).

More generally, however, Aristotle suggests that a relation grounded in erotic love will not be the highest form of friendship. He distinguishes a bond like friendship, grounded in a trait of character and involving choice, from a bond grounded in an emotion (8.5). And, while there can be friendship between lover and beloved, it will not be the highest form of friendship. It will be a friendship grounded not in character but in pleasure—and it is, therefore, likely to fade. "Still," Aristotle grants, noting how one sort of love may grow from another' "many do remain friends if, through familiarity, they have come to love each other's character, [discovering that] their characters are alike" (8.4).

It is important to note that *eros* and *philia* are indeed different forms of love, even if they may sometimes go together. In making a somewhat different point, C. S. Lewis suggested the following thought experiment:

> Suppose you are fortunate enough to have "fallen in love with" and married your Friend. And now suppose it possible that you were offered the choice of two futures: *"Either you two* will cease to be lovers but remain forever joint seekers of the same God, the same beauty, the same truth, or *else,* losing all that, you will retain as long as you live the raptures and ardours, all the wonder and the wild desire of *Eros.* Choose which you please."[4]

In recognizing the reality and difficulty of the choice we discern the difference between the loves. That difference Lewis captures nicely in a sentence. "Lovers are normally face to face, absorbed in each other; Friends, side by side, absorbed in some common interest" (p. 91). Friends, therefore, are happy to welcome a new friend who shares their common interest, but *eros is* a jealous love which must exclude third parties.

Lewis believes that friendship and erotic love may go together, but in many respects he agrees with Harry and with Aristotle that the combination is an unstable one. He suggests that friendship between a man and a woman is likely to slip over into *eros* unless either they are physically unattractive to each other, or at least one of them already loves another. If neither of these is the case, friendship is "almost certain" to become *eros* "sooner or later" (p. 99). This is not far from Harry's view of the matter. Having asserted that "men and women can't be friends—because the sex part always gets in the way," Harry adds a caveat when he and Sally meet again five years later: "unless both are involved with other people." But then, in one of his characteristically convoluted pieces of reasoning, he adds: "But that doesn't work. The person you're involved with can't understand why you need to be friends with the other person. She figures you must be secretly interested in the other person—which you probably are. Which brings us back to the first rule." A little more optimistic than Harry, Lewis suggests that lovers who are also friends may learn to share their friendship with others, though not, of course, their *eros.* Still, however, that does not address Harry's chief concern: the instability of friendships with members of the opposite sex when those friendships are not shared with one's beloved.

We ought not, I think, deny that friendships between men and women—friendships which are not also marked by erotic love—are possible. We ought not, that is, let a theory lead us to deny the reality we see around us, and we do sometimes see or experience such friendships. Nor need we express the view shared by Harry and Lewis quite as crassly as did Nietzsche: "Women can enter into friendship with a man perfectly well; but in order to maintain it the aid of a little physical antipathy is perhaps required."[5] Nor, surely, need we hold, as my students sometimes do, that friendship between men and women is possible only if at least one of the friends is homosexual—a view that will make *same*-sex friendships difficult for those who are homosexual, unless, of course, their experience of *eros is* in no way jealous or exclusive. At the same time, however, there is no reason to deny some truth to Harry's claim, even without the additional support provided by Aristotle and Lewis, for our experience also suggests that there is something to it.

The difficulties of combining *eros* and *philia* are the stuff of our daily life. Equalizing the relation of the sexes, bringing women into the academy and the workplace, has not made these difficulties disappear. Indeed, in certain respects they may have been exacerbated. Men and women are radically uncertain about how they are to meet in such shared worlds. Friendship requires an easy spontaneity, a willingness to say what one thinks, talk with few holds barred and few matters off-limits—precisely the sort of thing that some will find difficult on occasion to distinguish from sexual harassment.

I have discovered, however, that college students often wish to argue that Harry is wrong, that there need be no obstacle to friendship between the sexes. That may be because they have great difficulty managing erotic attachments, which are quite a different thing from sexual encounters. Fearful of the kind of commitment *eros* asks of us, fearful of being drawn toward one who is completely other than the self but to whom the most complete self-giving is called for and before whom one therefore becomes vulnerable, they take refuge in groups of friends—hoping thereby to achieve what parents of thirty years ago saw as the advantage of group dating: the domestication of *ergs*. But *eros is* a wild and unruly deity, unlikely, I think, to be tamed so easily.

It is wiser to grant the point. Friendship between men and women will always have to face certain difficulties that will not be present in same-sex friendships. There will almost always be what J.B. Priestley calls "a faint undercurrent of excitement not present when only one sex is involved."[6] This may even give to the friendship a tone not easily gotten any other way. Thus, as Priestley again puts it: "Probably there is no talk between men and women better than that between a pair who are not in love, have no intention of falling in love, but yet who *might* fall in love, who know one another well but are yet aware of the fact that each has further reserves yet to be explored" (p. 59). Priestley offered this opinion in a little book titled *Talking: An Essay,* published in 1926 as one of several volumes in the Pleasures of Life Series. But he might well have been describing what many viewers found appealing in *When Harry Met Sally.* Consider the scene in which Harry and Jess are talking while hitting some balls in a batting cage:

> Jess: "You enjoy being with her?"
> Harry: "Yeah."
> Jess: "You find her attractive?"
> Harry: "Yeah."
> Jess: "And you're not sleeping with her?"
> Harry: "I can just be myself, 'cause I'm not trying to get her into bed."

And yet, not too much later comes the party at which Harry and Sally dance together—and themselves recognize the presence of Priestley's "faint undercurrent," which we call *ergs*. This is a problem for friendships between men and women, even if it may also be enriching. *Eros* always threatens; for, unlike friendship, *eros is* a love that is jealous and cannot be shared.

If we grant this, we may not agree with Mary Hunt, whom I quoted earlier. She ascribes the difficulties facing friendship between men and women to "economic, political, psychological, and other differences"— unwilling, almost, to admit the power and presence of erotic attraction between men and women in human life. Nonetheless, it may be worth thinking briefly about what she recommends: namely, "new models of mutuality" which are most easily found among women friends. We ought not, she argues, take Aristotle's model of friendship and suppose that he simply forgot to include women when he talked and wrote of it—an omission we can then easily correct. We should not take his model and then just add women's experiences "as if they should have been there in the first place" (p. 93).

What is mistaken about Aristotle's model? Chiefly, it seems, that "[h]e considered friendship something that decreased in quality as it increased in quantity; the more intense the friendship, the fewer people with whom it was possible to enjoy it" (p. 92). Thus, according to Hunt, women need not worry about classifying friendships as carefully as did Aristotle, nor need they worry about whether friends are best friends or just good friends. "Only ruling-class men whose survival is not in question have the dubious luxury of looking up and down at their friends, companions, and acquaintances" (pp. 95-96). Women, by contrast, in a society which—in Hunt's view—is oppressive, cannot concern themselves with levels of friendship. For them the simple truth is that "friends, lots of them, are necessary for . . . survival in an often unfriendly environment" (p. 95). Paradoxically, however, to the degree that Hunt's assessment is correct, her thesis can have little to do with friendship between men and women or, even, between those of the same sex. For, on her account, women would have every reason to seek as many women *and* men as possible to be friends, and men who were not "ruling-class men" would be in similar circumstances. Neither would have reason to seek the kind of close, particular, and preferential friendships which Aristotle—and many others since—have considered the highest form of friendship.

What Hunt seems not to realize is that she is, in fact, like Aristotle in at least one important way. "How," Aristotle asks, sounding very much like Hunt, "could prosperity be safeguarded and preserved without friends? . . . Also, in poverty and all other kinds of misfortune men believe that their only refuge consists in their friends" (8.1). As it stands in the *Nicomachean Ethics,* of course, this is for Aristotle only one of the received opinions about friendship which he will refine, and it will turn out that this is not for him the highest form of friendship. More important, however, for Aristotle friendship is not only a particular and preferential bond which must be limited in number. He knows also a different kind of friendship which we call "civic friendship"; indeed, for him *philia is* the bond which joins together the members of any association. The concept of civic friendship deserves more attention than we can give it here. We need to ask whether it is coherent, whether we really wish to call it "friendship," and whether—if there is a coherent notion and we do call it friendship—it is helpful or harmful in life. Those who—like Hunt— emphasize such a concept of friendship may, despite their political concerns, have difficulty explaining one of the terrible things about injustice: how it may deprive us of the "luxury" of a *private* bond like friendship. But in any case, in her emphasis upon friendship as a public, political relation, Hunt is far more like Aristotle than she realizes, but, lacking his additional interest in those more private bonds we have in mind when speaking of friendship, she can shed little light on the problems of friendship between men and women.

These problems, I want to suggest, go deeper than the presence of erotic attraction alone. They involve the very nature of the bond of friendship. The friend is, in Aristotle's influential formulation, "another self" (9.4). At several points Aristotle considers whether friendship is more probable among those who are like or unlike each other. And, although he notes defenders of each view, he holds that friendship "implies some similarity" and that in the highest form of friendship "the partners are like one another" (8.3). In arguing that a person of good character should not—and ultimately cannot—remain friends with someone who becomes evil, Aristotle again appeals to the notion that "like is the friend of like" (9.3).

Anyone who reads Aristotle's discussion of the friend as another self is likely to find it puzzling in certain respects. It grows out of a peculiar treatment of self-love (in 9.4) as the basis of friendship, of love for the friend as an extension of the friendly feelings one has for oneself. And there are, in fact, aspects of his discussion that I would not claim fully to understand. What he has in mind, however, in depicting the friend as an alter ego is something *we* might discuss in terms of the social origins of the self. The friend is the mirror in which I come to know and understand myself. I have no way to look directly at myself and must come to see myself as I am reflected by others— and especially, perhaps, by close friends. In the friend I find that other self in whom I come to know myself. That is why friendship "implies some similarity" and why, at least in the most important kinds of friendship, "the partners are like one another."

Friends wish, Aristotle says, to pursue together activities they enjoy. "That is why some friends drink together or play dice together, while others go in for sports together and hunt together, or join in the study of philosophy: whatever each group of people loves most in life, in that activity they spend their days together" (9.12). I think Aristotle is largely correct here. We want in the friend someone who cares about the things we care about; yet we want the friend to be "another" who cares about these things, another with whom we can share them and with whom we come to know ourselves and our concerns better. The friend must be "another," but not entirely "an-other." Perhaps we do not, therefore, seek from the friend quite that sense of otherness which the opposite sex provides.

This takes us beyond the issue of erotic attraction into much deeper questions about what it means to be male or female. I do not know precisely how we can make up our minds about these questions today; we have a hard enough time just discussing them openly and honestly. A child of either sex begins in a kind of symbiotic union with its mother, without any strong sense of differentiation between self and mother. But as that sense of self begins to form, it develops differently for males and females. In attaining a sense of the self as separate and individuated we take somewhat different courses. Thus, Lillian Rubin argues, boys must repress their emotional identification with their mother and learn to identify with men, while girls, though repressing any erotic attachment, can leave the larger emotional identification with the mother intact.[7] The process of becoming a self involves identification with those who can be for us "another self"—those, as it happens, who share our sex. This does not, in my view, mean that friendship between men and women is impossible. It does mean, though, that J. B. Priestley was right to say of their "talk": "It will be different from the talk of persons of the same sex" (pp. 56-57). These differences are the stuff of bestsellers—and of much humor. Thus, for example, Deborah Tannen, who teaches linguistics at Georgetown University, could write a bestseller titled, You *Just Don't Understand: Women and Men in Conversation.* Full of illustrations in which one often sees oneself, Tannen's book suggests that for men life is "a struggle to preserve independence," while for women it is "a struggle to preserve intimacy."[8] The sort of problem this creates is illustrated clearly in a story like the following one Tannen recounts:

> Eve had a lump removed from her breast. Shortly after the operation, talking to her sister, she said that she found it upsetting to have been cut into, and that looking at the stitches was distressing because they left a seam that had changed the contour of her breast. Her sister said, "I know. When I had my operation I felt the same way." Eve made the same observation to her friend Karen, who said, "I know. It's like your body has been violated. But when she told her husband, Mark, how she felt, he said, "You can have plastic surgery to cover up the scar and restore the shape of the breast."

Where she felt the need for understanding and sharing, he discerned a problem to be solved.

If this can sometimes be disconcerting, we need not be too serious. And these differences have provided the occasion for much humor. Dave Barry, the columnist, can title a column "Listen Up, Jerks! Share Innermost Feelings with Her"—and most of us are likely to read it.[9]

Barry writes:

> We have some good friends, Buzz and Libby, whom we see about twice a year. When we get together, Beth and Libby always wind up in a conversation, lasting several days, during which they discuss virtually every significant event that has occurred in their lives and the lives of those they care about, sharing their innermost feelings, analyzing and probing, inevitably coming to a deeper understanding of each other, and a strengthening of a cherished friendship. Whereas Buzz and I watch the playoffs.
>
> This is not to say Buzz and I don't share our feelings. Sometimes we get quite emotional.
>
> "That's not a FOUL?" one of us will say.
>
> Or: "You're telling me THAT'S NOT A FOUL???"
>
> I don't mean to suggest that all we talk about is sports. We also discuss, openly and without shame, what kind of pizza we need to order. We have a fine time together, but we don't have heavy conversations, and sometimes, after the visit is over, I'm surprised to learn—from Beth, who learned it from Libby— that

there has recently been some new wrinkle in Buzz's life, such as that he now has an artificial leg.

Our world is full of attempts to remove such differences from life. In Tannen's words, "Sensitivity training judges men by women's standards, trying to get them to talk more like women. Assertiveness training judges women by men's standards and tries to get them to talk more like men" (p. 297). Better, perhaps, she suggests, to learn to understand and accept each other.

In this effort, I have found Priestley's old essay quite helpful. If talk between men and women is different from talk between persons of the same sex, it will not give the same kind of pleasure. But it may, Priestley suggests, compensate in other ways. The first condition of such talk is, he says, "that sex must be relegated to the background.... The man and the woman must be present as individualities, any difference between them being a strictly personal and not a sexual difference. They will then discover, if they did not know it before, how alike the sexes are, once their talk has dug below the level of polite chatter and they are regarding the world and their experience together and not merely flirting" (p. 57). That is, to revert to the terms I drew from Aristotle, they must find in the friend another self, another individuality, but one whose otherness is not so overwhelming as to threaten to engulf or invade their selfhood. No doubt this is not always possible, for reasons we noted earlier when considering the impact of *eros* on friendship. But when, for whatever reason, "passion is stilled," men and women may meet as individualities who care about the same things or seek the same truth.

There may, however, be something dissatisfying about the suggestion that a crucial aspect of our person—our sexuality—must, as it were, be bracketed for such friendship to be possible. And this would be unsatisfactory, I think, were no more to be said. Priestley goes on, however, to suggest that friendship between men and women can go beyond the play of individual personalities. "Secure in this discovery" of how alike they are, men and women "will then go forward and make another one, for at some point they must inevitably discover how unlike the sexes are.... This double play, first of personality and then of sex, is what gives intelligent talk between men and women its curious piquancy" (pp. 57-58).

In this second movement, when individual personality no longer brackets sexuality, Priestley ultimately discerns something more fundamental still—a third factor, which goes beyond the level of individual identity to a difference between men and women. "Men frequently complain," he writes, "that women's conversation is too personal" (p. 62). And, even writing in an age that knew not Carol Gilligan, Priestley finds some truth in this judgment. He says:

> [Women] remain more personal in their interests and less con-cerned with abstractions than men on the same level of intelli-gence and culture. While you are briskly and happily generalizing, making judgments on this and that, and forgetting for the time being yourself and all your concerns, they are brooding over the particular and personal application and are wondering what hidden motive, what secret desire, what stifled memory of joy or hurt, are there prompting your thought. But this habit of mind in woman does not spoil talk; on the contrary it improves it, restoring the balance.... It is the habit of men to be overconfident in their impartiality, to believe that they are god-like intellects, detached from desires and hopes and fears and disturbing memories, generalising and delivering judgment in a serene mid-air. To be reminded of what lies beyond, now and then, will do them more good than harm. This is what the modern psychologist does, but too often he shatters the illusion of impersonal judgment with a kick and a triumphant bray, like the ass he so frequently is, whereas woman does it, and has done it these many centuries, with one waggle of her little forefinger and one gleam of her eyes, like the wise and witty and tender companion she is. Here, then, is a third kind of play you may have in talk between the sexes, the duel and duet of impersonal and personal interests, making in the end for balance and sanity and, in the progress of the talk, adding to its piquancy. (pp. 63ff.)

In this sense, friendship between the sexes may take us not out of our-selves but beyond ourselves and may make us more whole, balanced, and sane than we could otherwise be.

Indeed, I think this is one of the purposes of friendship—one of the purposes God has in giving us friends. We are being prepared ultimately for that vast friendship which is heaven, in which we truly are taken beyond ourselves, and in which all share the love of God.[10] Something like this understanding of friendship, though without the strong theological overtone I have just given it, can be found in Katherine Paterson's *Bridge to Terabithia*—a book about friendship which is not simply a children's book.[11]

The friendship of Jess and Leslie in the book is between a boy and a girl who are a little too young for *ergs*. In different ways they are both outsiders in the world of their peers at school, and that very fact draws them together. They create—largely at the instigation of Leslie—a "secret country," Terabithia, in which they are king and queen. This country—a piece of ground on the other side of a creek, to which they swing across on a rope—is, in Leslie's words, "so secret that we would never tell anyone in the whole world about it" (p. 38). And, at least at first, it must be that way. Were they to follow Mary Hunt's advice, were no friendships of theirs to be special and particular, were they to have no secret country that others did not share, they would never come to know themselves as fully as they do. Thus, for example, Jess finds that his friendship with Leslie opens up new worlds for him. "For the first time in his life he got up every morning with something to look forward to. Leslie was more than his friend. She was his other, more exciting self—his way to Terabithia and all the worlds beyond" (p. 46).

Jess says that Leslie is his way not only to Terabithia but also to "all the worlds beyond," but he learns that truth only slowly and with great bitterness. When the creek is swollen from a storm and Jess is gone, Leslie still tries to cross to Terabithia on the rope. It breaks, she falls onto the rocks, and is killed. Grief-stricken and alone, without his alter ego, Jess can barely come to terms with what has happened. But he does, finally, and in doing so learns something about the purpose of all friendship.

> It was Leslie who had taken him from the cow pasture into Terabithia and turned him into a king. He had thought that was it. Wasn't king the best you could be? Now it occurred to him that perhaps Terabithia was like a castle where you came to be knighted. After you stayed for a while and grew strong you had to move on. For hadn't Leslie, even in Terabithia, tried to push back the walls of his mind and make him see beyond to the shining world—huge and terrible and beautiful and very fragile? (p. 126)

To learn to see beyond our own secret countries—to what is at the same time both terrible and beautiful—is, from the perspective of Christian faith, the purpose of friendship. And to the degree that friendship not only with those of our own sex but with those of the opposite sex may more fully enable such vision, we have every reason to attempt it, despite its inherent difficulties.

We should not, therefore, underestimate the importance of the most obvious location for friendship between men and women: the bond of marriage. There are many differences between our world and that shared by Socrates and Critobulus. By no means least of them is the formative influence of Christian culture, with its exaltation of marriage as the highest of personal bonds. To be sure, precisely because the husband or wife as friend is not only "another self" but as fully "an-other" as we can experience, friendship in marriage cannot be presumed. If there is any truth in Lillian Rubin's analysis, each spouse may fear the otherness of the partner and the loss of self that intimacy requires. The man fears engulfment, "losing a part of himself that he's struggled to maintain over the years" (p. 24). The woman fears invasiveness that threatens the boundary she has struggled to maintain between her self and others. Each is tempted to avoid such otherness, to settle for a friend more like the self. But if we can overcome that temptation—in this case, perhaps, with the aid of *eros*—we may find a bond that truly helps us see beyond ourselves and become more balanced and sane. With the aid of the commitment marriage asks of us, we may find that friendship is possible between men and women not only when passion is stilled but when it is satisfied and fulfilled. And it may even be true that within a life marked by such commitment we become more generally capable of friendship between men and women.

When Harry finally realizes that he loves Sally and wants to marry her, he ticks off the reasons: the way she's cold when it's 71 degrees outside; the way it takes her an hour and a half to order a sandwich; the way she crinkles up her nose when she looks at him. All these might be only the signs of an infatuated lover looking at the beloved, not of a friend who stands beside the friend and looks outward. But last in Harry's litany of reasons is that Sally is "the last person I want to talk to before I go to bed at night." And J. B. Priestley—though worrying that spouses' lives may be "so intertwined, that they are almost beyond talk as we understand it"—has a view not unlike Harry's: "Talk demands that people should begin, as it were, at least at some distance from one another, that there should be some doors still to unlock. Marriage is partly the unlocking of those doors, and it sets out on its happiest and most prosperous voyages when it is launched on floods of talk" (p. 60).

In marriage, if we are patient and faithful, we may find that "balance and sanity" which friendship between men and women offers, and we may find it in a context where *eros* also may be fulfilled without becoming destructive. Against the view of Critobulus we may, therefore, set the wisdom of Ben Sira (40:23): "A friend or companion is always welcome, but better still to be husband and wife."

Notes

[1] Xenophon, *The Oeconomicus*, in *Memorabilia and Oeconomicus* trans. E. C. Marchant (London: William Heinemann, 1923), 3.12.

[2] Mary E. Hunt, *Fierce Tenderness: A Feminist Theology of Friendship* (New York: Crossroad, 1991), p. 92. Future references will be given by page number in parentheses within the body of the text.

[3] Aristotle, *Nicomachean Ethics*, trans. Martin Ostwald (Indianapolis: Bobbs-Merrill Library of Liberal Arts, 1962),8.7. Future citations will be given by book and chapter number in parentheses within the body of the text.

[4] C. S. Lewis, *The Four Loves* (New York: Harcourt Brace Jovanovich, 1960), pp. 99-100. Future references will be given by page number in parentheses within the body of the text.

[5] Friedrich Nietzsche, cited in Ronald A. Sharp, *Friendship and Literature* (Durham, N.C.: Duke University Press, 1986), p. 73.

[6] J. B. Priestley, *Talking: An Essay* (New York and London: Harper & Brothers, 1926), p. 59. Future references will be given by page number in parentheses within the body of the text.

[7] Lillian B. Rubin, "Women, Men, and Intimacy," in *Eros, Agape and Philia*, ed. Alan Soble (New York: Paragon House, 1989), p. 22.

[8] Deborah Tannen, You *Just Don't Understand: Women and Men in Conversation* (New York: William Morrow, 1990), p. 25. Further references will be given by page number in parentheses within the body of the text.

[9] Dave Barry, "Listen Up, Jerks! Share Innermost Feelings with Her!" *Arizona Star*, 8 June 1992, p. 3B.

[10] I do not here seek to defend this view, but I have done so in *Friendship: A Study in Theological Ethics* (Notre Dame, Ind.: University of Notre Dame Press, 1981).

[11] Katherine Paterson, *Bridge to Terabithia* (New York: Avon Books, 1972). Citations will be given by page number in parentheses within the body of the text.

Bibliography: For Further Reading

Chapter 1: Gilgamesh

Primary Sources

The Epic of Gilgamesh. Translated by N. K. Sanders. Baltimore: Penguin, New York: New American Library, 1972.
Gilgamesh. A Verse Narrative by Herbert Mason with an Afterword by John H. Marks. New York: New American Library, 1972.

Discussion and Commentary

Heidel, Alexander. *The Gilgamesh Epic and Old Testament Parallels.* Chicago: University of Chicago Press, 1963.
Hyland, Drew. *The Origins of Philosophy.* Atlantic Highlands: Humanities, 1984.
Tigay, Jeffrey H. *The Evolution of the Gilgamesh Epic.* Philadelphia: University of Pennsylvania Press, 1982.

Chapter 2: Hesiod

Primary Sources

The Homeric Hymns, and Homerica. With English translation by Hแ Evelyn-White. Loeb Classical Library. London: W. Heinemanⁱ York: Macmillan, 1914; rpt. 1967, 1982.
The Poems of Hesiod. Translated by R. M. Frazer. Norman: Unⁱ Oklahoma Press, 1983.

Theogony. Translated by Hugh G. Evelyn-White. Cambridge: Harvard University Press; London: William Heinemann, 1914, 1967.

The Works and Days, Theogony, The Shield of Herakles. Translated by Richard Lattimore. Ann Arbor, Michigan: University of Michigan Press, 1959.

Discussion and Commentary

Fränkel, Hermann. *Early Greek Poetry and Philosophy.* 1975.

Jaeger, Werner. *Paideia: The Ideals of Greek Culture.* Vol. I. 2nd edition. Oxford: Oxford University Press, 1986.

Lamberton, Robert. *Hesiod.* New Haven: Yale University Press, 1988.

Pucci, Pietro. *Hesiod and the Language of Poetry.* Baltimore: Johns Hopkins University Press, 1977.

Solmsen, Friedrich. *Hesiod and Aeschylus.* Ithaca: Cornell University Press, 1949, 1967.

Walcot, Peter. *Hesiod and the Near East.* Cardiff: Wales University Press, 1966.

Chapter 3: Plato

Primary Sources

The Collected Dialogues of Plato. Edited by Edith Hamilton & Huntington Cairns. Princeton: Princeton University Press, 1961.

The Dialogues of Plato. 3rd ed. Vol. I. Translated by B. Jowett. New York: Oxford University Press, 1892.

Great Dialogues of Plato. Translated by W. H. D. Rouse, edited by Eric H. Warmington & Philip G. Rouse. New York: New American Library, 1956.

The Works of Plato. Selected & edited by Irwin Edman. New York: Modern Library, 1928.

Discussion and Commentary

Gould, J. *The Development of Plato's Ethics.* Cambridge: Cambridge University Press, 1955.

Guthrie, W. K. C. *The Greek Philosopher.* New York: Harper & Row, 1960.

Havelock, Eric A. *Preface to Plato.* Cambridge: Harvard University Press, 1963.

Jaeger, Werner. *Paideia: The Ideals of Greek Culture,* vols. 2 and 3. Translated by Gilbert Highet. New York: Oxford University Press, 1943.

Nettleship, R. L. *Lectures on the Republic of Plato.* London: Macmillan, 1937.

Pater, W. *Plato and Platonism.* London: Macmillan, 1910.

Shorey, P. *What Plato Said.* Chicago: University of Chicago Press, 1933.

Taylor. A. E. *The Mind of Plato.* Ann Arbor: University of Michigan Press, 1960.

White, N. *A Companion to Plato's Republic.* Indianapolis: Hackett, 1979.

Chapter 4: Aristotle

Primary Sources

The Basic Works of Aristotle. Edited by Richard McKeon. New York: Random House, 1941; Modern Library, 1947.

Nichomachean Ethics. Translated with analysis and critical notes by James E. C. Welldon. New York: Macmillan Co., 1897.

Discussion and Commentary

Adler, Mortimer J. *Aristotle for Everybody.* New York: Macmillan, 1980.

Allan, D. J. *The Philosophy of Aristotle.* 2nd edition. Oxford: Oxford University Press, 1970.

Burnet, John. *The Ethics of Aristotle.* London: Oxford University Press, 1900.

Cooper, John M. *Reason and Human Good in Aristotle.* Cambridge: Harvard University Press, 1975.

Jaeger, Werner. *Aristotle: Fundamentals of the History of His Development.* Translated by Richard Robinson. Oxford: Oxford University Press, 1962.

Joachim, H. H. *Aristotle: The Nicomachean Ethics.* London: Oxford University Press, 1954.

Kitto, H. D. F. *The Greeks.* 2nd revised edition. Baltimore: Penguin, 1957.

Loyd, G. E. R. *Aristotle: The Growth and Structure of His Thought.* Cambridge: Cambridge University Press, 1968.

Mure, G. R. G. *Aristotle.* London: Ernest Benn, 1932.

Randall, John Herman. *Aristotle.* New York: Columbia University Press, 1960.

Roger J. Sullivan. *Morality and the Good Life: A Commentary on Aristotle's Nicomachean Ethics.* Memphis: Memphis State University Press, 1977.

Ross, W. D. *Aristotle.* London: Methuen, 1923; 6th ed., 1955.

Steward, J.A. *Notes on the Nichomachean Ethics.* Oxford: Clarendon Press, 1892.

Veatch, Henry B. *Aristotle: A Contemporary Appreciation.* Bloomington: Indiana University Press, 1974.

Chapter 5: Seneca

Primary Sources

Epistulae Morales.   Translated by R.M. Gummere.   Cambridge: Harvard
    University Press, 1917.
Four Tragedies and Octavia. Tr. E.F. Watling. Baltimore: Penguin Books,
    1966.
Moral and Political Essays. Tr. John M. Cooper. New York: Cambridge
    University Press, 1995.
Moral Essays. Tr. R.M. Gummere.   Cambridge, MA: Harvard University
    Press; London: W. Heinemann, 1970.
Seneca.   Tr. Thomas H. Corcoran.   London: Heinemann; Cambridge, MA:
    Harvard University Press, 1971.
The Stoic Philosophy of Seneca: Essays and Letters of Seneca. Tr. Moses
    Hadas. Garden City, NY: Doubleday, 1958.
The Tragedies. Tr. David R. Slavitt. Baltimore: Johns Hopkins University
    Press, 1994.

Discussion and Commentary

Mendell, Clarence W. *Our Seneca.* New Haven: Yale University Press; H.
    Milford, Oxford University Press, 1941.
Motto, Anna Lydia.   *Guide to the Thought of Lucius Annaeus Seneca.*
    Amsterdam: A. M. Hakkert, 1970.
Lucas, Frank L. *Seneca and Elizabethan Tragedy.* Cambridge: The University
    Press, 1922.
Costa, C. D. N., ed. *Seneca.* London; Boston: Routledge & K. Paul, 1974.
Griffin, Miriam T.   *Seneca: A Philosopher in Politics.*   Oxford: Oxford
    University Press, 1976.

Chapter 6: Epictetus

Primary Sources

Discourses and Enchiridion. Based on the translation of Thomas Wentworth
    Higginson, with an Introduction by Irwin Edman. Roslyn, New York:
    Walter J. Black, 1944.
Epictetus.   2 volumes.   Translated by W. A. Oldfather. London: W.
    Heinemann; New York: G. P. Putnam's Sons, 1926-1928.
The Philosophy of Epictetus. By John Bonforte. New York: Philosophical
    Library, 1955
The Works of Epictetus. Translated by Thomas W. Higginson. Boston: Little,
    Brown & Co., 1866, 1890.

Discussion and Commentary

Arnold, E.V. "Epictetus" in *Encyclopedia of Religion and Ethics.* Edited by James Hastings. Edinburgh, 1937.

Arnold, E.V. *Roman Stoicism.* London: Routledge & Kegan Paul, 1958.

Bevan, E. *Stoics and Sceptics.* Oxford: Clarendon, 1913.

Copleston, Frederick S. J. *A History of Philosophy.* Volume I: *Greece & Rome.* London: Search Press, 1946.

Hicks, R. D. *Stoic and Epicurean.* New York: Charles Scribner's Sons, 1910.

Laertius, Diogenes. *Lives and Opinions of Eminent Philosophers.* Translated by R. D. Hicks. Cambridge: Harvard University Press, Loeb Classical Library, 1925.

Zeller, Edward. *The Stoics, Epicureans and Sceptics.* Translated by Oswald Reichel. New York: Russell & Russell, 1902.

Chapter 7: Cicero

Primary Sources

Letters of Marcus Tullius Cicero with His Treatises on Friendship and Old Age. Harvard Classics, Vo. 9. Translated by E. S. Shuckburgh. New York: P. F. Collier and Son, 1909.

On the Commonwealth. Translated by George Holland Sabine & tanley Barney Smith. Columbus: Ohio State University Press, 1929.

On Moral Obligations. Translated by John Higginbotham. Berkeley: University of California Press, 1967.

Studies in Latin Literature. Edited by T.A. Dory. London: Routledge & Kegan Paul, 1965.

Discussion and Commentary

Baily, D. R. Shackleton. *Cicero.* New York: Charles Scribner's Sons, 1971.

Boissier, Gastan. *Cicero & His Friends.* New York: G. P. Putnam's Sons, 1925.

Grant, Michael. *Cicero: Selected Works.* Harmansworth: Penguin, 1960.

Hunt, Harold Arthur Kinross. *The Humanism of Cicero.* Melbourne: Melbourne University Press, 1954.

Rolfe, John Carew. *Cicero and His Influence.* Boston: Marshall Jones, 1923.

Smethurst, S. E. Bibliographical reports in *Classical World.* Volume 51 (1957-58) 1-4, 24, 32-41; Volume 58 (1964-65) 36-45.

Chapter 8: Plutarch

Primary Sources

The Greek Questions of Plutarch. Translation and Commentary by W. R. Halliday. Oxford: Clarendon, 1928.

The Lives of the Noble Grecians and Romans. Translated by John Dryden. Revised by Arthur Hugh Clough. London: J. M. Dent and Sons; New York: E. P. Dutton and Co., 1932-1933; New York: Modern Library, 1967.

On Love, the Family and the Good Life: Selected Essays by Plutarch. Translated with an Introduction by Moses Hadas. New York: New American Library, Mentor, 1957.

Moralia. Translated by Philemon Holland (London, 1603). Introduction by E. H. Blakeney. New York: E. P. Dutton & Co., 1912.

Morals. Translated by "seven hands" (M. Morgan, *et al.*). Corrected and revised by William W. Goodwin. 5th ed. With Introduction by Ralph Waldo Emerson. Boston: Little, Brown, & Co., 1871.

Plutarch's Complete Works. New York: T.Y. Crowell and Co., 1909.

Plutarch's Moralia. 14 volumes. With English translation by Frank Cole Babbitt. London: W. Heinemann; New York: G.P. Putnam's sons, 1917.

Discussion and Commentary

Jones, R. M. *The Platonism of Plutarch.* Menesha, Wisconsin, 1916.

Moellering, H. A. *Plutarch on Superstition.* Boston, 1962.

Chapter 9: St. Augustine

Primary Sources

Augustine: Confessions and Enchiridion. Translated by Albert C. Oulter. *Library of Christian Classics,* Vol. VII. London: SCM Press Ltd., and Philadelphia, PA: Westminster Press, MCMLV.

The City of God. An abridged version from the translation by Gerald G. Walsh, *et al.* Foreword by Etienne Gilson. Edited by Vernon J. Bourke. Garden City, New York: Image Books, 1958.

The Confessions of St. Augustine. Translated by John K. Ryan. Garden City, New York: Image Books, 1960.

The Essential Augustine. Selected and with commentary by Vernon J. Burke. New York: New American Library, 1964; reprinted, Indianapolis: Hackett, 1974.

A Select Library of the Nicene & Post-Nicene Fathers of the Christian Church. Volumes I-VIII. Edited by Philip Schaff. Grand Rapids, Michigan: Eerdmans, 1974.

Discussion and Commentary

Bourke, Vernon J. *Augustine's Quest of Wisdom.* Milwaukee: Bruce Publishing, 1945.

Brown, Peter. *Augustine of Hippo: A Biography.* Berkeley: University of California Press, 1967.

Cochrane, C.N. *Christianity and Classical Culture.* Oxford: Clarenton Press, 1940.

Gilson, Etienne. *The Christian Philosophy of Saint Augustine.* Translated by L. E. M. Lynch. New York: Random House, 1960.

Tolley, W. P. *The Idea of God in the Philosophy of St. Augustine.* New York: R. R. Smith, 1930.

Warfield, Benjamin B. *Studies in Tertullian and Augustine.* New York: Oxford University Press, 1931.

Chapter 10: St. Aelred of Rievaulx

Primary Sources

Aelredi Rievallensis Sermones I-XLVI: Collectio Claraevallensis Prima et Secunda; recensuit Gaetatano Raciti, Corpus Christianorum. Contination Mediaevalis 2A Opera Omnia, 2. Turnholti: Brepolis, 1989.

De Anima. Edited by C. H. Talbot. Medieval and Renaissance Studies Suppl. 1. London: Warburg Institute, University of London, 1952.

Historical Works. Cistercian Fathers Series, No. 56. Ed. Patricia Jane and Marsha Dutton. Kalamazoo, MI: Cistercian Publications, 1996.

De Institutione Inclusarum. (Two English Versions) Early English Text Society, Original Series, 287. Ed. Alexandra Barratt. Oxford: Oxford University Press, 1985.

Mirror of Charity. Cistercian Fathers Series, 17. Tr. Elizabeth Connor. Kalamazoo, MI: Cistercian Publications, 1990.

Spiritual Friendship. Translated by Eugenia Laker, S.S.N.D. Kalamazoo, MI: Cictercian Publications, 1974.

396 *Friendship*

Discussion and Commentary

Squire, Aelred. *A Study* (of Aelred of Rievaulx). Cistercian Studies Series, No.
50. Kalamazoo, MI: Cistercian Publications, 1981.

Chapter 11: St. Thomas Aquinas

Primary Sources

Introduction to Saint Thomas Aquinas. Edited by Anton C. Pegis. New York:
Modern Library, 1948.
St. Thomas Aquinas: Philosophical Texts. Edited by T. Gilby.   New   York:
Oxford University Press, 1960.
Summa Contra Gentiles.   Translated by Anton C. Pegis.   Notre Dame:
University of Notre Dame Press, 1975.
Summa Theologica.   Translated by the Fathers of the English Dominican
Province. New York: Benziger Brothers, Inc., 1947.

Discussion and Commentary

Bourke, Vernon J.   *St. Thomas and the Greek Moralists.*   Milwaukee:
Marquette University Press, 1947.
Chesterson, G.K.   *Saint Thomas Aquinas.*   Garden City, New York: Image
Books, 1956.
Copleston, F.C. *Aquinas.* Harmondsworth: Penguin Books, 1955.
D'Arcy, M.C. *St. Thomas Aquinas.* Westminster: Newman   Press, 1958.
Gilson, Etienne. *The Christian Philosophy of St. Thomas Aquinas.* Translated
by L. K. Shook. New York. Random House, 1956.
Kenny, A. *Aquinas.* New York: Hill and Wang, 1980.
O'Connor, D.J. *Aquinas and Natural Law.* London: Macmillan, 1968.

Chapter 12: Michel de Montaigne

Primary Sources

The Complete Works of Montaigne.   Translated by Donald M. Frame.
Stanford: Stanford University Press, 1958.
The Essays of Michael Lord of Montaigne. Vol. I. Translated by John Florio.
London: J.M. Dent & Sons, 1910.
Montaigne: Essays.   Translated by M. Cohen.   Harmondsworth: Penguin
Classics, 1939.
Selected Essays. Translated by Donald M. Frame. Roslyn, New York: Walter
J. Black, 1943; renewed 1970.

Travel Journals. Translated by Donald M. Frame. New York: North Point Press, 1983.

Discussion and Commentary

Frame, Donald M. *Montaigne's Discovery of Man: The Humanization of a Humanist.* New York, Columbia University Press, 1955.
Popkin, Richard H. *The History of Scepticism from Erasmus.* New York: Humanities Press, 1964.

Chapter 13: Francis Bacon

Primary Sources

The Essays. Edited by John Pitcher. Harmondsworth: Penguin Classics, 1986.
ESSAYS and NEW ATLANTIS. Edited by Gordon S. Haight. Roslyn, New York: Walter J. Black, 1942, 1969.
New Organon and Related Writings. Edited by Fulton Henry Anderson. Indianapolis: Bobbs-Merrill, 1960.

Discussion and Commentary

Anderson, Fulton Henry. *The Philosophy of Francis Bacon.* Chicago: University of Chicago Press, 1948.
Bowen, Catherine Drinker. *Francis Bacon: The Temper of a Man.* Boston: Little, Brown & Co., 1963.
Broad, C.D. *The Philosophy of Francis Bacon.* Cambridge: Cambridge University Press, 1926.

Chapter 14: Baruch de Spinoza

Primary Sources

On the Improvement of the Understanding, The Ethics, and Correspondence. Translated by R. H. M. Elwes. 1883; rpt. New York: Dover, 1955.
A Theologico-Political Treatise and A Political Treatise. Translated from the Latin with an Introduction by R. H. M. Elwes. New York: Dover, 1951.

Discussion and Commentary

Broad, C. D. *Five Types of Ethical Theory.* New York: Harcourt, Brace, 1928. (Chapter 2)
Hampshire, S. *Spinoza.* Harmondsworth: Penguin, 1954.

Joachim, H. H. *A Study of the Ethics of Spinoza.* Oxford: Clarendon Press, 1901.

McKeon, R. *The Philosophy of Spinoza.* New York: Longmans, Green, 1928.

Wolfson, H. A. *The Philosophy of Spinoza.* Cambridge: Harvard University Press, 1948.

Chapter 15: Thomas Hobbes

Primary Sources

Dialogue between a Philosopher & a Student of the Common Laws of England. Edited by Joseph Cropsey. Chicago: University of Chicago Press, 1971.

Leviathan. Edited by Michael Oakshott. New York: Collier Books, 1962.

Man and Citizen. Edited by Bernard Gert. Garden City, New York: Doubleday and Co., 1972.

Discussion and Commentary

Brown, Kieth C. *Hobbes: Studies by Leo Strauss and others.* Cambridge: Harvard University Press, 1965.

Catlin, G. E. G. *Thomas Hobbes as Philosopher, Publicist and Man of Letters.* Oxford: Basil Blackwell and Mott, 1922.

Gooch, G. P. *Hobbes.* London: Humphrey Milford, 1940.

Peters, Richard S. *Hobbes.* Harmondsworth: Penguin, 1956.

Spragens, Thomas A. *The Politics of Motion: The World of Thomas Hobbes.* Forword by Antony Flew. Lexington: University Press of Kentucky, 1973.

Stephen, L. *Hobbes.* London: Macmillan, 1904.

Strauss, Leo. *The Political Philosophy of Thomas Hobbes.* Translated by Elsa M. Sinclair. Oxford: Clarendon, 1936; Chicago: Chicago University Press, 1936.

Taylor, Alfred Edward. *Thomas Hobbes.* London: Constable, 1908; Port Washington, New York: Kennikat Press, 1970.

Warrener, H. *The Political Philosophy of Hobbes.* Oxford: Clarendon Press, 1957.

Watkins, John W. N. *Hobbes' System of Ideas.* London: Hutchinson, 1965.

Chapter 16: Malebranche

Primary Sources

Dialogues in Metaphysics and Religion. Translated by Morris Ginsberg. London: 1923.

The Search After Truth and Elucidations of the Search After Truth. Translated by Thomas M. Lennon and Paul J. Olscamp. Columbus: Ohio State University Press, 1980.

Discussion and Commentary

Locke, John. "An Examination of N. Malebranche's opinion of seeing all things in God." *Philosophical Works.* Edited by J. A. St. John. London, 1972. (Vol. II)

Luce, Arthur Aston. *Berkeley and Malebranche.* London, Oxford University Press, 1934.

Radis-Lewis, Genevieve. *Nicolas Malebranche.* Paris: Presses Universitaires de France, 1963.

Rome, Beatrice K. *The Philosophy of Malebranche.* Chicago: H. Regnery Co., 1963.

Chapter 16: David Hume

Primary Sources

Dialogues concerning Natural Religion. Edited by Richard H. Popkin. Indianapolis: Hackett, 1980.

An Enquiry Concerning Human Understanding. Edited by Eric Steinberg. Indianapolis: Hackett, 1977.

An Enquiry Concerning the Principles of Morals. Vol. 4 of *Philosophical Works by David Hume.* Edited by T. H. Green and T. H. Grose. Aalen, Germany: Scientia Verlag, 1964.

Essays: Moral, Political, And Literary. Volumes 3 & 4 of *Philosophical Works.* Edited by T. H. Greene & T.H. Grose. Aalen: Scientia Verlag, 1964.

A Treatise of Human Nature. Edited by L. A. Selby-Bigge, revised by P. H. Nidditch. Oxford: Clarendon Press, 1978.

Discussion and Commentary

Broad, C. D. *Five Types of Ethical Theory.* New York: Harcourt, Brace, 1928. (Chapter 4)

Friendship

Broiles, R. D. *The Moral Philosophy of David Hume.* The Hague: Martinus Nijhoff, 1964.

MacNabb, D. G. C. *David Hume: His Theory of Knowledge and Morality.* New York: Hutchinson's University Library, 1951.

Mossner, Ernest C. *The Life of David Hume.* Austin: University of Texas Press, 1954; second edition 1979.

Smith, Norman Kemp. *The Philosophy of David Hume.* London, MacMillan Co., 1941.

Steward, J. B. *The Moral and Political Philosophy of David Hume.* New York: Columbia University Press, 1963.

Stroud, Barry. *Hume.* London: Routledge & Kegan Paul, 1977.

Chapter 18: Immanuel Kant

Primary Sources

Anthropology from a Pragmatic Point of View. Translated by James W. Ellington. Indianapolis: Hackett, 1974.

Critique of Practical Reason. Translated by Lewis White Beck. Indianapolis: Bobbs-Merrill, 1956.

The Doctrine of Virtue. Translated by Mary J. Gregor. Philadelphia: University of Pennsylvania Press, 1964.

Grounding of Metaphysics of Morals. Translated by James W. Ellington. Indianapolis: Hackett, 1981.

Lectures on Ethics. Translated by Louis Infield. Indianapolis: Hackett, 1963, see esp. his chapter on "Friendship," pp. 200-209.

Philosophy of Kant: Immanuel Kant's Moral and Political Writings. Edited by Carl J. Friedrich. New York: The Modern Library, 1949.

Discussion and Commentary

Beck, Lewis White. *Early German Philosophy.* Cambridge: Harvard University Press, 1969.

Broad, C. D. *Five Types of Ethical Theory.* New York: Harcourt, Brace, 1928. (Chapter 5)

Cassirer, Ernst. *Kant's Life & Thought.* Translated by Theodore M. Greene & Hoyt W. Hudson. New York: Harper & Row, 1960.

Korner, Stephen. *Kant.* New Haven: Yale University Press. 1982.

Lindsay, A. D. *Kant.* London: Oxford University Press, 1934.

Paton, H. T. *The Categorical Imperative: A Study of Kant's Moral Philosophy.* Chicago: University of Chicago Press, 1948.

Ross, W. D. *Kant's Ethical Theory.* Oxford: Oxford University Press, 1954.

Schilpp, Paul Arthur. *Kant's Pre-Critical Ethics.* Evanston: Northwestern University, 1938.

Chapter 19: G.W.F. Hegel

Primary Sources

Hegel: Texts and Commentary. Translated & edited by Walter Kaufmann. Garden City, New York: Doubleday, 1965.
Hegel's Philosophy of Spirit. Translated by T.M. Knox. Oxford: Oxford University Press, 1967.
Natural Law. Translated by T.M. Knox. Philadelphia: University of Pennsylvania Press, 1975.
Philosophy of Hegel. Edited by Carl J. Friedrich. New York: The Modern Library, 1953.
Phenomenology of Spirit. Translated by A.V. Miller. Oxford: Oxford University Press, 1977.

Discussion and Commentary

Findlay, J. N. *Hegel: A Re-Examination.* London: Allen & Unwin, 1958.
Kojève, Alexander. *Introduction to the Reading of Hegel.* Translated by James H. Nichols, Jr. Edited by Allan Bloom. Ithaca: Cornell University Press, 1980.
Lauer, Quentin. *Hegel's Idea of Philosophy.* New York: Fordham University Press, 1971.
Mure, Geoffrey Reginald Gilchrist. *An Introduction to Hegel.* Oxford: Clarendon, 1940.
Stace, W.T. *The Philosophy of Hegel.* New York: Dover, 1955.

Chapter 20: Arthur Schopenhauer

Primary Sources

On the Basis of Morality. Translated by E. F. J. Payne. Indianapolis: Bobbs-Merrill, 1965.
The Pessimist's Handbook:A Collection of Popular Essays. Translated by T. Bailey Saunders. Edited by Hazel Barnes. Lincoln: University of Nebraska Press, 1964.
The Philosophy of Schopenhauer. Edited by Irwin Edman. New York: Modern Library, 1956.
The World as Will and Representation. 2 Vols. Translated by E.F.J. Payne. New York: Dover Publications, 1966.

Discussion and Commentary

Copleston, Frederick. *Arthur Schopenhauer: Philosopher of Pessimism.* London: Burns, Oates & Washbourne, 1947.

Gardiner, Patrick. *Schopenhauer*. Baltimore: Penguin Books, 1963.

Chapter 21: Søren Kierkegaard

Primary Sources

Either/Or. 2 Vols. Translated by David Swenson et al. Princeton: Princeton
 University Press, 1959.
Kierkegaard: A Collection of Critical Essays. Edited by Josiah Thompson.
 New York: Doubleday Anchor, 1972.
A Kierkegaard Anthology. Edited by Robert Bretall. New York: Modern
 Library, 1936.
Concluding Unscientific Postscript. Translated by David F. Swenson &
 Walter. Lowrie: Princeton University Press, 1944.
Philosophical Fragments. Translated by David Swenson. Revised by Howard
 V. Hong. Princeton: Princeton University Press, 1936; 1962.
Works of Love. Translated by Howard and Edna Hong. New York: Harper &
 Row, 1962.

Discussion and Commentary

Barrett, William. *Irrational Man*. Garden City, New York: Doubleday, 1958.
Collins, James. *The Existentialists: A Critical Study*. Chicago: H. Regnery
 Co., 1952.
Evans, C. Stephen. *Kierkegaard's Fragments & Postscript*. Atlantic
 Highlands: Humanities, 1983.
Evans, C. Stephen. *Existentialism: The Philosophy of Despair & the Quest for
 Hope*. Grand Rapids: Zondervan, 1984.
Lowrie, Walter. *Kierkegaard*. New York: Oxford University Press, 1938.
Lowrie, Walter. *A Short Life of Kierkegaard*. Princeton: Princeton University
 Press, 1942.

Chapter 22: Ralph Waldo Emerson

Primary Sources

The Best of Ralph Waldo Emerson. Edited by Gordon S. Haight. Roslyn, NY:
 Walter J. Black, 1941.
The Complete Works of Ralph Waldo Emerson. Vol. II: *Essays*. Cambridge:
 The Riverside Press, 1904.
On Love And Friendship. White Plains, New York: Peter Pauper, n.d.
The Portable Emerson. Edited by Carl Bode & Malcom Cowley. New York:
 Penguin, 1981.

The Selected Writings of Ralph Waldo Emerson. Edited by Brooks Atkinson. New York: Modern Library, 1980.

Self Reliance. White Plains, New York: Peter Pauper, 1967.

Discussion and Commentary

Bishop, Jonathan. *Emerson on the Soul.* Cambridge: Harvard University Press, 1965.

Pachmann, Henry August. *German Culture in America.* Madison, Wisconsin: University of Wisconsin Press, 1961.

Chapter 23: Friedrich Nietzsche

Primary Sources

The Complete Works of Friedrich Nietzsche. 18 vols. Edited by Oscar Levy. New York: Russel & Russel, Inc., 1909-11.

On the Advantage and Disadvantage of History for Life. Translated with an Introduction by Peter Preuss. Indianapolis: Hackett, 1980.

Philosophy in the Tragic Age of the Greeks. Translated with an Cowan, Marianne Introduction by Marianne Cowan. Chicago: Henry Regnery Co., 1962.

Kaufmann, Walter. *The Will to Power.* Translated by Walter Hollingdale, R. J. Kaufmann and R. J. Hollingdale. Edited, with Commentary, by Walter Kaufmann. New York: Random House, Vintage, 1968.

Discussion and Commentary

Brinton, Crane. *Nietzsche.* Cambridge: Harvard University Press, 1941; New York: Harper & Row, 1965.

Copleston, F. C. *Frederick Nietzsche: Philosopher of Culture.* New York: Harper & Brothers, 1942; 2nd edition, 1975.

Danto, Arthur C. *Nietzsche as Philosopher.* New York: Macmillan, 1965.

Figgis, J. N. *The Will to Freedom.* New York: Charles Scribner's Sons, 1917.

Heidegger, Martin. *Nietzsche,* 4 Volumes. Translated by Krell, David Farrell Krell, *et al.* San Francisco: Harper & Row, 1979-1988.

Hollingdale, R. J. *Nietzsche: The Man & His Philosophy.* Baton Rouge: Louisiana State University Press, 1965.

Jaspers, Karl. *Nietzsche.* Translated by Charles F. Wallcraft & Frederick J. Schmitz. South Bend: Regnery/Gateway, 1979.

Kaufmann, Walter. *Nietzsche: Philosopher, Psychologist, Antichrist.* Princeton: Princeton University Press, 1950.
Morgan, George A. Jr. *What Nietzsche Means.* Cambridge: Harvard University Press, 1941; reprint New York: Harper & Row, 1965.
Salter, W. M. *Nietzsche as Philosopher.* New York: Henry Holt, 1917.
Wilcox, J. T. *Truth and Value in Nietzsche.* Ann Arbor: University of Michigan Press, 1974.

Chapter 24: George Santayana

Primary Sources

Atoms of Thought. Edited by Ira D. Cardiff. New York: Philosophical Library, 1950.
Birth of Reason and Other Essays. Edited by Daniel Cory. New York: Columbia University Press, 1968.
The Genteel Tradition at Bay. Brooklyn, New York: Haskell Booksellers, 1977.
Last Puritan: A Memoir in the Form of a Novel. New York: Charles Scribners' Sons, 1936.
The Life of Reason. New York: Charles Scribners' Sons, 1905-6.

Discussion and Commentary

Munitz, Milton. *The Moral Philosophy of Santayana.* New York: Columbia University Press, 1939.
Schilpp, Paul Arthur. *The Philosophy of George Santayana.* La Salle, Illinois: Open Court, Library of Living Philosophers, 1940; 2nd edition, 1951.

Chapter 25: C.S. Lewis

Primary Sources

The Abolition of Man. New York: Collier Books, 1962.
The Allegory of Love: A Study in Medieval Tradition. New York: Oxford University Press, 1958.
The Chronicles of Narnia. 7 vols. New York: Collier Books, 1970.
The Discarded Image: An Introduction to Medieval and Renaissance Literature. New York: Cambridge University Press, 1964.
The Four Loves. New York: Harcourt Brace Jovanovich, 1960.
Letters of C. S. Lewis. Edited by W. H. Lewis. New York: Harcourt, Brace & World, 1960.

Poems. Edited by Walter Hooper. New York: Harcourt, Brace Jovanovich, 1964.

That Hideous Strength: A Modern Fairy Tale for Grown-ups. New York: Macmillan, 1965.

Till We Have Faces: A Myth Retold. Grand Rapids: Eerdmans, 1964.

The World's Last Night and Other Essays. New York: Harcourt, Brace & World, 1960.

Discussion and Commentary

Gibb, Jocelyn, ed. *Light on C. S. Lewis.* New York: Harcourt, Brace & World, 1966.

Moorman, Charles. *Arthurian Triptych: Mythical Material in Charles Williams, C. S. Lewis, and T. S. Eliot.* Los Angeles: University of California Press, 1960.

Moorman, Charles. *The Precincts of Felicity: The Augustinian City of the Oxford Christians.* Gainesville: University of Florida Press, 1966.

Walsh, Chad. *The Literary Legacy of C. S. Lewis.* New York: Harcourt, Brace Jovanovich, 1979.

Chapter 26: Jean-Paul Sartre

Primary Sources

Existentialism. Translated by Bernard Frechtman. New York: Philosophical Library, 1947.

Nausea. Translated by Lloyd Alexander. New York: New Directions, 1964.

No Exit and Three Other Plays. New York: Alfred Knopf, 1949; renewed 1976.

The Philosophy of Jean-Paul Sartre. Edited and Introduced by Robert Denoon Cumming. New York: Vintage, 1965.

Situations. Translated by Benita Eisler. New York: George Braziller, 1958.

The Words. Translated by Bernard Frechtman. New York: George Braziller, 1964.

Discussion and Commentary

Desan, Wilfred. *The Tragic Finale.* Cambridge: Harvard University Press, 1954.

LaCapra, Dominick. *A Preface to Sartre.* Ithaca: Cornell University Press, 1978.

Warnock, Mary. *The Philosophy of Sartre.* London: Hutchinson, 1966.

Chapter 27: J. Glenn Gray

Primary Sources

Hegel's Hellenic Ideal. New York: King's Crown Press, 1941. Reprinted, New York: Garland, 1984. Also reprinted as *Hegel and Greek Thought.* New York: Harper and Row, 1968.

The Promise of Wisdom: An Introduction to Philosophy of Education. Philadelphia: Lippincott, 1968. Reprinted as *Rethinking American Education: A Philosophy of Teaching and Learning.* Middletown, Connecticut: Wesleyan University Press, 1984.

Understanding Violence Philosophically and Other Essays. New York: Harper and Row, 1970.

The Warriors: Reflections on Men in Battle. New York: Harcourt, Brace & Co., 1959.

Contributor. *European Philosophy Today.* Edited by George L. Kline. Quadrangle, 1965.

Contributor. *The Humanities in Higher Education.* Edited by Earl McGrath. W. C. Brown, 1949.

Contributor. *Ideas and Style.* Edited by Nathan A. Scott, Jr. Indianapolis: Odyssey, 1968.

Contributor. *Literature and Rhetoric.* Edited by Coulos, Somer and Wilcox. Glenview, Illinois: Scott, Foresman, 1969.

Contributor. *The Modern Vision of Death.* Edited by Nathan A. Scott, Jr. Atlanta: John Knox, 1967.

Contributor. *Naturalism and Historical Understanding.* Edited by John Anton. Albany: State University of New York Press, 1967.

Contributor. *Phenomenology and Existentialism.* Edited by Edward N. Lee and Maurice Mandelbaum. Baltimore: Johns Hopkins Press, 1967.

Editor and author of Introduction. *G.W.F. Hegel, On Art, Religion, Philosophy: Introductory Lectures to the Realm of Absolute Spirit.* New York: Harper and Row, 1970.

Translator, with Fred D. Wieck, and author of Introduction. *What is Called Thinking?* by Martin Heidegger. New York: Harper and Row, 1968.

Chapter 28: Hannah Arendt

Primary Sources

Antisemitism. New York: Harcourt Brace Jovanovich, 1970.

Between Past and Future: Eight Exercises in Political Thought. New York: Viking Press, 1968.

Eichmann in Jerusalem. New York: Viking Press, 1963; rpt., New York: Penguin, 1977.

The Human Condition. Chicago: University of Chicago Press, 1958.

The Life of the Mind. San Diego: Harcourt Brace Jovanovich, 1981.

Men in Dark Times. New York: Harcourt Brace Jovanovich, 1968.

On Revolution. New York: Penguin, 1977.

On Violence. New York: Harcourt Brace and World, 1970.

Discussion and Commentary

Kateb, George. *Hannah Arendt: Politics, Concience, Evil.* Totowa, NJ: Rowland and Allanheld, 1984.

Hill, Melvyn A., ed. *Hannah Arendt: The Recovery of the Public World.* New York: St. Martin's Press, 1979.

Young-Bruehl, Elizabeth. *Hannah Arendt: For Love of the World.* New Haven: Yale University Press, 1982.

Chapter 29: Mary E. Hunt

Primary Sources

Fierce Tenderness: A Feminist Theology of Friendship. New York: Crossroad, 1991.

"Friends and Family Values: An Old New Song," from *The Changing Faces of Friendship,* edited by Leroy S. Rouner. University of Notre Dame Press, 1994.

Editor. *From Woman-Pain to Woman-Vision.* By Anne McGrew Bennett. Minneapolis: Fortress Press, 1989.

Chapter 30: Gilbert G. Meilaender

Primary Sources

Faith and Faithfulness: Basic Themes in Christian Ethics. Notre Dame: University of Notre Dame Press, 1991.

Friendship: A Study in Theological Ethics. Notre Dame: University of Notre Dame Press, 1981.

The Limits of Love: Some Theological Explorations. Pennsylvania State University Press, 1992.

The Taste for the Other: The Social and Ethical Thought of C.S. Lewis (1978).

The Theory and Practice of Virtue. Notre Dame: University of Notre Dame
    Press, 1984.
"When Harry and Sally Read the *Nicomachean Ethics:* Friendship between
    Men and Women." *The Changing Faces of Friendship.* Edited by Leroy
    S. Rouner. University of Notre Dame Press, 1994.

Index

Achilles, 65, 102, 157, 288;
  Achilles and Patroclus, 65, 157
acquaintances, 81, 100, 105, 150,
  161, 220, 247, 260, 262, 265,
  276, 380
Adam, 195, 205, 245
Adimantus and Glaucon, 98
admiration, 109, 203, 240, 250,
  265, 268, 288, 300
adolescence, 19, 22, 30, 35, 54,
  88, 97, 115, 116, 117, 122, 130,
  131, 156, 157, 221, 251, 257,
  283, 307
adultery, 67
advice, 31, 89, 91, 96, 110, 159,
  163, 185, 228, 370, 386
Aelred of Rievaulx, Saint, x, xi,
  129, 130, 131, 132, 133, 134,
  135, 137, 139f.
Aeschylus, 157
affection, vii, 36, 41, 53-55, 61,
  70, 79, 84, 86-88, 90-95, 116,
  118, 131f., 135, 138, 146f.,
  155f., 158f., 163, 201, 207f.,
  210f., 240, 259f., 262, 282,
  286f., 290-292, 297, 299f., 303,
  315, 318, 322f., 332
affections, 86, 88, 91, 93, 96, 124,
  132, 150-152, 156, 166, 169,
  170, 209, 211, 260f., 290, 327,
affinity, 111, 261, 267, 283, 285-
  287, 327-329, 332
agapé (see "charity"), 388
AIDS, 369, 371, 374
Albertus Magnus, 143
Alcibiades, 104, 114
Alexander the Great, 51
alienation, 243, 284, 287
alienation, 354
altruism, vii, 206
ambition, 27, 87, 99, 107, 109,
  117, 139, 159, 179, 211, 221,
  335

Ambrose, Saint, 115, 148f.
amicitia (see "friendship"), x, 84,
  88, 129, 132, 246, 291, 129, 291
amor, 88, 132
amusement, 251, 303
anger, 6, 14, 24, 32, 50, 94, 105,
  109, 111, 116, 121, 241, 249,
  339, 351
animals, 31, 48, 52, 60, 71, 88, 95,
  103, 138, 180, 199, 207, 210,
  212, 231, 237, 242, 250, 284,
  303, 325, 365
Antony and Cleopatra, 98, 291
Aphrodite, 325; Aphrodite and Ares,
  321, 322, 323
Apollo, 108
Aquinas, Saint Thomas, viii, x,
  143f., 213
Arendt, Hannah, x, xi, 320, 335
Ares, 321-323, 325, 332f.
Aristippus, 155
Aristotelianism, 255, 298, 363, 365
Aristotle, viii, 1, 27, 51, 52, 65, 105,
  143, 154, 159f., 165, 171, 213,
  215, 234, 255, 288, 339, 346,
  354,
  376-378, 380-382, 384, 388;
  Eudemian Ethics, 51;
  Nicomachean Ethics, 51f., 375-
  376, 381, 388
arrogance, 121, 229
art, 31, 43, 69, 97, 102, 117, 123,
  126, 127, 171, 200, 234, 249,
  262f., 271, 279, 282, 284, 291,
  296, 300, 303, 339, 350
asceticism, 129, 233, 236, 292
attraction, 71, 91, 100, 132, 215,
  276, 333, 379-382
Augustine, Saint, vii, x, 68, 115,
  127, 139, 143, 146f., 193f.;
  Confessions, vii, 115f.
Augustinianism, 115, 193
Aurelius, Marcus, 77, 168, 256

judgment, 11, 71, 96, 107,
136, 159f., 168-170, 206, 217f.,
223, 227, 255, 281, 285, 310,
338, 340, 346, 357, 370, 385
justice, 7, 52, 58f., 80, 92, 137,
154, 156, 188, 235f., 238, 251,
255, 262, 266, 324, 338, 346,
355, 368, 371, 374,
Kant, Immanuel, x, 213f., 233,
356
Kantianism, 255, 258, 356
Kierkegaard, Søren, x, 243f.,
256, 305
killing, 12f., 15, 17-20, 154, 159,
170, 187, 305, 358, 386
kindness, 1-4, 42, 52, 54f., 57, 65,
79, 85f., 90, 95, 99f., 104, 107,
110, 112, 117, 123f., 130f.,
134f., 137, 145-147, 149, 157,
161, 167, 170, 179, 184, 186,
190, 203, 209-211, 221-223,
228f., 234, 238-240, 250, 253,
258f., 264, 281, 284, 287, 296f.,
300, 302f., 313, 315, 321, 324f.,
328, 330, 337-339, 342-344,
346, 348, 350, 363, 369f., 376f.,
379-385
kissing, 4, 14f., 79, 294
knowledge, ixf., 1, 3, 6, 29-31, 35-
37, 41, 44, 48, 53, 68, 72, 91,
107, 111, 122, 124, 131-133,
137, 157-159, 161f., 165, 197,
199, 206, 218, 223, 227, 231,
234-236, 238f., 242, 248, 252f.,
256, 261, 263, 277, 299f., 307f.,
313, 316, 324, 329f., 224, 339f.,
343, 350, 366, 381f., 286
laughter, 4, 5, 8, 32, 34, 73, 79,
103, 106, 111, 119, 160, 182,
188, 202, 224, 228, 239, 253f.,
303, 310
Leibniz, 173, 233
leisure, 85, 125, 130, 157, 165,
173, 249, 277f., 286, 298, 301
Lessing, G. E., 335-342, 344f.,
353-359

letters (correspondence), x, 34, 68,
83, 110, 115, 170, 173f., 190,
244, 257, 279, 289, 301, 311,
326, 321, 330, 335
Lewis, C.S., viii, 289, 375, 377,
388
Locke, John, 205, 206
loneliness, 69, 71, 276, 359
longing, 100, 120, 126, 253
love (see also "charity"), vii, 1f.,
7, 12, 18, 20, 29-33, 36-41, 43-
45, 47-50, 52-56, 59-65, 69-75,
78-81, 87f., 91f., 95, 98f., 103,
105f., 108-114, 116f., 119-126,
130, 132-138, 144, 145-152,
155-160, 163, 166, 168, 174-
179, 182, 185f., 195f., 198,
200-202, 204, 206-212, 214-
216, 221, 223, 225, 228f., 234,
238, 247f., 251f., 258f., 261,
264-266, 268-271, 274f., 283,
285, 304, 319-332, 332f., 339,
345, 354-356, 364-368, 372,
377-381, 385, 387; maternal,
32f., 224; paternal, 36, 160;
sexual (see "erotic love"); and
war, 323, 332
lovers, vii, ix, 1, 29-31, 37-39,
41f., 44, 49f., 56, 62-64, 70, 99,
103, 108, 148, 150, 156f., 168,
177, 259, 261, 286, 297, 300,
323f., 329, 331, 355, 365, 377f.,
387
loyalty, 6, 80f., 88-90, 93, 97,
105, 109, 111, 116-118, 121,
133, 145, 169, 173, 207, 227,
240f., 266, 269, 275, 283, 310,
313, 315,
323, 362, 387
Luther, Martin, 115
Lutheranism, 243, 375
lying, 24, 214, 235, 288, 317
MacIntyre, Alasdair, viii
Malebranche, Nicolas, 193
malice, 111, 203,214, 241, 317
Manicheism, 122, 314

CPSIA information can be obtained at www.ICGtesting.com
Printed in the USA
LVOW13s1103060214

372628LV00001B/16/P

9 780761 808183